Navigators
Quest for a Kingdom in
Polynesia

Dedication

To My Daughter,

Manaia Launoa (Iliganoa) Levi

*as a reminder
of her mother's undying love and care for her
and as a token of her father's love.*

Fata Ariu Levi

Navigators Quest for a Kingdom in Polynesia
First edition November 2020
Published by Ariu Levi

ISBN: 978-1-954076-02-0

Cover image by Faiga Tapusone Asiata

Cover design by Sheila Deeth

Edited by Sheila Deeth

Navigators Quest for a Kingdom in Polynesia

By Fata Ariu Levi

with a Foreword by

Susuga Papali'i Dr. Failautusi Avegalio.
Director, Pacific Business Center Program
Shidler College of Business
University of Hawaii System, Honolulu, Hawaii

and Afterword by

Afioga Vui Asiata Toeutu Faaleava, MPA, JD, PhD.
Director, McNair Scholars Program, Oregon
Assistant Professor, University Studies
Portland State University, Portland, Oregon.

Acknowledgements

To my village family, Afega and Tuana'i, the Honorable Aiga SaGauifaleai, and the reigning Honorable Chief Council Tuisamau: I am forever grateful for the gratitude, indulgence, and support given to me and to our family, in our efforts to better serve our village, district, the churches, and, in our joint responsibilities, the country. I thank you for your great job of caring for our village and the country.

To Gatoa'itele Savea, Founder and Owner of the *Observer*, Apia, Samoa, and recipient of the 1998 Commonwealth Press Union's Astor Award and Index on Censorship's Press Freedom Award: I take this opportunity to give credit to the Honorable Gatoa'itele Savea Sano Savea, Afega, Samoa, for his commitment to be the eyes, ears, and voice of the people of Samoa. This I do not say merely in passing. It's an observation I made when High Chief Savea founded his *Observer* newspaper company over 40 years ago. I can think of no one in Samoa who has endured more verbal and physical abuse because of his persistent nature and relentlessness in pursuing and publishing the truth, the real essence of our "freedom of expression." His indefatigable resilience is inspiring and admirable. In the Orator lexicon there are no words to express sincere thanks to you other than simply and humbly saying: Thank you, on behalf of all those who believe in the Truth.

To my family: I first want to thank my sister Selaina Miller for her love that has no boundaries and her unrelenting support of our family, my efforts to lead the family, and especially this book. Selaina is the rock on which our family is anchored, a matriarch of our family, and I love her very much. I also want to thank my younger sister Avasa (Kitty) Levi for her support of my work and the family. Susan Levi, mother of our daughter Manaia, is a tireless and loving mother, and her devotion to her care is a Herculean effort; I thank her for that and for always being supportive of my work from the beginning. I thank my brother, Orator Chief Faiga Tapusone Asiata, for his support and his contribution with the graphic art on the book cover.

Friends are more than friends to me; they are an extension of my family. My friends are evidence of my fortune and blessing, and they are far too many to list here.

Two friends to whom I owe so much, for my training in embracing Samoan culture and in becoming an Orator Chief, are my very dear friend Orator Chief Moemai Joseph Klies, of the Tagaloa family clan in the village of Vaiafai, Savai'i, and Mrs. (Shirley) Moemai Klies. Their untiring help, wisdom, and counsel supported my acclimation into my family Chief responsibility and the fa'aSamoa (culture) in the village and the Island. I absolutely could not effectively carry out my enormous responsibility without the support of Orator Moemai and Shirley, and for that I am forever indebted to them.

My personal family friends in Newport Beach, California, include Paramount High Chief Lilomaiava Mike Kneubuhl and Mrs. (Suzie) Lilomaiava Kneubuhl, whom I thank for their encouragement in getting this book done. Embracing me as a member of their extended Samoan family in Balboa Island, Newport Beach, California was an example of genuine Samoan love, and I treasure it forever.

Special thanks go to Rev. Henry Yandall and Rev. Mrs. Katie Yandall for helping start the Samoan culture dialogue with the youth group at their church in Carson, California. This became a catalyst in getting this book organized, based on the seminar curriculum for the dialogue. Their commitment to Samoan and Pacific Islands cultural development is to be commended for their belief, action, and love for the work of God.

I'm forever indebted also to my friend, Judge Linda Kuzma, for her support and encouragement and, of course, for reviewing the early draft of the manuscript and offering her suggestions. Linda has been helping and supporting my business ventures in getting intellectual property protections, and my work with my family in Samoa and culture.

I thank my "American Greek" friend in Newport Beach, Attorney Nicholas Frudakis, for always challenging me in the areas of classical antiquity and mythology, sharing his recall of his days at Berkeley to help me get this published.

And I would like to say thank you to my friend and business partner Steve Falk for being a great cheerleader in our business ventures and for supporting my effort to write this book.

Also, I thank my business ventures' co-founder, Tony Wang, for being a trusted friend for many years and through many ventures. Tony's support throughout our friendship for the last twenty-some years has been a tremendous help in many different ways. I can always count on him and forever thank him.

The short period of time since Guy and Trish Johnson welcomed me into their family and friendship has been a great pleasure, and I am enriched by their kindness and thank them for their generosity. Michael Jahabin is a business partner and a good friend to whom I am also so thankful for support.

My friend Jeffrey Aiono has been really committed member of our culture dialogue seminar and great supporter of my book effort. He will be a very effective chief for his family, some day in the future.

The words of John Donne's famous poem have been quoted ubiquitously as metaphor since their first publication in 1624: "No man is an Island." They express the truth of my working together with Sheila Deeth, editor of this book. This work needed the eyes and ears of an experienced professional editor with deep knowledge of the enormous landscape traversed in this book. The many sciences that it navigates demand a real expert to weave through the storyline in a language clear to readers. Sheila Deeth is my captain in organizing and pulling the silent messages out of my thoughts and delivering them clearly to readers. In bringing this project to fruition and publication, I am so happy and thankful that Sheila Deeth agreed to help me.

And thanks to the authors:

Lau Susuga Papali'i Dr. Failautusi Avegalio, fa'afetai mo le fanaafi o fa'amalama o le tapuaiga a Samoa ma Manu'a.
Lau Afioga Vui Dr. Toeutu Fa'aleava, fa'afetai mo le tuleiga o le tofa fa'atamaali'i ma le fa'autaga fa'aTumua.

Finally, my love and thanks go to my son, Marzel Joseph Levi, in Samoa, for being a good cheerleader and always praying for my good health. I hope this work will help illuminate your path. *I'a tafetoto ou ala!*

Fata Ariu Levi, Jr.

Foreword

Susuga Papali'i Dr. Failautusi Avegalio.
Director, Pacific Business Center Program
Shidler College of Business
University of Hawaii System, Honolulu, Hawaii

Navigators: Quest for a Kingdom in Polynesia is a compelling labor of love focused on retracing the origins of the past to better prepare for the future. Mary C. Bateson, the only daughter of Margaret Mead, author of *Coming of Age in Samoa*, expressed that same spirit; the past empowers the present, and the sweeping footsteps leading to this present mark the pathways to the future.

This is a personal research that retraces an ancient journey which is prefaced by a plethora of relevant literature and scientific references with citations listed in abundance. Orator Fata Ariu Levi's research draws extensively from classical history, recorded history and from the seven fields of science (formal sciences, natural sciences, engineering and technology, medical and health sciences, agricultural sciences, social sciences, and humanities).

That being said, Fata Ariu brings into the process a net that he casts over the historical reefs of conventional science and research. The essence of his net is *I'ike*, which in Samoan means attunement, synonymous with intuition. In Hawaii, 2,500 miles north of the Samoan archipelago, it is called *I'ke* with the same meaning. His I'ike is channeled by traditional practices supported by a heritage of noble orators and a genealogy traditionally linked to Polynesia's primogenitors, Tagaloa Lagi and Papa.

Fata Ariu shares an I'ike, in the first few pages of his book. *"I hear the constant and relentless whisper from the spiritual wind of our ancestors."* An I'ike is a profound experience among a people that believes death does not separate one from the living and that the wind carries the messages between the two dimensions; either as a whisper, a tap upon the shoulder, or cool breeze pleasant to the skin engendering an intuition or attunement.

Nobel Prize winner Albert Einstein was emphatic regarding his belief that *"The only real valuable thing is intuition."* He is also credited with a quote that strengthened my resolve as a young lecturer at the University Business College to hold on to my world with its I'ike and kinship ties to Papa, Earth Mother. *"The intuitive mind is a sacred gift. The rational mind is a faithful servant. We have created a society where we have honored the servant and forgotten the gift."*

Fata Ariu's net is unique in that the bare spaces between the net's strands are as significant as the strands themselves. The net not only harvests the material but also captures the spiritual treasures unmoved by time. The empty space merely makes room for the wind to nest as it carries the whispers of the wind that convey messages from the ancients and the sacredness of the other. I'ike, or attunement, is the gift of discernment.

I am reminded of a time when, as a new lecturer at the University of Hawaii College of Business Administration in 1989, the business and organizational paradigms were grounded in industrial era thinking, based on the machine metaphor that emphasized scientific analysis, quantification, and precision as the basis of efficiency. I was never able to fully embrace that mechanistic worldview in spite of extensive research and studies on that perspective. Having been raised in both Leone, American Samoa and with much time in Matautu Tai, Samoa, in a cultural context best described as a living or organic worldview, the dilemma of two opposing worldviews was a constant challenge, difficult to reconcile at the time.

The wisdom passed down by my elders told that all humans have two mothers and two fathers. The two mothers are our biological birth mother and Papa, our Earth Mother. In Polynesia, a newborn's umbilical cord is wrapped in *Ti* leaves and ritually buried in the sacred ground. The physical act of the burial ritual, conducted by elders, symbolically connects the newborn to Papa or Earth Mother.

Today, the modern meaning of *fanua* in Samoa is land. Its original and ancient meaning is placenta or afterbirth. *Ele'ele* today means dirt and *palapala* is mud. The original and ancient meaning of both words is blood. *Ma'a* today means stone, but its original meaning comes from the word *fatu ma'a* that means heart. The very language of my Samoan and Polynesian ancestors discerns the earth as living and as mother who birthed all life and material from the primogenitor of the heavens, Tagaloa Lagi. All elders of Polynesia are revered as the living stewards of the seeds of our living covenant to Papa the Earth Mother. It is believed that the life tree within our elders bears and carries the seeds of the living covenant that is passed on to each generation by breathing it into each new life.

All too often, Western science will make a so-called discovery after years of research, finally confirming what elders have been telling us for decades— for tens of thousands of years in some cases. The conceptual synergy of weaving traditional wisdom and ways of knowing together with empirical data, science, and technology enhances acuity and clarity with greater insight than if done so independently.

While native scientists do not conduct science in laboratories, they do systematically acquire scientific knowledge through observation, experiment, and theoretical explanation in a framework of natural law. The dominant paradigms of Western science, evolved from the 18th Century Age of Reason, had little tolerance for and no acceptance of perspectives outside of the boundaries of the scientific method. Fortunately, much has been changed with the introduction of quantum mechanics.

Dr. Greg Cajete, a Tewa Indian educator and author from the Santa Clara Pueblo, observed that Western man conducts science in a "low-context environment." They tend to isolate phenomena to study outside of their natural context, in a laboratory. In contrast, indigenous man conducts science in a "high-context environment," studying phenomena within their natural context. Dr. Cajete explains that the reason for this difference has to do with the purpose of science in the two cultures.

While both conduct science in pursuit of knowledge based on real observation and experiment, Western man removed phenomena from their natural context to study in laboratories, seeking knowledge enabling him to control nature for his own purposes. The indigenous man leaves what he studies in place, seeking knowledge that will permit him to integrate himself harmoniously into nature by discerning the rhythms, patterns, and currents of energy (*mana* in Polynesia) that guide life, (e.g. life patterns and cycles of fish, birds, plants, and those of the ocean currents, winds, and weather, etc.) so that he can conform to them with regenerative giving to assure balance, harmony, and sustainability for survival.

Ancient open ocean Polynesian voyagers knew the earth was round by the predictable movement of the stars, at a time the occidental world believed it was flat and balanced on the back of a giant tortoise. Polynesian seafarers perceived the universe as the whole that organizes the parts, as opposed to the prevailing reductionist belief, that is still held today, that the parts make up the whole. Wholistic systems thinking has already gained irretractable acceptance in the sciences. Indigenous cultures have always known of the participatory universe, while the industrial culture's scientists only recently discovered it. They now understand that pure objectivity, considered so fundamental to conducting good science, was illusory.

Indigenous science is participatory—fostering dialogue between humans, nature, and the unseen via attunement. It is taught to all people, not as something learned in limited years of schooling, but as a lifelong task through its traditional stewards of the sacred—primarily the traditional orators, family elders, village healers, regional guilds, and traditional leaders.

Fata Ariu reminds me, through the sweeping tapestry of his book that covers the ancient quest of our common ancestors, that I and all traditional leaders have a sacred obligation to promulgate measures to preserve and perpetuate the wisdoms of our Oceania and Samoan heritage. The Alii of Oceania must lead their *aiga* (extended family) to address and speak to the suffering of Earth Mother Papa, and not defer to the urgency of the scientist or the spinning of the politician. It is our responsibility, as the indigenous elder children of the earth, to speak to her suffering with actions to assuage her pain, restore her health, heal the vicissitudes of separation, and assure that the well of wisdom be forever preserved.

Fata Ariu's labor of love is a compelling response to the inexorable whispers, taps, and feelings of the spiritual winds to document his findings and experiences of Samoan and Manu'an culture and history. In his book, he has accomplished that and more. He has effectively engaged his oratorical heritage to affirm traditional wisdom and cultural perspectives woven meaningfully with modern science, knowledge, and technology, creating a more wholistic third option with value added. All are sustained and preserved in his book as part of the deep well of heritage and wisdom, stewarded by the great orators of Samoa and Manu'a—a well all are welcome to draw from, to learn the survival lessons of a quest that spanned past millennia, and encouraged to drink deeply from, to survive millennia more to come.

Susuga Papali'i Dr. Failautusi Avegalio
10/13/2020

CONTENTS

Images

Preface

Why I am Writing this Book

Navigators: Quest for a Kingdom in Polynesia

This book is the first of three books:
- Navigators: Quest for a Kingdom in Polynesia
- Navigators: Forging a Culture and Founding a Nation
- Navigators' Return: God's "Charge of the Light Brigade" Missionaries

In searching for a title for this first book, I found myself going back to Sir James G. Frazer's writing in the preface for Dr. B. Malinowski illustrious book, *Argonauts of the Western Pacific*[xi]. In his account of his study of the Trobriand Islanders, Frazer gives accolades to Dr. Malinowski:

"He has wisely refused to limit himself to a mere description of the processes of the exchange, and has set himself to penetrate the motives which underlie it and the feelings which it excites in the minds of the natives." He goes on to say, "It appears to be sometimes held that pure sociology should confine itself to the description of the acts and should leave the problems of motives and feelings to psychology. Doubtless it is true that the analysis of motives and feelings is logically distinguishable from the description of acts, and that it falls, strictly speaking, within the sphere of psychology; but in practice an act has no meaning for an observer unless he knows or infers the thoughts and emotions of the agent; hence to describe a series of acts, without any reference to the state of mind of the agent, would not answer the purpose of sociology, the aim of which is not merely to register but to understand the actions of men in society. Thus, sociology cannot fulfill its task without calling in at every turn the aid of psychology."

To describe the Navigators' migration by itself, without speaking to their motivation to find a Kingdom of their own, to secure their own freedom, would be to miss the important psychology of it all.

My Motive

My motive in writing this book is my own quest to exercise the responsibility of being an orator chief of our family, Fata Letunu Taliaoa Saena Poao Tagaloa (Saleimoa village).

This responsibility of my title includes being a custodian of the family history, genealogy, family lands, and titles; of the Samoan culture, history, legends and mythologies, and language; of the country's major families' genealogies; and, of course, of the island country's constitution and laws. This responsibility puts a heavy burden on chiefs, and on me in particular for I have been living away from the country and culture for the most part of my life until now.

This responsibility, vested in the Orator title, affords me the liberty to carry out my leadership duties as custodian and teacher of history, language, culture, folklore and legends, genealogies, and oratory to my family, and of being the orator in all our family ceremonies and affairs. This custodial responsibility extends to our village, district, and clan, and to monarch and country. And it motivates me with the responsibility of discovering and sharing answers to questions about the Navigators' history, language, culture, folklore and legends, genealogies, and oratory.

Who am I, and Where do We come from?

My journey began with the simple question: Who am I? And so, I shall answer that here:

Fata, Letunu, Taliaoa (Orator chiefs), and High Chief Saena Poao (great great grandfather) are the Chief titles that identify our family. Any title holder of one or more of these titles assumes an overall family identity. For example, while I have been bestowed the Fata and Letunu titles, I am identified as simply Fata, or Fata Letunu, of the Fata Letunu Taliaoa Saena Poao family clan in Afega and Tuana'i villages. Since I am one of two senior title holders and leader of our overall family, I can assume all three Orator titles at any setting. Likewise, my co-leader, Fata Taliaoa Laini Tugaga Sale, assumes the same family identity.

To simplify protocol procedures, I orate in one title, Fata, so that the other chiefs can properly address my title Salutation, as, in some cases, different titles have different Salutations. Many Chiefs carry several titles, bestowed on them by various branches of their family genealogy.

And so, my journey continues: Who are we? Where do we come from? And who are our ancient ancestors?

In my research to find answers to these simple questions, I hear the constant and relentless whisper from the spiritual wind of our ancestors to document my findings and experiences of Samoan and Manu'an culture and history. Acquiescing to this persistent call, I've decided to document my personal research effort in this writing.

Journey of the Book

The catalyst to getting this book organized and bringing it to fruition came in 1985, seven years before the title was bestowed on me—the title of Orator Chief of my mother's side of our family in Samoa (Western

Samoa). Learning and practicing to be a Chief is a lifetime process. The learning curve is usually steep and truly lasts a lifetime. It is a personal commitment and obligation. Leadership is recognized in terms of how proficient and eloquent you are in carrying out your duties as the leader of the family. You carry the title until you pass on.

In 2012, my pastor and family relative, Rev. Henry Yandall, asked me if I could help teach Samoan culture to the church youth group. Rev. Henry, of course, made his request knowing that I am an Orator Chief, and he thought that I would be qualified to hold this teaching dialogue. The seminar was held every other Sunday—two Sundays per month—for two years (2012 to 2014). The materials gathered for my seminar sessions are the foundation of this writing.

My Approach

An Aerial Survey of History and Culture

I have chosen to apply an 'aerial survey' approach to the history and culture of Samoans and Manu'ans in the context of the overall Polynesian race, of which we are a part. This spatial approach to the information will offer a bird's eye view of a very large, complicated subject.

The geographical map of Samoan and Manu'an migration paths covers thousands of square miles of ocean and land, and so a multi-dimensional approach is needed to understand the enormity and the vast extent of these migration paths. My intent is to zoom in on and observe the intra- and inter-relationships of the Navigators' locally observed norms, traditions, and cultural history, relative to those of other indigenous cultures along the migration path. Also, I'd like to observe any differences in their physical appearance vis-a-vis their physical land and oceanic environment. And, of utmost importance, I want to get a more detailed view of the Navigator's cultural and linguistic history as compared to that of other Pacific Island cultures and languages.

The Importance of Language

The whole idea of language—as in its having a single birthplace and thus growing, via human migration, across the globe—has stirred my curiosity for some time, since discovering Professor Joseph John Campbell's work in comparative mythology. Additionally, I was extremely interested in gaining an understanding of the inter-relationships of language development with that of culture, given the isolated environment of Samoa and Manu'a. In particular, I want to look at which development came first: the language or the culture? Or are they inextricably linked, like one coin with head and tail faces?

Topics of Interest

I was particularly interested to seek out and understand the following:
1. To identify the patterns and evidence for diffusion, or fusion, of the many cultural attributes and ethnicities encountered along the migration path of the Navigators.
2. To understand the development of Polynesian culture that occurred in each place where the Navigators paused along the migration path.
3. To understand the impact of natural disasters and changes in climate on the geographical migration paths, and how these impacted planning, organization, economics, people, and culture.
4. To understand the relevance of genetic mutations and genealogy as the Navigators intermarried with other indigenous people encountered on their path through different cultures, societies, and ethnicities.
5. To see how history and the oral transmission of events affects religious rituals, customs, norms, and the practices which sustain the culture.
6. To see how all the above factors affected the Navigators' way of life, both economically and in sustainability.

The Archipelago of the Navigators

The French Explorer Louis-Antoine Bougainville coined the name "Archipelago of the Navigators" on 3 May 1768. Writing in his journal, as he reached the Manu'an Island group, he called his island discovery "l'Archipel des Navigateurs," because he admired the dexterity of the Manu'ans as they maneuvered their canoes swiftly around the French ships.[xii]

The Question of Isolation

The isolated locality of the Samoan island chain throughout its ancient history—a period of over 3,500 years since our ancestors arrived in these islands—gives rise to a common misconception that our cultural development has, for the most part, taken place in isolation. With minimal contact with the outside world, this belief became ingrained in the mind of the Navigators, and is perpetuated in the independent attitude of the people, and in the belief that their world—the islands—is the center of the world. This reinforces their sense of uniqueness, and the belief that the world evolved around them.

I observed this attitude many times, and it appears to be common among people from many ancient cultures, from the cradles of ancient societies and civilizations—for example Greek, Roman (or Italian), Egyptian, African, Indian, Chinese, etc. Each society believes their culture is the cradle of the ancient world.

From this inward and limited perspective, the Navigators gained the idea that they were different, that theirs was the origin and cradle civilization of all of Polynesia. This, of course, promoted storytelling and embellishments of their migration history and cultural origin relative to the whole of Polynesia.

How Assumptions of Uniqueness affect the Search for a Migration Path

The answers to the question of the Navigators' origin and their migration path to their current homeland elude many social and physical scientists' research efforts. But the era of "ubiquitous information" on the Internet, coupled with advancements in technology and science in virtually every field affecting our lives, has been a godsend to piecing together and connecting the dots of the mystery of Polynesian migration.

Information about other Polynesian histories, cultures, languages, human genetics, and migration paths must be gathered, amalgamated, and compared, in order to find the truth. For we cannot always see the size of the forest for the trees, metaphorically speaking.

As it is, the chronicling of historical events is dependent on the writer's point of view, with, often, only a sample of events or anecdotal evidence accrued over a period of time. Having said that, I am reminded of the statement of Cicero, the great Roman orator and philosopher: in his view, time was variable, constantly moving as events occur in time and place; the history of these events being memorialized by the citizens and passed down to future generations—"History is the witness to the passing of time."[xiii] To this witness are added the footprints of the Navigators' paths, language, cultural similarities and genetics, which give further evidence of their migration journey—these are the tidings they brought with them and gifted to their descendants.

Unlike many countries of the world that are full of ancient monuments—defining and documenting their history and civilization within the timeline of human evolution—Samoans and other Polynesians have very few examples of such abundant fortune. Their only proof is themselves: the people, their homeland, culture, and language bearing evidence of their existence in isolation for thousands of years. This is the "mystery monument" that has so occupied scientists since the colonization of these Pacific islands during the Enlightenment period (mid-1700s through to 1800 A.D.).

Defining Samoan history, in isolation, without examining the totality of the Polynesian group, negates the value of corroborating evidence from common ancestors and the migration path. Looking at other Polynesian histories and cultures as a group will give us more common data points to connect with, in order to further define and substantiate patterns that may lead to possible conclusions. The single common thread, woven through the fabric of their respective Polynesian cultures, is that they share the same ancestors. That is, they are of the same people, Polynesian, and we shall see what the geneticists have to say about it.

Looking for a Polynesian Thread

My hope is to assemble and collate the available data—from already established research studies and conventional knowledge in the fields of anthropology, ethnology, comparative mythology, linguistics, and genetics of the Polynesians—into a common language for everyday readers to appreciate the Navigators' migration from their ancient to their current homeland. To be sure, I am not conducting new field research or laboratory experiments in any of the above disciplines. However, I have been collecting information about the subject matter for over 35 years. The variety of generational and other research studies about Polynesian migration have afforded me a reservoir of information, fragmented as may be, to put this effort together and launch this writing.

Comparing information gathered about the Polynesians' migration with the current body of conventional knowledge about other ancient societies and cultural practices is vital to this effort. Also, comparing the data with current norms and views of life is critical to illuminating the path of this ancient journey. It is my desire to be an effective Orator Chief and custodian of Samoan histories and culture. And this purpose motivates me to take this exciting journey.

While I am not publishing a thesis or even a dissertation, I am cognizant of the rules and standards of good research methodology in literature and social science. I am far from being an expert in any of the fields that I will traverse, but I will stay true and honest to the sources of the materials that help illuminate my conviction and beliefs about why, how, and when these Polynesians crossed several continents, and their final "leap of faith" journey into the East Pacific, in the midst of the largest ocean in the world. I want to highlight comparative themes and historical events from other cultures and societies that further illustrate the parallel development of the Polynesian initiative. Drawn from a plethora of information on comparative mythology, linguistics, anthropology, ethnology, and genetics concerning the Polynesians and their "mystery migration," I hope to simply point out the obvious and so illuminate the point.

My aspiration comes from my inspiration in learning about the ancient classical period and the way this influences my vision of how to view the ancient history and cultural development of Polynesians, in general, and of the Navigators, in particular. Proverbially speaking, the world is getting smaller, due to inter-connectivity and the ubiquity of information. But the scientific fact is that we all came out of one place, Africa, and this is fundamental to the search for the ancient ancestry of Polynesians.

Looking for a Polynesian "thread" in the world's "Out of Africa," "Out of India," Out of Levant... Out of the Pontic Steppe, Out of the Eurasian Steppe, Out of mainland Asia, Out of the Malay Archipelago, and, finally, out of the West Pacific and into the East Pacific Ocean... is no doubt a daunting and challenging task. Nevertheless, there have been abundant research studies undertaken in the fields of anthropology, ethnology, linguistics, archaeology, genetics, and geology over the last three hundred years. Thus, many important findings are now accepted as conventional knowledge, so the only thing left to do is to "connect the dots" and summarize the results into a book.

My Responsibility

Responsibilities and History of an Orator Chief

My responsibility as an Orator Chief commands a great deal of humility, as is commanded of any chieftain title holder in both Samoan and Manu'an societies. In my title, *Fata* adds more pressure because it designates me, by decree, as Paramount Orator Chief of the Malietoa monarch, one of two constitutional monarchies and royal houses of Samoa (not including the Kingdom of Manu'a). Together with my fraternal brother, Orator Chief Maulolo, and with the Council of Chiefs Tuisamau and Auimatagi, we share this oratorial and custodial responsibility on behalf of the Malietoa, Gatoa'itele, and Vaetamasoaali'i monarch—this monarch was the Paramount Royal Chief who received Christianity from Reverend John Williams of the London Missionary Society, London, England in 1830.

Oral History and Ancestry of an Orator Chief

These two fraternal titles—Chief Fata and Chief Maulolo—both represent high ranking chiefs, and Senior Orator Chiefs, and Elder leaders of the clan's district, Tuamasaga. The Circle of sitting Malietoa monarchs begins with Malietoa, the title holder, then the Fata and Maulolo title holders, respectively.

According to oral history[xiv] (recorded by Dr. Krämer in *The Samoa Islands, Volume I* 1901), these permanent designations were decreed to Fata and Maulolo around 1275 A.D. by the first Malietoa Saveatuvaelua, their brother-in-law. The two orators and their sister, Luafatasaga, were descendants of Manu'a's deity, Tagaloalagi—that is, of Tagaloalagi's daughter Sinalagilagi and Malalatea. Malalatea was the son of Fe'epo, and

7

brother to Leatiogie. Leatiogie was the father of the three brothers—Savea, Tuna and Fata—who helped free the Samoans from the Togan (or Tongan) yoke in 1225 A.D., according to legends promulgated by the Tuamasaga and Malietoa clans. Hence, these were the ancestors of Fata, Maulolo, Luafatasaga (their sister) and Va'afuti or Va'afa'i. The elder brother, Va'afuti (also known as Va'afa'i), is known as the explorer whose descendants are legendary in the old history of Samoa.

The genealogies of the two brothers, Malalatea and Leatiogie, sons of Fe'epo, were reconnected by the union of their sister, Luafatasaga, to the first Malietoa Saveatuvaelua. This further reinforced the Manu'an connection to the Malietoa royal family, with TuiManu'a, through the Tagaloalagi.

The Samoans were subjugated by the King of Toga (Tuitoga—in Samoan legends Toga and Tonga are the same) for over 400 years until his defeat (by the Samoans) around 1225 A.D. This oral history is memorialized in the founding of the Malietoa dynasty. The Malietoa monarch's genealogy and clan cover almost every major family of Samoa—with about 300,000 people living in Samoa and across the globe, primarily in New Zealand, Australia, and North America. The first five generations of the Malietoa—Malietoa Savea, Gagasavea, UilamatutuFaiga, Uitualagi and La'auli—reigned over Samoa for around 150 to 200 years since its founding, and his genealogical tree grew into a forest.

There have been around 45 generations of Malietoa title holders since its founding. (Samoans would say, who is counting? Which side of the Malietoa family is counting?)

Malietoa Vaiinupo was the title holder who reigned over all of Samoa and Tutuila when the first missionaries dropped anchor at the lagoon harbor in Sapapaali'i, Savai'i in 1830.

My Genealogy

My Genealogy (Mother's Side)

My Fata title is inherited from my mother's side: Through my grandmother, Ta'io, on my mother's side, my great grandfather (Ta'io's father) was Letunu Samasoni Saena, son of the Paramount High Chief Saena Poao. He is a descendant of the original Saena Faiga, who was the grandson of Malietoa Sagagaimuli (son of Malietoa Falefatu) and Sinalemanaui, sister to Malietoa Taulapapa (1560 A.D.).

The first Saena Poao was the second son of Saena Faiga from his marriage to Mualeoa, daughter of Fe'e So'oialo of the Vaimauga district, Upolu. My great-great-grandfather Saena Poao (1780-1845 A.D.) was the son of Paramount High Chief Tagaloa I'ata'atimu from the village of

Saleimoa, who married Saena Poao's daughter from village of Tuana'i, and that is how he inherited the Saena Poao title.

The Tagaloa title of Saleimoa is inherited by a descendant of Tagaloausufono and that royal Sina, granddaughter of the first consolidated ruler of all Samoa, Tafa'ifa (Queen) Salamasina. My great-grandfather Letunu married Talitiga Iliganoa (whose only sibling was the brother Warrior Orator Chief 'Aulavemai of Vaimoso). Talitiga Iliganoa was the daughter of Orator Chief Motuapua'a from Tafitoala village, Upolu, and of Iliganoa, daughter of High Chief Loau. Loau, from the Faleula and Saluafata villages, was the son of High Chief Simanu Afoa Fanene, and so the grandson of Prince Afoafouvale Tupua.

My grandmother's name, Ta'io, comes from the proverb that resulted from the brave action of her uncle 'Aulavemai in the war between Paramount Royal Chief Mata'afa and Paramount Royal Chief Tamasese, contesting for the Ruling Crown of all Samoa in the late 1800s. The proverb says: *Ta i uta, Ta i tai, Ta i o le faleaitu a 'Aulavemai ae le'i taga'i Faleata*—He, the Warrior 'Aulavemai, strikes (*ta*) and carries out his war magic club (*faleaitu*), to the mountainside (*uta*), to the seashore side (*tai*), and strikes over there (*ta'i'o*), but Faleata village didn't observe it—my own translation: He came carrying a large load which consisted of two large baskets (woven from coconut leaves) full of decapitated human heads of the enemies.

My daughter's middle name, Iliganoa—from my great-grandmother—is derived from the High Chief Loau's princess title, Iliganoa. My grandfather on my mother's side is Tavita Niu from the Elise Island (also called Ellice Island) of the Tuvalu Archipelago. His father was Baker, son of Reverend Baker from England, a missionary to the Island of Toga. His mother was a daughter of High Chief Niu, a descendant of Apemoemanatunatu-III Folasaaitu.

Apemoemanatunatu is legendary in Samoa and Toga and Elise as the Samoan explorer who came from Fasito'otai, Upolu, and landed in Toga. He led and won the war, on the side of Tui Haapai, against his brother, Tui Nukualoha, and he subsequently married Tauaho, the daughter of Tuitoga Haapai. His second marriage, to the twin daughters of the Paramount Chief Namumea of the Elise Island (Ellice in the European form), produced seven children: the elder son, Tepa, is an ancestor to my grandfather's mother (Lafai Ape Tonumaipe'a).

My great-grandfather's Orator Chief title, Letunu, makes the title holder the authority and custodian of the Fata Title in the village of Afega, Upolu, since the original legendary title of late 1200 A.D. Most of the court cases are centered on who are the genealogical holders of the Letunu title. Today, based on a landmark decision in 1990 that was reaffirmed in 2017, the Fata title family covers four main branches. Our branch is the Letunu family clan, and this Letunu title genealogy is how I come to inherit the Fata Orator Chief title.

My Genealogy (Father's Side)

I will be disowned by my father's side of the family if I don't mention my responsibility to uphold my father's family genealogy. Samoans always remind us there are two sides to a person's family: a mother and a father.

My father is Ariu Levi, son to Ariu Levi Moso Moegu of Olosega Island, Manu'a, and Selaina Moliga Leasau of Taū, Manu'a. My grandfather is a descendant of the ancient Tagaloalagi, Tuimanu'a, TuiAtua Moso and TuiOlosega. My grandmother is the daughter of Moliga and Liseoge Leasau. Her mother Liseoge Leasau is descended from Tuimanu'a Salofi (son of Tuimanu'a Taliutafa, according to Dr. Krämer's book[xv]), who reigned in Manu'a in the early-1700s. Tuimanu'a Salofi appears in our family genealogy around the mid-1700s. Some Manu'ans referred to him as Taliutafa—always ask the direct descendants.

Our family, in the village of Taū, carries three Prince titles: Moliga, Leasau and Nuanua. These titles are the names of the three sons of Tuimanu'a Li'a, who reigned in the mid-1500s—though there is some debate on the correct Tuimanu'a. Through time, these titles have been interwoven in the families and history of Manu'a, but the core of the three titles remains intact with our family, the Moliga clan. Since Tuimanu'a Salofi these titles have been held, mostly, by the members of the Moliga clan. Their combined salutation is: the Honorable Prince Brothers (*Pupuali'i*) of the Tuimanu'a, Tau, Manu'a.

My Experience

New York City, 1983: Mead vs Freeman

I remember one chilly morning in late January 1983 in New York City, when I came in to work at our office in mid-town Manhattan at 42nd Street across from Penn Central Station. I was greeted with one of my associates asking me, laughingly, as if it were a joke, in a voice clearly heard across an office fitted for a staff of twenty: "Hey Ariu, did you catch the news last night when CBS' Dan Rather was moderating a debate on who you are, what you are, and what you are going to be?" Of course, I did not catch the news the night before, but I immediately glanced over the New York Times headline: "New Samoa Book Challenges Margaret Mead's Conclusions."

The joke was clearly on me. Here I am, a Samoan acclimating into my U.S. citizen way of life, and now I have to listen to the experts debating whether I grew up in a free sex (Margaret Mead's belief) or a violent society (Freedman's theory)! Of course, it didn't help matters that the "Wild Samoan" wrestling phenomenon was at its peak in New York City at the time.

I recalled my memories of my first social science course, in college at Pacific Union College (PUC), a Seventh Day Adventist college in the Napa Valley at Angwin, California. The assignment was to read the Coming of Age in Samoa by Margaret Mead and prepare to discuss it, following with a standard written report. I remember the professor asking for my opinion about the book. I remember my answer even now: in my naiveté, I thought the Christian way of life had ruled the island's moral code, ever since Christianity arrived in Samoa and Manu'a. (I should say that I was born into a Seventh Day Adventist family, practicing a very rigid faith; and that is how I ended up at PUC.)

I followed the Mead vs. Freeman Controversy for some time. It was the biggest controversy in the social science field of anthropology, probably ever since the never-ending "nature vs. nurture" debate. The controversy affected me personally and profoundly because, not only am I Samoan, but my father's family village, Taū, Manu'a, was the control environment for the research. In fact, my father was a young teenager when Margaret Mead conducted her field research there. He shared with me that he was one of the boys assigned to run errands (at 9 years old) for the Village Guest, Margaret Mead. Many of my father's uncles, aunties and cousins were involved in support of Dr. Mead's research. In fact, in reviewing the sample participants listed in the book, I found many of the girls' names were from our family in Taū, Manu'a.

My father's family in Taū at that time—the Moliga/Leasau/Nuanua (three sons of Tuimanu'a) and Lefiti (Le alala Lefiti ma le Pupuali'i)—was compared to that of the Biblical Abraham due to its size and growth. The Moliga clan was the single largest family in the of village Taū, Manu'a, at the time. Also, Taū is the capital of Manu'a, where Tuimanu'a resides. Thus Mead's 1925-26 research effort in Taū was based on interrelated families, with strong family connections and traditions of respect and obedience to authority, which made it easy for Mead to organize her project with the support of the village chiefs.

Mead and Freeman's Conflicting Messages

Mead and Freeman both studied Samoans in a post-Christian period. They did not devote themselves to study or understand the anatomy of the peoples' development in the time before settling in the Pacific, because that was not part of their purpose. They were not studying Samoans to understand Samoans, but rather to further their understanding of the Western world. The Samoan and Manu'an story, that we are uncovering now, is a lot more complex and reveals marvelous and profound characteristics—characteristics that afforded the Navigators the achievements which sustained them through the last 3,000 years.

My great-grandfather and great-grandmother (Moliga and Lise Leasau) were among the early group of Manu'ans to be educated and then ordained in the mission seminary college in Malua, Upolu. Subsequently they were sent as missionaries to New Guinea and the Solomon Islands.

They were followed by my grandparents (Reverend Levi and Selaina), who served as missionaries to Papua and the Solomon Islands. The missionaries from this family, as well as from other related families in Olosega—such as Moegu, Moso and Malemo Iosefa and others—belong to a long line of missionaries from Manu'a to Melanesia. So, the laboratory atmosphere of Mead's research effort was, in fact, a very religious, paramount chief-controlled environment. Obedience was the rule, not the exception, in this atmosphere. Lying in an interview with someone in authority was not recommended and could not be undertaken lightly.

Just having the Tuimanu'a sanction Mead's study was critical to establishing creditability. No one could refuse Paramount Chief Tuimanu'a. Disputing participation in the iconic study by a sage of Mead's caliber would defame the Tuimanu'a's uncompromising authority, for Mead had been introduced to Manu'a by the Government of American Samoa, so she was well-respected, and getting the study done with the full cooperation of the citizens was Tuimanu'a's responsibility.

Subliminally, in my subconscious, I always knew that someday I would confront this itching nerve and scratch it. For I had always thought that the European researchers were studying the Samoans for their own, completely different (not Samoan) objectives. As it turned out, Margaret Mead stated, in her last Edition (1967), that she did not write her book, describing her field research in Manu'a, for the Samoan audience or market. She wrote it for the social sciences, catering to the challenge posed by the phenomenon of rebellious adolescents in an industrialized society. This made her a very successful leader in her field in the United States and Europe.

Dr. Mead's message to the Manu'ans might be summarized as: a closely netted and isolated community, where all members have kin relationship to one another, gives rise to a more cohesive and balanced life to usher in the young generations.

Dr. Freeman, on the other hand, wrote his book describing his research intended to refute and discredit a giant. Dr. Freeman's message to the Samoans is: the daily pressure of Samoan culture, balanced with Christianity as a way of life, leads to reflexive violence—rather like Ivan Pavlov's conditioned reflex or response—resulting in a high rate of crime and suicide.

Answering Mead and Freeman

My motivation in writing this book is, in some sense, to give my answer to these two sages. I had to go to the United States to learn about the cultures in which these social scientists anchored their respective sets of beliefs. Now I can confirm that human behavior is as old and complex as man himself, from his humble beginning to the marvels of his creative and destructive power. But understanding the ancient origin and purpose of a people is fundamental to knowing who they are, in any stage of their development. Both Mead and Freeman ignored at least half of the true

Samoan and Manu'an history and culture in their respective analyses. They both started with the Samoans of the 1900s, after Christianity, and ignored the 1,500 previous years which molded and developed their way of life and culture, from their arduous migration to settlement of their new homeland in isolation.

How could they ignore this? For every Samoan and Manu'an knows where their umbilical cord is buried. *O le tagata ma lo na fa'asinomaga—* Every Samoan has a "designation" or "identity," defined by family, village, title, salutation and the land or earth where they were born or where their umbilical cord is buried, all the way down to the core of the earth—my translation.

My Commitment

I am aware of the risk of disclosing and sharing the history and genealogies of people whose belief opposes this. These are sacred heirlooms of a country's dignity. For many families, it has been taboo, or strictly forbidden, to disclose such things openly, while, in the case of the Island of Manu'a, it is customary not to disclose them. They have been orally transmitted, in the lexicon of oral language, from generation to generation. But even writing them down in the English language risks inaccuracy, opening the storylines and messages to misinterpretation, and failing to extract the true meanings and spirit of the legends. I am cognizant of the obvious contraindications, but I have accepted the risk, with the hope in mind that I can serve those for whom English is now their primary or only language. It is my aspiration to bring water from the "well of the ancient past" to those who are thirsty for knowledge of their ancestors, in a language of the country they have adopted (which, for many of them, is English).

Salutation

Having said that:

On behalf of all reigning Paramount and Orator Chiefs of Samoa and Manu'a, the venerated Families of Samoa and Manu'a, and their respective Paramount Princes and their royal families, the Elder Chronicle Orators, honorable citizens of all Samoa and Manu'a, *tulou! tulou! tulouga lava!* (meaning: Your honor! and a form of prostrating one's self to addressing the Country).

I humbly ask your indulgence, for I am embarking on a journey, with the hope in mind to quench the thirst of those Samoans and Manu'ans that have emigrated and embraced new homelands in English-speaking countries such as the United States, New Zealand, Australia and many others, and of their future generations.

Introduction

<u>Oratory Calling</u>

Who is the Wind?

So, I shall call on the Samoan ancient Prophetic Spirit, the Oracle Tree, *Le Fau Gagana*, to summon the powerful Winds, *Matagitetele*, of Ancient Samoa. *Matagitetele* is the herald of the Creator, delivering the sacred Words to the people of Samoa and Manu'a. The Wind will deliver the message, quenching that thirst for knowledge of their beginnings and cultural development, so they may see light, illuminating the path traveled by their ancient ancestors.

The Wind is older than the Earth, according to common beliefs of the Polynesians. It is the messenger of the Gods and Warrior Spirits to the people. It is said: the Wind first produces a vibration; that single vibration begets a sound that echoes across the vast Pacific Ocean, the habitat of the people of Polynesia; the Wind blows in the white clouds, providing a navigational compass, and in the dark clouds, providing rain to fill reservoirs with drinking water and to cultivate the land for food crops; the Wind communicates climate, seasons, and daily weather prospects; it aggravates the ocean tides, influencing them to be calm or angry.

Although the people do not know the cause and effect of, or the source of the Wind's coming and going, still, having observed all these things, for thousands of years and many generations, their observations are passed down orally, in history, as messages from the gods. These messages, carried by the Wind from the ancient past, are ubiquitous across the ocean and islands, delivered to all living things: *Ua logo le na i Atea, logo fo'i i ama*—Proclaim (the message) to Atea, to the place the ancient Polynesians came from; proclaim it to the portside of the canoe (that's where a sailor would sit to balance the canoe),and let the message be known to the people (on the portside), and also in Atea, the ancient home of the Polynesians—my translation. The message delivered by the Wind is heard in the ancient world by the traveler in the canoe.

The Wind is worshiped, feared, and given reverence as though it were a deity. This belief is not unique to the Polynesians. Mythologies can be found throughout the ancient world that define and incorporate the Wind as being integral to their storylines, particularly in classical antiquity.

In Bulfinch's Introduction to his popular book, *Illustrated Mythology* (based on his famous *The Age of Fable* published 1867) he gives the name Hyperboreans to the happy-face people inhabiting the northern part of the earth, in the beginning or birth of Greek society, meaning those who live beyond the North, from the word hyper, meaning beyond, and Boreas, meaning the North Wind.[xvi]

For the Navigators, the North Wind brings a cool and life-refreshing breeze.

Creation of the Earth

In the beginning, at the dawn of time, when the Earth is covered with water and fire, and, in its belly, is breathing life, the story of Genesis begins—"And the earth was without form, and void; and darkness was upon the face of the deep." Then, periodically it "sneezes," or has "seizures," caused by sipping oxygen through cracks in the tectonic plates that insulate the fury of magma in the core of the Earth.

"Mucus" of magma erupts and shoots up violently, like a "geyser" of fire. And the "flood of fire" flows freely, slowly, and unrelenting, as if the Earth is "vomiting" molten rock, which finally comes to rest in the cool abyss of the Pacific Ocean. Then Fire is tamed by Ocean water. Together they beget Lava, a continuous form of rock.

Then *Malama mai Aga'e* (the Light from the East) and *Malama mai Aga'ifo* (the Light from the West) burst through the heavens like a phoenix and create a union that begets the Cliffs. Then Cliff is united with Boulder, birthing Pebbles, Rocks, and Soil. Then Soil meets Water and begets the Marshes, and a Fertile Land is born.

Geological Creation and Chemosynthesis

According to Lydia M. Boschman, a geologist at Utrecht University in the Netherlands[xvii], the places where plates of the earth's crust are pulling apart form instabilities, allowing molten rock to pour through. The freshly born crust pushes older crust away toward the edge of a continent, and so a deep ocean bed is born. The ocean crust, crashing into the continental crust, is sucked down under the plate to become liquid and rise again.

In early 1979, a team of astrobiologists, led by Robert Ballard of Woods Hole Oceanographic Institution, announced the discovery of deep-ocean hydrothermal vents. They identified a process called "chemosynthesis"—that is, life powered by sulfides, by chemical energy, instead of by sunlight as in photosynthesis. They observed this in oases that had sprung up around the volcanic springs of the deep, revealing a whole new ecology powered by chemosynthesis. Author Charles Pellegrino described this as "The Europa Theory," in *Ghosts of Vesuvius*.[xviii]

On the heels of this discovery, astrobiologists Clair Edwin Folsome and Cyril Ponnamperuma became the first to propose that abundant heat and ever-expanding mineral deposits near deep-ocean volcanic vents were, almost from the day of the earth's formation, the source of life's origins.

This represented a major paradigm shift from the long-held belief of physicists, from the ancients—Euclid, Thales of Miletus, and Archimedes—

to the scientific revolution in Europe in the 1600s; from theories put forward by the likes of Newton and Maxwell, till William Whewell first coined the terms "physicist" and "scientist" in 1840, to the ushering in the new ideas of quantum mechanics, which the iconic Albert Einstein expanded into a whole new paradigm.

The Scientific Origins of Life

To risk over-simplifying a highly complex scientific discipline: In the old paradigm, everything begins in space, and the fundamental origins of life are protons, electrons, and neutrons, which, when combined, are the source of energy.

Before the much-discussed and now accepted theory of the origin of life—by chemical oxidation, or oxidative chemical reactions now known as chemoautotrophs—we were taught that the source of life's building blocks was the energy of sunlight, or photoautotrophs, referring to forms of life that generate energy by combining inorganic materials such as ammonia and methane etc. with oxygen.[xix] We have understood this as the process of photosynthesis. I like to refer to it as the carbon-based source of life, for carbon atoms have six protons, while hydrogen atoms have one proton and oxygen atoms have eight, making such combinations effective. Human life is believed to be carbon-based.

When you simplify this and reduce it down to basic building blocks, the interactions of basic energy-chemicals drive the life-producing cycles that feed the life-sustaining chain and those multiple processes that contribute to life as we know it today: what we have long known as photosynthesis.

This is where faith-based beliefs meet science. Science has already taken the position that it has confirmed the process of evolution of human beings over several million years—DNA sequencing processes bear this out. But, from my humble, naive perspective, I have asked: where do these energy-chemical particles come from?

God's plan of creation should be evident in the answer to this simple question, yet it poses an enigma to science. Believing that the so-called "bursting" of some very, very big star, some billions of years ago, together with its resulting death, gave birth to the chemical energy that eventually became the source of life's building blocks, is really a faith-based belief. To accept this—to allow science to convince you of the facts about this process—you have to be educated in astronomy and astrophysics, or else you accept it on faith.

The problem is the inherent exclusivity of science, its exclusive hold on facts. If this is the "truth," and if only the few can comprehend it, not the masses, one must ask: did God really mean to keep His creation understandable only for the very, very few elites? No, because faith remains essential. It still requires faith to accept science.

The Biblical Origin of Life

As the NRSV Bible states in Psalm 90: "Lord you have been our dwelling place in all generations. Before the mountains were brought forth or ever you had formed the earth and the world, from everlasting to everlasting you are God. You turn us back to dust, and say, 'Turn back, you mortals.'"

Pellegrino asked, in *Ghosts of Vesuvius*, if anyone could really believe that we arose from the dust of the stars, or from the dust of the earth. Then he reminded his readers that the earth, our cradle, has had billions of years and entire oceans to work with. For in the basements of the oceans resides a system of volcanic vents that, even to this day, weaves a lengthy path, somewhat like the seam on a baseball, over more than 40,000 miles (65,600 kilometers) of the seafloor.

The Movement of the Stars

Consistent, over several moon's "waxing" and "waning," "sunrises" and "sunsets," the *Holy Book* states, in Ecclesiastes 1:5 (NRSV), "The sun rises and the sun goes down, and hurries to the place where it rises."

The Greeks gave the name, Erebus, to the darkness of the sky, born like the earth from the void.

With simple, naive, and almost childlike observation, we see that when the stars show their faces in the darkness, it seems as if they are speaking, in a sparkling digital fashion, almost like conversing with the moon. And in the early evening, the sound of the crickets almost feels as though the sparkling stars are singing, like a choir, welcoming the night. In orator phraseology: *Ua fepulafi mai fetu o le lagi a'e pepese mai fetu o le afiafi*—the Orator would say: "Oh how beautiful! The sparkling of the stars in the heavens and chorus of the stars of the evening"—my translation—referring to the sounds of the crickets in the evening that seems so well-orchestrated with the sparkling of the stars. It's as if the stars were pantomiming the cricket's chorus.

The celestial bodies appeared to travel from one location to another when the moon showed different sides of her face. The sun rises, always from the same place that the moon also comes up from—i.e. from the east (moonrise might be east-northeast or east-southeast, depending on its phase). And directions were only known by how the heavenly bodies traveled across the sky; they come out of and go into the ocean every day, so the oral wisdom whispers.

Ancient belief holds that the earth is bounded by the ocean and the ocean is vast—the heavens are a dome, and the ocean is flat; it has boundaries that the heavenly bodies fall over at night and come up from again the next day. For the people had observed these things for thousands of years and passed them down by "word of mouth" from one generation to another. Memorizing the traveling movements of the heavenly bodies in the dome—the stars, as they didn't know about planets—facilitated their learning. Their hut house was often used as a classroom dome, with fruits or coconut shell oil lanterns hanging from the ceiling to represent stars and their movements, to instruct the young people. The classroom was a transition from the hut house dome to the dome of the heavens at night. And next would come night-time fishing excursions.

The people recognized the vastness—the monumental magnitude and immovability of the earth—from their vantage point vis-a-vis the Pacific Ocean, at a time before the Old Testament was written in the Hebrew Bible, where Psalm 93:1, 96:10, and 1 Chronicles 16:30 all include text stating that "He has established the world; it shall never be moved." Likewise, Psalm 104:5 states "You set the earth on its foundations, so that it shall never be shaken."

So, the Southern Cross or Morning Star rises at different places during different phases of the moon. Joe Rao, of SPACE.com's Skywatching[xx], describes how the four stars in the constellation Crux have come to represent the lands that lie below the equator. So, because the earth was believed not to move, the motion of stars could be used to define different parts of the earth.

The Nature of Time

The people would know when winds from the east would come and go, for the East Wind brings with her heat in the morning and warmth at night. Then it is followed by the winds from the west, the same direction where the sun and moon set, and by southwest winds as well, bringing wet and cold air from the southern hemisphere. Winds from northwest would join hands, metaphorically, with southeast winds to bring fair, calm, and soft breezes.

But they all come and go. For time was seen only in the repetitively changing face of the heavenly cosmos. And the coming and going of winds indicated the season, cycle, and changes in climate. This is how time was known to the people, for there was no time-keeping apparatus.

Clearly, the Polynesians did not have the knowledge of Galileo Galilei, the sixteenth century scientist whose epiphany with the swinging crystal chandelier seemed to swing to the cadence of his heartbeat. Galileo went home and set up two pendulums of equal length; he swung one with a large sweep and other with a small sweep, and found that they kept time together, hence the accidental discovery of the timepiece (as described in Isaac Asimov's *Intelligent Man's Guide to Science*).[xxi]

The Navigators knew the "time" of day by observing the movement of the "shadow of the trees" from west to east, relative to the direction and location of the sun, and by watching the sprouting of deciduous vegetation on the earth as a sign of life's progression.

According to Genesis 1:11 (NRSV), "Then God said, 'Let the earth put forth vegetation: plants yielding seed, and fruit trees of every kind on earth that bear fruit with the seed in it.' And it was so." Geologists put these events at around 200 million years ago—in "the dark backward and abysm of time," to use the words of England's national poet laureate, William Shakespeare in his play "The Tempest" (1611)[xxii].

A Digression on the Value of Oral History

Not Just Legend

I am compelled to digress for a moment, for there are many people that may view oral history to be purely legend or anecdotal. But, in the words of the old North African (Tunisian) philosopher Ibn Khaldun in the 13th century, "the oral message is more accurate than the written one."[xxiii] According to Warren E. Gates (writing in 1967) and Mohamad Abdalla (writing in 2007), the pious Arab Muslim historiographer, a direct descendant of the Prophet Muhammad, must have been influenced by Socrates, the classical Greek philosopher credited as one of the founders of Western philosophy. Socrates also vehemently argued that oral history is more correct than written documents.

William Harris (in *Ancient Literacy,* 1989), introduces Phaedrus, written by Plato, documenting conversations and discourses between Socrates and Phaedrus (444-393 B.C.):[xxiv]

The final discussion between Socrates and Lysias (a speech writer, 445 – 380 B.C.) addressed the technology of writing. Socrates recounted a myth about the god Theuth, credited with discovering writing and transmitting it to the Egyptians. But when Theuth presented writing to King Thamus of Egypt, praising it as a device that would increase wisdom and memory, King Thamus replied that writing would increase forgetfulness instead. For instead of working things through for themselves, internalizing and understanding them, students would come to rely on writing to inform and remind them of things. As well, writing might expose them to many ideas without them being fully thought out. Socrates criticized writing because it is not speech: the written word cannot discern between audiences, and it cannot respond to questions or criticism.[xxv]

The philosopher continues by stating that writing represents "not Truth but only the semblance of Truth." Written words "seem to talk to you as though they were intelligent," the philosopher said, "but if you ask them anything about what they say, from a desire to be instructed, they go on telling you the same thing forever."

Written words are often cited as references and as proof, and over time they become gospel. But "Oral history provides information about the impact of events on the lives of ordinary people that would not necessarily be found in the document left by the elites," as noted by

Alexander Stille in his New York Times article, "Prospecting for Truth in the Ore of Memory." [xxvi]

Quoting Mary Marshall Clark, director of the Oral History Research Office at Columbia University, who was commenting on the work on oral history of Alessandro Portelli (an Italian oral historian in the early 1950s), Stille invites us to see, in oral history, not just eyewitness accounts that can be judged either true or false, but also the themes and structures of the stories being told.

William Harris recounts that Plato, while documenting Socrates' viewpoint, clearly recognized the importance of writing both for its mnemonic value, and for creating, preserving, and distributing complex expositions such as his Dialogues. Harris describes how, in many non-literate cultures, in order to remember their history and their folklore, individual people had to develop the skill of remembering words with great accuracy. "As cultures change over the centuries and millennia, our methods for storing and sharing information have naturally changed, and they will probably continue to change."[xxvii]

Just to close, as I opened, with my favorite philosopher:

The Middle East historian and economist, Ibn Khaldun, begins his famous book, *Muqaddimah,* with a thorough criticism of the mistakes regularly committed by his fellow "historians" and the difficulties which await the historian in his work. He notes seven critical issues (*Muqaddimah*: Wikipedia Website encyclopedia), stating: "All records, by their very nature, are liable to error due to:

1. Overconfidence in one's sources
2. Partisanship toward a creed or opinion
3. The failure to understand what is intended
4. A mistaken belief in the Truth
5. The inability to place an event in its context
6. The common desire to gain favor of those of high ranks, by praising them, by spreading their fame
7. The most important is the ignorance of the laws governing the transformation of human society"[xxviii]

This iconic Islamic philosopher is considered by many of his contemporaries and modern academicians to be the authority on Middle Eastern history, the development of tribal culture, and, among many other credits, the economic development of the Arab Muslim world in North Africa. His detailed, expert knowledge of tribal-based cultural development, from his travel and research into Arabic-speaking nomadic peoples of the Middle Eastern deserts (the Bedouin tribes), lends credibility to a view that lies outside Western-based thoughts.

And so we owe the acceptance of oral history to Socrates, Ibn Khaldun, and also to Allan Nevins, a historian at Columbia who founded the oral history office there in 1948.

This now widely accepted field of oral history led to our enjoyment in reading *Roots* by Alex Haley, *Hard Times Working* by Studs Terkel, and *Children of Sanchez* by Oscar Lewis, and many others, which were all based on interviews.

Oral Tradition in History

I believe the classical Greek historian, Herodotus (484-425 B.C.), knew all along that there would be readers of his works in the future who would criticize them because they were based on hearsay and anecdote. The Roman orator Cicero called Herodotus the "The Father of History," but he was also called, by his critics, "The Father of Lies." Nevertheless, his literary contribution to the world of Classical Greek history will be forever appreciated by current and future generations.

As James Romm, author and Professor of Classics at Bard College, New York, wrote, Herodotus maintained the common ancient Greek cultural assumption that the way events are remembered and retold—as myths and legends—creates a valid picture, even if not a completely factual one.[xxix] For Herodotus, myth and history must work together to attain true understanding.

As for his critics, Roy Arthur Swanson writes that Lucian of Samosata, a Greek-speaking Assyrian author, "attacked Herodotus as a liar in his 'Verae Historiae' and denied him a place among the famous on the Island of the Blessed."[xxx]

I believe Herodotus obsessed over details in order to compensate for the lack of documented evidence. Hence his descriptions of his encounters and discourses throughout his sojourn were written with sedulous care. As stated in G. Rawlinson's *The History of Herodotus*, "The fact of an immigration, and the quarter from which it came, are handed down from father to son, and can scarcely be corrupted or forgotten, unless in the case where the people sink into absolute barbarism."[xxxi]

Reliability of Samoan Oral History

Samoans believe that their oral history is self-audited and eventually self-corrected by the respective family members. The belief is that the "owner" (source family) of the legend, folklore, genealogy, etc. will always be motivated by self-interest to maintain its accuracy, and to correct any errors that may have been introduced, intentionally or unintentionally, by others, for these genealogies, family history, and folklore are heirlooms, foundational to the organizational structure of the family. Thus, they are guarded and kept in secrecy.

It is not unusual to argue a title (such as that of a Chief) in a special court system—the Land and Titles Court that mediates and legally decides indigenous property rights and inheritance of a family's titles. In my personal experience, our family has been in court to resolve titles and land disputes for over 35 years for one title, Fata, and over 25 years for another title, Taliaoa—both titles deriving from the village of Afega in Upolu, Samoa—and for over 27 years for the title, So'oialo, in the district of Vaimauga in Upolu, Samoa. To quote Psalm 94:15 in the NRSV version of the Holy Scriptures: "for justice will return to the righteous, and all the upright in heart will follow it." So, fortunately, the results were in favor of our family at large with the final legal decisions (2016, 2013 & 2004).

The point is, people care very much about their heirlooms and the inheritance of the family titles, because these things define their identity and property rights. So, you do whatever it takes, for however long it takes, and no matter how many appeals have to be filed with the court, to fight for what you believe about your identity. It is this legal adversarial relationship, coupled with persistence and resilience, that the people believe will yield the truth—most of the time.

Dr. Augustin Krämer, in his *The Samoa Islands, Volume II,* tells that one thing he learned from earlier missionaries—Turner, Pratt, Stair, Ellis, Powell, and Violette—is that individuals do not invent stories and legends; they are the common property of the Samoan people. All the different variations, whether embellishments or distortions, maintain the same quality of story at the core. Indeed, he found the various traditions to have been uniformly retained since the arrival, 70 years earlier, of the missionary John Williams in 1830. Clearly verbal transmission is accurate and effective and should be looked on with full confidence.[xxxii]

An Old Orator Saying

As the old orator says: "In the quest to quench your thirst of the culture and family genealogies, don't drink the unripe coconut for it is bitter and sour, but drink the green and ripe coconut for it is sweet," *Ia utu vai i le fuiniu ae aua le utu vai i le fuisa'a*. A more modern version is, "Don't drink from another family's water well but from your own for that is the truth of your own family history, genealogies, and ancient family relationships."

History's Mosaic

The Archaeological Mosaic

I remember touring the beautiful archaeological sites and ruins of the cities of Pompeii, Herculaneum, and Stabiae, of the Roman Empire, in Italy. The eruption of Mount Vesuvius covered a circle of about 25 miles radius, burying those cities in 79 A.D. The magnificent sets of mosaics, in the ruins of various homes, speak volumes to the daily life of citizens of the Roman Empire at the time. The evidence of a rich, mighty, and sophisticated culture and organization is magnificent.

Likewise, when we look at the enormity of the Pacific Ocean we might imagine how the incredible richness of the archaeological mosaic, lying beneath the ocean, could speak to us about the hundreds of thousands of voyages that have traversed the ocean. The tidings that lie in the ocean depths will eventually illuminate the path traveled by the ancestors, with colorful stones of this mosaic that traces "The Great Migration"—a migration that is a mystery and a conundrum to the modern world.

The Era of Discovery

Understanding the mystery of Navigators' migration is a task that has eluded and intrigued many men of science, ever since the discovery of the mighty Pacific Ocean in 1520 A.D. by Portuguese explorer and navigator Ferdinand Magellan. His discovery in 1521 A.D. marked the first time that the islanders learned there were other islands in this vast Pacific Ocean colonized by their predecessors.

In 1616 A.D. a Dutch explorer, Willem Schouten, navigated through what is now called the Bismarck Archipelago (named in honor of the German Chancellor Otto von Bismarck, when the islands were annexed as part of the German protectorate of German New Guinea in 1884). The Bismarck Archipelago lies in the southwest Pacific Ocean, and Schouten made contact with the indigenous people of Melanesia, in Papua New Guinea. Thus began the era of discovery and colonization, as Europeans descended on the Pacific Islanders.

And now the story of the Pacific peoples would undergo major changes, until their isolated habitats would be transformed into the last ocean world to be conquered.

The Path Passed Down from the Gods

The mosaic path has been passed down from the gods, to the oracles, to the warriors and orator chiefs of the ancestors, by words delivered to the people by the soothing, whispering wind, in the early dawn before the first cock crows. The legends, folktales, and mythology, all told by word of mouth at early dawn, of a culture, people, and their homeland, are the oral evidence of their ancient existence. It is the land of mythology, as ancient as the wind that carries the myths down through the generations. It is as old as the story of man and his beginning.

Much like the parallel stories of other ancient societies, the mosaic path begins with the creative thought process of imagination, with the embellishment of mythology and storytelling. And so we are left with oral history and traditions. A close examination of these rich oral traditions will take us to the ancient well of the Navigators' ancestors, giving us more colorful stones in the vibrant mosaics of Samoan and Manu'an history. Using in the words of James Joyce, the motifs of the kaleidoscope that we find in these legends and mythologies are "ever the same yet changing ever."[xxxiii]

Samoans and Manu'ans believe they are different from other Polynesians; however, the more we dig into the well of the ancient past, the more we will find they are a branch from the same ancestral tree.

The Historical Migration

Beginning the Story

Long, long ago, somewhere in the Molucca group of Islands, between the Gilolo Passage to the east and the Molucca Passage to the west, in the far-east of the Malay Archipelago (now called the Malaysian Archipelago), a group of homogenous people, with a common ancestry, has long been planning to make a migration eastward to the mighty Pacific Ocean, in search of a new home.

These migrants have flocked into the Asiatic Archipelago (which covered the whole of Southeast Asia and South India), traveling from mainland Asia. Many different ethnicities have assimilated, juggling for position in many areas throughout the archipelago. (This has been verified by the initial Polynesian genome marker, which notes mainland ancestry.)

This is where the Polynesians begin to explore the whole region, going as far north as Taiwan and the northeastern islands in the China Sea, and as far west to the coast of the South African continent, where Madagascar is today. The Polynesians, or the people that we now call Polynesians, initially settled around the Strait of Malacca, which lies between Malaysia and mainland Indonesia, where they stayed for over 300 years. In effect, the Polynesians pushed out the Negritos (the previous occupants) eastward, into and through the Java Peninsula, then further east to the Indonesian Archipelago. Then, when Malayans arrived from the mainland and migrated down toward the Malacca Strait, they, being more aggressive, pushed the Polynesians into the same Java Peninsula and into the islands of the Indonesian Archipelago.

So we see, this intrepid journey is only a beginning of the people's long migration path—a path that will take them thousands of miles and years, leaving many layers of evidence of their generations, until they arrive in Southeast Asia, or specifically at their starting-off point for the Pacific, the Malay Archipelago. The catalyst to their constant movement, island-hopping throughout the Indonesian Peninsula, will be a combination of war and their constant search for the freedom of a permanent homestead.

With the Help of Tagaloalagi

The supreme god is called Taga-loa-lagi: *Ta-ga* refers to *tagata* meaning human; *loa* means ancient; *lagi* means heavens. Hence, Tagaloalagi denotes a supreme human being that resides in the tenth—the highest— heaven.

Long ago, in the time of the ancient wind, the people ask their supreme god, Tagaloalagi, to show them trees that are strong and agile for canoe building. The god, Tagaloalagi, summons:

- the *koa*, for the hull
- the *ulu* (breadfruit tree, which has very strong and supple wood) for the bow, and also for the stern (*manu*)
- the *fau* (hibiscus) for the crossbeams (*iato*)
- the *niu* (coconut tree) for coconut husk fibers (sennit)
- and the *lau fala* (pandanus leaf plant) for weaving the sail.

In the depth of the night, the people hear the sound of trees falling, and the ruckus of what seems like construction work being carried out in the dark. At sunrise, the people rush to survey the forest, looking for signs of trees lying on its floor, but there are neither trees nor any sign that the forest was ever touched. However, at the beachfront lies a beautifully carved-out double-hull canoe ready to be launched, with the sail ready to be rigged for the journey. As the legend tells, the people are reverently thankful to the spirit, that the god has answered their prayers and built the first canoe. But they are also aware the boat must be put to the test in the mighty ocean, for the idiom of the time is: the true test of a boat for a long journey is to count how many seas or oceans it has traveled and endured.

The Task of the Matriarchs

The women of the village, led by the Elder women (wives of Elder leaders of the family village), begin to discuss the plan for weaving the vessel's sails out of pandanus tree leaves. Leaves lie out to dry in the sun for three to four weeks before they are sliced into small vertical strips like fibers; over time, this repetitive process will create soft fibers, good enough to weave the sail "mat."

The daunting task of scraping the leaves begins after they have been soaked in salt water. The rough leaves' membranes are scraped off to get to the fiber, which is similar to cotton or wool. These fibers are interlaced, some passing in one direction with others at a right angle to them. It is the same process that weavers of cotton and wool fibers use in producing canvas, clothing materials, and rugs etc. The task is done only by senior and experienced women, for they have the patience and knowledge to be efficient.

Weaving the sail mats is done by hands that have built many sails in the past, with the knowledge that, for every vessel launched to the sea, the sails' obedience to the commands of the wind will be tested. Elderly women work diligently on weaving and on joining overlapping fibers for mainsails and jibs, which are often the weakest points. These experienced hands are strong, with thick calluses on the palms, wrinkles from age, and evidence of motherhood in the nurture of children, family, and the people. These are the matriarchs of the families and culture.

The matriarch is the mother of life and truth.

The Task of the Men

While the village women are diligently tending to their chores, the chiefs summon the men of the family and village to discuss, debate, deliberate, and plan the voyage. Navigators of the Pacific Ocean understand that for every voyage there must be a destination. For they know the clouds for launching; the stars for sailing; the paths of fish; the winds for their bearings; the ocean swells for the current; the sea birds, fishing schools, and landmass directions; the rooster crow for the dawn of day and signs of land; for these are the instructions from gods.

After much discourse and opposing views, some are not convinced that the proposed, arduous voyage is necessary. Some prefer to stay and fight for their home, land, and way of life. Others need more definitive signs from gods, while still others are somewhat indifferent to the decision.

As the sun casts shadows to the east while dying into the west, the Elder Chief in his wisdom knows that the topic must be slept on, or put to sleep, *fa'amoe le toa*, for the night is long, and wisdom will wrestle and negotiate with emotions and reasoning till morning. He has this hope in mind, that sleep will bring forth sound ideas, critical to the decision that lies ahead.

Thus, the Samoans and Manu'ans use a well-practiced management approach to deliberations and negotiations to derive a decision. The process takes days, even months on end, and several years elapse, while the driving motive remains—the desire for a new homeland, out there beyond the bright sunsets and sunrise clouds at the end of the known Earth, that itching nerve of ambition to know what is out there in that vast ocean, and an unquestioning tolerance for ambiguity to venture out and discover what is out there.

27

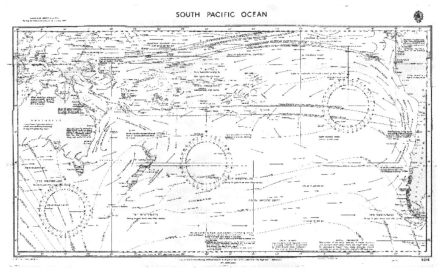

Figure 1 Admiralty Chart No 5216 South Pacific Ocean, Published 1942[xxxiv]

Sailing the Trade Winds

The waiting period is over. Destiny has arrived. The appointed time has come. The wind from the east of the southern hemisphere (from the coast of South America) gives way to long awaited westerly, northwesterly, and southwesterly winds. These seem to stir up the ocean currents to move east and then due northwest toward the northern hemisphere; then they circle back southwest to the southern hemisphere, as observed by anthropologist Ben Finney, in a July 1986 excursion on the Hokule'a, a replica of a Polynesian sailing canoe.

In the Americas, these winds are commonly known as "El Niño" (Spanish for Little Boy or Christ Child) and "La Niña" (Little Girl in Spanish). El Niños occur irregularly and are part of a complex series of climatic changes which affect the equatorial Pacific Ocean and related regions every few years, typically during the Christmas season, hence the name—the "Little Boy" phenomenon. An opposite effect of heating and atmospheric pressure anomalies occurs during La Niña.

The Navigators observed that there are times when the trade winds blowing east to west would pick up momentum, blowing warm air westward, and gathering up in the West Pacific around Indonesia and the Philippines. Then the trade winds would reverse, and warm air would blow eastward and northeastward. This would be the time to sail eastward and into the East Pacific Ocean, using the westward trade winds for a trip back to the Indonesian Archipelago. These observations are recorded in the memory of Polynesians oral history.

The Anthropological View of Migration

Human Migration in History

The story of human migration is fundamentally the story of the human race, from its origins to the present. It is an integral aspect of life since the "Out of Africa" migrations. And within it lies the story of how the Polynesians reached the Asiatic Archipelago.

History has revealed much about the impetus propelling human migration. The consensus of anthropologists is that "hunter-gatherer" humans follow their food supply and are therefore always on the move, their journeys ranging from a few miles' hunt to epic travels across oceans and continents. Droughts, plagues, floods, or other natural disasters trigger migrations as well. Slavery, escape from slavery, invasions, and exile enforce migrations. And adventurers seek new land, fame, fortune, or power. The formations of empires, colonies, and nation states takes people across the continents.[xxxv]

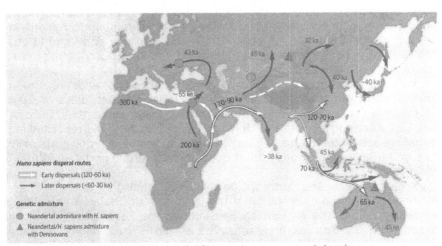

Figure 2 Out of Africa migratory model[xxxvi]

The First Two Migrations

The different migrations into the Asiatic Archipelago begin with the first "Out of Africa" migration through the South Arabian Desert; this followed the southern coastal landscape of greater India, which guided the North African migrants to settle and populate the Malay Archipelago and the Australian continent (becoming the aboriginal Australians) around 100,000 years ago. Long established conventions have suggested this happened around 65,000 years ago, but new archaeological excavations have given rise to a new date.

The second migration into the Asiatic Archipelago began when the group of people, including the Polynesians, arrived from mainland Southeast Asia. This migration traversed through the continent of China, travelling all the way from North Africa, through the Levant, and up into the Near East and the Pontic-Caspian steppe, then crossing the greater Eurasian steppe, through China and down South East Asia. This migration took place during the period between 50,000 and 15,000 years ago and is estimated to have arrived in the Asiatic Archipelago around 33,000 years ago.

DNA Evidence for Migration Paths

The complex tapestry of the peopling of East Asia—which encompasses a wide variety of environments, peoples, cultures, and languages—has preoccupied the scientific world during the last 150 years, as scientists try to unravel the mystery of human migration around the globe. But genetic studies by the HUGO-Asian Pan-Asian SNP Consortium, looking at mitochondrial DNA (mtDNA) and non-recombinant regions of the Y chromosome (NRY), are confirming that the two early migrations into East Asia and Southeast Asia mentioned above do describe the initial settlement of East Asia.[xxxvii]

Pedro Soares et al., writing in *Ancient Voyaging and Polynesian Origins*, point out that the ancestry of Polynesians, regardless of their origin, appears more complex the more we learn about their history, genetics, intermarriage etc.[xxxviii] If we go back far enough, current thinking is that we are all a mixture of many lineages of mankind, which originally diverged from a single lineage that goes back to Africa, perhaps 200,000 years ago.

Archaeologists and anthropologists agree that the arrival of the Polynesians and the colonization of the islands in the Malay Archipelago, in effect, pushed the Negrito Melanesians to the East Pacific. (Negrito comes from the Spanish and translates as "little black person.") Many Negrito Melanesians had already settled in the East Pacific since the arrival of the first migration, between 30,000 and 60,000 years ago, after the Toba super-eruption, around 75,000 years ago.

The subsequent arrival of the Mongoloid migration from Northeast (mainland) Asia into the Asiatic Archipelago, between 5,000 and 8,000 years ago, marked the birth of the Malayan people in the archipelago. The Mongoloid Malayans were a more aggressive people, and they in turn pushed the Polynesians into the mountainous regions and further east toward Indonesia and the Pacific Ocean.

It is this struggle with the Malayans that eventually led to expansion across the various islands in the Indonesian Archipelago and became a launching pad for Polynesian migration into the East Pacific Ocean.

A History of Exploration over the Oceans

It turns out the world's massive oceans are the last frontier that man, both ancient and modern, had to conquer, or learn to make peace with.

Around the time of the beginning of Egypt's Old Kingdom (founded by Pharaoh Sanakht) and the construction of the first Great Pyramid of Khufu (built at Giza between 3000 B.C. and 2500 B.C.), the Egyptians learned to make peace with the River Nile and the Mediterranean Sea. But they did not venture out to the Atlantic Ocean or the Indian Ocean until Queen Hatshepsut (1478-1458 B.C.) commissioned an exploration to the Indian Ocean, destined for Nubia and Somalia and the land of Punt,[xxxix] a land that was accepted as a fact and believed to exist somewhere down and beyond the Gulf of Aden. The Queen was an ambitious ruler who realized that successful reopening of trade routes with Punt could finance her reign and cement her place in history. Reports dating back from the time of Sahu-Re dynasty around 3000 B.C., nearly fifteen hundred years earlier, and other fragmented pieces of data, plus the wealth of Egypt, helped her properly organize and equip the expedition.

Egypt's five-ships expedition had a much more advanced design than those of previous primitive vessels. It was not clear how far down the coast of Africa the expedition reached—some say the southeast coast of Somalia, though the expedition's cargo points to somewhere on the African coast from Kenya, even to Mozambique, in the vicinity of Madagascar, which would make it the first known open-ocean exploration to the Indian Ocean, between the continents of India and Africa. The details of the voyage are not known, but some of the sailors might have abandoned the expedition and stayed on in places where they sojourned, thus transmitting knowledge to other remote areas around the globe.

The time of this trip coincides with the period of rather busy island-hopping across the Asiatic Archipelago by the Austronesians or Polynesians, this being right around the corner from where Queen Hatshepsut's expedition reached on the coast of South Africa.

The Phoenicians, meanwhile, had been honing their skills in trading goods, such as purple cloth and cedar wood, up and down the Mediterranean Sea and Asia Minor in 1400 B.C. Then in 600 B.C., Pharaoh Necho II and his Phoenician sailors circumnavigated Africa, and founded a Phoenician colony at Mogador (now called Essaouira) on the Atlantic coast. This is where the voyager Navigators encountered a native seafaring people in the Indian Ocean and Arabian Sea. And in 150 B.C., Ptolemaic mariners from Egypt learned, from Indians and Arabs, the art of sailing the Indian Ocean on its monsoon winds.[xl]

Let us not forget that, in a totally independent Mediterranean maritime evolution, the Irish also developed their own seaworthy vessel, well-adapted to the cold, choppy waters of the northernmost Atlantic. The Irish had established refuges along the islands west of the Norwegian Sea (the Shetlands, Faeroes, and Iceland) during the eighth and ninth centuries A.D. (so post-Christian, pre-Viking). Although there is little to no significant documentation on the Irish exploration during this period, we should not ignore the accomplishments of the Irish generation of cleric navigators. There are those who have maintained that Saint Brendan—or one of a century's worth of his contemporaries, followers, and disciples—may even have beaten the Vikings to the New World. And Erik's Saga, which mentions a White Men's Land while recounting Viking expansion several centuries later, may have originated with an Eskimo encounter with Irish anchorites.[xli]

The recognition of major oceans as possible highways and bridges to economic trade in goods from faraway lands did not occur until modern man took up the challenge, making a leap of faith to build better equipped vessels to circumnavigate the world's major oceans (the Atlantic, Indian, and Pacific) in 1281 A.D. Seafaring Mongol invaders met fierce resistance from Japanese warriors around the Island of Kyushu, where fierce winds aided the Japanese by devastating the Mongol invasion fleet.[xlii] But traffic between Asia and Europe spread like an uncontrollable infectious disease and sustained a lucrative trade in spices and other goods, promoting further advances in navigation.

While the Venetian, Marco Polo, was trekking the Silk Road to China in 1260 A.D., the impending transatlantic exploration by the Europeans was imminent. Marco Polo may very well have been the first "Latin" to cross the Asian continent. He was also the first European to describe the Malay Archipelago, and the first to report the presence of an island empire east of the Asian continent.[xliii]

Before Marco Polo, Niccolò, and Maffeo had even begun their journey back to Venice, a Franciscan friar, John of Monte Corvino, headed east as a representative of Pope Nicholas IV. Traveling across Persia to the Persian Gulf, he continued by water past India, through the Straits of Malacca, along the South China Sea, and finally into the Yellow Sea, reaching Khanbalik in 1294 A.D. John of Monte Corvino would be the first European and Christian to traverse the Malay Archipelago and the Indonesian Archipelago up to the China Sea in the modern era.

In 1420 A.D. Prince Henry of Portugal (the Navigator) began the push to explore and conquer the "natives," wherever they may be, in foreign lands across these oceans. The economic reasons for the push to discover a new way to the Orient was to obtain and maintain the supply chain of spices, silk, perfumes and other exotic goods for the European market, probably thanks to the Ottoman Turks conquering Constantinople in 1453 A.D., which shut off overland routes (the Silk Road) from Europe to Asia Minor, the Eurasian Steppe, India, China and Southeast Asia. All this was a continuing result of religious wars going back to the Christian Crusader Campaigns—the first through the sixth—from 1096 A.D. to 1291 A.D.

In 1492 A.D. Christopher Columbus and agents from Genoa believed that sailing west across the Atlantic would lead to the East Indies, but, to their surprise, they landed on an island in the Caribbean, making it to North America on subsequent trips.

The quest, or thirst for discovery, together with entrepreneurial curiosity about the unknown world, quickly led to religious proselytization, followed by the installation of imperialism. Economic progress demanded that the oceanic highways and bridges connecting the globe must be conquered. The impact of conquering the major oceans spawned developments in celestial navigation, astronomy, oceanography, meteorology, geography, geology, and the physical and social sciences. Man's understanding of the world began to go global. And, as we shall see in the course of our journey, there are several layers of exploration that account for human migrations in general, and the Navigators' Eastern Pacific migration in particular.

<u>Fire and Water</u>

The Pacific Ocean as a Deity

Of course, the Navigators, or Austronesian people, have been traversing the ocean waters for thousands of years since their ancestors spent over 13,000 years navigating the Indian Ocean to the Asian Archipelago and on to the Malay and Indonesian Archipelagos. The ocean waters are nothing new to them. The ocean is a highway of life.

The ocean, which provides them a living, seems endless in all directions. They know it is a vast body of salt water that lies ahead, but they do not know it's the largest ocean in the world, one that will later be called the Pacific Ocean. They do not know that it encompasses approximately one-third of the earth's surface, having an area of 167.2 million square kilometers (63.8 million square miles), making it significantly bigger than the earth's landmass of some 58 million square miles.[xliv]

The people know and respect the Ocean as a god, for it holds the key to life and death. It breathes and moves, peacefully and serenely. And at times, it becomes angry and violent. The people give reverence and obedience to the Ocean's commands. It is the path and beginning of their journey to the future homeland that lies ahead, gifted to them by the Ocean god.

The Navigators have long been associated with water systems, whether rivers or oceans. They are people of mariner descent. Their ancient ancestors navigated waterways throughout the Asian Archipelago and mainland Asia, all the way to the Nile and major rivers foundational to the development of early civilizations and man's migration out of Africa. They perfected travel by waterways and ocean. It's in their blood. They feel, see, smell, and taste the water, salt or fresh, and are proficient in negotiation with it.

A Fiery Marriage between Two Crusts

The earth began from nothing (ex nihilo in Latin), and then, several billion years later, the waters filled the earth. The water was too hot to provide a habitat for living things. The story is one of struggle, confusion, and chaos:

The earth's surface consisted of an upper crust, made up of dense basalt lavas, or as the mortals (or geologists) call it, the "oceanic crust," with a bottom layer made up of lower density sedimentary rocks and granites that the mortals (or geologists) call "continental crust." The slow movement of crusts converged and begat the earth's "plates," which would evolve into major "tectonic plates." The adversarial relationship, some would say acrimonious marriage, of the two earth crusts—the "oceanic crust" and "continental crust"—would eventually cause the denser (oceanic) crust to "humble" itself and "bow down," slipping downward to sink into the weak "ductile layer" in the upper mantle, forming a "subduction zone." The convulsions, stemming from this constant adversarial marriage, caused fracturing in the brittle subduction zone (which can extend to depths of 700 km) producing earthquakes.

Water, released from the upper layers of a descending plate, interacts with the surrounding mantel edge of the continental crust, eventually creating magma that rises to the surface, forming volcanic arcs around that edge. Mortals (or geologists) estimate that this miracle-like process took place 750 million years ago.

The intermixing of magma and crustal materials begets volcanic rocks that are known as andesite. The presence of andesite reveals the volcanic arc in a half-moon like andesite ring that circumscribes the Pacific Ocean, running from New Zealand to Easter Island, colloquially known as the "Pacific Ring of Fire."

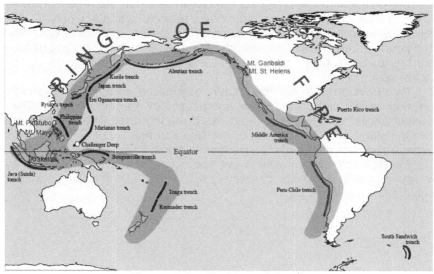

Figure 3 Pacific Ring of Fire[xlv]

The Tectonic Tango

About 1.2 billion years ago, the somewhat rough dancing movement—analogous to the Brazilian tango, perhaps—of the earth's tectonic plates reconfigured the earth's landmass into a couple of supercontinents, one of which was "Rodinia," a Russian word meaning "homeland." Mortals (geologists) have named this period of earth's history, calling it the Proterozoic Era (around 750 million years ago).

Rodinia suffered an epileptic-like attack and split into three large pieces which drifted away from each other, creating new oceans in between. One of these is the Panthalassic (Greek for "all" and "ocean"), the ancient predecessor of the Pacific Ocean.

The supercontinents' convulsions produced the supercontinent of Pangea around 270 million years ago, according to one of world's leading researchers on paleogeography, Dr. Christopher Scotese, a member of the "Paleomap Project."[xlvi] So, by 165 million years ago the first ocean floor, described as the "Pacific plate," was produced from a spreading center in the Central Pacific, ultimately growing to become the largest oceanic plate on the earth.

The three other plates, to the east of the original spreading center, are Cocos, Nazca, and Juan de Fuca. These three, plus the "Pacific plate," became foundational to the evolutionary development of the islands of the Pacific. The Pacific islands emerged as a linear chain of volcanic islands above the tectonic plates.

The Pacific Plate and Resulting Archipelagos

The convergence of these tectonic plate margins caused a subduction, with one plate moving under another and magma forced to the surface.

167 million years ago, the sea floor spreading to the west of Pangea formed the largest ocean floor: the Pacific plate.[xlvii] This new floor emanated from a Y-shaped ancestral East Pacific Rise and its extensions, creating three major oceanic plates named clockwise from the north: the Kula, the Farallon and the Pacific.[xlviii]

The Kula plate was absorbed by the Cocos and the Juan de Fuca. The northern part of the Farallon was absorbed by the largest plate of all, the Pacific plate, while the rest was absorbed by the North American plate. These absorptions resulted in volcanic islands that lie above the linear volcanic chain across eleven archipelagos. Of these, the following ten are of most significance for they are the roots of the respective island homeland: the Solomon Archipelago, the Fiji/Rotuma Archipelago, the New Caledonia Archipelago, the New Zealand Archipelago, the archipelago of Japan, the Izu-Bonin Archipelago, the Palau Archipelago, the Society Archipelago, the Galapagos Archipelago, and the Hawaiian Archipelago.

35

Hotspots and a Volcanic Archipelago

Volcanic hotspots appear where lava pushes up under the mantel and creates a volcano. These hotspots are continually supplied by plume (hot magma welling up from under the mantel). One of these hotspots is where the Samoan and Manu'an chain of islands was born 23 million years ago.

The location of the Samoan hotspot is 30 km from Taū, Manu'a. The Island of Savai'i dates from around 2.3 million years ago; Upolu Island from 2.3 million years ago; and Tutuila dates from around 1.53 million years ago. The Manu'an Island chain is dated at around 1.6 million years old.

The miracle of creation did not stop here. The grand design continues, because the island chain needs to support life, including an inevitable, impending human migration. The foundation of life in these far remote islands is anchored in coral reefs that can sustain a bio-ecosystem, where the processes of life energy can develop.

When the volcanic magma finally comes to rest and becomes lava, this rock becomes the foundation of the island landmass. At the same time, the reefs act as ocean citadels, to protect the landmass. They protect the coastlines from the damaging effects of wave action and tropical storms. Additionally, they provide habitats and shelter for many marine organisms. Collectively known as an ecosystem, the reefs form a fortress that buffers the sandy beaches, which are the boundaries between the ocean and the landmass.

It takes around 100,000 to 500,000 years for the reefs to develop, according to geologists and oceanographers. So, if these islands were formed between 2.5 and 1.3 million years ago, the surrounding reefs began to form around 1 to 2 million years ago.

The Importance and Preservation of Reefs

The ocean and its reefs are not just worthy of respect, but they are also worthy of our care, and in need of our care. For the reefs are the boundaries between the ocean and the landmass. They protect the coastlines and provide habitats and shelter for many marine organisms. They are where the ocean meets the land.

The three most common types of coral reefs are fringing reefs, barrier reefs and atolls. The majority of reefs in the Samoan Island chain are fringing reefs. If we think of the ocean as a source of the food supply chain, sustaining the life of the inhabitants of an island, then the reefs have to be the factory or manufacturer of the seafood supply. It is a simple metaphor. Thus, if we neglect to care for the reefs, the effect will be to destroy the seafood supply. Likewise, if we pursue policies that undermine the health of the reefs and ocean at large, the food supply will become less sustainable, ultimately affecting human survival.

The human impact on coral reefs, through neglect and environmental mismanagement, is significant. Damaging activities include coral mining, pollution (organic and inorganic), overfishing, blast fishing, and the digging of canals changing access into islands and bays, all of which have exacerbated the demise of the reef ecosystem.[xlix] A worldwide study by Clive Wilkinson of the Global Coral Reef Monitoring Network, in 2008, estimated that 19% of the existing area of coral reefs has already been lost, and that a further 17% is likely to be lost over the coming 10 to 20 years.[l] Only 46% of the world's reefs could be currently regarded as being in good health, and about 60% of the world's reefs may be at risk due to destructive, human-related activities.

Interestingly, the threat to the health of reefs is particularly strong in Southeast Asia and the East Pacific Ocean, where 80% of reefs are endangered, according to Wilkinson's study. The factors that affect coral reefs include: the ocean's role as a carbon dioxide sink, atmospheric changes, ultraviolet light, ocean acidification, viruses, impacts of dust storms carrying agents to far-flung reefs, pollutants, algal blooms, and more.

Reefs are threatened well beyond coastal areas. It's evident that climate change and warming temperatures cause coral bleaching and, if severe, destroy the coral and the whole of a reef.[li] Studies from NOAA (the U.S. Department of Commerce's National Oceanic and Atmospheric Administration) in their Coral Reef Conservation Program (CRCP)[lii] indicate that the current condition of coral reefs in American Samoa and the Manu'an Islands is as follows:

- Good condition overall: corals and algae, fish, climate, and human conditions
- Doing well: Benthic cover and coral populations
- Moderate to severe impact: environment situation impacting the fish
- Depleted: Sharks and other predators throughout the world and American Samoa is no exception
- Negative impact: Climate negatively affects coral reefs due to temperature stress and ocean acidification

The study also confirmed the active participation of the local communities in resource management plans, and in ordinances to govern the health of the coral and reefs, as well as the beaches and costal shores.

In another study, the 2016 Tara Pacific Expedition, looking at the Samoan Islands (Upolu, Savai'i, Apolima, and Manono), found that coral cover was extremely low (1%) at approximately half of the sites and below 10% at 78% of the sites. Acanthurus (a colorful fish found in tropical oceans near coral reefs) and Zanclus Cornutus (the Moorish Idol fish), were significantly (10%) smaller near Upolu than around nearby islands. But marine protected areas had higher coral cover, so local action in managing the reefs is useful tool in supporting the ecosystems and reducing anthropogenic impacts.[liii]

The message from these studies is a cautionary sign for reef ecosystem health in remote locations on this planet, reinforcing the need to immediately reduce anthropogenic impacts on global sites.

Reverence for the Ocean

One of the important elements in the foundation of the Polynesian race is the Pacific Ocean. Everything about the Polynesians' enigmatic origins, mysterious migrations, and their development in isolation is set against the backdrop of the Pacific Ocean. How they managed to conquer and use the Pacific Ocean to their advantage is a study in survival. And understanding the ocean's violent evolutionary environment sheds light on understanding their culture and way of life.

These islands are the gifts of the Pacific Ocean. The Pacific Ocean gave life to these migrant people from the west. Worshiped as a god by the Polynesians, the Pacific Ocean responds with love, blessings, plagues, anger, peace, war, and a birthplace. It is feared and loved simultaneously. It can be predictable, and yet it is volatile.

The first humans conceived and born in this vast East Pacific Ocean were Polynesians. The first human that died and was buried in the East Pacific Ocean was a Polynesian. The lives sacrificed to this deity are too numerous to count, through thousands of generations. The mere size of the Pacific Ocean evidences the majesty of God's creation. The Ocean's complex evolutionary intricacy baffles the imagination. It demands reverence, and it is worshipped by the indigenous population.

A fundamental belief with both Samoans and Manu'ans about the Ocean is that it is their inheritance from their ancient ancestors, a gift from the god. A Samoan proverb, *O le tagata ma lo na fa'asinomaga*, describes how "a person is defined by his family (title), village, sacred residence, and meeting ground all the way down to the core of the Earth"—*O le tagata* (a person) *ma* (and) *lo na* (their) *fa'asinomaga* (designation and identity, where designation and identification implies family, village, physical residency) *Maota/Laoa, Malae* (titles—high and Orator Chiefs and princes and princesses—salutations, genealogy, heirlooms—fine mats and special names of the Ava cup, etc.). It's a proverb that defines the whole of the Samoan culture—my translation.

This belief is held consistently throughout Polynesia. The Polynesian people are inextricably interconnected by their ancestry, and also bound together by their home space, the Pacific Ocean. It is the source and support of life. And beneath the Pacific Ocean are the ancient mosaics of the colorful history of their race.

The ocean represents their heirloom and tidings from their ancestors, gifted to the people by the gods. In their mythology, the god opens the orator's mouth and breathes into his lips to empower him with the gift of words to sustain the culture—with a database of information about language, culture, history, and ancestry. It's interesting that now, in an era of instantaneous information, the most expensive product traded in any economic market worldwide is still "information."

The ocean has created an earthly space for the sacred burial of adventurers, warriors, and conquerors of this largest ocean in the world. Thus, veneration is given to the Pacific Ocean out of respect toward the birth of life and to departed ancestors.

The Migration of the Navigators

From Long White Cloud to Dark Shadow

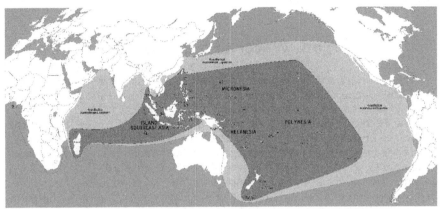

Figure 4 Austronesia with hypothetical greatest expansion extent (Blench, 2009)[liv]

The migration of the Navigators of the Pacific Ocean, to discover and eventually colonize the islands, in the Eastern Pacific Ocean, which would become known as Polynesia (from the ancient Greek *polus*, meaning "many," plus *nesos* meaning "island"), began with a route snaking through the Malay Peninsula, off the coast of Java, heading eastward and north of Papua New Guinea. The Navigators would traverse through thousands of islands (around 25,000) in the Malay Archipelago for another 1,000 years before they saw the "long white cloud" over the middle of the Arafura Sea. (The Arafura Sea is bordered by the Torres Strait and, through that, by the Coral Sea to the east, the Gulf of Carpentaria to the south, the Timor Sea to the west, and the Banda and Ceram seas to the northwest.)

Some Navigators would follow the long white cloud through the Torres Strait, heading eastward over the continental shelf between Australia and New Guinea. The continental shelf is that part of the continent that is underwater; it was part of the land during the ice ages, in the glacial periods, but passed under the water in the interglacial periods. At present we are in an interglacial period.[lv]

Other Navigators would continue north on the Banda Sea toward Maluku; navigating for another 500 years up to the Molucca Sea, where they sojourned on Taliabu and Obi, and on toward North Maluku. This became another staging area, before they launched on to the greater East Pacific Ocean.

These seafaring island people crossed the Wallace Line and settled in the Bismarck Archipelago for another 600 years. They settled in the Solomon Island Archipelago, while others would settle the islands in the north, where Caroline Island and Marshall Island are, or the now-called Micronesia. The Navigators would follow and obey the clouds and winds until they entered the Coral Sea. Their vessels were propelled by winds that would come and go, until the cock crowed in the odd darkness of the night; and they would not stop until the dawn of early morning sunrise, when a dark shadow silhouetted what lay out in a far distance, what appeared to be landmass.

From Water to a Birthplace

Interestingly, the birthplace of ancient societies is usually where there is an abundance of water and rich swamp areas, fertile for farming. The origin of life, it seems, lies in water.[lvi]

The Fertile Crescent of Mesopotamia, a moist and fertile land, is the birthplace of Iraq; likewise, where the Euphrates joins the Tigris River is where life began, leading to metropoles in the Middle East. Many scholars believe this is where the "Garden of Eden" is located. The Nile River became the source of pyramid empires to the Egyptians; the Indus River Valley gave India the beginning of a pivotal civilization that is the gateway to the Far East., where Baluchistan would have been part of a cultural continuum extending from the Tigris to the Indus;[lvii] and, finally, the Yangtze River and the Yellow River Delta are the source of China's development, producing a sophisticated civilization that the world is still uncovering, ancient gifts and tidings from the past that continue to crystallize the brilliance of the mosaic image of its colorful history.

The Mekong River begins its flow up in the Tibetan Plateau and snakes down, through six countries of Southeast Asia and mainland China. The flow of the Mekong River has honed the maritime skills of indigenous people in the six South East Asian countries (China, Myanmar, Thailand, Laos, Cambodia, and Vietnam), all of which are foundational to the amalgamated group of indigenous people, the origin of the Pacific Island people.

The Importance of Mythology

Thomas Mann (1875-1955), the German novelist and essayist and winner of the 1929 Nobel Prize for Literature, is often called the greatest German novelist of the 20th century. Of his many notable works, *Joseph and His Brothers* is especially relevant to our journey to investigate and reimagine the Navigators' migration across the South Pacific Ocean.[lviii]

Thomas Mann's reinterpretation of the journey of the "appointed people" of God starts with the human weakness of jealousy—of Joseph's brothers to committing a violent act, and finally the Midianites selling Joseph to the Ishmaelites—an event that brought Joseph to Egypt, paraphrasing Genesis 37:12-36. How much of that was coincidence, that a descendant of Isaac should be sold to the people descended from Isaac's older and firstborn brother, Ishmael, son of an Egyptian mother?

Mann reveals a profound understanding of tribal collective action and the need to understand the motivation leading to the Israelites' migration into Egypt. He understands the myth and its schemas, saying, as many psychologists would agree, that "the myth is the foundation of life; it is the timeless schema, the pious formula into which life flows when it reproduces its traits out of the unconscious."[lix] So too, Samoan and Manu'an mythologies are evidence of their "immemorial imaginations" of their existence, from the beginning of time through to their current reality.[lx]

The Importance of Fame

Delos, important in classical mythology, is the most important archaeological site in the pre-Olympian era of Greek mythology. It is a holy sanctuary, the birthplace of the twin gods, Phoebus Apollo and his sister Artemis. And it is located near the center of the Cyclades Archipelago, a Greek island group in the Aegean Sea. Delos is famous from the Homeric *Hymn to Delian Apollo*, as referenced by Hesiod and Thucydides.[lxi]

Now, in seeking to understand how the Samoans and Manu'ans came into existence, I want to make a distinction between the Manu'an and the Samoan, because the Island of Manu'a is an independent kingdom, separate from that of the Island of Samoa (which includes the Islands of Savai'i, Upolu, Tutuila and Aunu'u, Manono, and Apolima). And I want to point out that Manu'a, in our mythology, "is like Delos" in the Greek, as Dr. Augustine Krämer said, a most important and sacred archaeological site in Polynesian mythology. Manu'a should be famous too.

The Importance of Investigation

"There is no race upon the earth which, in proportion to its numbers, has been a subject of so much interest and such minute investigation as the Polynesian. This is owing not only to the interesting character of the race, but also to the mystery, as yet unsolved, which shrouds their origin, and their extreme isolation" wrote Professor W.D. Alexander, of Punahou College, Honolulu, Hawaii, in his preface to *An Account of the Polynesians Race. Its Origin and Migration and the Ancient History of the Hawaiian People to the Time of Kamehameha I. Vol. III*:[lxii] W.D. Alexander is also the author of *the Brief History of the Hawaiian People.*[lxiii]

The homogenous group of Pacific Island peoples has long been the subject of physical and social scientific research into its origins, culture, and history. Ever since the great explorer Captain James Cook discovered these islands, now known as Polynesia, back in June 1769, the mystery of how these people migrated, colonized, and developed their culture in isolation, in the largest ocean in world, has provided a valuable real-life specimen for comparative anthropology, ethnology, and linguistic research. While they are treated and referred to as research subjects, the people of Polynesia go about living their lives as normal, as their ancestors did thousand years before, plus-or-minus some adjustments to the environmental and cultural changes.

The Important Question

But who are these Manu'ans and Samoans? How did they get to their current respective island homelands? How long ago did they occupy these islands?

In an oral-based society, the answers vary, of course, throughout Polynesia. In fact, scientists have labored to find an answer to their question of their migration and origin for the last 200 years.

Manu'ans and Samoans would provide an answer that describes a god, Tagaloalagi who resides in the tenth heaven. Meanwhile Tongans, Tahitians, Hawaiians, Marquesans, and other Polynesians would respond by describing the long treacherous voyage on dugout or double-hull canoes that came from Southeast Asia through Indonesia down to the Pacific.

The truth is that there is no cohesive history of the Pacific Island people, or the Pacific region. The ancient history of the Pacific people is fragmented and is kept orally by each island's indigenous inhabitants. Their migrations to discover their current habitats were originally undertaken by small groups, often consisting of families or clan. Settling in these isolated islands kept them insulated from other kinfolk who might have journeyed on to other islands. So the history of the origin of these people—now called Micronesian, Melanesian, and Polynesian—is now scattered throughout the 62.46 million square miles of the Pacific Ocean. While their origin and history are told by their oral traditions, the vicissitudes of generations and histories have eroded memory into a faint, early dawn chant, the mythologies of the past.

The Last Conquest

And so, we come to the last world territory to be "conquered," the 62.46 million square miles that lie between Asia and the American continent, with 25,000 islands with indigenous populations and unique cultures. At a glance, these island peoples seem different from each other. However, on a closer look, common threads are discovered among their oral traditions and cultures, and, of course, their group of languages.[lxiv]

Conquest marks the beginning of the examination of these Pacific peoples, leading to the documentation of their respective origin, history and culture by explorers, missionaries, anthropologists, ethnologists, archaeologists, geologists, geneticists, and linguists. But, while there were, and still are, many social and physical scientists undertaking studies to refine their understanding of the origin and history of the Pacific peoples, a clear picture is yet to evolve of this beautiful mosaic of an amalgamation of people sharing common attributes of their beginnings, cultures, and language family. This is the beginning of the development and articulation of the history of a region, be it Southeast Asia or Oceania.

As the world continues to gravitate toward a "trading block," cocooning the Americas, European Union, Africa, Asia, Pacific, and more, I believe an effort to continue synthesizing the history of the Pacific—Melanesia, Micronesia and Polynesia—is critical to the cultural identity of the Pacific people. It needs to be taught in K12 schools and universities.

The colorful mosaic of these people and their diverse origin, history, and culture needs to be shared with the world. The history of 25,000 islands and indigenous people, as a cohesive group of diverse people with a common migration history and similar cultures, will yield the world many tidings from the "well of the past," to borrow Thomas Mann's phrase.[lxv] The value of understanding diversities and commonalties among a large group of fragmented homelands should give us lessons for our path to the future.

The Urge to Know More

It is important to know the origin of the various launches and reasons for migrations, and to know their details. The spirit of colonization or entrepreneurship, the urge to discover new homelands, is clearly an aspect of these people worth studying; it provides many parallels that can be drawn with our modern life paradigms. Studying cultural development only as it happens in isolation offers a far from complete scientific understanding. Rather, understanding the human behavior of this diverse group of people through time, and how it influenced their cultural development is our desired objective.

And, while there is a significant delay in confirming science's agreement with history—specifically that of the Navigators' migration history across the Pacific, as told in their folklore through oral transmission—I believe time will allow us to synchronize the results and confirm the truth. In a quest to explore the differences that define individuality and self-identity, we will be left with a testimony confirming that human population and culture diffused across Southeast Asia and continued into the South Pacific with the Polynesians, much as with all other human migrations since leaving middle Africa.

Reaffirming the scientific facts that humans traveled, and that we are all descended from Scientific Eve and Scientific Adam in the middle of the African continent, we will see that, yes, we are all citizens of one world—which is a convoluted way of defining inclusion.

Conclusion

So, what guideposts we should look for to help us decipher the Navigators' journey and path? We have many studies which are available to us from the social scientists of the late 1800s, and we shall look at them for guidance. Although they are fragmented, the studies having been done during different timeframes, they nevertheless give us empirical data and, indeed, some evidence or imprints of the Navigators' migration path. While these studies represent events in time, in each respective scientific investigation we should be able to corroborate them with cultural similarities in the neighboring cultures and societies along the path and, of course, with the oral legends and mythology about the migration, to learn and reveal who we are and where we come from.

Tracing the Migration Path

Layers of Migration

Introduction

Somewhere in the midst of human migrations, around 100,000 years ago, an homogeneous group of people began to break away from the Sub-Saharan desert of the North African continent, seeking a path to an unknown destination. They belonged to a clan that was born into one family at an ancient time in the Arabian Desert. Their quest would take thousands of years, crossing several continents, cultures, and societies, and would forever influence the culture of this group, who would come to be known as the people of the Pacific Islands.

The precise paths of this migration are still a subject of considerable debate among scientists, but the paths are etched into the minds, hearts, and souls of the Pacific Islanders; they flow and circulate in their veins. For within those ancient paths, buried under many layers of thousands of cultures and societies, lie the lineaments of Pacific Islander footsteps, bearing witness to their journey and ancestral beginning.

How we Search for a Path

Searching through the layers of human migration to find a thread of common ethnicity, people, and culture, is clearly a complex, "needle in the haystack" problem, particularly when it relates to a small group of people such as the Polynesians. The problem is further complicated when we consider the many layers of migration that have occurred, traversing many different routes, as we look for that path or "thread" that will identify a race of people and the origin of their particular migration. The impossibility of this task may seem obvious, but to the inquisitive mind, no mountain cannot be scaled, and no haystack cannot be demolished.

There are many steps to this process:

- Evidence from anthropology
- Ethnology and evidence of ethnicity
- Evidence from archaeological excavations
- Comparison of mythologies
- Evidence from the records of genealogy
- Extrapolation of historical evidence to establish timelines
- Ethology and evidence of ethos, customs, and behavior

- Geography and Geology—the way the physical world has changed
- Sociology and psychology
- Semiotics and the way communication develops
- Linguistics and the development of language
- Genetics and comparisons of DNA

The Search for Evidence

I want to trace the various human migrations, through their many different timeframes, in order to arrive at a timeline for the Polynesian migration. I will look at the evidence for each migration, to determine its timeline and relationship to a path to the Asiatic Archipelago. I will use the word "layer" to denote the evidence left behind by separate groups of migrants who may have made similar migrations leading to different parts of the globe. We can visualize different migration waves arriving at different times, leading to a watershed moment in the Asiatic Archipelago. Thus we might reconcile the layers left behind by populations arriving in the region.

Then comes the Polynesians' arrival and subsequent departure to the Indonesian Archipelago and on to the Eastern Pacific, leaving behind a colorful archaeological mosaic that speaks to us of the hundreds of thousands of voyages in which they have traversed the ocean.

A major challenge to reconstructing the mosaic of the Polynesians' ancient past is posed by in the climate of the equatorial zone and the southern hemisphere. Near the equator there is very little distinction between summer, winter, autumn and spring. The temperature is usually high year-round, except on the high mountains in South America and in Africa (the Andes Mountains and Mount Kilimanjaro respectively). But the temperature can still plummet during rainstorms. However, in tropical regions there are typically two seasons: the wet or monsoon season, and the dry season. But many places close to the equator lie on the ocean and are thus rainy throughout the year, since "seasons" can vary depending on elevation and on proximity to the ocean.

The equator passes through the three largest oceans in the world: the Pacific Ocean, the Atlantic Ocean, and the Indian Ocean. With habitats that are, metaphorically speaking, smaller than a pebble or rock in comparison to the vast Pacific Ocean surrounding them, the challenge in preserving archaeological artifacts and heirlooms is obvious—many artifacts are made of perishable materials to begin with, and the weather (humidity and salt water) wreaks havoc on these materials, which are so critical to reconstructing the ancient *motif* of early Polynesians.

Joseph Campbell points out, in his *Oriental Mythology* book, how, in northern, temperate zones, objects constructed from stone, pottery, and metal survive and play a large part in the culture, but in the equatorial zone the materials used to build the culture were mostly natural and perishable.[lxvi]

The High Culture Zone

Another problem arises as scientists are frequently biased toward the "high culture zone" in their thinking, influenced by the abundance of ancient archaeological sites in the northern hemisphere (Arabia, Egypt, the Fertile Crescent, Anatolia and Europe) which yield great rewards for very reasonable time spent in research. If we look at and compare the overall accomplishments of all research into the Polynesians in the Pacific in the last 200 year period, we find only the following two things:

1. The analysis of Y-Chromosomes and mitochondrial DNA, which is indeed a scientific breakthrough
2. and the discovery of the Lapita trading network, attributed to archaeological and anthropological findings.

Compared to the myriad investigations and discoveries of the "high culture" ancient societies of the northern hemisphere, these two are minimal. And this attitudinal bias induces a shift in the financial capital available for research projects in the northern hemisphere because it is easier to yield greater profits and results there, rather than with research projects directed at South Pacific islands. This, in turn, results in fewer studies being undertaken, making our task more difficult.

Cultural Context and the High Culture Bias

The reality is that, for several thousands of years, the "world" was defined in the upper hemisphere, north of Tropic of Cancer. This was the center of human cultural evolution, or so it was believed at the time. This may very well be due to settlements from early migrations out of Africa, which made it the center of the world. So, as human migration continued flowing across the globe, knowledge of other societies and cultures came as an epiphany to those discoverers and rulers of the old Kingdoms. However, the more knowledge gained, the more the web of human interconnectivity and cultural relationship will be illuminated and understood.

More recent confirmation of cultural diffusion (recorded in the late 19th century, by Joseph Campbell) simply shows that we all came out of one place, "out of Africa," and that other cultures and societies do exist outside the realm of the "high culture civilizations." This paradigm of "cultural diffusion" allows us to view the world as if in a kaleidoscope, whereby the basic elements are light and reflection. When a kaleidoscope is manipulated, it produces different patterns of beautiful colors. Likewise, human anatomy displays a pattern; we are the same, and how we differ from each other is the miracle of human anatomy interworking to produce a "multicolored" human race.

The German ethnologist Leo Frobenius, in his writing in 1929, makes the case that our understanding of ancient history is based first in archaeological findings, and later in documents and cultural context. Do we not hear Socrates whispering to remind us not to depend on written history, because over time its mistakes have become cast in stone? Referring to documented history as giving evidence of their own "little egos," Frobenius adds that the interpretation of written documents does not hold an accurate mirror up to the world; it is easier to study the obvious, because it is less controversial than venturing into an unknown, where fewer artifacts and heirlooms provide evidence from the ancient past.[lxvii]

Frobenius concludes by pointing out that the "grandiose high cultures of antiquity" represent only a belt around the world, reaching from 20 degrees to 45 degrees north—i.e. a region confined to an area north of the Tropic of Cancer. But south of this belt are cultures from West Africa, through India, the Malay Archipelago and Melanesia, which have survived to this day, with cultural traits that don't derive from the archeology or the cultures of the north. Their cultures represent a world of their own, as distinct as is the plant world from the animal world.

As we make the case for cultural diffusion in the comparative mythology section, we shall find a plethora of parallel themes, story lines, objects and subjects of Samoan and Manu'an mythology, which ring in resounding confirmation of the conclusions of these illustrious and prodigious men of science—scientists who followed their vision and passion to shed light on the "well of the past," to illuminate our understanding of self and of how we capitalize on our differences for the betterment of humanity.

I anchor my search on that same foundation as Joseph Campbell's comparative mythology proposition, on the profound quotation from Thomas Mann: "Myth is the foundation of life."[lxviii]

The Motif in my Research

"A motif is a symbolic image or idea that appears frequently in a story. Motifs can be symbols, sounds, actions, ideas, or words."[lxix]

When I first envisioned this writing project, after deciding on the subject matter, I had imagined it as though I were composing a symphony. It might not be that big, but in my imagination, I wanted to compose and then conduct a finished work. Specifically, I was thinking of Ludwig van Beethoven's prodigious Symphony No. 5 in C minor, Op. 67 ("Symphony of Fate"), composed in 1808. The opening motif (what the musician also refers to as "leading motive") is only four notes, perhaps the most famous four successive notes around the world, and while Beethoven does introduce variations on the main motif, he always returns to the motif itself.

If we look at the challenges of orchestrating the "Migration Path" storyline, we can imagine we are "juggling" the following "notes":

- Migration Path
- Culture
- Comparative Mythology
- Language and Genetics

On the "deepest" view (like Campbell's) I want to point to the gray color of the "void" to find the mosaic. And on the "shallowest" view, or the "local" and personal view (again, like Campbell's) I want to point out the motif in many variants of the theme.

Thus, as I wove the storyline, I often found myself going back and bringing forward a variant of the motif, now reimagined, amplified, turned about and reborn in each of the above major sections.

My motive is to clarify the image of the motif for myself, and to convey that clarity to others through a mosaic image.

Anthropology

The study of human evolution, including biological and physiological characteristics

Pre-Historic Humans

New Technology in Archaeology and Anthropology

Conventional understanding of human migration from Africa or, more specifically from North Africa, is well-established, providing answers to questions of birthplace, migration path, physical characteristics, mental knowledge and thinking skills, environmental conditions, and an approximate timeline. That said, the proposed "ancient" timeline continues to be pushed further backward and re-dated, thanks to advances in technology.

New technologies assist social scientists in discovering more archaeological sites, which reveal more facts and more precise evidence as to the timeline of our ancient ancestors. For example, "Satellite Archaeology" combines smart computer programming and artificial intelligence with satellite imagery, mapping, and topological analysis, to point out and reveal thousands of new sites.

Dr. Sarah Parcak, Professor of Anthropology and Director of the Laboratory for Global Observation at the University of Alabama at Birmingham, is the leading expert in the field of satellite remote sensing application. Since 2003, she has used satellite imaging to discover sites going back to 3000 B.C. Using satellites, researchers can map and model features that are totally hidden on the ground by buildings, forests, and soil. She points out that satellites aren't just another "gee whiz toy," but rather they're a valuable scientific tool yielding results from Egypt to Syria to Italy to Easter Island. Satellite imagery can transform every aspect of how we perceive and understand our past.[lxx]

I am encouraged by this technology and its future application to unraveling the mysterious thread of the ancient past of the Polynesians.

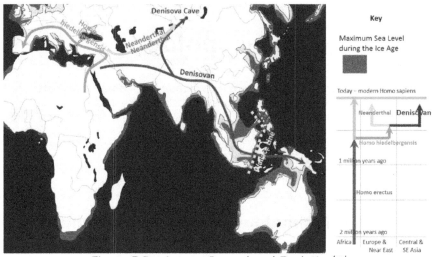

Figure 5 Denisovan Spread and Evolution[lxxi]

Before "Out of Africa"

"Out of Africa" migrations have occurred in many waves (leaving many layers of civilizations) at different times in the history of the world. In my opinion, these layers provide the essence of the deep "Well of the Past"—the deeper you go down, the more "tidings" (or data) you discover.

The most critical discoveries we make in the search of our history are "fossils." As our ancient ancestors lie dead and undisturbed, their "fossils" are the "witnesses" to the "time and space" of our rather young beginnings. So, as we unearth human fossils, we must be careful not to mix up the "layers" of our ancestors, confusing which layers came before others. For they are the only thing we have to prove that we existed in the world's history. Otherwise, what we learn would be based only on faith.

Investigating these discoveries, we find two "Out of Africa" migrations which affect Southeast Asia and ultimately impact the Asiatic Archipelago, the area that would become home and a kingdom to the Polynesian people. But, before embarking on a study of these two "Out of Africa" migrations, it is important to summarize conventional wisdom on the earlier human migrations that populated the world before the arrival of our "modern" human species.

The 1st Layer

It is commonly agreed that evidence of the 1st "layer" of migration out of Africa can be found in the Southern Levant (Mesopotamia Middle

Eastern area), occurring between around 1.4 million year ago and 250,000 years ago.[lxxii]

This is where evidence of the first domesticated dog was uncovered.[lxxiii] But another significant discovery here is the controlled use of fire. While it would later be determined that fire was first used for cooking only around 20,000 years ago, prior to that—around 200,000 years ago—fire was worshipped by early humans as a deity from the time of its first discovery.[lxxiv]

Denisovans and Neanderthals

The "Denisovans" and "Homo floresiensis" or "Flores Man"—nicknamed the "Hobbit"—must have long occupied the landmass of Asia and Southeast Asia before the later layers of migration from North Africa arrived some 60,000 to 70,000 years ago. Current theory is that Denisovans and Neanderthals are both descended from the ancient human, Homo heidelbergensis, and that they left Africa 300,000 to 400,000 years ago. Scientists further posit that the two groups left Africa and split shortly afterward. One group ventured northwestward into West Asia and Europe and became the Neanderthals. The other branch moved east, becoming Denisovans. Scientists who support this theory believe that Homo heidelbergensis, remaining in Africa, became Homo sapiens—our ancestors—and did not begin their own exodus from Africa until about 60,000 or 70,000 years ago (in later layers of migration).[lxxv]

In 2008, paleoanthropologists digging in a cave in Southern Siberia unearthed a 40,000-year-old adult tooth and a pinkie bone of young girl, aged five to seven years old when she died. Comparing DNA with the genomes of modern humans showed the girl was related to Neanderthals but different enough to give rise to a new classification of ancient humans, called Denisovan after the cave where the bones were found.

The DNA marker of the Denisovans is significantly present in the Indonesian Archipelago, in places such as New Guinea and Papua New Guinea, and among the aboriginal people of Australia, and the Torres Strait Islanders. These "new" human species, taken collectively, further complicate the already convoluted conundrum of the ancient history of Southeast Asia and Oceania, and could very well cause a re-telling or re-writing of the history of the region.

Homo Floresiensis and Hobbits

Homo floresiensis (named after the Island group in which the paleoanthropologists unearthed remains in Liang Bua Cave, Indonesia) was originally discovered by a priest and part-time archaeologist Theodor Verhoeven, during the 1950s and 60s. But, given his amateur status, Verhoeven failed to persuade the archaeological establishment of the importance of his find. In the 1990s, other researchers used modern techniques to date tools from the Soa Basin to about 840,000 years ago, thus confirming the original proposition and claims of the priest and part-time archaeologist Verhoeven.

In 2003 a group of archaeologists from Australia and Indonesia, sponsored by National Geographic, focused on Liang Bua, in the uplands of western Flores; the cave yielded rich artifacts and an entire "Hobbit" skeleton—the skeleton of a small-bodied hominid, who would have stood about 1.1 meters (3 ft 7in), from the Late Pleistocene era.[lxxvi]

The relevance of these archaeological findings to my efforts to connect the dots, and to retrace the Polynesian migration, is the locational proximity of the "Hobbit" to the launching point and paths of the Polynesians onto the East Pacific Ocean. The salient facts of the Homo floresiensis or Hobbit discovery are:

- Firstly, that the island was not connected to the landmass or bridge to South East Asia and mainland Asia or northern Australia; and
- Secondly, that the small size, or dwarfism, of the islanders' physical characteristics, like pygmies, seems to support the idea that they had limited access to food resources, due to their isolation. So their growth could have been stunted by disease or malnutrition.

Researchers have concluded that this group of ancient humans was the last to go extinct, around 54,000 years ago. The latest research, under the Australian Research Council grant in 2010, concluded that Homo floresiensis is not part of the Homo erectus family. It is much more archaic and may have evolved before Homo habilis.

Legends of the Hobbits

People on almost every South Pacific island believe that their legends about hobbits and dwarves are true. So here is one such myth:

This occurred at the Island of Savai'i in the village of Paia in the district of Samauga. One day Mauai, of Paia village, took his dog and went hunting for wild pigs. As he moved further into the forest, the dog began to get excited and anxious to get his master to follow him into a cave. Mauai obediently followed his dog.

Suddenly, behold, a bearded small man appeared in front of the cave. Mauai thought he was seeing a spirit, for the bearded man stood no more than two to three feet tall. Likewise, the small man could not believe what he was seeing—a man that stood like a giant.

The bearded small man told Mauai that he was the chief of his little-people clan. As chief, he was very concerned about having the people's village cave become known by everyone in Paia village, let alone by everyone in the district of Samauga. So, the little-people's chief and Mauai made a pact to keep his habitat a secret, in return for which Mauai would get anything he yearned for.

At one evening meeting with the little-people village, Mauai accidently offended the little-people with his speech. By that time, the villagers of

Paia had begun to question Mauai as to the source of his prosperity. While showing off to them, he had revealed the identity and whereabouts of his benefactors. So, the little-people packed up their village and vanished from sight, never to be heard from or seen again.

The Menehune legend is a story of Hawaiian dwarf people, very much like the Samoan story above. The parallel legend speaks to parallel culture, language, and common ancient ancestry.

The main reason I choose to discuss these here is because of the small or dwarf people of the Florēs Island of Indonesia. The location of the island of Flores, in the middle of the Austronesian and Polynesian migration into the Indonesian Archipelago, makes it conceivable that the dwarfs made the same migration on to Oceania together with the Polynesians.

Homo Luzonensis

I would be remiss if I didn't also mention the recent unearthing of Homo luzonensis in the Philippines, which indicates that there were even more human species living alongside each other, coexisting before the "family tree" was whittled down to just modern humans. The excavation at Callao Cave in Luzon, in the Philippines, unearthed remains of two adults and one juvenile, now dated to 67,000 years ago. The authors of the study analyzed all the fossils collected, including foot and hand bones, teeth, and a partial femur.[lxxvii]

The odd mix of traits in these specimens throws the entire hominin family tree into "intriguing disarray," with molar and pre-molar teeth presenting similarities to Homo sapiens, Homo erectus, Homo floresiensis and even the Paranthropus (from around 2.6 to 0.6 million years ago), and curved and monkey-like toe bones showing similarities to Australopithecus afarensis (3.9 to 2.9 million years ago).

The age of this species, Homo luzonensis—dated at 67,000 years ago—means that they roamed the earth at the same time as other hominins, such as Homo sapiens, Neanderthals, Denisovans, and Homo floresiensis. This further supports the growing conviction that Homo erectus is not the only hominin species that traveled out of Africa.

Some scientists now think that, like Homo floresiensis, Homo luzonensis lived on an island that could only be reached with a sea crossing. It is possible that both species (floresiensis and luzonensis) evolved from Homo erectus populations who lived and evolved in these isolated islands for a long time.

The 2nd and 3rd Layers

Evidence of the 2nd Layer of civilization is found in the Middle Paleolithic period, around 48,000 to 250,000 years ago. It can be seen in the Mousterian culture in the Levant (often associated with Neanderthal man) and is known from numerous sites throughout the region.

The 3rd Layer of civilization is evidenced in later Middle Paleolithic human remains, including both the Neanderthals in Kebara Cave, Amud Cave, and Tabun, and the anatomically modern human remains from Jebel Qafzeh and Skhul Cave (remains, designated AMH, which display a complete and intact anatomy).

The 4th and 5th Layers

The 4th Layer is evidenced by anatomically modern human remains dated in the Upper Paleolithic Period, around 48,000 to 20,000 years ago, in the Levant.

The 5th Layer arises in the Epi-Paleolithic Period between 20,000 and 9500 B.C. Significant cultural variability is found, together with a wide spread of microlithic technologies. Small stone tools, about a centimeter or so in length and half a centimeter wide, usually made of flint or chert, were made by people from 35,000 years ago to 3,000 years ago in Europe, Africa, Asia, and Australia. And this microlithic tool kit is associated with the appearance of the bow and arrow in the area.

Kebaran culture—also known as Early near East—shows affinities with the earlier Helwan phase in Egyptian Fayyum, and may be associated with the movement of people across the Sinai, associated with climatic warming after the Late Glacial Maxima of 20,000 B.C.

The latest part of the Epi-Paleolithic era, from 12,500 to 9,000 B.C., is the time when the Natufian culture flourished, and also when more permanent settlements among hunter-gathers developed in a process called sedentism.

It's clear, from this preponderance of accumulated layers of evidence, that the prehistory of the Levant area is fundamental to understanding the migration and cultural development of early modern humans. Therefore, it is critical to unravel the threads of this multi-layered ancient carpet, with the hope in mind of meticulously pulling out those threads that might be relevant to the ancestry of the Polynesians.

The Importance of the Levant

The prehistory of the Levant includes the various cultural changes that occurred there, as revealed by layers of archaeological evidence. These changes precede recorded traditions in the area of the Levant.

Archaeological evidence suggests that Homo sapiens and other hominid species, which originated in Africa, took a route through the Sinai desert and the Levant to colonize Eurasia. This is one of the most important and most occupied geographical areas in the early history of human migration. Not only have humans of many cultures and traditions lived here, but also many species of genus Homo.

In addition, this region is the center for the development of agriculture, a significant stage in human evolution and migration.

Agriculture allowed humans to graduate from hunters and gatherers into formal organizations with the ability to deliberately cultivate land—planting and harvesting and engaging with food preparation and storage.[lxxviii]

Modern Humans

Two Waves of Modern Human Migration

The first migration, or "wave," of "modern humans" out of Africa occurred between 115,000 and 130,000 years ago, but the migrants apparently either died out or retreated, according to recent studies in a multi-disciplinary effort by various scientists.[lxxix]

The second migration wave occurred around 100,000 years ago, following the so-called Southern Route. This route initially crosses the River Nile into Southern Arabia; then it follows the coastline of India, navigating around the Indian Ocean toward Southeast Asia, where Burma and Thailand are today; it continues on downward to the Malay Archipelago, where Sumatra and Java are; and eventually leads to the continent of Australia.

This second migration takes place prior to the catastrophic Toba super-volcanic eruption, which happened around 75,000 years ago. The super-volcano was located near where Sumatra and Indonesia are today. Current archaeological evidence indicates that this migration began in Northern Nubia, leading scientists to further posit that a part of this migration went up into India, and, after a period of time, continued moving northwest to populate the Levant, Europe and the Near East.

The Toba Volcanic Eruption

Not all scientists subscribe to Toba Catastrophe Theory. The theory holds that the super-volcanic eruption caused a bottleneck in world population growth, unleashing a global winter up to ten years long and a cooling period up to 1,000 years long.[lxxx] But wherever the science comes down on the importance of this eruption, the fact is it occurred at a very significant time, and its impact on the environment and the ecological systems of Southeast Asia must have been devastating, disrupting the whole way of life of the region, and affecting the population for tens of thousands of years after its eruption.

I believe the Toba volcanic eruption may very well have reconfigured canyons under the ocean in the Malay and Indonesian Archipelagos. This, of course, would affect the ocean currents around the Wallace Line (which will be discussed later), and thus it would become a major obstacle to crossing over into the East Pacific Ocean.

It's a known fact that ocean gyres in these parts of the Wallace Line and north east Papua New Guinea have some of the strongest ocean currents in all of the South Pacific Ocean, with a force is equivalent to seven times the Amazon river's flood combined.[lxxxi]

The presence of these features should be contrasted with the predictable weather, which allowed travelers to stop their caravans and build temporary shelters in the sand dunes until storms subsided, when crossing the 3,600,000 square miles of the Sahara Desert, which earlier hunter-gatherers had to endure. With the Pacific Ocean, there are far more factors—wind, temperature, ocean currents, movements of the heavenly bodies, etc.—to be managed or negotiated successfully, in order to traverse the waters safely.

The Cushite Connection

One important aspect of establishing the source of migration, out of Africa or Sudan, or now Nubia (a name that comes from the Egyptian word for gold[lxxxii]), for tracing the migration of the Polynesians, is to see if any similarities in culture and other characteristics can be found between the Polynesians and the people that originally migrated out of this region into the Indian sub-continent and on to Levant and the Near East.

The Hon. Judge Fornander, with his three-volume treatise written in 1877-1884, put forward the proposition that Polynesian ancestors may be traced to the Cushite people and to the culture in Ethiopia, Africa.[lxxxiii] In the Hebrew Bible, the Kush or Cushites are descendants of Ham, son of Noah (Genesis 10). At the time of Fornander's writing, very little was known about this ancient culture, other than what Egyptologists had said about the Kingdom of Kush. However, the Hebrew Bible makes several references to Cushites, including one where Moses marries a Cushite woman in Numbers 12:1. Jeremiah 13:23 refers to an Ethiopian, using the same Hebrew word translated "Cushite." So, Judge Fornander makes a passionate argument, even with only faint evidence, that this migration, across the Nile into Southern Arabia, represents the tribal people that would go on to be ancestors of the Polynesians.

New evidence has now been uncovered, through archaeological digs as part of the Grand Ethiopia Renaissance Dam project (also known as the Millennium Dam excavation project). And now Cush is generally accepted to refer to the area south of Egypt, above the cataracts on the Nile, a place where a black African civilization flourished for over two thousand years.[lxxxiv]

Deserts of Arabia

Dr. Jeffrey Rose, professor and world acclaimed archaeologist and expert on antiquity at the University of Birmingham, U.K., together with his team of researchers, discovered stone tools in the sand dune desert of Nubia. The tools were made using technology from what is now called the "Nubian Complex," by nomadic hunters from the Africa's Nile Valley. Nubian technology is a unique method of making spear points, previously only found in North Africa.[lxxxv]

Accurate dating of Dr. Rose's Nubian discovery is made possible using optically stimulated luminescence (OSL), which can determine the last time a single buried grain of sand has been exposed to light, by measuring the amount of energy trapped inside it. This technique revealed the tools to be 106,000 years old, proving they come from exactly the same time the Nubian complex flourished in Africa.

The implication of Rose's discovery is that it pushes the date for human migration much farther back in history—dating it about 45,000 years earlier than geneticists previously thought, to around 60,000 years ago.

For myself, I am not questioning when human migration first happened, but where. I suggest that the great "modern human" expansion to the rest of world was launched from Africa rather than from Arabia.

As Dr. Rose points out, it had not previously been considered that the link to Africa would be found in the Nile Valley, and that the migration route, instead of following the coast, might go through the middle of the Arabian Peninsula. But the Arabian deserts would have been blooming at that time, with fertile grassland providing food resources for hunters and gatherers. Water trapped in the sand dunes by the Indian ocean's monsoons would have made them a "land of a thousand lakes!"

Rose describes the landscape as truly unique, a romantic "lost world" filled with mysterious ruins, a "living museum of artifacts," and surely a place one would want to show off to one's descendants.

Early Maritime Migration

The dating of modern human expansion, whether from Africa or Arabia, through various specific paths, is being re-examined, given new data from geneticists, archaeologists, linguists, ethnologists, and anthropologists. These new findings provide new clarity, as if with a telescope, on determining the ancestry of the Polynesian people and their migration.

Places on the migration path are seen more clearly now than ever before. The timeline and the numbers of waves of migration can now be more closely estimated. The accepted paths of human migration eastward have been corroborated by more recent studies, namely by Dr. Rose of Birmingham University, Professor Joseph Campbell, and other scientists, establishing the presence of several paths:

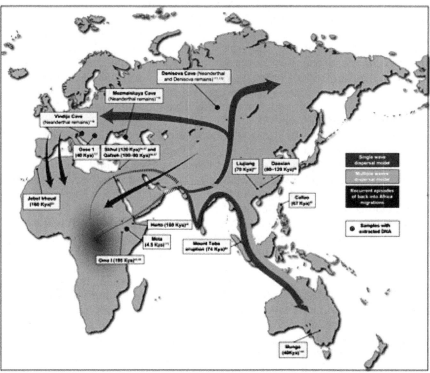

Figure 6 Putative migration waves out of Africa[lxxxvi]

- The migration of the Proto-Australoid goes from Africa through Arabia and crosses over Baluchistan, into the Indus Valley, crossing the Deccan Plateau down to South India into the coastal Indian Ocean, and finally to the Malay Archipelago, then on through Ceylon and Melanesia. Professor Stuart Piggott writes that current opinion tends to the view that Australia received her aboriginal population via migration through Ceylon and Melanesia, from Southern India. Dr. Rose's more recent research findings point to the same navigational vector path.
- The second path—important to the quest of tracing the origin and migration of the Pacific Island peoples—takes the northeastern route from the Caucasus mountain range, down through Baluchistan (Pakistan again); crossing over the east side of the Indus Valley, then continuing east and descending through the river systems of Irrawaddy, Salween, and Mekong; landing in Laos, Yunnan and Cambodia.

Both migration streams eventually meet in the Indian Archipelago, long before the arrival there of the Mongol or Mongoloid Malays. Then this easterly migration splits into two paths:

- One path turns northeastward into China. This trajectory eventually turns south through Lijiang, China, and down to the island of Taiwan, and into the Pacific Ocean.
- The other trajectory turns southeastward to Burma and continues southeast to Laos, and then south into the Indian Archipelago, going through the now submerged Sunda Strait and the Indonesian Peninsula, where Java and Sumatra are located. (This is described by Fornander, Campbell, and Piggott).[lxxxvii]

This southeastward migration followed the Mekong River and was driven by maritime natives and traders. The costal routes from the south Indian Ocean to the Malay Archipelago, to the costal routes of Southeast Asia (Thailand, Vietnam, Laos and Cambodia) all the way up to Taiwan, formed a busy shipping highway, populated by seafarers and mariners—the same seafaring people that made the initial launch northeast into the Pacific Ocean and populated the Philippines.

It is important to remember that this long-term maritime seafaring produced long-established skill-sets, these being the very skills that gave the Polynesians confidence to make that leapfrog journey into the mighty Pacific Ocean.

The Navigators in the Java Sea

When the Navigators finally entered the Java Sea, Banda Sea, Timor Sea and Arafura Sea, there were two routes open to them, leading into the Eastern Pacific Ocean. According to anthropologists Churchill, Percey, Smith and Rivers (writing between 1911 and 1916),[lxxxviii] the two routes are as follows:

- The Torres Straits or the Togafiti Stream (as per Rivers): This stream passed from Indonesia along the southern coast of New Guinea through the Torres Straits, finally to Viti Levu, in the Fiji group around 1000 B.C. Mementos of their passage are left in the Polynesian names of various places. Anthropologists (such as Rivers, Churchill, Smith and Percey) believe the Marquesas immigrated through the passage.
- The Gilolo Passage: Outlying remnants of their own race are found on scattered points of the Papuan Archipelago. The Islands of Lifou and Uea of the Loyalty group, and Noumea of New Caledonia were inhabited during the earlier migrations that traversed through this passage. This route traversed north of New Guinea and through the Bismarck Archipelago, where the Navigators (Samoans) and the Hawaiians staged their voyage into the Eastern Pacific Ocean around 2000 B.C.

Gratitude to Those Who've Gone Before

I pause momentarily now, to render humble gratitude to the "wisdom of the past," as advised by the Manu'an deity Tagaloalagi, and to mention Robert Freiherr von Heine-Geldern (1885-1968), who was known after 1919 as Robert Heine-Geldern. He was a noted Austrian ethnologist, ancient historian, and archaeologist. More, perhaps, than any of his contemporaries, Robert Heine-Geldern is credited for helping shape the literary, cultural, and historical dialogue of a single region, Southeast Asia. This place was his motive, ambition, and passion. And yes, we owe a lot to him for casting that first "compass azimuth" to the "harbor light" of Southeast Asia and Austronesia.[lxxxix]

And we must not forget Professor Joseph Campbell (1904-1987), who describes the path of the Polynesians' migratory expansion, snaking through the Far East at Anyang and the northeastern corner of Honan, where we find the earliest levels of the Chinese High Neolithic and hieratic city state. Here there is evidence of the Yangshao culture in full bloom (dating from around 2200 to 1900 B.C.), and the Yangshao complex may be the first place responsible for domestication of the pig.

Among other elements carried from the southeast European, Danube-Dniester zone were a number of distinctively painted pottery motifs—including the double ax, spiral and swastika, meandering and polygonal designs, concentric-circles and checker patterns, wavy-water lines, angular zigzags, and organizations of bands. Spear and arrowheads made of slate are also found from there; arrowheads and awls of bone; a technique for building pile dwellings along river and lake shores; a particular technique for cutting stone, together with a type of square-cut ax made using this technique. This stone-cutting skill would, in the further course of human migration, appear throughout the Malay Peninsula, Indonesia, and good part of Melanesia, as well as, in a modified form, throughout Polynesia.

The second, parallel phase of that same stream of life—the one that brought the Yangshao complex to Kansu, Shensi, Shansi, and Honan—turned south onto the Malay Peninsula. Heine-Geldern tells how this branch, before reaching "Further India"—an old term referring to Mainland Southeast Asia, specifically countries including Cambodia, Vietnam, Thailand, Myanmar, Malaysia, Lao and others in the India Asiatic Archipelago—must have passed through western China. He goes on to describe the migrants as "a folk and culture wave of prodigious force," arriving in East Asia from the West in the late Neolithic period. They transformed the entire ethnic and cultural structure of the region, laying the foundations of Chinese culture and empire, as well as influencing all the Further Indian and Indonesian cultures. Finally, he says, they went on to Madagascar, New Zealand, East Polynesia, and maybe even America as well. Thus, even small groups can provide the impulse that continues to work for millennia, across continents and seas.[xc]

The convergence of the Yangshao (2200-1900 B.C.) and the Austronesian culture waves with the migration wave from the West produced an onward migration that combined all the tools, the vessels (such as outrigger canoes), and the know-how to forge westward to Madagascar and eastward to Polynesia. Heine-Geldern points out that the characteristic square-cut axes with their various modifications, including some magnificent ceremonial forms, found on the Island of Java, provide examples marking a high point of Indonesian Neolithic stone-craft. The population of the area must have been relatively dense, achieving a considerable cultural peak, and engaging in vigorous trade, as can be seen in evidence from Madagascar to Easter Island, and from New Zealand to Japan.

And so, we are led to look at the ways ethnology, ethology and archaeology will contribute to our search for the Navigators' path.

Ethnology

The study of human characteristics,
and relationships between ethnic groups

The Origin

For over 400 years, the Pacific Islander's intrepid voyage across the Pacific Ocean has been a subject of research and controversy regarding several things:

- their origin
- the time period
- and the motivation for making this arduous journey

Much is still unknown about the path of the migration, the people's affinities, and their cultural development in isolation; many things still need to be researched

Scientists (including anthropologists, ethnologists, archaeologists, linguists, biologists, geneticists, and historians) have all agreed that the evidence points overwhelmingly to the "Mediterranean people" having made their first appearance in the Far East at a time when the Bronze Age (3300–2100 B.C.) was in full flower in Crete, Egypt, and Mesopotamia. Evidence can be found in the northeastward spread of culture, mythology, livestock and food products, tools, weapons of war, and transportation materials.[xci]

So, let's start our search with them.

The People

The Mediterranean Type

This original group or race for us to consider is the "Mediterranean People." Professor Stuart Piggott (1910-1996) defined them to include people-groups stretching from Iberia to India, and described a characteristic "type" dating back to the late Natufian culture of 13000-11000 B.C.[xcii] The Natufian culture may have separated from other cultures in the Southern steppes of Northern Africa and Asia, spreading westward and eastward, and evidence of the Natufians is found in pre-agricultural settlements in the Levant, which covers the whole of the Middle East including Palestine.

Archaeological evidence suggests that Homo sapiens and other hominid species originated in North Africa, and that one of the routes taken to colonize Eurasia went through the Sinai desert and the Levant. This would make the Levant one of the most important and most occupied areas in the history of the world.

Archaeologist Ofer Bar-Yosef from the Hebrew University in Jerusalem, Israel, has studied the prehistory of the Levant,[xciii] looking at human occupation of the Pleistocene archaeological site, Ubeidiya (located some 3 km south of Lake Tiberias, in the Jordan Rift Valley in Israel). The site dates from some 1.5 million years ago and preserves traces of the earliest migration out of Africa of Homo erectus—close ancestors to modern humans. Discoveries include hand-axes of the Acheulean type—named after the site of Saint-Acheul on the River Somme in France, where artifacts from this tradition were first discovered in 1847. The archaeological remains reveal that the prehistory of the Levant includes various cultural changes that must have occurred there, prior to recorded traditions.

Professor Piggot concludes that predynastic Egyptians were part of the migration of the Natufian population in the Levant, and that their purest representatives at the present day are in the Arabian Peninsula.[xciv] In India he believes they form the dominant element in populations in the north, and are widespread elsewhere among the upper classes. Such people, he writes, are of medium to tall stature, of slender build, with dark to light olive-brown complexion, long head and face with a narrow and relatively pronounced nose, black hair, and eyes characteristically large and open with color ranging from black to brown. Describing them as a "long-headed Mediterranean type," he finds archaeological evidence of them everywhere in Western Asia, associated with the earliest agricultural settlements.

Archaeological evidence, from the painted pottery of Baluchistan (Pakistan) to the painted wares in the Harappa Culture, points to an eventual homogeneity among these early agricultural economies and communities. So, the appearance of the early "Mediterranean" type in prehistoric India points to expansion from the west. This is significant to tracing the Polynesian migration, as this description of physical characteristics is found in people in the west and northwest of India—the same people, cultures, and geological areas traversed by the Polynesians on their way east.

Arrival of the Aryans

Professor Joseph Campbell draws a parallel conclusion from an archaeological find. A seven inch high, broken statuette from Mohenjo Daro represents a priest-like figure wearing a shawl that extends over the left shoulder, leaving the right bare—which is still the proper way to indicate reverence, both in India and throughout the Buddhist world, when approaching a shrine or holy person. The statue, typical of early Sumerian statues of priestly personages, and the trefoil design of the shawl, also appear in Mesopotamian art. However, Campbell makes the distinction that these designs did not exist in later Indian tradition, suggesting they represent a culturally and socially superior second race which, by the time the Aryans arrived (in the Indus Valley and India), may have been to some extent absorbed.[xcv]

From the Ancient Past

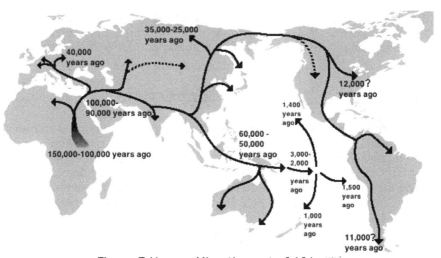

Figure 7 Human Migration out of Africa[xcvi]

Scientists are unanimous now in stating that human migration began in central east Africa—from Lake Turkana, Kenya (1,800,000 years ago) or from Lake Baringo, Kenya (4,500,000 years ago), or from Laetoli, Tanzania (3,600,000 years ago)—and arrived at Ubeidiya, Israel some 1,400,000 years ago, and Qafzeh, Israel some 92,000 years ago.

A right-turn in this migration, heading southeast toward Narmada, India (500,000 years ago), resulted in the people of Eurasia. This Eurasian-based group continued on to middle China. Then one group made a right turn, moving from the northwest and going southeast, continuing toward East Asia (Taiwan) and down through South East Asia to the Malay Peninsula, Indonesia, Java, and to the Pacific Ocean. A second group from the Eurasian migration moved northeast to Lantian, China, and up to Zhoukoudian, China. Subsequently they made another right turn to the Pacific Ocean. The descendants of this migration went on to populate Japan around 30,000 years ago.

The descendants of the Malayan-based group split up again. One group made a right turn toward the Pacific Ocean and peopled the Philippines (30,000 years ago), then traveled onward to settle the Mariana Islands, and the rest of Micronesia. The other group, which came down through Borneo, Burma, would eventually become the ancestors of the people, of the Navigators, of Polynesia.

From the Malay Peninsula

When the migration arrived at the Malay Peninsula, we find acute and profound similarities in cultural and physical attributes. The common language basis gives evidence of a people that share the same ancestry, culture, language, and mythological foundations. This is not to be confused with the Malayan language; we will make the case that the Polynesian language is not kindred to it in our language comparison later.

The Hindu Connection

Ganesh Damodar Savarkar (also called Babarao Savarkar) is an Indian freedom fighter, a contemporary and collaborator of Gandhi, and founder of Abhinav Bharat Society (a far right conservative Nationalist organization). Hindu nationalists, led by Savarkar and Madhav Sadashiv Golwalkar (1906-1973), were "eager to construct a Hindu identity for the nation," and vehemently argued that the "original Hindus were Aryans" and that "they were indigenous to India." They further maintain the continuity of the Indian race throughout its long history, with no disruption by an "Aryan Invasion" causing fragmentation in the race and history.[xcvii] In other words, Indian movement northwest to "Urheimat" and the Pontic Steppes is the beginning of the Indo-European and Indo-Aryan languages.

One methodology employed by the "Indigenous Aryan" group to prove their case is to use the lists of Kings and respective genealogies to establish the continuity of history through the reigns of successive kings. This is corroborated with the traditional chronology of India's ancient history to show continuity

Michael Witzel, of Harvard University, writes that Megasthenes, the Greek ambassador to the Maurya Court at Patna around 300 B.C., reported having heard of a traditional list of 153 Kings covering 6042 years, which goes back to the fourth millennium B.C.[xcviii]

The Language

The Indo-European and Indo-Aryan debate

While the academic debate continues regarding which origin comes first of Indo-European and Indo-Aryan—"Out of India," or "Out of the Pontic-steppes, Caspian-steppes, or Caucasus Mountainous and/or Eurasian steppes"—this will have little impact on the study of Polynesian migration. What it is important to us is the specific descriptions of the small groups of migrants and of their cultural attributes, seeing how they were able to adapt to and influence other indigenous groups.

Additionally, agreement on the period of the Rig Vedas (the oldest scriptures in Hinduism) as the early Vedic period (1750-1000 B.C.)—making them prior to the "old Sanskrit" (1000-500 B.C.) and classical Sanskrit (300 B.C.) periods—allows us to better identify when the Polynesian language developed, prior to the Navigators continuing their migration eastward and to South East Asia.

"The Beginning of Knowledge," also referred to as "The End of Knowledge," is the Vedanta (meaning the end of Vedas), with a philosophy describing the ultimate knowledge, "to know the self as separate from the body and its culture. If a person doesn't know his own self, the soul, whatever else he may know is mere information (datum)."[xcix]

The Dravidians or the Indo-Aryans?

The current consensus among Indologists is that the Dravidians were indigenous in India prior to the Aryan incursion. They were eventually driven up into the mountains by the Aryan invaders.

Thomas Burrow, a well-known Indologist at the University of Oxford, England, has published a list of ancient cities of the Indus Valley with names ending with a word *armaka*, which means "ancient, ruined city" in ancient Sanskrit. These include the ancient name of Mohenjo Daro as Kukkutarmaka or Kukkutarma. The word *Kukkut* in the Proto-Dravidian language means cockerels or roosters. Thus, Kukkutarma means "ruined city of cockerels."[c] These findings support the argument that Dravidians were present there.

The "Out of India" theory of Indo-Aryan migration postulates, instead, that the Indo-Aryans were the indigenous people of India, forming the Indus Valley Civilization. David Frawley, teacher, author, founder and director of the American Institute of Vedic Studies in San Fe, New Mexico, writes that Aryans entered the Indus Valley before 4500 B.C., thus becoming integrated with the Harappans.[ci]

Understanding Indo-Aryan migration is important to the story of the Polynesians, as conventional knowledge claims that the Indo-European language came out of India. The discovery of the Indo-European language family was made by William Jones, a British lawyer dispatched to India to integrate Indian laws and British common and commerce laws, during the colonial period in the late 18th century.[cii]

Sir William Jones studied Sanskrit and Sanskrit texts at the ancient Hindu university at Nadiya. He noted the similarities between Sanskrit and Persian, English, Latin, Greek, and Gothic. After three years of study, he concluded that the Gothic and Celtic languages had the same origin as Sanskrit, just as old Persian does.[ciii]

Many of the Enlightenment sages, including the pioneers Voltaire, Immanuel Kant, and Karl Wilhelm Friedrich Schlegel, subscribed to the idea that India was the *Urheimat* (or origin) of all Indo-European languages.

Out of India

The "Out of India" theory of Indo-Aryan migration has changed into the now well-supported agreement that Indo-European–speaking people migrated from the Pontic Steppes into Europe, the Levant, south Asia (India), and east Asia. This agreement is based largely on the development of historical linguistics, and in particular on the palatal rules or laryngeal theory—this technique involves the analysis of:

- the sound of pieces of a word in a general occurrence of ablaut (apophony)
- vowel gradation
- and vowel mutation, alternation, and internal modification.

It is the alternation of sounds within a word that indicates grammatical information (often inflectional).

These linguistic analyses are supplemented with archaeological data and anthropological arguments, which together provide a coherent model now widely accepted.[civ]

While there is heated debate between those who support the "Out of India" migration versus those who now embrace the theory of Indo-European migration from the Pontic Steppe into Europe, the Levant, the Near East and the Far East, the important point is that this migration path corroborates the path that Professor Joseph Campbell and others mentioned earlier.

It should be noted that the Pontic Steppe, or Pontic-Caspian Steppe, is the vast steppe-land stretching from the northern shores of the Black Sea as far east as the Caspian Sea; from Moldova and western Ukraine, across the Southern Federal District and the Volga Federal District of Russia, to western Kazakhstan. This forms part of the larger Eurasian steppe, adjacent to the Kazakh steppe to the east. it is part of the Pale-Arctic temperate grasslands, savannas, and shrublands ecoregion of the temperate grasslands, savannas, and shrublands biome. The Pale-Arctic is the largest of the Earth's eight-ecozones.[cv]

We will look more closely at how linguistics helps us find a migration path later. But first, we will look at archaeological confirmation of the Navigators' migration paths postulated above.

Archaeology

*The study of human history and pre-history
from artifacts and other physical remains*

The Road to Migration

Dating a Civilization

Scientists, in both the physical and social sciences, have, over time, sometimes confirmed and sometimes updated their ideas about the birth of man and the dawn of civilization. In a few cases, they have narrowed their dialogue, based on the abundance of physical and scientific evidence. Advancements in technology have led to numerous discoveries that continue to push back the timeline of the origin of man and of the development of civilized societies. For example, archaeological remains—pottery, weapons, stone tools etc.—can now be dated with increasing confidence, which helps us in tracing and dating the Navigators' migration path.

Initial radiocarbon dating (C-14) of Catal Huyuk, a proto-city in Anatolia (Turkey), in the 1960s, gave a result of 6000 B.C., with the ancient city of Jericho (Israel) dated around 6300 B.C. Now, based on new archaeological findings since the 1970s, Catal Huyuk is re-dated at 7250 B.C. and Jericho at 8000 B. C. Another site, the Gobekli Tepe (also in Turkey), has also undergone a significant change in interpretation.

So, while it might be safer and less risky to stay in the comfort zone of "conventional belief," sometimes it is important to recognize additional factors at the edges of investigative studies, leading us to acknowledge and learn from progress in research studies.

Gobekli Tepe

The Gobekli Tepe site continues to hold the interest and inspire the curiosity of social scientists looking to understand human migration and its impact on various societies where people sojourned. When I first followed studies of the Gobekli Tepe archaeological site, scientists had dated it from around 9000 to 6000 B.C. and believed a group of farmers had built the site. At that time, scientists were all in agreement that this was a temple site used for religious ritual practices, with Klaus Schmidt,

73

a member of the German Archaeological Institute, writing, "This is the first human-built holy place." [cvi]

It seemed logical to believe this, though it stretched the timeline of the birth of agriculture in the Fertile Crescent valley back from its earlier estimate of 5000 B.C. It made sense to think of a natural human development in community, progressing from farming into religious rituals of worship. This would lead to the building of temple-like structures, and thus Gobekli Tepe would become a place to congregate for worship. And this, we know, would lead to developing a town and finally a city.

Now however, with new discoveries made possible by modern technology, Klaus Schmidt reports that the Gobekli Tepe site has been definitively re-dated to between 11000 and 10500 B.C. This predates the site of Stonehenge by 6,000 years. More significantly, for my efforts, this confirms that the builders of the Gobekli Tepe site were hunter-gatherers, as opposed to farmers, which means the site precedes the agriculturalists in the Fertile Crescent valley.

The implications here for human migration—across the Levant, Pontic Steppe and Eurasian Steppe—are that the hunter-gatherers seem to have been more sophisticated than was originally thought.

The importance of sophisticated knowledge and experience accumulated over long periods of time should not be underestimated. We know, from basic psychology, how important experiences and environmental factors have been in the development processes of human cognition. And, while human migration across the globe is still a conundrum and an enigma to all of us, the mystery of the Polynesians' migration is no less mind-boggling than trying to interpret the Gobekli Tepe site and others.

The Circle of Life

The Gobekli Tepe temple center was unearthed by a team of scientists in Turkey/Kurdistan. The site evidenced a well-developed settlement that seemed, as was then thought, to have been driven by organized farming and agriculture, implying a well-defined division of labor and man's discovery of his superiority over animals. Even in the new hunter-gatherer context, derived from the new dates, the site still evidences well-defined cultural structures. [cvii]

The growth of settlements into towns, and eventually cities, provides the motivational spark for religion and the development of a moral code. This paradigm shift in religious thought creates a need for a place of worship, hence the building of a temple. And this leads to questions about the circle of life, particularly its final stage in the idea of resurrection: that is, out of nothing comes birth, then life—virgin, adulthood, and old age— then death followed by resurrection. At which point the metamorphosis of life begins over again.

Moving Onward

Efforts in archaeological dating yield a result of around 3000 B.C. for Neolithic villages along the Indus River (in modern-day Pakistan), and for village life along the Yellow River and Yangtze River Delta in China. The Mohenjo Daro and Harappa cities (in Pakistan) are dated some 500 years later. Meanwhile, during same time period, the people of New Guinea began cultivating yams, taro roots, and domesticating pigs and chickens.[cviii]

Scientists had already dated the arrival of modern humans in New Guinea and Australia to around 60,000 B.C., to a time when the lands were connected, before the icecap melted in 10,000 B.C. Aboriginal rock paintings are dated around 45,000 B.C. And the Solomon Islands were settled in around 28,000 B.C.

The First Erected Land

Around 2000 B.C., the Great Migration arrived and settled various Pacific Islands, where they introduced those yams, taro roots, and breadfruit. At this time, the Austronesians reached Vanuatu, where they established hierarchical chiefdoms.

The name Vanuatu means "first erected land," where *vanua* means "land" in all of Polynesia (though the spellings might change). *Tu* is a Polynesian word for "stand erected" as in "the first that stands erected." Thus, the Island of Vanuatu is (by name) the first island discovered in the Polynesian migration; they called it the first island erected in the middle of the Solomon Archipelago.

Manu'an Mythology tells of the decree by the first Tuimanu'a—some believe it was Tagaloalagi's decree—delegating the Paramount Authority to the Chief of the Island of Toga. He gave it the title *Tu*, meaning "stand erected on the Island of Toga." Hence the king is "here," *i,* called *Tu-i-Toga* (*Tuitoga*). The decree further proclaimed *TuiFiji* (King of Fiji), *TuiFiti*, *TuiHawaii*, *TuiManu'a*, *TuiAtua* (king of the district of Atua), *TuiAana*, *TuiSamoa* and others (though there is no "title" word spelled "Tui" in the Samoan dictionary.[cix] The Samoan and Manu'an word *fanua* (like *vanua*) means land.[cx]

At this point, the most recent updates in scientific evidence come from analysis of Y-chromosome DNA extracted from human remains found in the various archaeological sites. It has been established from Y-chromosome DNA that Polynesians share their DNA with the people of Southeast Asia, in particular with Malayans, thus confirming the migration path of the Austronesians (people of Malay Peninsula).[cxi] This result is confirmed in the influence of cultures that seem strategically located along or close to the migration path, down toward the Malay Archipelago, Indonesia, and eastward to the Pacific Ocean.

The White Cloud and the Lapita Trading Network

The timeline continues with the settlement of the Fiji Islands by Austronesian mariners around 1500 B.C. and the establishment of the Lapita trading network in the western Pacific Islands, again by 1500 B.C., again by Austronesian mariners.[cxii] Radiocarbon (C-14) dating has established a date between 1530 and 200 B.C. for settlements of some kind on the Island of Saipan in the Marianas, some 1,500 miles east of the Philippines, where, by around 1100 B.C., the Austronesian people were speaking in a variety of Malayan, Indonesian, Filipino, Polynesian, and other Oceanic languages.

About now, the ocean swell is about to peak, and the mighty wave is about to break. The presence of the *Aotearoa*, or the long white cloud as the Maori would say, is hovering over the Pacific Ocean, directed by the wind toward Polynesia. This wind of change propels the mariners of the Great Migration and picks up momentum as they move across Polynesia.

Archaeological Findings

A Connection with the Americas

Several archaeological discoveries in early 1960s are worth noting at this juncture, leading us to make a connection with the Americas, even if only on a cultural diffusion level, and laying a foundational path that crosses the Pacific Ocean to the American continent.

A piece of Japanese pottery was picked up on the beach off the coast of Ecuador. After this, subsequent excavations yielded many more fragments, all of them in the early Jomon (cord marked) style of around 3000 B.C. According to Joseph Campbell, these were the earliest examples pottery registered for the New World at that time, including a number of ceramic female figurines which represented the earliest figurines—even the earliest works of art—to be unearthed in the Americas.[cxiii]

The significance of this important discovery is the possibility of an early trans-Pacific diffusion of cultural traits to the New World.

Archaeological Finds on the Islands

Archaeological findings from a site in To'aga (Ofu Island, in the Manu'an Island Kingdom) were radiocarbon-dated at between 1700 and 400 B.C.[cxiv] These included ceramic pottery, tools made from rock, and hearth remnants indicating signs of community life. Stone quarries have been found at Tataga-Matau—4 large and 6 smaller quarries to date. And basalt from Tutuila has been found in Tokelau, Taumako, Tokelau, Fiji, Western Samoa, Manu'a Island and Cook Island.[cxv] These basalt stones were used to produce tools such as adzes and weapons. It appears that the Samoa Island group was trading these items with other traders throughout the Lapita Trading Network.

At a site behind the village of Vailele, on the northeast side of Upolu, Samoa, pottery and tools made from rock were excavated in 1957 by archaeologist Jack Golson with members of the I'iga Pisa family from Savai'i. These artifacts were carbon-dated to 1000 B.C., showing evidence of human occupation there at that time. Another site, behind the village of Luatuanu'u, Upolu, Samoa, about seven miles northeast of Vailele, yielded artifacts that, again, showed human occupation there in around 1,000 B.C.[cxvi]

Findings at a site at Falefa, a village on the northeast side of Upolu, Samoa, were radiocarbon-dated to between 800 and 400 B.C.[cxvii] And in the village of 'Aoa, Tutuila (American Samoa), a rich set of artifacts and ceramics were carbon-dated to between 1,440 and 800 B.C.[cxviii]

Additionally, beautiful clay ceramic pottery with crude designs was found during the excavation of the docking pier for the ferry at Mulifanua village, on the west side of Upolu, Samoa. This was carbon-dated to around 1,000 to 800 B.C.[cxix] This corresponds again to the timeframe of the Lapita trading network.

The Lapita Trading Network

The Lapita Trading Network is an economic system that the Pacific Islanders constructed to trade goods such as food and livestock, as well as tools and weapons technology, and to share knowledge of environmental and navigational skills.[cxx] In order to travel from island to island one has to master navigating the ocean to be able to exchange merchandise. Thus, the trade network spawned economic activities which led to further developments in society, such as village communities and a centralized authority (the monarchy) over an island. The Lapita Trading Network includes Fiji, Tonga, Samoa, Marquesas, Vanuatu, and Papua New Guinea, and archaeologists are in agreement that this existed from around 1500 to 1000 B.C.

Languages based on Malayan-Polynesian (now referred to as Austronesian languages) correspond to the same time-frame as the Lapita Trading Network, making this the Pacific Islanders' equivalent of the "Silk Road" in the Pacific. Language, of course, was critical for communication in a successful and productive trading system.

Carte synthétique des migrations en Océanie

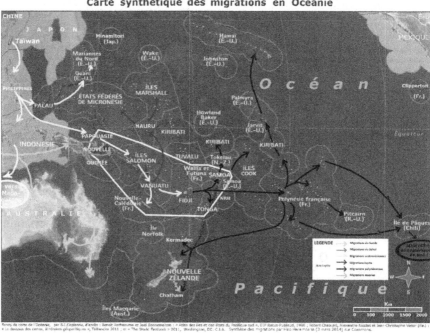

Figure 8 Carte synthétiques des migrations en Océanie[cxxi]

The Lapita Archaeological Debate

As with most scientific discoveries, the more new findings illumine the research subject, the more they also cause controversy. The discovery of more than 200 sites of what is now called the Lapita Trading Network—snaking throughout the southwestern Pacific Islands to the east Polynesia islands of Toga, Fiji and Samoa—adds another dimension to deciphering the mystery of the origin of the Polynesians.[cxxii]

The name Lapita comes from for *xapeta'a*, meaning "a place where one is digging." The first site where pottery of this type was found was in the Foue peninsula on Grande Terre, the main island of New Caledonia[cxxiii]. The pottery style is generally associated with peoples who had well-developed skills in navigation and canoe building and were horticulturalists, according to the consensus of scientists who have labored diligently to understand this cultural development. To paraphrase Andrew Pawley writing in his *The Origin of Early Lapita Culture: The Testimony of Historical Linguistics*, such pottery includes earthenware vessels with red-slipped surfaces, made in a characteristic variety of shapes, including large carinated jars (round base joined to inward sloping cylinder), globular bowls, spherical pots, flat-bottomed dishes, and pedestal stands. A minority of vessels were decorated with precise and elaborate geometric motifs, done by dentate stamping (the repeated application of a set of toothed implements).[cxxiv]

The Lapita culture was carried to Fiji then to Toga and finally to Samoa where the first distinctively Polynesian culture evolved.

On the one hand, we can determine that these intrepid voyages were made deliberately, and therefore had to be planned and organized—a conclusion that stands in opposition to previously held views that the Navigators' migration was purely accidental. However, on the other hand, the findings spawn controversy among archaeologists as to whether Polynesians were the people who established the Lapita Network, or whether it was established by some other group of people originating out of Melanesia and the Bismarck Archipelago.

The timeline established by dating the (already scarce) artifacts indicates that the Lapita network precedes Polynesian migration to East Polynesia by 800 to 1,000 years. Further comparative analyses—of tools (adzes) and apparatus for fishing (hooks), pottery for food preparation, cultural implements such as jewelry, and basalt quarries for making tools and weaponry—all heighten the debate, given differences in the cultural tools and fishing methods. For example, the Lapita artifacts show that Lapita people used bows and arrows, and spears and nets for fishing, while Polynesians used fishbone for hooks and harpoons, and adzes for tools and weapons.

Samoan legends frequently mention that "dark skin people with their bow and arrows and spears are frightful enemies," also mentioning different methods of fishing, such as hooks (*pa*) and lagoon fishing (using coconut leaves to weave like a net to entrap the fish).

Just when you think a discovery is going to clear up the puzzle, instead it adds another layer of complexity.

Back to the Origin

The evidence seems to indicate that these islands were initially discovered by traders during the Lapita network timeframe. If, in fact, these original traders stayed and colonized these islands, they may represent the foundation of the Polynesian race.

In legend, the history of Samoa began with the intermixing of Fijians, Togans, and many other Pacific islanders such as Tokelauan, Niuean, Elise Islanders, and Kiribati Islanders, before the reign of the first Tuimanu'a around the first century A.D. It is clear, from these legends and from the oral history of Samoa, as told through family history and genealogies, that Samoans knew very well which parts of the chain of islands were populated by which other pacific islanders.

For example:

- Savai'i was populated by Fijians and Togans early on in its history, beginning with Fotulafai and Funefea'i, brothers from the Sagaga district in Upolu Island.

- The other district in the island of Upolu that was predominantly populated by Fijians is Falealili, named after its founder, Liliolelagi. Liliolelagi came from Fiji via Savai'i, and his mother, Laufafaetoga, was half Samoan half Togan.
- TuiSamoa, the first Malietoa Savea's nephew-in-law, also from Fiji, was decreed by Malietoa Savea to go to Falealili and establish a family branch there.

The genealogical story continues: Tupa'imatuna married Laufafaetoga, who bore Taua, Utu, Legaotuitoga and Liliolelagi. Liliolelagi's union with Fanuaalemoa, daughter of Tuigate'i in Falealili, resulted in a son Punaoa. And Punaoa married Taupifagalau, who gave birth to the famous warrior Manusamoa and his sister Tautiapagofie. Taupifagalau and her sister Sinaauvale (Manusamoa's aunt) were the daughters of Tagaloa Funefea'i and his wife Ulalemamae of Manono Island.

Manusamoa is the warrior from the district of Falealili known for his bravery in wars in their district. Malietoa Tuilaepa (around 1620 A.D.) needed a warrior to lead a war campaign against another warrior in Manono and Island district, so he called on Manusamoa. Manusamoa accepted Malietoa Tuilaepa's request and, in his preparation, he pulled a whole tree (equivalent to a *koa* in strength) and single-handedly split the tree in half and made each side a warclub. When they heard of this on Manono Island, they were petrified, and so the two warriors went into battle for several days. They were equally powerful and relentless, and then, on the fourth day, the Manono Warrior fell defeated. Manusamoa decreed the other half of the split tree club to the village of Iva, Savai'i, for their bravery and support, and also because of his family relationships, hence the name, High Chief Orator Tofilau—the split warrior club.

Sinaauvale (Manusamoa's aunt) married TuiAtua LeTaua, giving birth to the Warrior Orator brothers Alei and Pata—these brothers became known as Leifi, and Tautoloitua; then, when they conspired to assassinate Tafa'ifa Salamasina they were ordered never to use these names again; the brothers were caught in their own trap and were executed by burning right where they are buried; and their villages renamed the orator title Chiefs to Tafua and Fuataga.

So, from the beginning, Samoans have always known that these village people have mixed ethnicity. They are Togan and Fijian.

Still, the mystery of the origin of the Polynesians continues to elude us all. It is unclear whether the scientists who occupy themselves in researching the mystery are blinded by their own biases or are too easily satisfied that further research will yield only marginal value. However, the real story lies in the oral history of the Polynesians. We need to collate and correlate the archaeological findings with those of genetics, linguistics, cultural similarities and differences, mythology, and history. Weighing the evidence, in a sound, methodical manner, will shed light on the unfolding conundrum of the origin of the Polynesians.

Mythology

The study of myths, especially of how they are connected and promulgated between cultures

Introduction

The Dawn of the Great Migration

While there is significant archaeological evidence of Samoans' occupation of the Samoan chain of islands, it is still unclear where the Samoans originated from. What Samoans believe is that they came from somewhere on the East-West wind, while Manu'ans firmly believe they are descendants of Tagaloalagi, the god of the heavens. However, close examination of folklore, mythology and oral history will reveal deep running threads of a foundational "mat" held in common, providing a conversational platform for rhetoric analogous to that of Greek philosophers in pursuit of wisdom or cultural fabric—or, as the Samoan Chiefs would call it, the *fala lafo*—where *Fala* means "mat," and *lafo* means "to spread out, to seat and converse to seek wisdom and truth"—or *fala talatala*—to seek the truth of its cultural tenets.

The Oral History of the Ancient Past

The ancient history of Samoa is virtually undocumented and thus our knowledge of it relies totally on oral legends, folktales, and mythology, passed down anecdotally from the distant past. The Samoan term for the ancient (distant) past is *Vavau*. And mythology—the record of that past—is the foundation of Samoan and Manu'an culture.

Mythology is the voice of historical events, recorded over an extremely long history. It's foundational to the development of language in isolation. It's the database of the orators. It's the poem of the poet. It's the musical note of the composer, bringing together sound, pitch, rhythm, cadence, and beat. It's the verbally recorded instruction manual, or the archive of the shamans, making it the relationship databank of relationships for the whole culture.

Mythology has its own structure and architecture, designed for easy reference. Language, oration, history, customs and formalities, religious rituals, frameworks of family structure, evidence timelines, and

81

generational history maintained through time in isolation, all use components from mythology. Relationships of data and its usage in mythology can be thought of as similar to the "object-oriented code" design of computer software—a paradigm shift in the early 90s which became a predecessor to Service Oriented Architecture (SOA) in software design, where service components are significantly more scalable than previous software design technologies:

Object-oriented systems are constructed to a particular architectural design discipline. Code, at a system level, is built onto functions which are organized and defined together with the data, in object modules or software components. For example a database containing customer account profiles might need code for passing messages (messaging), doing calculations, selling, buying, etc., and this code might be defined for different types of customers, working on parts of the data that are common to all. The data-types and associated "methods" are the objects, or instances of a class—in this case, the "class" of client accounts. Objects "inherit" the data structures and functions from the class, making the code "reusable" over many different instances, even though it may take different forms depending on the use or application.

Samoan formal Chieftain language is likewise organized by function, protocols, vocabulary, hierarchical structure, events, etc. Therefore, events such as weddings, celebrations, ceremonies, funerals, visiting trips, conferences, symposia, and church events all have their specific protocols and language structure and vocabulary. Thus, the Chief first determines the function's "object," for example, a funeral. Then the Orator immediately begins the orchestration of the overall event, organizing speeches, timeline, protocols, families, genealogy, ceremonies, salutations, language and formal vocabulary, resources, gifts, etc. The chieftain idiom says, "the Orator turns and twists their body over twenty times in their sleep at night, once they are informed of the occasion or event." That's how much preparation they have to worry about.

Similarly, all chiefs, orators, shamans, and other people can access and use mythology in their everyday lives.

Why Myths are Important

The question arises: is Samoan and Manu'an mythology any different from the mythologies of the cultures and societies we traversed, in our quest to trace the Navigators' migration path? Do the themes, storylines, characters, and purposes or motivation agree; do the structure and poetic oration sound the same to the ears; do the stories conjure up the same images in our minds? For that is what legends and myths do for us, as humans. They allow us to remember the past and imagine the future. They give guideposts behind us and a harbor light ahead.

What is Mythology?

Dr Samuel Noah Kramer, the world's leading Assyriologist and a world-renowned expert in Sumerian history and the Sumerian language, created a list (included at the end of this book in the Tables and Notes section) of mythological types, based on Sumerian mythology.[cxxv] In reviewing his list, a universal archetype of mythology is revealed, as in the following structure:

Origin and Beginning

1. The creator or Supreme God or Deity
2. The council of Deities (descendants) representing different parts of the genealogical tree
3. Definition of the various offices held by pious members of the supreme family of Deities.
4. Genealogy of the Deities to beget humanity
5. Authority of the ruling Deities
6. The rule of Man, including families and genealogy

Items #1-20 on Kramer's list give the functional descriptions and characteristics of this phase of development of Sumerian Mythology.

Cultural component

1. The organization of families, based on the genealogy of the first family
2. Rules, norms, rituals, taboos, and protocols
3. Development skills and assignment of work
4. Division of labor and delegation of responsibility
5. Governors and rulers
6. Governance and enforcement
7. Language and speech
8. Human behavior, emanating from everyday living, leading to culture
9. Childbirth, youth, adulthood, old age, death, and resurrection
10. Tools and weapon-making
11. Agriculture and hunter-gathering
12. War and colonization

This component incorporates Kramer's List items #21-51, 65-68.

Religion and philosophy

1. Guiding principles
2. Rituals and dogmas
3. Moral principles
4. Boundaries of things
5. Spiritual enlightenment and resurrection
6. Shamanism, totemism, and animism
7. Spirits and daemon

In this component we find items #35-37, 41, 43, 44, 52-64 from Kramer's List. Some items fall into more than one component, of course, but viewing his list in this summary structure allows us to gain an arial view over comparative mythology and thus gives clarity on cultural diffusion across cultures and society.

Documenting the Myths

It should be noted that the written language of Samoa was only developed for the purpose of translating the Bible from English to Samoan, and the resulting Bible was published between 1842 and 1848.

Manu'ans first heard of Christianity from two Tahitians whose boat was stranded and landed in Manu'a in 1827. At once, there were many Europeans—mostly missionaries such as Rev. G. Pratt, Dr. Schultz, Rev. G. Brown, J.B. Stair, G. Turner, and W. Ellis, together with many other authors—who took a keen interest in documenting mythology and folklore during their tenures in Samoa.

This resulting body of documentary fragments and scattered literary works (mostly in European libraries) is what we have to rely on, in any serious research into the ancient history of Samoa—together, of course, with the legends, folklore, mythology, genealogy and events of history passed down from ancestral generations by word of mouth—the whispering of the wind in Samoan.

Of course, for some academicians the oral history is considered purely anecdotal. But not for us.

Cultural Diffusion

Professor Joseph Campbell, of Columbia University, spent most of his academic career laboring in the field of comparative analysis of mythologies of cultures around the world. When I discovered his life passion—that is, his study on comparative mythology—it resonated within me, and it has had a profound influence on my research into the Polynesian migration story.

During my research, I found Professor Campbell's *The Mask of God* Series and also his Public Broadcasting System (PBS) television series "The Power of Myths," with Bill Moyers. I was also greatly motivated by Dr. Augustin Krämer's well-known and productive reference work for the Samoans, *Die Samoa-Inseln* (The Samoa Islands), published in 1903, in Kiel, Germany. Dr. Krämer pointed to one particular area of potential further study—one among many—being the study of the rich mythology of the Samoans and Manu'ans.

Mythology is one area that has helped move forward the "continuum agenda" of anthropology. This theory postulates that the world's great human migration started in Africa and continued globally to the "four corners" of the Earth, as it says in says Isaiah 11:12 (NRSV): "He ... will assemble the outcasts of Israel, and gather the dispersed of Judah from the four corners of the earth."

The Random House Dictionary defines "cultural diffusion" as the natural process whereby cultural beliefs and social activities are spread from one group of people to another, causing world cultures to become mixed throughout different ethnicities, religions, and nationalities. And Professor Campbell, working in the field of comparative analysis of mythologies of cultures around the world, did more to publicize the idea of how comparative mythologies can further our understanding of human migration and cultural diffusion across different societies around the world.

I've been a fan and, to a large extent, a proxy student of Professor Campbell's academic theory: Simply stated, the parallel images of legends, folktales, and myths, from cultures around the world, are evidence of the diffusion theory—they display a linear migration path, snaking through many cultures and ethnicities, to influence culture in many areas. These images and recurring themes are, in reality, repeated instances of the same motifs that have transcended national borders and crossed cultures—a diffusion of culture resulting from human migration.

Underlying messages in different myths and legends may be the key to unlocking the mystery of that great human migration. The hidden meanings of poetic words deserve to be re-examined, that we might better decipher these subliminal messages of the story told in history. This proposition has preoccupied me for some time, throughout my quest to understand the ancient history and the development of the Samoan and Manu'an peoples.

Gods and Heroes

"Myth is the foundation of life," said the German novelist, Thomas Mann.[cxxvi] Legends are remnants or fragments of stories about real events whose details have eroded in the memories of people over time. The creative process of recalling these historical events, through poetry and storytelling, coupled with embellishment by storytellers and the eloquence of poets or orators, is itself the history of people and their society.

These legends are about heroes and anti-heroes, gods and goddesses, or warriors and villains—not about common men. They allow the imagination to compose an incredible story of the event that justifies the action or theme, while making its characters more than ordinary men. Although they often offer variants on a theme, the variations are usually in the local scenery. Therefore, the local version is believed, by the local group, as the true event.

As Bergen Evans points out, in his *Dictionary of Mythology* (1970),[cxxvii] farmers depended on the goodwill of the Greek goddess Demeter (goddess of vegetation and fruitfulness) or the Roman goddess Ceres (goddess of grain) to make their crops grow; sailors depended on Poseidon (god of the sea) to bring them home safely; pregnant women trusted Hero (a priestess of Aphrodite who drowned herself after her lover drowned when the wind put out the light of the lantern) or Lucina (the

Roman goddess of childbirth). Everywhere—sky, sea, mountains, plains, groves of trees, and even the underworld—was populated by invisible, supernatural creatures whose whims determined human affairs.

The Legacy of St. Thomas Aquinas

Long ago, Saint Thomas Aquinas (1225-1274) was the first to synthesize Aristotelian philosophy with the principles of Christianity,[cxxviii] in a methodology accepting that antiquity is not an old wives' tale or an amusing fantasy. I refer to this as the "two sides of the same coin" approach—one side being Christianity and the other being the culture. The stories are real and important, bearing witness to the events of history and the developments of society as they are believed by the people.

Saint Thomas Aquinas was canonized a saint in 1323 A.D. and officially named doctor of the church in 1567 A.D. He lived in the epicenter of 13th century radical theological renewal, brought about by the social, cultural, and religious evolution of the West—a time of doctrinal crisis that confronted Christendom, when the discovery of Greek science, culture, and thought seemed about to crush it.[cxxix] It's important to acknowledge his legacy and contribution in continuing the rise of the Christian "river" against the seductive nature of Greek culture, thought and philosophy on the generation at the time. In this intellectual battle Aquinas appears to have single-handedly fought with the Church, creating a paradigm shift in the bridge-building blocks to bring about an environment of coexistence between Church doctrine and natural human culture, history, thought, and science. This bridge afforded the integration of science into faith and of faith into human thought or science.

While I risk over-simplifying Saint Thomas Aquinas' legacy and contribution in the above, not to acknowledge it would be an equally great risk. His contribution, in creating an atmosphere of balance, ushered in and accelerated developments in human thought, leading to revolutionary and evolutionary progress in virtually every aspect of human life since the 13th century. His is the very foundation of our journey through comparative mythology, culture, linguistics, and genetics, to better understand the Navigators and their journey.

Samoan and Manu'an Mythology

The Sun god

If you were to ask a Samoan and or a Manu'an where they came from, they would not respond to you by saying they migrated here, in dugout canoes, from some land out in the Pacific Ocean. They would simply tell you they came from Tagaloalagi (the mythological god), who resides in the Tenth Heaven. Tagaloalagi, also known as the sun god, formed the Samoans and Manu'ans into his ideal men.

Samoan folklore tells how the sun became too hot, so people were beginning to die from the heat. To save them, a young girl had to marry the sun. From this marriage was born the sun god, Tagaloala and his brother Aloalolelā.

When you begin to dissect other cultures' versions of creation— Mesopotamian, Egyptian, or Hebrew for example—you'll soon come to the conclusion that they run parallel to each other. Interestingly, crude as it may be, the Samoan version also has parallels with these ancient cultural stories. The Samoan creation story, for example, has always assumed the existence of a god. Samoans didn't imagine that, all of a sudden, there was the firmament, and out of the firmament came heaven—no. Their story always assumed that there was a god, and that god was Tagaloalagi. There was no confusion here. Now, whether this creation story was created 3,000 years ago or 100 years ago, the amazing thing is its consistency with other versions of the creation story in other ancient societies; the premise—god's existence—is identical.

The Spirit

Idol worship becomes the next topic of many myths in cultures in ancient history, with stories of half-human and half-spirit warriors in Samoan mythology too.

The spirit, I believe, is the second stage of the creative mythology process that Mann refers to as "the foundation of life, the timeless schema, the pious formula into which life flows when it reproduces its traits out of the unconscious."[cxxx] The first stage, creating a deity as a source of life and every living thing, is then followed with the second stage of transition, bridging the relationship between humans and the deity. The genealogical connections between man and the gods are critical to the organization of human culture, and this development runs in parallel across all human societies; we will highlight this along our journey.

The important thing to note is that the timeline of Polynesian migration into the Asiatic Archipelago makes this mythological, half-human half-spirit phase of cultural development a precursor to the mythological creativity of Classical Antiquity in the Near East. We must look further back, to the origin of human migration from Africa, to find the source when the human psyche first "reproduces its traits out of his unconscious."

Cultural diffusion, as an integral component carried by the waves of human migration, continues to speak to us in this silent, relentless manner. The "well of the past" continues to provide us with tidings wherewith we unravel the conundrum of the origin of mankind and his life development.

Genealogy and Salutations

In Samoa there are several chief titles and respective salutations derived from a belief in Spirit, in particularly from stories of half-human half-spirit warriors of mythology, with the distinction that a son of the "half-spirit, half-man" chief is simply the "son," not the Prince as most sons of a Paramount Chief would be called. In such a case, his father is the "half-spirit, half-man." The original title, "half-spirit, half-man," would imply a person of cruel behavior. But when the son inherits the Salutation, it doesn't mean or imply that he is a cruel person.

There is also a Title, "half-spirit, half-man," which means someone is a half-spirit, half-man chief.

Aiono Dr. Fanaafi LeTagaloa's *O le Fa'asinomaga* is a complete list of every village's Titles and Salutations, so you can go to the island and then the village, and you will find the village Titles and Salutations.

Examples include:

- Lua le Maga in the village of Asu, Tutuila, Son of half-spirit, half-man, *Afio le Tama a le Aitu ma le Tagata* [cxxxi]
- There is the famous son of Malietoa Uilamatutu (also known as Malietoafaiga, where *faiga* means cruelty; son of the first Malietoa Savea or Malietoa Saveatuvaelua) whose name is Luatua in the village of Saleimoa, Upolu. His salutation is *O le aitutagata* (meaning a spirit-man)[cxxxii]
- High Chief Liufau's salutation in Aua in Tutuila is *Afio le Matua le Tama a Aitu ma Tagata* (meaning Veneration, Honorable Elder High Chief Liufau, the Son of the Spirit and Man). [cxxxiii]

Familiar Myths

So, we look at the period where folklore and mythology started to create the warriors—female and male warriors, gods and goddesses or other deities—and they all begin with a story.

The Greeks spoke of Zeus, their mighty god that ruled above all the others. And other ancient cultures including Mesopotamian, Egyptian, Roman, Indian, and even Chinese have stories of gods and goddesses, deities and warriors that were half-human and half-spirit mythological figures. Timelines may differ among them, but it's evident that they share the same recurring themes in the stories.

The theft of fire, different versions of creation, the virgin birth, the development of a warrior growing from poverty into a mythological figure, and finally the beginning of a mighty foundational family in a society—these are all themes in the mythology of other ancient cultures as well as Samoan. Tool-making, weaponry, and human genealogy from plants—humans born from or becoming plants—are also stories that have been told as folklore. Sir James G. Frazer called it "the effect of similar causes acting on the similar constitution of the human mind in different countries and under different skies" in *The Golden Bough*.[cxxxiv]

The Story of Sina and the Eel

By the time human migration arrives at the lush tropical rain forest of Southeast Asia and the Pacific, the mythological serpent or snake of ancient Mediterranean traditions had been substituted with the eel, as seen in this story:

It is one of the most famous stories told in Samoa—the legend of Sina and the eel, describing the way we discovered the coconut. The legend is almost exactly the same in the Tuamotuan version of Hina's adventure, a story which introduces characters like Te Tuna (the Samoan word for eel), Maui, Hina or Sina, the Monster Eel, and the birth of the coconut tree. The story is recounted in Joseph Campbell's *Primitive Mythology*, where Campbell points out that almost exactly the same legend is also told in Indonesia.[cxxxv]

First, let's enlarge our focus to show the continuum of the theme; we find the Toga Island version of the eel, which says the eel is a male child of a human couple, and he has two sisters. The eel, living in a water pool, springs up toward his sisters, eager for affection, but the girls flee out of fear and disgust. As the eel pursues the sisters, they jump into the sea and become two rocks, which may be seen to this day, off the shore of Togatapu. Then the eel continues swimming to Samoa and ends up in a water pool in Savai'i, where Sina, the virgin maiden, makes friends with the eel.

The Samoan version begins here, ending with the growth of the coconut tree from the head of the eel, which is buried (after his death) by Sina, in accordance with the wish of the eel. When the husk is peeled off the coconut, one will see the three indented marks on the head, representing the eyes and nose and mouth of the eel.

In Mangaia, one of the Cook Islands, the mythology gives the maiden's name as Ina (a dialect variant of Hina and Sina), and says she likes to bathe in a certain pool: The great eel swims past and touches her. This occurs again and again, until one time he throws off his eel form and stands before her as she bathes, revealing himself to be a beautiful youth named Tuna (the Samoan word for eel). Their relationship eventually ends with Tuna's parting wish to have his decapitated head buried in a place where Ina can visit him daily. Ina complies with the eel's wish and, after a while, a green shoot appears and grows into a beautiful tree that, in the course of time, produces fruits; this is the first coconut tree.

In the Manu'an legend, Sina is violated by a fish which is really the lizard Pili. According to Dr. Stuebel, Pili is the son of Tagaloalagi and Muliovailele, whose name appears in the story of how the ava plant was found. Rev. Turner, however, names Pili as a son of Tagaloalagi and of Tuimanu'a's daughter, Sinaleana.[cxxxvi] In Rev. Turner's account, Pili is the progenitor of the brothers Tua, Ana, Tuamasaga and Tolufale, who became the organizers of the Upolu and Savai'i Islands

The Manu'an legend maintains the theme of a fish, eel, or lizard living in the water pool, and of Sina who bears the progenitor of the organizers of Samoa.

The Story of the Bread-Fruit Tree

In all cultures, we find origin myths of animals, humans, inanimate objects, real estate properties, and environments. And our theme of plant-origin stories would not be complete without the birth of the breadfruit tree:

According to Hawaiian legend, a man named Ulu had a sickly baby boy, whose life was endangered due to the scarcity of food. Ulu went to the god, Mo'o (this is the same as Pili in Samoa). He prayed at the temple at Pu'ueo for help for food and, when he returned, told his wife he had heard the voice of the god and that, when the volcano goddess, Pele lit the night sky above Mount Kilauea, then the "cloth will cover my head." At his death, Ulu's wife had to bury his head near a spring of running water, and his heart and entrails near the door of the house, hiding other parts of his body similarly. Then she was to listen throughout the night, perhaps hearing the sound of heavy fruits falling to the ground, which would tell her Ulu's prayer had been granted and their son would be saved. Ulu immediately died, and his wife sang a lament and obeyed all his instructions. In the morning, her house was surrounded by a thicket of vegetation and breadfruit.[cxxxvii]

Indonesia has a similar breadfruit story, with just a slight difference to the Samoan version. The existence of similar stories helps us determine the truth of the stories and the migration path taken by those who carried the stories with them.

Creation Myths

Mythological, Historical or Literary?

Manu'ans conceptualized the story of their creation and origin, building their incredible mythology to rationalize their beginnings and existence in their isolated environment. The creation process of such a tradition has its foundation in the human psyche, going back to how our minds work, and how the conscious and subconscious minds conceive of images and ideas that are then manifested in mythological stories. Dr. Carl Jung and Dr. Sigmund Freud taught us about this in their respective bodies of work.[cxxxviii]

This same foundation is demonstrated in scientists' research into the field of Comparative Mythology. It allows us to draw parallels with creation mythology found in other cultures. Thus, when we speak of mythology from various high-level cultures—such as Greece, Egypt, Mesopotamia, Sumer, and Akkad—we can immediately go to the part of their mythology that describes their respective "creation."

Professor Campbell writes of the strange dichotomy whereby we study mythological figures and perceive them to be literary figures. But we consider figures in the Bible, such as Moses and Jacob, as belonging purely to the spiritual realm.[cxxxix] Zeus and the myriad deities of Classical Literature are given great importance, so why would we not accept the mythological god of the Samoans and Manu'ans and their story of creation as being of equal importance?

The Manu'an Creation Poem

Manu'ans recite, with great conviction, an old Manu'an "Poem of Creation" about the god Tagaloalagi. Tagaloalagi was also known by his other names: Tagaloanimonimo (invisible heaven), Tagaloafa'atupunu'u (creator of islands), and Tagaloala (the sun). His name can also be written TagaloaLelagi, which means something like "the one and only" Tagaloalagi. His presence is ubiquitous in the legends of origin of almost all of Polynesia.

The Manu'an Poem of Creation states that the heavens opened up, and the god, Tagaloalagi—who resided in the tenth heaven (the first through ninth heavens being occupied by the children of Tagaloalagi)—looked down and summoned the winds of the dry season—*vaitoelau*, *mataupolu*, and *matalepola*—and the winds of the wet season—*matu*, *tuaoloa*, and *pi'ipapa*; he called, also, on the rolling and crashing, angry, smashing surf; and he summoned the high-rising, feared waves; and then he commanded them to be still and calm, for Tagaloalagi wanted to rest.

At this junction, Tagaloalagi called out to the heavens for a few small pebbles which he organized into islands, naming them as follows: Manu'atele was first (Manu'a "at large" (tele) is another name for Manu'a), then Upolu, Tutuila, and Savai'i. He created the various sacred meeting and resting grounds for himself and his Chiefs.

Tagaloalagi pulled up thousands more islands, by their necks, from the abyss of the ocean and distributed them throughout Polynesia—the Tongan Archipelago, the Fiji Islands, and the rest of the little islands.

Tagaloalagi flew over these Islands, and surveyed the landscape, and "weighed and measured the space between them, and he saw it was good."

And so... Tagaloalagi sent down the creepers to populate Tutuila, Upolu, and Savai'i. When the vines decayed, they produced maggots, but he saw the maggots did not have a soul, feet, hands, head, or heart. So, he dispatched his messenger, Tuli (the Golden Plover), to see what was wrong with the maggots, and Tuli ((*Le Tuli o le Tagaloa)* told him they do not have a soul. So Tagaloalagi pulled out limbs and gave them appendages, and then he brought down the soul and, behold, humans became a living soul.[cxl]

Note, *Le Tuli o le Tagaloa* is a title given to the servant of Tagaloalagi. Shortened to Letuli, it is a Paramount High Chief title in the village of 'Ili'ili, Tutuila Island.

We should notice also, creation takes place totally on the ocean, which seems to indicate a period of time when all things are born from water after the flood. According to Dr. Ananda K. Coomaraswamy, many cultures share a belief that life originates in water, a belief that would have arisen very naturally in the case of peoples living close to water (around the Nile, the Euphrates or the Indus River for example), for whom seasonal rains and the flow of rivers were so clearly essential to life and vegetation.[cxli]

The Samoan Creation Genealogy

Samoans, on the other hand, tell their creation story through one of the oldest family genealogies in Samoa, the TuiAana (the district of Ana).

At a time when the earth was full of darkness, the union of the ancient Lights from the East (*Malamagaga'e*) and the West (*Malamagaga'ifo*) begat a lava rock, of bluish sheen, that transformed into *Lupe* (a pigeon—pigeons, chickens and roosters are important to the Navigators' voyaging, because they can indicate landmass and the position of the sun).

Lupe (the pigeon) united with *Papatu* (upright cliff), giving birth to *A'alua* (two tree roots, as in the roots of family trees). *A'alua* married *Papamau* (a solid cliff), giving birth to *Papafoagia* (a demolished cliff). *Papafoagia's* union with *Ma'ata'anoa* (scattered rocks) gave birth to *Papae'ele* (cliff soil). *Papae'ele* with *Palapala* (swamp, the most fertile land) begat a female, *Papamavae* (the fissuring cliff, being a cliff where life can be conceived). It is clear, reading the sequence, that this took place after the Flood.

Papamavae, a female, married *Imoa* (a male rat—a name that is common in Samoa) and bore a female, *Salasala* (meaning cut off, or that which the rat gnawed off. The rat is one of the oldest animals, next only to the lizard, *Pili*, and there are reptilian mythologies across many ancient cultures—for example Egypt, Mesopotamia, Greece, India, etc.—that parallel the Samoan lizard and rat legends).

Salasala, the first woman, married *Tagaloanimonimo* (invisible heaven) and begat *Tupufua* (a free man—we should note this is where *Tagaloanimonimo*, of the Manu'an story, makes his appearance here in the Samoan genealogy). Then *Tupufua* married *Leletaimalie*, a lady from TuiAtua ancestry, who gave birth to *Leo-Pili* (descendant of *Pili*) of Manu'a.

In the family genealogy of the Malietoa (a much later Warrior Paramount Chief), early ancestors also include *Ma'ata'anoa,* scattered rocks, and *Imoa*, the rat.

Thus, the belief is that we are a byproduct of a heavenly creator god, Tagaloalagi, and his wonders created out of the abyss, carried over to the earth, and culminating in the rat, *Imoa*, and then the first woman who begets *Tupufua*, who is known to be the first free man. The story displays an incredible logic in its construction of the heavenly Lights and Mother Earth, through the union with a hard rock, producing soft soil for *Imoa*, the rat that represents a male figure to produce a female human, *Salasala*.

Other Creation Stories

Now, let's think about how all this parallels the creation stories of other "high level" ancient societies—Egypt, Mesopotamia, Greek, Persia, India, etc.

An abundance of evidence and a great body of knowledge has been amassed by all the research scientists—archaeologists, anthropologists, ethologists, ethnologists, and biologists—with respect to these ancient societies. We are mesmerized by Greek mythology, and overwhelmed by the intellect and creativity of the Egyptians and their Kingdoms of Old; we praise Mesopotamian and Sumerian creativity for the invention of writing, the wheel, and accounting, and for the Akkadian war machine in the First Empire. Clearly, we are astonished and profoundly impressed by their contributions to mankind, from the enlightened beginning of human development and evolution to the accomplishments of this great migration. Indeed, we immediately and intuitively recall the familiar mythological figures:

- The Greeks proclaim Gaia and Uranus, and the Titans, as their mythological ancestors.
- The Egyptians name Atum, Re, and Ptah as their origin—their ancestors.
- For the Hebrews, Yahweh, Elohim, and the Holy God are names given to their creator.
- Likewise, the Mesopotamians list Enki and Enlil and Ninhursag as the mythological gods of their beginning.
- And India's Vishnu, Shiva and Brahma are well-known mythological gods of their origin.

And all these mythologies have their respective version of Genesis, the creation.

Greek Creation

When we speak of Greek mythology, we are amazed and humbled by the well-known classical myth, told to us by Hesiod, the 8th Century Greek poet and historian: This is the story of Gaia (Earth) who, in the beginning, brought forth of herself, without consort, Uranus (Heaven); they were separated by their sons, Kronos (Saturn), Urea (Hills) and Pontus (Sea). Gaea then conceived, by her son Uranus, the race of the Titans which included Oceanus and Tethys, of whom Metis was born; also Cronus, Rhea, Themis, and, in a special manner, Aphrodite; thence the fully convoluted derivation of the gods and goddess of the Greek pantheon.

This genealogical ancestry produced the demigod warriors who begat human offspring. Thus, Alexander the Great, on his deathbed before his untimely death, wanted to ensure his genealogy came from Zeus via Peleus then Achilles, and through his mother Olympias the Queen of Epirus. So, appropriately, his Egyptian title was Zeus Ra, just before his passing.

Egyptian Creation

Speaking of Egyptology, we recall the *Philosophy of a Memphite Priest* by Professor James Henry Breasted, later confirmed by Professor Adolf Erman and dated to the Old Kingdom: "There came into being on the heart and tongue of Ptah, something in the image of Atum."

Then Atum brought forth Shu and Tefnut, then begat Geb, Nut, Osiris, Isis, Seth, and Nephthys. Thus, wrote the Father of History Herodotus(484-425 B.C.), we arrive at the first king of Egypt, Menes, at the time of the Narmer palette; the generations continuing down to the first Pharaoh, Aha-Mena, builder of a great civilization and the ubiquitous pyramids.[cxlii]

Mesopotamian Creation

Dr. Samuel Noah Kramer has shown—in his studies of Sumerian tablets in the libraries of Europe, the Near East, and America—that the Mesopotamian creation myth begins with the goddess Nammu, the "Mother," who brought forth Ki (Earth) and An (Heaven). An is the male Heaven, the upper portion, and Ki is the female Earth, the lower portion. Ki and An begat Enlil, the air-god, who separated and tore them apart. This marks the beginning and foundation of the Mesopotamian theology of creation.

Indian Creation

India, with its impressive ancient Indus Civilization, has been studied much, particularly in Professor Joseph Campbell's *Oriental Mythology* in *The Masks of God* series. The hymns of the Indo-Aryan Rig Veda introduce its gods:

Varuna (all-encompassing the universe), Agni (god of fire), Soma (god of liquor), and Savitri (the Sacrifice), were the negotiators of Creation, and the predecessors of Brahma the Creator, Vishnu the Preserver, and Shiva the Destroyer of Illusion. The three gods of the Trimurti (Sanskrit, meaning "three forms") are effectively a chief triad of Hindu deities, in a pantheon of about thirty million.

Born from the lotus in Vishnu's navel, Brahma is often portrayed as a four-faced god sitting on a lotus flower. With his own hand, he is said to have written the Rig Veda on leaves of gold. This is a collection of 1,028 ancient Sanskrit hymns to the gods. After Brahma laid and hatched the egg of the Universe, according to speculation in some Hindu writings, the work was in Vishnu and Shiva's court.

Vishnu, the preserver god, has had nine major avatars (or incarnations); the tenth (and last) avatar will be Kalki, the rider of the white horse who, with sword blazing in hand, will put the end to all sin and sinners. Among Vishnu's avatars were his seventh, Ramachandra or Rama; his eighth, Krishna; and his ninth, Buddha.

Vishnu is probably the most popular Hindu god, willingly incarnating himself to save the world and mankind from various giants, demons, tyrants, and other calamities. "When order, justice, and mortals are in danger," said Vishnu, "I come down to earth." Many Hindus worship him as the supreme deity.

Completing the Trimurti, Shiva, the destroyer god, is a composite figure. His fierceness is counterbalanced by kinder, gentler qualities that make him a favorite deity of ascetics and a patron of the arts, letters, music, and dancing. His most famous representations show him as a white, four-armed figure performing his cosmic dance on the body of a prostrate, nasty little demon whose back he has broken. The dance of Shiva symbolizes the eternal alternation of destruction and creation in the Universe since, in Hindu thought, destruction always implies a subsequent restoration.

Chinese Creation

The illustrious ancient history of the Chinese presents many of the same conundrums in its story of creation as the Levant societies. To paraphrase Dr. Li Chi of the National Taiwan University, China is the land of mythological mysteries, with a documented continuous history of 5,000 years.[cxliii] To understand Chinese mythology is to unravel these mysteries and decipher China's unique and complex culture and history.

Professor Joseph Campbell began his coverage of Chinese mythology in his book, the *Mask of God: Oriental Mythology*, with the Period of Ten Great Monarchs that were assigned in the early Chou-time mythology, which terminates in a "Deluge." The ten monarchs are as follows:

- Fu Hsi (famous for the invention of symbols, on which the *Book of Changes* is based; he used nets for hunting and fishing)
- Shen Nung (he "ruled the world" for seventeen generations)
- Yen Ti
- Huang Ti (he invented the fire drill, burned the forest to clear the brush, burned the marshes, and drove out wild animals)
- Shao Hao (he reigned for seven years and introduced the ritual of regicide)
- Chuan Hsu (he had eight sons. His son Kun, the "Great Fish" was unsuccessful in dealing with the Deluge. But Kun's son Yu, the Great Yu, was given the Great Plan from Heaven to solve the problem of the Deluge. Yu dug the soil and led the water to the sea.
- K'u (he had two wives who each conceived a son miraculously).
- Yao (the Divine Yao, he was reverential, intelligent, accomplished, thoughtful, sincerely courteous, and obliging)
- Shun (he reigned for 28 years and is an ancestor of a great house)
- Yu (son of Kun, son of Chuan Hsu; Heaven gave him the Great Plan to solve the Deluge)[cxliv]

I believe Joseph Campbell's purpose in starting his comparative mythology discussion with the ten monarchs was because they are the "primeval heroes," foundational to Chinese mythology. Campbell draws many parallels between the storyline of the ten monarchs and the ten Sumerian kings, and with the Biblical patriarchs, with the shared legend where the last monarch of the series overcomes the "Deluge." He pointed out how remarkable it is that both Noah (in rabbinic literature) and the Great Yu, each became lame in the course of their labors during the Deluge. How they were each injured by the solar beast (or lion) magnifies the parallel.

China's indigenous faith, as it is occasionally described, is the ancient religion and philosophy called Taoism, one that emphasizes harmonious living with the universal way—Tao. [cxlv] The following provide a sample of Taoist Chinese Mythology:

- Ba Xian: The "Eight Immortals" are Taoist deities. One famous storyline tells of them, each individually, crossing the Eastern Sea and coming into conflict with the Eastern Dragon King[cxlvi]
  - He Xian'gu (female)
  - Han Xiang Zi (music)
  - Lan Caihe (ambiguous)
  - Li Tieguai (male)
  - Lu Dongbin (leader)
  - Zhongli Quan (death)
  - Cao Guojiu (prince)
  - Zhang Guo Lao (old age)
- Dou Mu Niang: The mother goddess of The Big Dipper stars, she is the progenitor of the stars and constellations
- Ling Bao Tian Jun: One of the Three Purities in Taoism, the name means "Heavenly Lord of the Divine Treasures"
- San Guan: The "Three Officers" of Heaven, Earth, and Water
- Tai Shang Lao Jun: Taoist Title of Laozi, the mythical founder of Taoism, one of the most supreme divine trinity in Taoism.

Biblical Creation

We herald all these historical and cultural stories as monumental and fundamental to the beginnings of mankind. We think of these characters as literary figures, and we look for a natural order among the mythologies of human development and the Great Migration.

In contrast, when we study Abraham, Noah, Moses, Jesus, and Peter, etc., some think of them as purely spiritual and supernatural, and find it hard to argue them as objective history, whereas in fact, as Professor Campbell explains, the fabulous elements common to contemporaneous Eastern Mediterranean traditions can be seen to have derived from earlier civilizations of Mesopotamia—a result that the modern science of archaeology could not have predicted.[cxlvii]

Again, we are quick to accept Zeus, Ra, Nammu and Enki, the Vedic, and the other mythologies and deities of the great societies of the Levant and the East, giving them historical and cultural importance, because of the preponderance of evidence as to their stories. But the deeper we dig into the well of our ancient ancestors, the more we discover how we are a branch of the same of Tree of Life, and the more we find the well "bottomless."

We accept the story of Genesis, also, because we've accepted the Word of God and Christianity. But our investigation does not alter our view of the objectivity of Hebrew history in the Bible, even if it's subject to our believing, hoping, and faith in God.

Counting Heavens

Interestingly, the Samoan stories have similarities and parallel structures to all the other mythologies. First, they state that the gods—Tagaloalagi, Tagaloala—and deities—TagaloaUi, Taeotagaloa, Fe'e (eel), Po (dark or night), and Ao (light or daylight)—all started with a single god.

Second they include a deluge—Dr. Krämer places them in historic time periods of which the first consists of Po, Ao, Heaven, Deluge and Tagaloalagi; the second period consists of Tagaloalagi's descendants; the third begins the Tuimanu'a, TuiAana and TuiAtua genealogies, and the fourth consists of the other major families of Samoa and Manu'a.[cxlviii]

And thirdly, they include the separation of different "Heavens"—in the Manu'an myth, there are ten heavens, of which nine are each occupied by the other deities, and the tenth Heaven is the residence of Tagaloalagi.

Muslims refer to the concept of multiple heavens as well, listing seven heavens, with each described by what it is made of—pure silver, pure gold, pearl, white gold, silver, ruby, and divine light. Prophets and angels preside over each heaven—Adam and Eve, John the Baptist and Jesus, Joseph, Enoch, Aaron, Moses, and Abraham, in the same order.

The Jewish seventh heaven, also called "the heaven of heavens," is farthest from earth and is considered to be the abode of God and the loftiest angels. Ezekiel 1 and 10, in the Old Testament, speak of Cherubim, who wield a flashing sword to keep the banished Adam and Eve away from the Tree of Life. In Isaiah 6:2, the Seraphim are described as having six wings: two to cover their faces, two to cover their feet, and two for flying. However, in Ephesians 1:21, Colossians 1:16, and 1 Thessalonians 4:16 in the New Testament, St. Paul adds seven more orders: Principalities, Powers, Virtues, Thrones, Dominations, Archangels and Angels. These nine orders of angels were assigned to the various heavens, hence nine heavens occupied each by an angel and a tenth heaven of pure spiritual fire and light where dwells the Kingdom of God.

The ancient Babylonian astrologers identified the five planets visible to the naked eye (Mercury, Venus, Mars, Jupiter, and Saturn) with five of their chief gods. These, together with the gods of the sun and moon, were seen as inhabiting seven heavens, another example of multiple heavens.

97

Creation Parallels

One amazing parallel in the world's mythologies lies in how creative reasoning affects the authoring of such myths. An abundance of mythologies is committed to memory, to ensure their existence is preserved—just as, historically, say, Alexander the Great sought to preach Hellenism throughout the known world. And many parallels can be drawn between the mythologies and theologies of creation throughout the great Levant, the Near East and, of course, the Far East and South East Asia.

For example, the concept of separating things or tearing them apart (Earth vs. Ocean, and Water vs. Fire for example)—then the idea that this separation took place in the water (the deluge or the abyss, implying events during or after the great Flood)—followed by the mention of various part of the anatomy (limbs, heart, legs, head) and of movement without anatomical parts are all present in the Samoan and Manu'an stories of creation. The creative imagination and psyche of the Samoan and the Manu'an people brought them to the same conclusion about their origin— a conclusion very similar to that drawn by the Greeks and the great ancient societies of the Levant, India, Africa, mainland Asia, South East Asia, and the Americas. But when the missionaries—many of them learned men of science—wrote their erudite treatises on Polynesian mythology, they referred to these stories only as "myths," ignoring their importance.

In Samoan belief the myths are sacred. Samoans will continue to hold onto their mythology and to the Manu'an poetry, which recites their beginning, and to TagaloaLeLagi's creation. (Tagaloa-*Le*-lagi means "The one and only" Tagaloalagi.) to echo the words of Gerhart Hauptmann, poetry is the art of causing the sacred Word to resound behind words[cxlix] ("Dichten heist: hinter Worten das Urwort aufklingen zu lassen").

Migration path of Mythology

The scientific consensus of social and physical scientists, based on evidence from anthropology to linguistics, is that the "ancient" (1st wave) of Polynesian migration to the East Pacific took place during the Neolithic period (3200 to 1150 B.C.)[cl] They agree that the Polynesians stayed isolated till the arrival of European explorers in the mid-1500s, which means they did not have the benefit of cultural diffusion for over 2,000 years.

The prevailing religious practices in the Far East and Southeast Asia during the Neolithic period included deities in the form of idols, powers of shamanism, nature (later known as animism), multiple gods, demigods, warrior heroes, totemism, headhunters, the spirits of dead ancestors, and worshiping the soul, among others. Austronesians were already participating in several of these religious or cultural practices, and so the Navigators were exposed to or might even themselves have practiced the worship of dead ancestors, together with shamanism, totemism, animism, and belief in the human soul before their migration journey.

The expansion of peoples coming from southwest and central India, after the Proto-Europeans (or Proto-Aryans) totally reconfigured and redefined the originally Dravidian Indus Valley cultural society, would have led to the birth of the Hindu Religion. This resulted from a major migration into the Asiatic Archipelago. And this cultural diffusion had a major impact on the Asiatic population, leaving a permanent imprint in the memory of Polynesians before their great migration to the East Pacific, then during and after their arrival in their isolated islands home.

It should be noted, the only monotheistic religion at this period came from Egypt's Pharaoh Akhenaten (around 1353 B.C.) where Aten, a single God, was worshiped.[cli] It was much later than this, during the Israelites' exodus from Egypt to Jerusalem, that Moses received the Ten Commandments and proclaimed monotheism, with a single God for the Jews. By this time, the Navigators were already aware of their own story, of the repeating cycle of every living thing and of the heavenly bodies, each coming and going in accordance with different weather cycles. For them, the quest for understanding the source of everything in the universe already pointed to the heavens.

As we examine Manu'an creation mythology, with creation by Tagaloalagi, we must keep in mind this background knowledge, in order to gain some understanding of the psyche of the Manu'ans, leading to their creating a mythology that justified their existence from a single god. Their mythology evidenced a much older cultural society than we had imagined. Their psychological inquisitiveness had gone beyond the question of where they came, or migrated from, to the question of where does life itself comes from. This step is fundamental to the cognitive development process of religious beliefs and rituals and represents the first essential function of mythology.

In the most "elementary" way, to use Sigmund Freud's terminology, the four essential functions of mythology can be discerned as "eliciting and supporting a sense of awe (strong religious or spiritual quality) before the mystery of being."[clii]

The second function of mythology is to provide a cosmology—an image of the universe that will support and be supported by this sense of awe. The cosmology has to correspond, however, to the actual experience, knowledge, and mentality of the culture involved. Joseph Campbell points out that when the "priestly watchers of the skies in ancient Sumer" studied the order of the planets around 3500 B.C., the entire system of mythology in the Near East moved away from the simple primitive themes of the hunting and planting tribes; the change represented a paradigm shift from the "elementary" level of demonic dread, to, on the highest level, "mystical rapture."

The third function of mythology, according to Joseph Campbell, is to support the current social order—the group and its collective efforts and decisions. And the fourth function is to initiate the individual into the order of realities of his own psyche, guiding him toward his own spiritual enrichment and realization—that is, to give time for the individual to rebuild the ego because it has long been suppressed to cater to the collective initiative.

When we view the myriad legends and myths of the Navigators, as the backdrop for reviewing Manu'an creation mythology, we should be able to identify the transformation taking place in their cultural development as a reflection of the four functions of mythology. Thus, we can identify the logic of the orator and the prosody of the poet.

The most relevant study, in our analysis of the stages of cognitive development of Manu'ans and Samoans during and after their arrival in Polynesia, is that undertaken by Dr. Bronislaw Malinowski (1884-1942), looking at the Trobriand Islanders' primitive economic system of exchange (bartering) in his *Argonauts of the Western Pacific* treatise.[cliii] Dr. Malinowski gives an erudite account of how the indigenous people of the Trobriand tribe went about developing an economic system of exchange to sustain their way of life. Dr. Malinowski did not draw on where and when the Trobriand natives derived the cognitive knowhow to create such a system of exchange in goods and services. But we now know that the revolutionary Lapita trading network was functioning in the same group of islands around 1500 B.C. The people had to have learned about the "law of supply and demand," visibility in both demand and supply, market intelligence, logistics and fulfillment, and more. This gives us the reason why Gilgamesh, the Sumerian king of Uruk, invented coin currency, the "bullae," and bookkeeping around 3300 B.C.[cliv] Rational thinking on the part of the participants is an important assumption, in this and other principles of economics. So, the bartering system in economic development actually goes back to the migration of early "hunter-gatherers" out of Africa and became more refined during the agricultural revolution that accelerated human development across the globe.

The Trobriand natives were in isolation during the early Neolithic period, much like the Navigators, while their ancestors were already living on the main island of Papua New Guinea, as discussed earlier. The Trobriand natives were also isolated from cultural diffusion taking place in and around the Indonesian and Malay Archipelagos. It's important to keep in mind the attitude of the indigenous people of Papua New Guinea—for the Melanesians, this was a "preferred isolation" since they founded their kingdom in Melanesia between 45,000 and 32,000 years ago. To a large extent, even today, they still maintain that attitude of independence.

So, did Dr. Malinowski miss the "big picture," the application of the barter system of exchange across a much larger group of traders, covering a much larger geological ocean area, of which the Navigators were a member? Keep in mind, we are still looking at the Neolithic period, when the Lapita trading network was developing—that is, when they were going through the process of identifying unique products and services with enough of a "demand curve," as well as satisfying their own needs for products in order to make the long arduous ocean journey to trade. This is fundamental to economic development.

During the time of the Lapita trading network across the Pacific, Samoans were trading in black "obsidian" rock—obtained from quarries in Tutuila Island, it was great for spears, fishhooks and for cutlery—and in "ocher"—used for coloring tree-barkcloth with siapo designs, obtained from quarries in Tiavea and Aleipata villages in Upolu. Archaeological discoveries in Tutuila have confirmed this. So, are we still not convinced that the Navigators were capable of the kind of imagination needed to derive this great mythology of Creation?

The Manu'an Poem of Creation

"Over the rolling and crashing surf, angry and smashing surf, choppy sea, and incoming waves, swelling up high, but not destructive; high rising in low plotting waves; splendid waves, frontal waves, feared waves breaking on the reef banks; waves from the west and from the east; waves that rise; ships reaching out for people; and talking waves and their companions to spring waves, followed by their spray of the rocks.

"That's why they call them companion waves.

"Where are the waves? In heaven, the golden plovers rest from the seas; Tagaloa wants to rest. The waves below frighten him. The earth has not yet been created.

"Which is the place that comes first into being? Manu'a is first, then Savai'i, followed by Malae Alamisi, the Tongan Archipelago, the Fiji Islands, and the little islands around the East Pacific Archipelago. Alamisi is in Samataiuta, Savai'i; it is the dwelling and resting place of Tagaloalagi and of his retinue:

"Tagaloalagi steers toward Samataiuta. He flies across his islands in the west. He weighs and measures if the spaces between the islands are the same. Tagaloalagi climbs on your mountains but stays on the mountain of Manu'a. Unthinkably long, the island sea lies under the winds, and Tagaloalagi is startled by the terrible waves. He calls to heaven for a few small pebbles; Upolu is only a small rock, and Tutuila is a small pebble. He enlarges the islands by lifting them up as a resting place for chiefs, all of whom look toward Tagaloa.

"Tagaloa (short for Tagaloalagi) sends down the sacred bindweed to populate Tutuila, and Upolu, Atua, and A'ana, together with Tuamasaga. But the fruits of the creeper are maggots, soul-less beings that move their bodies but cannot sit; they have no heart.

"The *tuli* bird (the origin of Tulialetagaloalagi which is now a Paramount title in 'Ili'ili village in Tutuila Island) reports to Tagaloalagi that the land is beautiful but that there is a problem. There are no edible plants. So Tagaloalagi answers, "Come, take this staff *to'oto'o* and strike the creepers." The bird goes down and strikes the creepers which fall to the ground in pieces. Then Tagaloalagi tells the bird to look again. The bird sees that the creepers have decayed, and maggots have developed among them.

"Tagaloalagi tells the bird to go down with the devil, whose name is Gai'o. So, the devil makes humans out of maggots. The devil names the human beings after the bird *tuli*: hence, *tuli-lima,* the elbow, and *tuli-vae,* the knee.

"Tagaloa hears, up above, that human beings have come into being from the *Fuesa*—the sacred vine. So Tagaloa comes down in the west and brings them speech and form. He brings down the soul that it might illuminate the body, and that you might await Tagaloa when he descends to walk about." (My rendition of the poem)

And so the Manu'ans are cognizant of the foundation of life being maggots. They notice that when living things decay, living maggots come from the decayed, and become the foundation of human life. The logical process begins with photosynthesis producing plants or creepers, which die and decay, going back to bacteria to produce life again.

The detail of how certain parts of human anatomy are created is relatively advanced compared to other creation myths. The planting of the soul in the maggots is also an advanced intellectual concept. We know, from the religious practices of the west and from the east, that humans worship the soul. And so, everything in the descriptions of this Manu'an creation myth points to worship in nature—worship of nature, soul, spirit and the dead ancestors.

But how does the poem continue?

"Fititele is in the islands of the east; everywhere mountains are scattered, but none different. They are all like Manu'atele.

"Tagaloa creates the cliffs and counts 110 islands. But which island was formed first?

"Manu'atele: the land away from the wind, the Matasaua on Manu'atele and the lee land in 'Ofu and Tufue'e.

"Fiji and Tonga: the smooth cliffs and the stark plants spread out leaves which supported the falling sky.

"Savai'i: as broad as a tethered leaf; in vain its mountain surpasses in height the big mountains, but they are nothing special. They are shoots of Fatulaii in Manu'a and Fatueleele.

"So that no one will make false claims, the first chief is Alele, Tagaloa's son. He slides down to the *male o vevesi* (meeting ground for war); it is quiet in the *malae o toto'a* (meeting ground for peace). Peacefully set there, Tagaloa's circle of chiefs watch who will receive the first cup of kava.

"Losi, you fish in the sea and take the best fish up to heaven. Is this a meal for his circle of chiefs? Take all the fish to heaven, with the exception of Politoa, that is for Tagaloa. Tagaloa's people assemble for the *fono* (meeting) at the *Malae*. (In heaven is the *Malae Osia*, the *Malae Tafuna'i*, the *Malae Papa*, and the *Malae o vevesi*. The *malae o toto'a* is the meeting ground for peace.)

"To the carpenter goes the first kava of his title; happy voyage for his boat that he lays the keel. Tagaloa sits on his throne with his title; down below the carpenter is grateful for his title and carries it away from Tagaloa's gathering. The Faletufuna, which is the circle of chiefs and carpenters, are all here.

"Who has the first tools? The first ship heads to Manu'a; it is tied by the Faletufuna. There are many thousands of carpenters, but only one leader.

"The god comes down, bursting the rafters; in ruins lies the house that shattered; cliffs and sea both meet like the moon, the inconstant one, and the sun, which was formed and changes no more. The sea grows; the water grows; heaven grows.

"Tagaloa comes down for a visit. He laments to the west and he laments to the east. He sobs because there is no place for him to stand.

"Savai'i and Maunaloa, then Fiji is formed, then the Tongan Archipelago, but Manu'a was made first." (Adding my own interpretation to the reference material, this is my rendition of the Manu'an Creation Poem.)

The Importance of Myths

How Myths Reveal a Society's Development

It would be an egregious error in judgment for me not to discuss the mythological stories of creation of Manu'ans and Samoans. These stories evidence the characteristics of an ancient society, as compared to the higher level societies recognized by the world. They give us a reference point for starting this exciting story of the journey of these people, bringing their culture and the story of their beginning across the Pacific Ocean. It is not my purpose to debate the validity or the literary worth of these "Great Societies" mythologies, as compared with those of Samoa and Manu'a. Rather, I wish to draw a parallel showing the unrecognized creative psyche of the Navigators of the Pacific in their evolutionary development.

The richness of Samoan and Manu'an mythology is indicative of a people that were already well-equipped with the intellect to organize and lead a major journey, and to design a vessel, and to map out a course, using wind direction and pinpointing the stars to navigate their arduous journey across the largest ocean in the world, the Pacific Ocean—and we should remember it took 2,000 more years for the Portuguese to develop similar skills and technology, such as using a compass.

How Myths Relate to an Orator

I have a rule that I tell young orators, and that is to be sure you use a proverb that you clearly understand. You have to make sure not to reference the genealogy of the people in the audience, because if you can't defend it, you're in trouble. So how do I practice my own religion? I pick the proverbs or the sayings, or the parables, that I know belong to my village, my clan. Fortunately, the Malietoa genealogy covers all of Samoa including Upolu, Tutuila, Fiji, and even Tonga, so I have many to choose from.

How Myth becomes a Human Story

We've discussed the Sun god earlier, and the origin of the coconut and palm tree (the Story of Sina and the Eel). Let me now tell you a story of Malietoa Molī and how the word Molī came about.

In Fagasā, there was the kingdom of Mageafaigā. There were 10 seats in his circle of chiefs, and in the middle of that was a lamp. The second Malietoa wanted to defeat Mageafaiga. So, he sent out his troops, three times, to defeat Mageafaigā, and all three times they failed. So, one day Malietoa decided to figure out how to defeat Mageafaigā himself.

The Malietoa clan had a tradition of collecting a bunch of ripe bananas. The ripe bananas would be carried from village to village. Whoever would partake of a banana from the bunch, this person had to fight in battle on behalf of the Malietoa.

One day, the banana bunch was being carried around the villages until it arrived at Fasito'otai village. The young warriors were gazing upon it and said, our mother has been asking for some bananas. Well, their uncle heard of this and he warned them that they really don't want to take a banana. Ignoring their uncle's words, the young warriors plucked ripe bananas from the bunch for their mother. The uncle's name was Li'o, and these two young men were To'otai and To'outa—hence the village names, Fasito'outa and Fasito'otai.

The three men understood now that they had a problem. Sure enough, in the next few days the messenger from Malietoa came for the two brothers. With their uncle's blessing, they went, and the Malietoa told them of his need to defeat this warrior. It became their duty to plot a way to defeat Mageafaigā.

They decided one brother would attack from the harbor and the other would attack from the mountainside, which was on the other side of Nu'uli. Lo and behold, the warrior Mageafaiga received news from the beach that there was a fleet coming from Upolu. But what he failed to realize was that he was being attacked from both sides at once.

It was a spear that caused the demise of Mageafaigā. Before he passed away, he admitted defeat to Malietoa and asked for the names of the two brothers. Upon receiving this information, Mageafaigā renamed these two brothers—To'outa and To'otai—naming them Ape and Tutuila. Ape was the one that arose every morning to make sure all the preparations were done. Tutuila was the brain behind the master plan.

Mageafaigā bequeathed all 10 seats and the lamp to be taken to the Malietoa. Malietoa received these, along with the name of the lamp—in Samoan, it is *molī*. Hence, the name of Malietoa Molī, son to Malietoa Vaiinupo, the Paramount Chief that hosted the missionaries at Sapapaali'i, Savai'i in 1830. If you date this story, it takes place in around 1290 or 1300 A.D.

There are very few families in Samoa where you will ever see hear that name, *Molī*. But mythology and folktales turn into decrees that are promulgated, and then become designations. If you go to Leulumoega, or Fasito'outa, or Fasito'otai in the TuiAana district, you will hear their salutations: *Falefitu a Ape ma Tutuila, Ape ma lou Fale Fitu, Tutuila ma lou Falefitu, Leulumoega ma lou Faleiva; ae Falegafulu ia Molī*. This is how these salutations were founded. And now, you don't call these two warriors To'outa and To'otai, but rather refer to them as, *Ape moemanatunatu* and *Tutuila le matemate ma lua Falefitu*. The folklore and mythology have become a human story, a part of history.

Myth and Animals

The Samoan Sua

Some people are curious as to what Samoans do with the pig in their culture, particularly in the Sua ceremony. Why is the pig a part of their sacred ceremonies?

The pig was brought over by the Navigators when they left the Fiji and Rotuma Islands. This is the only domesticated animal that was, in olden days, exclusively used for offering sacrifices to the deity (god), to the Paramount Warrior half-spirit and half-man, and to Paramount Chiefs. This ritual practice is evident in the "Sua" presentation of the meal of the god, Warrior and Paramount Chiefs. Thus the Sua represents the mythology of the pig, as the sacred animal for sacrifices to gods and Paramount Chiefs. The pig, chicken, pigeon and dog are the domestic animals or pets the Navigators brought with them in their migration journey.

The story of the pig also stems from other mythologies. In classical Greek mythology there is a story about Persephone, daughter of the goddess Demeter, who was kidnaped and taken to the underworld by Hades. A thousand pigs were sacrificed during Demeter's celebration ceremony after she found Persephone.

Pigs have become sacrificial animals throughout many cultures. So, it's not surprising to note the Samoans still use the pig for sacred ceremonies today. Of course, the pig is domesticated and also used for food, but it's a form of sacrifice as well.

So, the Sua ceremony is conducted basically like a ritual offering made on behalf of a person of honorable status, and it shouldn't come as a surprise that the pig is an offering. It is an ancient religious ritual that goes back to Classical Greek Antiquity.

Animal Sacrifice in Ancient Cultures

The first animal that was offered to the gods was not the pig; it was the bull. There is a story in Greek mythology about a half-human half-bull that's called the Minotaur. A lion later became a substitute for the bull in myth. The lion is often seen eating the head of the bull in Greek drawings on pottery and cups and statues.

There were also sacred chickens, as I discovered on Hebrew coins with plaques portraying a rooster that the Israelites worshiped. This was during the time that the prophets were complaining about how the Israelites still worshiped idols when they were in Babylonia. I discovered these coins bore images of the heads of chickens or roosters. Apparently, this also ties to one of the earlier birds used by Noah during the flood.

Interestingly, as we read in the creation poem, TagaloaLeLagi uses a similar bird called the Tuli bird (golden plover) as an ambassador, and later, of course, there is the legend of Lufasiaitu and his sacred chickens.

The Story of the Demigod Lufasiaitu

In the beginning, at a time when darkness filled the sky after the deluge, the light from the east united with the light from the west, and produced Lupe, the Samoan pigeon. The legend has it that the pigeon and the chicken were the only birds alive.

Lupe's union with loose rocks (*ma'ata'anoa*) produced swamp (female, *Palapala*), a fertile swamp conducive to producing and sustaining life.

Swamp's union with fertile land (*Nu'u*; a village) produced *Tagata*, a human being born out of nothing, also known as the first human, born out of nothing (*Tupufua*).

Tupufua married *Sulu-i-mauga* (the light shined over the mountains) and begat Lu. At this juncture, the Samoan and Manu'an genealogical pedigrees unite. For Tagaloalagi's children have occupied the first through the ninth heavens, while Tagaloalagi resides in tenth heaven.

The legend of Lu introduces several mythological ideas that have shaped the imagination of Samoan and Manu'an folklore, perpetuating their ancient history and culture. It is the Samoan legend of the rooster— or *moa*, a general word for chicken—and it is often referred to as the source of the name *Sa* (sacred) *Moa* (Chicken).

The demigod warrior Lu, later known as Lufasiaitu—*Lu* (his name), *fasi* (thrashing or beating), *aitu* (spirit)—lived in Uafato village in the District of Fagaloa, Atua. He is also a descendant of the legendary and ubiquitous Pili in Polynesia.

Lu gathered up the chickens from across the island and built himself a chicken enclosure or farm. He made his chickens *tapu* or prohibited; no one was permitted to eat the consecrated (*sa*) chicken. But then the people of Tagaloalagi, on their return home to heaven from a fishing expedition, discovered Lu's sacred chicken farm and decided to help themselves to the chickens. Upon Lu's discovery that his chickens had been stolen, his wrath descended on Tagaloalagi's people, starting with those residing in the first heaven. He waged war on them.

As Lu thrashed and whipped the people, they retreated upward to the next heavenly tier until they reached the ninth heaven, where

Tagaloalagi's princess *Lagituaiva* resided—*Lagi* meaning sky, *tua* meaning circle, *iva* meaning ninth.

At this point, the omnipotent Tagaloalagi saw that Lu was approaching the tenth heaven, the location of his sacred throne. Thereupon Tagaloalagi said to Lu, "I beg your forgiveness. I offer you my princess Lagituaiva as a ransom for my people and my kingdom." At which point, the beautiful princess threw herself down, lying across Lu's warring path as an obstacle to gain his attention, with the hope of stopping him and his rage.

Lu now inherited that additional part of his name— Lu-*fasi-aitu* (Lu the destroyer of spirits). Upon looking at the beautiful princess lying in front of him, he was mesmerized and touched by her bravery and her honorable sacrifice, made for her father and their people. While Lu was temporarily stunned by this act of "human sacrifice" made by this beautiful princess, Tagaloalagi spoke out saying, "Lu, may the burden be lifted. Take my daughter as atonement for the sins of Sa Tagaloalagi." Almost immediately Lufasiaitu replied, "Tagaloalagi, your people will live, their sin forgiven, because of Princess Lagituaiva's brave sacrifice."

In this version, Lagituaiva is also known as *Fa'alavaleamoaileala* from *Fa'a lava le amoa i le ala*—the chicken lying prostrate on the sacrificial path. This marriage produced a girl named *Moa* (chicken or rooster), who married the first Tuimanu'a and began the Tuimanu'a family name, Moa, according to Manu'an tales.

The Sun God

The above legend, of the demigod Lufasiaitu, is always recited as the rationale for the naming of the group of islands *Sa*-(sacred) *Moa* (chicken or rooster). While the name is a literal translation of Lufasiaitu's chicken farm, it doesn't speak to the profound importance of the chicken or rooster as the harbinger of the coming of the Sun god.

In Greek mythology, told to us by Hesiod, alectryon is an ancient world for rooster:

Ares, the god of war, was carrying on an illicit affair with Aphrodite, the deity of love. Being fearful of being caught in the act by Helios, the Sun god, Ares appointed a young man named Alectryon to watch for Helios. Unfortunately for Ares, Alectryon fell asleep and Helios came and uncovered the love affair of Ares and Aphrodite. Ares, out of anger, condemned Alectryon to be a rooster, to watch and announce the arrival of the Sun god.[clv] Alectryon (the rooster) was often referred to as a symbol of the sun god (the god Ra, as the Egyptian would call it).

This story was further interpreted to mean that the sun is the enemy of the dark.

The Significance of the Rooster

The time period, around 700 B.C, is approximately the same time period when the Mesopotamians were also worshipping the rooster as being equivalent to the sun god, according to Herodotus' *Histories,* published around 450 B.C.

The Hebrews also worshipped the rooster god, again as being equivalent to the sun god, as evidenced by the image of the rooster on Hebrew coins. Professor Joseph Campbell writes that the "cock head is a solar symbol" representing his reproductive prowess, and Jewish legend, in the Talmud, speaks of learning "courtesy toward one's mate" from the rooster—due to the observed behavior of the rooster when he finds something good to eat; he calls his hen to eat first.[clvi]

In India, in Tamil folklore, Tabuh Rah (Balinese Hinduism) involves animal sacrifice, where ritual cockfights usually take place outside the temple during the worship ceremony.

In China, the bird has traditionally been considered a good sign, as its crow meant the break of dawn and beginning of a fresh start. It's also believed that it chases ghosts and evil spirits, which flee at the mere sound of the rooster's crow. Chinese mythology attributes the following virtues to the rooster: knowledge, military might, courage, benevolence, and credibility, according to Patel Utkarsh, Professor of Comparative Mythology at Mumbai University, India.

As we move further down East Asia, Professor Utkarsh adds that documents from the Koryo Kingdom (918-1392 A.D.) in Korea tell of roosters being reared in the royal court to keep time, as no clocks existed in that era. Travelers would take roosters with them on trips, so they would awake in a timely manner.[clvii]

Finally, arriving at the East Pacific Ocean and the Island of Micronesia, we find the legend of the rooster in the Island of Chuuk, whereby in the war between the Chuuk and the Pohnpei, the rooster "god" helps the Chuuk defeat the Pohnpeian.

Thus the rooster was ever revered as a "god." And the representation of the sun deity using the rooster, found across ancient civilization and told in oral mythology, resonates with the Samoan legend of the founding of its name, Sa-Moa (sacred rooster).

We should also note the similarities between the Egyptian name for the sun god (Ra) and the Samoan word (La) for the sun. The sun god was also worshipped by the Samoans and Manu'ans, by the descendants of Tagaloa-La, grandson to Tagaloalagi and descendant of the TuiManu'a, also known as the family of Moa (the chicken or rooster). In Manu'a, one of the many honorific salutations of the family of Tuimanu'a is "Veneration, Mighty family of Moa, Your Honorable Tuimanu'a." The Orator can choose any one of the Salutations based on the construction of his or her oration.

In the Hebrew world, Luke 22:34 reminds us of Christ's prophetic revelation to his disciple Peter that "the cock shall not crow this day, before thou shalt thrice deny that thou knowest me."

Myth and Culture

The Girl who Married the Warrior

Sometimes proverbs are derived from mythology and folk stories, and proverbs provide another way in which language is developed. Proverbs help the people to remember their stories by creating clever sayings, parables, and phraseologies which describe the events. Hence, as we find in Samoan mythology, a talking tree, animals changing into different forms, plants and trees growing out of animals, and creatures like the coconut.

There is a Samoan saying: *Ua tautala* (speak) *le fau* (hibiscus tree) *gagana* (language), *ua logo* (proclaim) *le na i Atea, logo fo'i le na i ama* (meaning: the hibiscus tree spoke up to give instructions as to how to find the longhaired Warrior, Taemanutava'e, proclaim it to Atea, the ancient homeland of the Polynesian, and proclaim it to the portside of the outrigger—my translation). A second proverb, *Ua valuvalusia le a'a o le fau*, is a proverbial instruction for the blind man to rub the hibiscus tree trunk, hence the tree speaks up and gives instructions.

These sayings come from the myth of Oleaifale'ava, the blind man, his wife Leulupu'a, and his daughter Lea'auta. They journey together to find the longhaired Warrior Taemanutava'e who then weds Lea'auta; the couple produce Va'afuti, Fata, Maulolo, and their sister Luafatasaga, who married the first Malietoa Saveatuvaelua.

This is an ancient story. The young warrior ran away into the forest at Sili, Savai'i, and lived there. He was a powerful warrior, half-spirit and half-human, and his story, the story of Taemanutava'e, echoes throughout the Pacific, as follows:

There was a young girl, from the village of Faga, who became quite intrigued with this warrior. So, she urged her parents to seek out Taemanutava'e in the forest. Her father, Oleaifale'ava, was blind, and her mother was unwilling to waste time on her daughter's curiosity. So her parents were hesitant about her request but ultimately agreed to go into the forest. Hence, the name of this legendary journey from the village of Faga, *Le Malaga mai Faga*, which goes like this:

They went around from Safotulafai, and they began to name every place they ventured through. These particular lands, or now villages, were all named from this story. They stopped and rested underneath a coconut tree and fell into deep sleep. The old men felt heat upon his hand and he quickly began to wake his wife and daughter. He said, "Hey! Hey! Hey! Wake up; we overslept. The sun is almost straight up! I feel it piercing through the coconut leaves. So, get up and let's go, before it's too late." So they packed up their things and, before they left, the old man named this place, saying, *'O le mataniu-feagaima le ata*, meaning *mataniu* (coconut leaves) *feagaima le ata* (sunlight piercing through), hence: Let this land be called *mataniufeagaimaleata*—the sun is beginning to shine through the leaves of the coconut tree.

A spirit ghost bird, *ve'a* (also called *tuli*—the servant of Tagaloalagi in the Manu'an Poem of creation), followed them throughout their journey—it was related to the old man because his genealogy extends from Tagaloalagi: Tagaloalagi's union with Sinaalaua of Savai'i led to a daughter Sinalagilagi. Sinalagilagi married Malalatea, giving birth to a girl Lelapueisalele and her brother Oleaifale'ava, the blind man.[clviii]

The old man began to wonder why the *ve'a* was making so much noise. His daughter paid no attention to it, as she continued to bathe in the water by the rocks. Now the rock was shaped like a bowl, and the bird began to settle in its bath as well. So they named the place, *'O le mea* (a place, referring to Malae Fuifatu) *na fuifui ai le manu*—or *manuali'i,* which means "the place where the spirit bird bathed in the rock." It is now the location of the sacred meeting place of Safotulafai village. *Fui* means bath and *Fatu* is another word for stone.

They had now arrived at the village and realized that they had a problem; it was in the middle of nowhere. But the spirit bird, ve'a, told the old man to go over to the big tree and scratch the trunk, and the old man complied. Then the tree woke up and said, "Hey, who is scratching my trunk?" The old man replied with, "We are here looking for the warrior Taemanutava'e." And the tree responded with, "Well, you are not going to find him down there. However, go over to the other tree by the bank of the dried-up river and beat the trunk until you hear thunder and see lighting. When the rain starts pouring down, wait until the river flow is clear, after the mud has washed down to the ocean. When you see hair floating down the wave of the river, you must take hold of it and tie it to the roots of that tree; then hold on to the hair and follow it upriver and you should find him."

The old man obeyed the spirit tree, and went right over to the other tree, and began to beat the trunk with good-sized logs. Suddenly, thunder and lightning began and, shortly thereafter, rain started pouring down; and after some considerable period, the river began to rise up.

The hair began flowing by, and the old man tied the hair to the roots of the tree. They began to follow the hair upriver. Around the bend, they saw this great specimen of a superhuman, handsome warrior, standing in the middle of the river, taking a bath.

The warrior was shocked to see the old man and his wife and daughter, and he appeared angry, but to no avail because his hair had tied him to that spot. Finally, the warrior Taemanutava'e said, "What do you want?" The old man began with this long-winded story of their journey across Savai'i to find him, because his daughter was enamored by his legendary story and thus wanted to see him in person. And so the warrior wanted the daughter Lea'auta for his wife, and she consented.

When the young girl and her father were resting on a cool grass-like vine, called the *fuesaina,* the old man looked at his daughter Lea'auta and thought how they had done all this for her. And he said, "Look at how far we've come. I hope your genealogy becomes royalty"—in Samoan, *a tonu e tau tupu lo'u gafa.* This was a prophetic statement, fulfilled in her genealogy.

Taemanutava'e married Lea'auta, the young girl. Soon after their marriage they begat sons Va'afuti, Fata and Maulolo, as well as Luafatasaga, their only daughter. Luafatasaga married the first Malietoa Saveatuvaelua, and bore Malietoa Uilamatutu or Malietoa Faiga, whose genealogy continues to the present day. Thus was fulfilled the prophetic statement made by the old man, father of Lea'auta, when he said, "I hope your genealogy will be royal." Henceforward hers is the genealogy of royalty that continues today, and the dynasty of the Malietoa begins from this mythological story

Sacred Meeting Places

There are several villages in Savai'i whose names derive from the story of Taemanutava'e and Lea'auta, such as Fogapoa, Tuasivi, Fatausi. And the land called *Mataniu feagai ma le ata*, later called *Sapapaali'i*, is the actual "sacred ground" where Christianity arrived in Samoa. *Le taeoa mataniu feagai ma le ata* is the name of it and it comes from part of the same myth.

My passion is to identify the foundation of the Navigators' beliefs and mythology and how they are manifested in the Navigators' history and origin. I want to find the ways that Samoans and Manu'ans constructed their mythologies or *fagogotagiaō—fagogo* (legend) *tagi* (crying, singing, or acapella storytelling) *ao* (before dawn), hence a legend crying or singing in a manner perhaps similar to today's "rap music," monotonic storytelling, in acapella before dawn (between 3:30 and 4:00am!).

In the creation story, when Tagaloalagi called out to the heavens for pebbles which he organized into the islands, Manu'atele, Upolu, Tutuila, and Savai'i, he created the various sacred meeting and resting grounds (*Malae*) for himself and his chiefs at the same time.

Malae is the sacred meeting ground for a village, and the *malae* is surrounded with High Chiefs' *maota*, or residences. *Malaetele* and *Malae o Vavau,* both in Manu'a, are the ancient meeting grounds of Tuimanu'a and his kingdom. In Savai'i, the sacred meeting ground is the *Malae Alamisi* in Samata (actually in the middle of the two subdivisions, Samata-uta (inland) and Samata-tai (seashore)). There is a different word, *tia,* for the paramount Chief's resting, or burial place, where *tia* means a burial mound or rock pyramid.

In Fagasā, the name of the sacred meeting ground, the *malaefono-malae* (sacred land for *fono)* is Malaepule. In my village, the *maota* are Tanumafili and Vaito'elau.

Death and Resurrection

"Sacred meeting places" make us think of birth, death, and resurrection, right? Sounds familiar? It's like the natural order of things in life and in mythology—also the natural metamorphosis of philosophical thoughts. It doesn't matter what part of the world you come from, this order applies in every country and gives rise to specific protocols, from days of old. And death is followed by "spiritual" resurrection—that is, the dead turn into spirits that roam the world.

This is where Samoan culture differs from Christianity's view of resurrection. In Samoan culture, the belief about spiritual resurrection is that the living can still communicate with their loved ones who have passed on. They exist, to them, in a spiritual form.

Pulotu is the Samoan version of Hades, where the dead reside, but there is no deity of the underworld in Samoan and Manu'an mythology— only a name of the underworld place, *Pulotu* or *Fafā o Sauali'i*, the Abyss of the Underworld Spirit, or the Samoan Elysium.

Samoan and Manu'an belief holds that the Spirit of the Underworld exists and summons dead souls to be guided to Pulotu, or Elysium, directing the chiefs to one path and ordinary citizens to another. But the legends do not view or refer to Pulotu as a sinful place, simply as a place for departed souls.

Resurrection, for Samoans, is evidenced by the belief that their ancestors speak to them on a daily basis. Samoans call on their ancestors when in need. The spirits of their dead ancestors watch them and know what they are doing. Sometimes they speak their mind when they are not happy. So this is the Samoan and Manu'an idea of resurrection—that the spirit of the dead comes back and visits, everywhere and anywhere. And in this, the missionaries found parallels with Christianity—the practice of believing in God and of constant communication with God through prayer. I will write more about this is my third book.

There is only one Samoan and Manu'an legend in which a dead person comes back to life, as a person rather than a spirit. This is when the god Tagaloalagi split the body of Pava's son for disrupting and disrespecting the Ava protocols and then later resurrected him back to life after Pava pleaded for his son's life. Otherwise, there are legends of half-human half-spirit demigods, actors in a storyline where they come back to life but only in spirit. But Samoans and Manu'ans never confused their god, Tagaloalagi, with the various demigods in their mythology. They practiced monotheism, believing in one god, Tagaloalagi, that resides in the tenth Heaven.

The Greek gods and deities judge you and determine which part of Hades you will go to, but Samoans and Manu'ans didn't have an evil deity that had to be banished to an evil underworld. In Samoan and Manu'an mythology, bad actors were defeated and put to death or they were banished, and that was the end of it. For in the words often recited by the orators: "the language, and all of its cultural appointments have already been determined and settled in Pulotu." *'O upu o Samoa ua uma ona malepe i Pulotu.*

Monotheism and Christianity

Samoan and Manu'an legends are monotheistic. They believed in one God, Tagaloalagi, who lived in the tenth heaven. Every attempt made to rebut Tagaloalagi's will by humans (Samoan and Manu'an), whether leading to triumph or defeat, always ended up with some form of decree from Tagaloalagi, to gift or delegate authority or freedom to the human, rather than deliver punishment.

In the same way, the kingdom of Israel accepted and embraced the gift, from God, of the Ten Commandments, received by Moses at Mount Sinai around 1300 B.C. The Ten Commandments state above all, "You should have no other gods before me," hence the birth of monotheism within Judaism, which eventually became the moral code for Islam and Christianity.

I believe there are many parallel concepts—one God, residing in the highest heaven, one creator, etc.—found in the monotheistic religion of the Samoans and Manu'ans that allowed them to easily understand the message of Christianity and accept it readily. Thus, they realized that resurrection would occur to the spirit of a man (dead or alive), the righteous one rising after the final judgment. They accepted that the saved will be rewarded to enter the Kingdom of God and that sinners will be destroyed by the everlasting fire. And they believed in one God.

Mythology Conclusion

On a personal level, when I look back on my early life growing up in Samoa before immigrating to the United States, I was around my grandparents most of the time and thus I frequently experienced the rituals of storytelling in the early morning. So by the age of 14, when we left for United States, I was already familiar with many of the legends or mythology and folklore—Professor Campbell describes this as "the Imprints of Early Infancy."[clix] Most of the legends that I learned were particular to our family's titles, ancestry, history and genealogy. That is where it all began, at home, at an early age, and specific to my family history.

Now I am pondering how I should write a summary to this mythology section of my book. I'm struck with the realization that my generation (the baby boomers) of Samoans and Manu'ans, who spent our early teenage years on the island, might be the last generation to have experience of early morning storytelling rituals, and this worries me. The erosion of old practices is rapid, and grasping at them leaves us on slippery slope.

The current generation learns its stories through books. Unfortunately, books can't convey the rhapsody of the refrain, and their own version of "rap" music does not sound in the voice of the Elder poet—they miss the personal and profound levels of the story.

Thus, for me, as I recall my own experience in hearing these legends, I can identify with the idea of experiencing them at a very personal level, because almost all the legends and myths I was told relate to the family, village and clan: The legend of the blind man and his daughter and their trip from the Village of Faga; The Legend of the Warrior Taemanutava'e, who refused to have his hair cut; The Legend of Va'afuti or Va'afa'i and his son Li'ava'a and Tu'uleama'aga;[clx] the Legend of Fata and Maulolo and their sister Luafatasaga; and so many others. I relate to and see the story at the "local scenery" level, as Professor Campbell puts it, because it is personal and it pertains to our family and clan titles, genealogy, and history. Thus, as I continue to increase my understanding of the science, sources and anatomy of mythology, I find myself seeing the "deepest and the foreground"—as Campbell describes it[clxi]—the far and the endless, and the gray and mysterious color of the void.

As I mentioned in the Preface, I'm not writing a thesis on comparative mythology, but it is my hope to tell the world that, if you are interested in understanding how a tiny little group of people, an Island Nation, has developed a culture, history, language and way of life almost exclusively, from its origin, based on mythology, legend and folklore, in isolation, then you should stay with me in our journey to the end of my three-book series.

Genealogy

The study of lines of descent traced through ancestors

Pulotu and PapaAtea

Pulotu

We have mentioned Pulotu, the Samoan version of Hades or Elysium. It is the abode of the departed chiefs and ordinary people, each with a respective path to the land of eternity. And it plays an important part in mythology and in genealogies. As we shall see, Pulotu is where Saveasi'uleo and his wife Tilafaiga reside, as decreed by the parting covenant between Saveasi'uleo and his brother Ulufanuasese'e.

Judge Abraham Fornander recounts a version of the Tongan story of creation that says "they were ... descended on their group, from their gods, but that the gods themselves dwelt on an island far to the north-west called Pulutu. This name strikingly points to the Island of Buru, near Ceram, of the Bandai group in the Asiatic Archipelago."[clxii]

The Papuans, of Papua New Guinea, refer to the abode of departed spirits with a similar name, "Mbulu." And on Marquesas Island, Fornander tells us the "Ta-ke nation" say "they were created in a country far, far to the west, *iao-oa*, called Ta-ke-hee-hee." They have two different traditions reporting the same fact. Quoting Fornander again: "one mentions thirteen places of stoppage and sojourn during their migration east-ward, *iuna*, ... and the other mentions seventeen places. In one of their legends or religious chants, that of the creation of the world, *te Pena-pena*, by the god Atea, the then known world extended from Vavau to Hawaii "*me Vevau i Hawaii*," and after the earth was made, or rather brought to light, the order was given—*Pu te metani me Vevau...* (Blow winds from Vavau...)"

The consistency of the names and meanings for the abode of departed spirits is clear. It's a consistency that holds from eastern Polynesia to the west and north-west to Fiji, Papua New Guinea, and the Asiatic Archipelago, and it provides evidence of the path in the great Polynesian migration.

PapaAtea

Hon. Judge Abraham Fornander points out the important part played also by PapaAtea in mythology and genealogies. Fornander proposed that the period of Papa and Atea might point to the arrival of Polynesians into the East Pacific Ocean. He highlights the fact that "the generally-received genealogies of most of the leading Polynesian groups lead up to Wakea, Atea, or Makea, and his wife Papa, as the earliest progenitors, the first chiefs of their respective groups."[clxiii]

Fornander continues by estimating, using the Hawaiian genealogies leading up to Wakea, a time range from 230 B.C. to 160 A.D. for the arrival of the Polynesians at their respective abodes.

This genealogy differs from other Polynesian island genealogies recorded by Fornander, in that it begins with Atea and Papa. It does not, however, indicate which of the respective islands are older or younger. Samoan and Manu'an genealogies do not mention PapaAtea as a progenitor of the Samoans and Manu'ans. However, it should be noted that Reverend Pratt's *genealogy of Papatu,* in his *Genealogy of the Kings and Princes of Samoa*, lists 19 forerunner generations of the TuiAtua genealogy, and states:

"Ele'ele people got together. And Ele'ele'mu (burned soil) married Ele'ele'mea (brown soil), and Papatu (upright cliff) was created. From Papatu's union with Papa'ele (muddy cliff) was born Papatea (white cliff). Papatea married Papaga, giving birth to Lagi (haven), Fati, Elo, Masa Malu leTuapapa and Taufaalematagi (a daughter). It was Taufaalematagi that was sent to fetch water belonging to Alao who was already in Samoa. Taufaalematagi ended up marrying Alao and gave birth to Salevao and Saveasi'uleo"[clxiv] and to Ulufanuasese'e (whose story will be told later). However, these pedigrees have been determined to be too ancient to be verified.

Samoan legend continues the genealogies of these characters into major Samoan family lineages, as in the case of Salevao and Saveasi'uleo. Samoan and Manu'an legends and folklore always refer to Atea as a far faraway place, very much the same as in the island group, "Vavau," as in *va tea* meaning far far away.

If we were to include the 55 generations of the TuiAtua genealogy, which include the legendary 19 generations mentioned above, then, using Dr. Augustin Krämer's 30-year base generation age, we would arrive at 180 A.D. for the date of arrival in Samoa. A margin of 300 to 400 years puts the time period between 220 B.C. and 180 A.D. It's interesting to note that this estimated time for Samoan arrival in the Pacific appears to corroborate well with the time given by Judge Fornander for Hawaiian arrival.

All this is far from scientific, as piecing together the legends of oral history is a challenge. In the words of Judge Fornander: "The Wakea period eclipsed or obscured all previous movements or migrations in an easterly direction." He further states, "The Wakea era, however, was undoubtedly one of great disturbance, displacement, and change in the ancient Polynesian homesteads. The very fact that so many of the principal tribes have retained his legend, though under different forms, and have attempted to localize him and his wife on their own groups, proves to me that he was anterior to, or at least contemporary with, some great popular movement preceding or attending the first considerable exodus into the Pacific, the memory of which was linked to his name, and thus handed down to posterity."[clxv]

Importance of the Pulotu-PapaAtean War

According to Samoan legend, the battle between Pulotu and PapaAtea represents the first war in remembered history. The story also indicates that there were people already inhabiting some parts of the (Savai'i and Samoa) Island group at the time of the war.

Pulotu is the Samoan equivalent of the lands of Hades and Elysium in Greek mythology, and PapaAtea is the "rock island gifted from the firmament." When the daughters of Tui Pulotu, King of Pulotu, were sent to fetch water and were mocked and humiliated by the PapaAtean people, this caused a war.

Historians and orator chiefs in Samoa and Manu'a disagree about the geographical locations where the events of the Pulotu-PapaAtean war took place. Some believe Pulotu is on the west side of the Island of Savai'i. Others say that it's in the eastern part of Manu'a. But with scientific evidence abounding, the image of the Navigators' mosaic storyline is coming into focus, confirming this ancient mythology.

This Samoan and Manu'an legend is one of the oldest, and the only one that describes, cryptically, a storyline indicating that they (the Navigators) came from somewhere in *Vavau* (meaning ancient beginning place). Over time, as many generations passed, the legend became nothing more than just a good piece of mythology, rapidly eroding from people's memories. However, we continue to search for the Navigators' origins and migration path, and the methods of scientific research allow us to go back and re-analyze the myth based on evidence available from all the relevant fields of science.

The Story of the Pulotu-PapaAtean War

Here is the story:

The Paramount Chief of Pulotu was angry and ordered his warrior chiefs to launch an all-out war, organizing a war party, with the wise Pulotu warrior Elo, against Tui PapaAtea and his people. Upon hearing this, Tui PapaAtea responded aggressively and quickly launched an attack on Tui Pulotu's people. Seeing Tui PapaAtea's massive war fleet approaching, Tui Pulotu instructed his warrior Elo "not to engage the warring party at sea but to wait until they come on land"—*'Aua le taia i le tai a'e fa'aa'e i fanua*.

This advice became a proverb frequently used by orators, meaning both to be patient, and that your strength is on the land. In peaceful times, this proverb means one should welcome the arrival of guests on land and into your house, as opposed to on the shores and the docks.

Warrior Elo paid heed to the paramount chief's advice. When the ships landed on shore, Elo and his war party launched their attack. The battle was fearsome, and casualties were plenty on both sides; blood ran like a river on Pulotu, land and sea.

The two warriors of Tui PapaAtea, Utuma and Utumou'u, saw that they were outnumbered, with no means of resupplying their forces. They began to retreat back to the fleet for an orderly escape.

The PapaAteans were soundly defeated by the Pulotu, and the two PapaAtean warriors were pursued by the Pulotu warrior Elo. They landed on the east coast of the Island of Upolu, Samoa, where, instead of being killed by Elo, they chose to be transformed into tiny island rocks, rising up on the coast between the villages of Solosolo and Luatuanu'u .

Analysis of the Pulotu-PapaAtean War

All the Samoan and Manu'an chiefs and writers (Apemoemanatunatu, Fuimaono Naoi'a, Tofaeono Tanuvasa, and the authors of "Samoa Ne'i Galo") document the mythology concerning the Pulotu-PapaAtean War in virtually the same way. However, my current analysis of this myth yields new light on the storyline as follows:

- The names Pulotu and PapaAtea can be confirmed with the same name common to all Polynesian folklore (in Hawaii, Fiji, Toga, Tahiti, Vanuatu, and others); I base this on Fornander citing King Kalakaua, David Malo, Hon. Kamakau, Thomas Williams and James Calvert, W. D. Alexander, Rev. Ellis and others in his *An Account of The Polynesian Race, Vol. I.*
- The story corroborates Fornander's Wakea storyline and time period. In fact, it was Fornander's perspective on the Wakea folklore that compelled me to re-examine the Pulotu-PapaAtean war to find the common thread in these two stories (Hawaiian and Samoan).
- Pulotu in Savai'i is where Saveasi'uleo and Ulufanuasese'e made their famous decree: "We must part in order to keep peace between us. We shall meet again, not at the head or origin of our lineage, but the tail of our lineage."
- The PapaAtea rock was decreed (by the Spirit deity of the ancient ancestors) to be the Rock of Nafanua. (Appointments and delegations of authority are revered and venerated when decreed by the gods, as opposed to by the Paramount Chief.) The term PapaAtea refers to the original "Rock Birthplace" of the first war that led to the settlement of Samoa and Manu'a. Thus, PapaAtea is metaphorically the "Island Rock" on which Samoa and Manu'a rest.
- Also, the storyline says Pulotu and Atea (or PapaAtea) were already part of the Samoa and Manu'a island group.

- The story further makes connections with the deity Tagaloalagi. It describes Tagaloalagi giving Warrior Elo the stars *Utu* and *Va* to guide the ocean journey. When Elo reports to his leader, Pulotu, that PapaAtea's Warriors, Utuma and Utumou'u have been severely beaten and defeated and have, of their own choosing, turned themselves into two island rocks in the eastern part of Upolu, Pulotu instructs the Warrior Elo to go back and make sure PapaAtea's people are chased down and destroyed. Hence, the term *fa'apapatea*, meaning to destroy and defeat like the PapaAtean.
- When the warrior Elo goes back and continues chasing the PapaAtean people, one couple name Tutu and Ila seek refuge on an isolated island with no name; they settle in and call it Tutuila. Another couple (Ma and Nono) find refuge on a tiny island lying between two big islands; they hide and settle there and call it Manono Island. Likewise, another couple (U and Polu) find refuge on another island which they settle and call Upolu. Lastly, Sa and Vaii make haste to a big island, to hide there before Elo catches up with them and puts an end to them. Sa and Vaii find refuge and settle the island and name it after their names, Savai'i.
- The legend says that when Warrior Elo goes back to his master, Pulotu, he discovers that an earlier couple named Ma and Nua have already settled in a small chain of islands and called it Manu'a.
- The legend is very specific in not mentioning Pulotu and PapaAtea as being chiefs, implying there were no chiefs (no leadership system including chiefs) at the time.
- The legend also makes note that the period is before the deity Tagaloalagi established residency in Manu'a. Indeed, as we have seen, it describes the peopling of the various islands in the chain.
- Additionally, the legend seems to imply that the reign of Pulotu lasted a "long period of time." In Samoan and Manu'an history, based on mythology, the "first" period is defined as the time of the establishment of Tagaloalagi's residency in Manu'a, followed by Galea'i, also of Manu'a; then Tuimanu'a, followed by the Saveasi'uleo and Ulufanuasese'e decree at the Savai'i Sea; then the time of the TuiAtua and TuiAana genealogy; and then the "Warrior Queen" Nafanua. But the Pulotu-PapaAtean war myth appears to be older than any of the human legends known at the time.

This myth has the ring of a real and normal storyline that actually describes a migration in the sort of detail that could be corroborated by scientific evidence, revealing the Navigators' origins and migration. It also corroborates other Polynesian mythology about their origins and migration. This further implies that the Pulotu-PapaAtean war puts the migration in the 400 B.C. to 100 A.D. time period, using the 55 generations of the TuiAtua and Dr. Krämer's method, with 1830 as his base year and 30 years per generation, plus or minus errors and extrapolation.

Direction and Purpose

The legend of the Pulotu-PapaAtean war highlights the fact that war was a cause of the subsequent migration of the Navigators to their current homeland. It's the only legend that describes, albeit cryptically, a process of departure whereby a group landed and populated a known place, called Upolu, Samoa.

The legend also references locations (Atea or PapaAtea, Pulotu, Mbulu, and Puvlutu) and directions (from the west or northwest) taken in the war and subsequent flight to safety, which directed the discovery of a new home. These directions clearly point westward to Fiji, Papua, and the Malay Archipelago.[clxvi]

Genealogy and Inheritance

The Descendants of Lu

Remember the story of Lufasiaitu (Lu who thrashed the spirits) and Lagituaiva (Sky of the ninth circle of heaven)—the story of Lu's sacred chickens? It's where the name *Sa* (sacred) *Moa* (chicken) comes from. And the names of Lu's descendants tell their stories:

The union of Lufasiaitu and Lagituaiva produced: Lu-nofo (Lu that sits up), Lu-ta'oto (Lu that lies down), and Lu-tausili-i-nu'u (Lu that first arrived and built the village).

Lu-tausili-i-nu'u married Lagi-aunoa (Emptiness of heaven) and begat Lagi-mafola (female, the firmament).

Tagaloalagi's union with Lagi-mafola produced Pilipa'u (Pili that fell from heaven). Pilipa'u married Sina-le-sae'e (Sina that arrived on earth), the daughter of TuiManu'a (the paramount authority of all of Manu'a), begetting Pili-a'au (Pili who swims across the ocean).

Pili-a'au's union with Sina-ale-tava'e (Sina the white tropical-fish-eating seabird, phaeton aethereus[clxvii]), the daughter of TuiAana Tava'etele (he who is paramount authority over the Region of Aana), produced five boys; Tua, A'ana, Tuamasaga, Tolufale and Munanitama.[clxviii] (Note, Dr. Krämer adheres to Bulow for a more complete and reliable legend of Pili, rather than to Turner.) They would inherit each of the three Regions of the Island of Upolu, the islands of Apolima, Manono, and Savai'i. This was proclaimed via the legendary decree of their father, Pili, that Tua would get the TuiAtua region, A'ana would get TuiAana, Tuamasaga would get the middle region, Tolu-fale (the third house of authority) and would inherit the islands of Apolima, Manono, and Savai'i, while the young brother, Munanitama, was dispatched to assist Tuamasaga from the south side.

Thus we should note, Lu is the ancestor of Pili.[clxix] And *SaTagaloalagi* refers to the family clan of Tagaloalagi (*sa* refers to "the family clan"— often a large family clan, as in *SaFata* (family clan of Fata), *SaTupua*, *SaTuimanu'a*, or *SaMalietoa*).

Saveasi'uleo and Ulufanuasese'e

Another major family of Samoa is the Tonumaipe'a. The Tonumaipe'a began to rise up during the reign of Tuitoga Manaia. The genealogy of this family is once again carried through the women and told through myth, beginning with the legend of the brothers—Saveasi'uleo with a tail like a sea eel, Salevao and Ulufanuasese'e.[clxx] The story is as follows:

Saveasi'uleo had several brothers who loved to surf. But Saveasi'uleo was filled with anger, from jealousy, because his parents "threw" him— after a "blood clot" miscarriage during the second trimester—into the ocean. The blood clot was swallowed by an eel, and the eel transformed into a half-eel, half-man (Saveasi'uleo). He always felt his parents cast him into the ocean because they didn't love him, hence his cruelty and cannibal appetite.

Saveasi'uleo, in his anger, devised a plan to murder his brothers. He turned himself into an eel. As his brothers surfed, one by one Saveasi'uleo dragged them down into the depths of the ocean to feast on their bodies.

One of his brothers scolded Saveasi'uleo for murdering their brothers. It was then that a famous decree was pronounced at sea: Saveasi'uleo ordered this brother to stay in Savai'i to take care of the rest of the family, while Saveasi'uleo would leave and go to Manu'a, and carry on the genealogy there. The rest of Saveasi'uleo's surviving brothers became paramount warriors called the Alatau'a.

Ulufanuasese'e and Sinalalofutu-i-Fagaiofu became the parents of the twin girls Taema and Tilafaiga (or Taematilafaiga, since they were conjoined twins). Their story describes the origin of tattooing. Tilafaiga and Taema were known to have once shared a body—as conjoined twins— until an unknown man scared the two girls so much they tried to run opposite directions, and their bodies separated.

In Manu'a, Saveasi'uleo married Tilafaiga, often referred to as Pi'ilua. (Saveasi'uleo was Tilafaiga's uncle.) Tilafaiga and Saveasi'uleo begat two girls, Nafanua (the warrior queen whose story is told next) and Sua'ifanua. Sua'ifanua, also known as Sua'ifanuanafanua, married TuiTonga and begat Latuivai. Latuivai's union with Mimisapua, sister of Lefolasale'i'ite— both of them descendants of Sinalagilagi, Tagaloalagi's daughter (from the village Faia'ai)—brought forth Faletapaau and Taigalugalu. (Note: There is a part of the traditional house where the roof drains the rain. If you sit close to the drain, the rain will drip on you. This is called *tapaau*. *Faletapaau* is a term that refers to the paramount chief. In ceremonial practices, the chief is the one to sit next to *tapaaufasisina*. Also, *Taigalugalu* means the ocean tide is rising—*Tai* meaning ocean tide, and *Galugalu* means rising or waves.)

Taigalugalu's union with Lilomaiavaseve of Safotu produced a girl named Foalo, which means to make peace. Foalo married Lologavivao of Samata, Savaii, and begat Maisina.

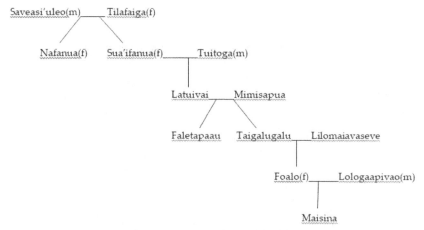

Figure 9 Genealogical Table

The Genealogy of Le Aumoana

The story of the blind man (Oleaifale'ava) and his daughter (Lea'auta or 'Olea'auta) is set around 1165-1225 A.D. About 335 years later, there is a famous decree of La'uluNofovaleane, that takes place around 1460-1500 A.D.

From La'uluNofovaleane's first marriage, to Fulusiailagitetele, the daughter of Tuma'ai from Safotulafai, he begat Tuaetali. Tuaetali begat her son, Tapumanaia.

From La'uluNofovaleane's second marriage, with Lefaagapulu, the daughter of Pulusauleloga, he begat Fatupuigati. Fatupuigati begat her son, Pesefeamanaia.

From La'uluNofovaleane's third marriage, to Pouliotaua, the daughter of Tu'u of Safune, he begat Maupenei and Maupenei begat a son, Aumoana. And Maupenei's son, Le Aumoana (meaning "the one and only Aumoana"), had a much bigger head compared to the other boys.

To teach their sons to crawl, the three women took them to the rocks near the ocean. As the waves would hit against the rocks, the infants had to crawl to protect themselves from getting hit. While the boys were on the rocks, Maupenei's sisters would ridicule Aumoana for having such an unusually big head. The size of his head was out of balance, relative to his body, so much so that it hindered his ability to crawl. Maupenei heard her sisters taunting Aumoana and began to cry.

La'uluNofovaleane, Maupenei's father, was aware of the mockery taking place. La'ulu favored Maupenei and Aumoana, and he became very upset, seeing the situation unfold for so long. He commanded his three daughters to meet with him. It was then that La'ulu revealed his decree over his children and grandchildren. The decree stated:

Tuaetali and Tapumanaia will be the Aualuma for Lufilufi and Leulumoega; and Fatupuigati and Pesefeamanaia will be the Aualuma for the "Vae o le Nofoafia," with the family of Lilomaiava in Sagafili village. However for Maupenei, her son, Le Aumoana, will be anointed and appointed to be Aualuma of the mighty SaLeMuliaga family. He is the boy of decree.

Aualuma is a formal organization in a village—a company of single ladies who are the custodians of the village heirlooms and culture protocols and ceremonial procedures. The young man's organization is called the *Aumaga*—the servants of the village Chiefs Council.

As times passed, Le Aumoana's genealogy became the origin of the Tupuivao, Mataafa, and Salevalasi families.

Historical Records

The study of history as recorded by those writing books and papers

The Warrior Queen

The Samoan Version of Boudicca of the Iceni, the Celtic Tribe

The legendary Samoan "Warrior Queen" Nafanua might be considered a Samoan version of Queen Boudicca of the Iceni in Great Britain. Her legend is foundational to the early development of Samoan "modern" history. This is the phase of Samoa's history which evolved into the beginning of the major families, whose lineages would intertwine, leading to consolidation through marriages and the eventual arising of a consolidated ruler of all Samoa (Tafa'ifa Salamasina TuiAana Tamalelagi).

The prophetic rise of the "warrior queen" Nafanua fulfilled the farewell parting words decreed by her ancestors (the brothers: Saveasi'uleo and Ulufanuasese'e) at the Pacific Ocean shore, at the Leone Tai, Alataua and Pulotu at Falealupo, Savai'i: "We must part in order to keep peace between us. We shall meet again, not at the head or origin of our lineage, but the tail of our lineage." This means that "we," the head and origin of our lineage, will not meet again, but perhaps our respective descendants will cross paths and genealogies.

The warrior Nafanua is the daughter of Saveasi'uleo, and her brief genealogical history is as follows:

- Masa of Tufutafoe village married Popoto; the issue was a girl Taufaalematagi.
- Alao married Taufaalematagi; their children were Saveasi'uleo and Ulufanuasese'e and others. Their story is the legend where one brother scolded Saveasi'uleo for murdering their brothers. A famous decree was pronounced at sea: Saveasi'uleo ordered his brother to stay in Savai'i to take care of the rest of the family, while Saveasi'uleo would leave and go to Manu'a, and carry on the genealogy there. The rest of Saveasi'uleo's surviving brothers became paramount warriors called the Alataua.
- Ulufanuasese'e married the Sina of Falelatai village; their children were Taema and Tilafaiga, the conjoined twin girls. These Siamese twins are quite well-known in the history of Samoa for their journey throughout the Samoan and Manu'an chain of islands producing

several paramount families and chiefs in every island where they sojourned. Their story is the story of how tattooing came to Samoa and Manu'a.

- Saveasi'uleo married Tilafaiga; their children were two girls Nafanua and Sualefanua.[clxxi]

Nafanua was known for the many wars she fought and triumphed in, but the most notable war was the one in which she defeated the formidable opponents Aeaisisifo and Aeaisasae at Alataua, Savai'i. After conferring with her father Saveasi'uleo about fighting the war to free their extended family's district from the harshness of the neighboring district's warring tribes, she was gifted with weaponry in the form of three war clubs called: *Ulimasao* (meaning to guide), *Fa'auliulito* (meaning to strike and kill with) and *Tafesilafa'i* (meaning to guard the troops with). These war clubs had in them the *mana* spirit (power), so that Nafanua was literally thrashing the enemy.

The enemy began to retreat and, by daylight of the fourth day of continuous battle, the battle had reached the district of Falelima village, and had already crossed the Falealupo and Neiafu villages. As the warrior queen Nafanua pressed the troops forward, fighting with the knowledge that victory was near, a wind came up suddenly. Nafanua was huddling to her war club, and the wind blew the warrior queen Nafanua's attire off her shoulder, exposing her breasts.

The shocked Nafanua was filled with shame and dropped to the ground to cover herself. Then the battle on both sides of the battleground came to a screeching halt. The troops were shocked and filled with disbelief to see that Nafanua was a woman warrior.

Nafanua quickly recovered and realized that she had arrived at the boundary in Faia'ai village, the *Papaifualaga* that her father Saveasi'uleo had decreed she must not cross. This village was the boundary of the Paramount Chief (Tauiliili) of their clan (sacred residence), and she must not cross it. And so the warrior queen Nafanua said the troops and warriors must stop and retreat, because the enemy had already retreated in defeat.

And so began the reign of Nafanua in the history of Samoa. She had assembled a large group of warrior fighters and troops to wage war on enemies and protect her extended genealogical family districts. Any monarch of her family, seeking warriors to fight a battle, would send a senior orator chief to ask for assistance from the warrior queen Nafanua, to help wage war with their enemy.

If Boudicca and Nafanua are both looked on as figures of different mythologies, we might wonder if their stories were carried with migrating tribes to those two different locations. However, Boudicca is now believed to be a genuine historical figure, and so is Nafanua. The fact that they are historical people means that we do not need to redirect our view of the migration path in the light of their stories. Rather we should study their stories to learn the history of the people.

The Four Paramount Title Crowns

The Warrior Queen Nafanua is progenitor of one of the foundational families of Samoa, the Paramount Family and title Tonumaipe'a of Alataua district of Savai'i. The first Paramount Chief Tonumaipe'a (1440-1460 A.D.) married Leatougaugaatuitoga, daughter of Gatoa'itele and LeSanalala. Their children were Tauiliili (who inherited the head of family position), Tupa'ivaililigi (the ambassador of Nafanua), and Levalasi, who married her first cousin TuiAtua Mata'utiafa'atulou. Levalasi and Mata'utiafa'atulou adopted the daughter of Levalasi's cousin, TuiAana Tamalelagi, as their own daughter, Salamasina. The mother of TuiAana Tamalelagi was Vaetamasoaali'i, Levalasi's auntie.

It is during this part of Samoan history that all of the four paramount title crowns of monarchs—Papa of TuiAtua, Papa of TuiAana, Papa of Gatoa'itele and Papa of Vaetamasoaali'i—ended up being held in custody by Nafanua, until she wanted and agreed to bestow all four titles on Levalasi. But Levalasi wanted to bestow the titles on her adopted daughter Salamasina.

The Gatoa'itele title had been decreed by their mother to the three children—Vaetamasoaali'i, Leatougaugaatuitoga (mother to Levalasi), and their brother Lalovimama (who was father to TuiAtua Mata'utiafa'atulou who married his first cousin Levalasi). Thus they were now all connected together through marriages (as were their titles). They were all cousins, and their grandmother was Gatoa'itele.

This is the collective genealogy that brought the island country together under one ruler.

Nafanua and the Kingdom of God

There are many historical events that are attributed to Nafanua. But one story that has been immortalized in the Malietoa monarch is this:

Around 1570 A.D., Malietoa Taulapapa heard that the warrior queen Nafanua was sending the high priest and orator messenger Tupa'i to bestow all four royal titles on Levalasi—and, of course, Levalasi wanted to bestow these on her adopted daughter Salamasina. When Malietoa Taulapapa got wind of this, he immediately dispatched his fleet of canoes to take him to Nafanua, on Savai'i Island, to seek a title gift from the warrior queen Nafanua. But unfortunately, by the time Malietoa Taulapapa arrived at Nafanua's residence at Alataua, the high priest had just left for Leulumoega village in Upolu, where Levalasi and Salamasina were living.

Malietoa Taulapapa began with a long Salutation and Oration to the warrior queen Nafanua, asking to be considered for the Malietoa Monarch title. Nafanua, after hearing Malietoa Taulapapa, felt sad for him, but the decision had already been made. There were no titles left with her, for Tupa'i, the high priest, had just left with all the titles. And so Nafanua gave Malietoa Taulapapa the gift of a prophecy, as follows:

"Malietoa Taulapapa, I am sorry that you came too late. Tupa'i is on his way to Leulumoega to bestow all four titles onto Levalasi. But, come; be patient and wait for your Kingdom from Heaven"—my translation. In 1830 A.D. the "Messenger of Peace" vessel, bringing the missionaries and Reverend John Williams to Samoa, brought a new "Kingdom" and was received and accepted by Malietoa Vaiinupo, a direct descendant of Malietoa Taulapapa. 270 years they, the Malietoa clan, had waited till they received their Kingdom.

There are others who believe that it was Malietoa Fitisimanu that came to Nafanua for the titles. But the history is clear that the only time Nafanua held all four titles as custodian was at the end of all the wars (the TuiAana Tamalelagi war, the TuiAtua Mata'utiafa'atulou war, the Vaetamasoaali'i war and the Gatoa'itele war). In each of these she gave military assistance to achieve victory. This all took place, probably, between 1500 and 1580 A.D.

History's Heroes and Villains

Heroes and Warriors

Every culture has heroes, villains and warriors: likewise the Samoan culture. The need for heroes, for people to look up to and models to reflect upon, is one thing that inspires creative minds. We start to create these mythological figures to immortalize historical events and the characters and actors who played a part in them. And, of course, there are anti-heroes that are often more popular than heroes.

But which came first: the hero or the myth? Or does the event ignite the creative imagination and drive the authorship of the story?

Remember Pulotu, the Samoan Elysium? The decree of Saveasi'uleo and Ulufanuasese'e and the subsequent legend of Nafanua point to Pulotu as a seat of Nafanua's sacred Rock, as the origin of the beginning of modern Samoan history—all the pious salutations and the dignity of the four Papa Families were decreed in Pulotu (the Warrior Queen Nafanua's sacred seat). This is the beginning, source, and origin of modern Samoa—of Samoan history.

So we see with Samoan folklore, when a story is told through many generations, the mythological story all of a sudden becomes a more human story. It begins with an incredible theme and ends with the origin of a real live person or family, or with a real object. It tells a part of the real history, which helps us navigate history to find the Navigators' migration path.

Anti-heroes

So we give credit to the heroes in the literature and annals of Samoan and Manu'an history, but then we neglect to honor, let alone mention in an honorific manner, the anti-heroes that have equally contributed to the country's developmental history. This is partly because we don't always understand or appreciate these anti-heroes' actions that caused the shift in the trajectory of the country's history. For example (taking these examples from Krämer's *Apemoemanatunatu Tonumaipe'a, Fuimaono Na'oia,* and *Tofaeono Tanuvasamanaia*):

- Should we view PapaAtea as an anti-hero or an enemy of Pulotu? Do we forget how, even in defeat, his tribal clan ended up peopling the island chain (Tutuila, Manono, Upolu, Savai'i and Manu'a)? Is he a hero or anti-hero? I would say we owe our homeland beginning to PapaAtea.
- Should we also view Saveasi'uleo, the cannibal brother of Ulufanuasese'e, as an anti-hero because of his cruelty, or as a hero? Because of his prophetic decree, their genealogy would define the progenitors of Samoa's and Manu'a's major families. The conjoined (Siamese) twins would not exist without Saveasi'uleo and, of course, the warrior queen Nafanua would not have existed; maybe the founding of the first Tafa'ifa consolidator authority ruler (Tafa'ifa Salamasina) wouldn't be a reality.
- Tupuivao, son to Queen TuiAana and TuiAtua Taufau (granddaughter of Tafa'ifa Salamasina) was known for cruelty, obstinacy, disobedience and a lack of wisdom that forced his mother the queen to relinquish her son Tupuivao's inheritance to the crown. Instead she decreed her TuiAtua Papa and TuiAana Papa titles to her nephew Faumuina, her sister Sina's son. This became a pivotal decision reflected in the genealogical inheritance of the TuiAtua and TuiAana Papa for 150 to 200 years, until the reign of Tafa'ifa Tupuafui'availili.
- The two Paramount Orator Chiefs, Apemoemanatunatu and Tutuilalematemate, of Fasito'otai village, kidnapped Vaetamasoaali'i's son, adopted him to be their Paramount Chief, and called him Tamalelagi. Later he inherited the TuiAana title and Papa—he was the father of Salamasina. This horrific act caused a war between Vaetamasoaali'i clan district and TuiAana district but, in the end, it became a critical step to achieving the first Tafa'ifa consolidation.
- Then there are the Orator Chiefs Talo and Ofoia, of Falealili village, who kidnapped Tafa'ifa (Queen) Salamasina's son, Tapumanaia II, and made him their Paramount Chief. While the A'ana district were ready to forge war to bring back their heir, a parent to the Tafa'ifa crown, Tafa'ifa Salamasina, remembering that her biological father TuiAana Tamalelagi had been kidnapped from his mother Vaetamasoaali'i, showed the wisdom of a Tafa'ifa ruler and called off the war party, citing the fact that her father had been kidnapped for good reason—they needed a Paramount Chief of royal blood as their

leader. This Tapumanaia-II, also known as Satele, is the progenitor of Tafa'ifa Tupuafui'availili, also known as the male (son and) heir of Tafa'ifa Salamasina, that carries the TuiAtua and TuiAana Papa still today. The anti-heroes performed unpopular actions at the time but changed the course of history.

- Orator Chiefs Leifi and Tautoloitua of Aleipata village connived to orchestrate the marriage of their Paramount Chief TuiAtua Mata'utiafa'atulou to his cousin Levalasi, in spite the tapu on relationships between close family siblings. Levalasi is the one to whom Nafanua designated the Tafa'ifa, but Levalasi wanted her adopted daughter Salamasina to inherit. The coercive power of these Orator Chiefs forced the Tafa'ifa families to accept the shame and the marriage. The result was that Levalasi and her husband (her 1st cousin) TuiAtua Mata'utiafa'atulou adopted their niece Salamasina, the first Tafa'ifa. This event, shameful because of its incestuous relationship, became paramount to achieving the first Tafa'ifa.

Trade Routes

Trade Routes (1519)

Historical trade routes offer another way to gain insight into Polynesian origins and migration, and they allow us to link events on the islands with events in other parts of the world. These written records begin when early European discoverers first ventured into the Pacific Ocean.

Ferdinand Magellan, a Portuguese explorer, navigated across the Atlantic Ocean, continuing through a dangerous passage at the top of South America into the Pacific Ocean, in 1519 A.D. This took place at a later date than Columbus' accidental discovery of America in 1492.

Subsequent to Ferdinand Magellan's unfortunate altercation with Philippine natives that cost his life, a Portuguese and Spanish trading fleet of galleons began navigating the Pacific Ocean, crisscrossing between Europe, Asia, the Philippines and Central America, transporting gold and silver from the Americas in exchange for cotton, silks, and other European goods. Magellan named the Philippine island group after his country's king, the Spanish King Philip II.

Trade Routes (1524)

Historical records can be compared with and validated by oral histories. Hawaiian culture has oral stories of a few ships that were blown by windstorms and landed on the Hawaiian Islands as far back as 1524 A.D.

William DeWitt Alexander related, in his *Brief History of the Hawaiian*,[clxxii] that the beginning of the 2nd Period (1450 A.D.) of ancient history, during the time of Keali'iokaloa (elder son of Moi-Umi who had just recently passed), a foreign vessel was wrecked at Keei, South Kona, Hawaii. Only the captain and his sister reached the shore in safety, and the natives observed them kneeling down on the beach, remaining in that posture as if prostrate to a god. Whence, the name of the place was called *Kulou* (Hawaiian for humbling and giving respect to the gods), or *tulou* in Samoan. The strangers intermarried with the natives and became the progenitors of certain well-known families of Chiefs, such as Kaikioewa, former governor of Kauai.

Spanish historians confirm that Cortez, the conqueror of Mexico, fitted out several exploring expeditions on the Western Coast about this time. The first squadron, consisting of three vessels commanded by Don Alvarado de Saavedra, sailed from Zacatula for the Moluccas, or Spice Islands, on October 31st, 1527 A.D. These ships sailed in company but, when they were a thousand leagues from port, they were scattered by a severe storm. The two smaller vessels were never heard from again, but Saavedra pursued the voyage alone in the "Florida" to Moluccas, touching land at the Ladrone Islands on the way, where Saavedra and his crew massacred the natives. It seems certain that the foreign vessel, which was wrecked about this time on the Kona coast, must have been one of Saavedra's missing ships, for there were no European navigators in this early period.

Trade Routes (1542)

The Spanish navigator Juan Gaetano discovered the Caroline Islands (Islas del Bey) in the year 1542 A.D. when he piloted a vessel for Ruy López de Villalobos.

The account of this second voyage has never been published, but there is an ancient manuscript chart in the Spanish Achieves on which a group of islands is laid down on the same latitude as the Hawaiian Islands, but over ten degrees too far east in longitude, with a note stating the name of the discoverer and the date of discovery. The southernmost and largest island was named La Mesa (the table), which is probably Hawaii with its high tableland. North of it was La Desgraciada, "the unfortunate," or Maui, and three small islands named "the monks" which were probably Kahoolawe, Lanai, and Molokai.

A similar chart was discovered in June 1743, when the British warship "Centurion," under Lord Anson, captured a Spanish galleon from Acapulco near the Philippine Islands, on her way to Manila. A manuscript was found on board, containing all the discoveries which had been made in navigation between Mexico and the Philippine Islands. In this chart, the Hawaiian Islands are laid down in the same position as in the old chart in the Spanish archives. A copy of it is to be seen in the account of Lord Anson's voyage which was published in London in 1748.

These islands did not lie on the track of the Spanish galleons, for on leaving Acapulco the galleons steered southwest, so as to pass far to the south of the Hawaiian Islands; on their return voyage they sailed northward till they reached thirty degrees latitude, then ran before the westerly winds till they approached the coast of North America. But the navigational errors are not surprising when considering that chronometers were not yet invented at the time.

Trade Routes (1616)

On the west side of the Pacific Ocean, now known as the Bismarck Archipelago, the first European to visit these islands was the Dutch explorer William Schouten in 1616. The land was annexed as part of the German protectorate of German New Guinea in 1884 (the same period when Samoa was under an implied diplomatic condominium of Germany, Great Britain, and the United States of America).

The Skills of the Navigators

Let's not forget that the understanding of wind and ocean currents that the Spanish mastered in their trading voyages in the 16th century, and that others mastered later, are very similar to the skills the Navigators of Polynesia had to have already developed to conquer the Pacific Ocean. This topic is now a focus of scientists researching the origin and migration paths of the Polynesians into the Pacific Ocean.

Ethology

*The study of cultural ethos,
social organization, and behavioral customs*

Culture Comparison

Relationship between Samoan and other Pacific Islanders

Throughout all the ancient history of Samoa and Manu'a, there is no mention that Samoans ever occupied, or even temporarily settled in, the Fiji Island group. Nor had Samoa ever been colonized by the Fijians. However, the genealogical connections between the Fijians, Manu'ans and Samoans are plenty, and are foundational to the major families of Samoa and Manu'a.

For example, intermarriages between the Samoan Tupa'imatuna—son of Lealali and great grandson of Pili-LeSo'opili (Pili the So'opili, also known as TuiAana Pili who decreed that Alali—short for Lealali—should to go to Savai'i to populate and rule over it), so, of Manu'a and TuiAana lineages— and the daughter Laufafaetoga of the king TuiTonga, and her later marriage to TuiFiji, king of the Fijians, produced children that came to Savai'i and settled the west part of the island. The children of these marriages are:

- Ututauofiti (according to Krämer) or Utuofiti, the eponymous founder of the mighty village of Matutu. Samoan legend says that Utuofiti became a fearsome warrior guardian of the village that Tuifiti resides when visiting his children in Savai'i, hence the additional of "tau" to his name. The legend continues with *Ma* (and) *tau* (fight/war or Vanguard) *o* (of) *ututauofiti*, hence *Matautu* (Vanguard) or *Matautuofiti* or *Mataututauofiti*
- Tauaofiti, the founder of Sataua
- Legaotuitoga, the founder of SaLega village
- Liliolelagi, founder of Falealili on Upolu Island
- Va'asiliifiti (son of Tupa'imatuna and Laufafaetoga), the elder who went on to Upolu and married two women, Fe'egaga and Fe'easoa, from the Sagana and Saleimoa villages, producing the brothers that populated and conquered Savai'i
- Fotuosamoa: Laufafaetoga remarried her Samoan husband, Tupa'imatuna, and bore a girl while journeying back home to Savai'i,

133

Samoa. The daughter's name is Fotuosamoa; hence the name of the village of Safotu (not to be confused with Safotulafai village).

The homogeneous characteristics of Pacific Island cultures, languages, economic systems, and way of life has been exhaustively studied and documented, ever since men of science descended upon the Pacific Islands in the early part of the 19th century. Some areas of controversy still need further research and confirmation—such as whether the other Polynesian Islanders (Hawaiians, Tahitians, etc.) migrated from Tonga, or Samoa and Manu'a, or took another path altogether to discover their current homeland. But the fact remains: the Polynesians are of one "race," with common genealogical ancestors.

With the limited availability of sample specimens from ancient Polynesian habitats, scientists have had to collate evidence from cultural similarities, language origins, folklore, human DNA, archaeological specimens, and other relevant information that researchers have sedulously gathered, to piece together the migration story. But their finds have corroborated Polynesian mythology and oral history, confirming that the Polynesians are kin to each other.

Cultural Diffusion

Family and Society

In 1898, W.H.R. Rivers was recruited by Alfred Cort Haddon to head up a team of British scientists for a Cambridge University expedition to the Torres Strait in the Indonesian Archipelago. During this Cambridge Anthropology Expedition to the Torres Strait (CAETS), Rivers found a passion for anthropology and pioneered the study of kinship genealogy as a fundamental aspect in formulating an organization of cohesive units and sustainability in a family clan, tribe, or social culture.[clxxiii] (The 100th anniversary of CAETS was celebrated August 10-12th 1998 at a conference hosted by Dr. Keith Hart, who was then the director of the African Studies Center at Cambridge.)

During the same period, 1898, Augustin Krämer, a German physician, was launching an ethnological project, documenting the cultural norms, religious rituals, and details of family genealogy across villages in Samoa and Manu'a. While Rivers was proposing a theory of structural functionalism—i.e. a system where cultural customs, rituals, protocols, taboos, ordinances and practices (referred to as functions), when adhered to by tightly-woven kinship structures, serve to create a much more sustainable culture—Krämer was busy documenting and witnessing functionalism in practice in Samoan and Manu'an culture.

Krämer observed that Samoans and Manu'ans are able to sustain and perpetuate the continuity (and continued survival) of their culture, history, and language through meticulously detailed knowledge of family kinship and genealogy. He did not venture to ascertain when the Navigators adopted and honed this kinship practice and behavior, but all indications showed they already had these traditions when they migrated over as family groups or clans. And the parallel efforts of these two physicians and social scientists help pinpoint the ethology and behavioral patterns that sustained the Navigators through their perilous migration journey.

Family kinship is organized in similar ways across all human migrations, but the real differences are in how extensively kinship is practiced and adhered to over time. Through well-developed cultural norms, religious rituals, language, history and folktales, or functions, a community and society can have significant chances of survival.

Much as Rivers observed with the Melanesians, the Navigators had limited terminology describing kin. Words such as mother, father, elder, sister, and brother are "genetic" terms, referring not only to immediate family members, but also extending to "cousins" however far removed, and to extended relatives. "Elder" is a generational term, but it is also used as a formal title to address any grandparents or folks in the older generations to show respect. Titles are identifiers and are addressed accordingly because they define family, responsibility, and relationships within family, clan, or tribe. The focus is always centered on the family. It's the family that defines everyone's identity.

To put it in another words, individual identity is defined through family. For example, all the Salutations of the Island's families include the villages; they always begin with the main or Paramount family, then follow with the Salutations of the rest of the family titles, village, and extended family.

Thus one can understand why the Navigators' language is, to some extent, impoverished with respect to a lexicon defining and identifying kinship structures. It's because the family is the point of identification relative to all family relationships in the clan or tribe. Genealogy is the "glue," or, as the Samoan would say, the "weaves" of the fishing nets constantly rewoven or repaired to ensure that the family web is solid and works effectively.

I will discuss these attributes in detail with the next book, *Navigators: Forging a Culture and Founding a Nation*.

An Isolated Society

In 1933, Professor Radcliffe-Brown based his book, *The Andaman*, on work undertaken with the Andamanese of Andaman Island, a remote location off the Andaman Archipelago in the Bay of Bengal, some 250 miles south of the last headlands of Burma. His well-respected field work (still, even today, required reading in college anthropology courses) notes how an isolated society seems to have discovered the fountain of structured functional development, of culture and way of life.[clxxiv]

Although Radcliffe-Brown intended to prove his claim—that, in an isolated society, the innate need to have order in community will induce the development of well-established structural organization of the community and society—he, nevertheless, firmly believed this is a natural progress in a tribal-based organization. This belief is akin to that of the Muslim Historian, Ibn Khaldun, who observed similar forms with the structure of Bedouin Society in the Western Sahara desert in the 13th century.[clxxv] This, of course, is in opposition to the ideology of cultural diffusion and evolution that was percolating then in the nascent fields of anthropology and ethnology.

The importance of Cultural Diffusion

The influence of cultural diffusion cannot be minimized. The imprints of culture, whether at an "elementary" or "ethnic" level, are fundamental to the human psyche. This idea of a "personal unconscious" and a "collective unconscious" ascribed to a cultural group—an idea that might also be known as 'archetypes'—was put forth by Adolf Bastian (1826-1905), back in 1868, and was elaborated on by Carl Jung, in his *Psychology of the Unconscious*.[clxxvi] Jung viewed this unconscious as existing in our dreams and imagination, providing a prototype for our creative unconscious mind to work on, leading to "the rapture in our imagination"

In 1923 Carl Jung wrote that the procedures and processes, integral to the collective functioning of a community, come from both inborn and environment imprints, and are regressed (the logic of going back and learning from experiences) over time. Thus, as people and cultures progress onward across geographical boundaries, their customs and religious rituals become permanent. Thus the imprints of their mythological images continue to travel with the people.[clxxvii]

The intrinsic value of drawing parallels and recognizing similarities of specific cultural attributes, organizations, and mythologies is that it helps us recognize the power of influence. The idea of adopting best practices comes into play, to maximize the value of the individual and the community as whole. Then the accumulation of knowledge over time gives an advantage to both community and individual. The cognitive process is reaffirmed, as well as the wisdom that will protect the individual and community throughout a long and difficult migration.

Customs and Society

How Customs are Carried by People

Cambridge University's 1989 expedition to the Torres Strait in the Indonesian Archipelago turned out to be a "Dream Team" of the best of Cambridge University's social and physical scientists ever to be assembled in a specific geographical location. They were: C.S. Myers, William McDougal, Sidney Ray, C.G. Seligman and, of course, W.H.R. Rivers. And it is here that Rivers became so keenly interested in anthropological field work and the pioneer of kinship studies as foundational to the development of organizational structures in tribe, clan, village and family.

Rivers studied Polynesian migration from the sociological perspective (looking at the social behavior of society, its origin, development, and organization, etc.). He concluded there were several streams of different groups of people that migrated into the Indonesian Archipelago, influencing migrants into the East Pacific Ocean.

Firstly he listed the aboriginal people of Melanesia, of whom practically nothing is known. Then came a stream of people passing through Melanesia and into the Pacific. These were identified as people who buried their dead in a sitting posture, and they might have been the original inhabitants of Polynesia. Many of these remained in Melanesia, combining with the Melanesians to form a dual composite people."[clxxviii]

Rivers then identified a stream of ava- or kava-drinking people, composed of two groups immigrating at different periods. One group mummified their dead, while the other buried them in the more familiar extended position. Small successive groups of apparently peaceful people, mostly men, came to the islands and were well received. These groups represented a "higher culture," and before moving on they introduced new ideas and new beliefs. Whereas the earlier "dual" people dealt in magic, believed in spirits that were not the spirits of people, and held that the spirits of their dead lived underground, the ava people, on the other hand, were religious, dealing in religious ceremonies rather than in magic rites. The ava people believed in ghosts, the spirits of dead men, and that the spirits of their dead passed to other places either on the earth or above it (exactly as in the Samoan and Manu'an belief system).

According to Rivers, the Ava drinking people were followed by betel-nut chewing people; after them came cremation people, but the influence of these two cultural migrations was apparently confined to northwestern Melanesia. Anthropologist Robert Wood Williamson, writing in 1924, believed Rivers could have been describing the same two streams of the Ava people as Churchill.[clxxix]

Anthropologist Jean Gelman Taylor, of the University of Toronto, believes Sundanese Austronesians—an Austronesian ethnic group native to the Indonesian province of West Java, DKI Jakarta, and Banten (at the western part of Java)—reached Java, traveling from Taiwan via the Philippines, between 1500 and 1000 B.C. But other ethnologists and geneticists date the Austronesian migration from Taiwan at around 4,500 years ago. The region was inhabited from the Mesolithic era, around 20,000 years ago.

Taylor, writing in 2003, notes that most Polynesians partake in the consumption of the Ava and its ceremonies.[clxxx] But Samoans did not discover the Ava plant and its potent roots until the Fijians introduced it around 1100 A.D. The plant itself (Piper methysticum) is indigenous to Papua New Guinea and Melanesia. However, historians believe it originated on Vanuatu Island and spread to Micronesia and Fiji.

Chewing the betel-nut is a custom that is common throughout Melanesia and the rest of the Indian Archipelago, East India, and East Africa. The fruit nut comes from an Areca catechu palm tree. Often betel-nut is combined with leaves of the Piper methysticum (ava) plant to enhance its overall psychoactive effect of well-being and physical stimulation. But Samoans and Manu'ans do not partake in the custom of chewing the betel-nut.

Burial Customs

Samoan folklore tells that TuiAtua Lufasiaitu—the one who, according to legend, declared the chickens to be sacred, from which declaration, *Samoa,* comes the name of the Island of Samoa—was buried in a seated posture, together with his tropical fruit parrot named Sega, just as Rivers said of the stream of people that passed through Melanesia.

Also, there are two families in Samoa who, the missionary Reverend Turner discovered (in 1845), had practiced mummification some 60 years before the arrival of Christianity—again, just as Rivers described the practice among the Ava people. The first of these families is on the Island of Savai'i where Paramount Orator Chief Letufuga resides. The second is on Amaile, Upolu, where the ancestors of Paramount High Chief TuiAtua Mata'afa were discovered, by Reverend Turner, to have practiced mummification. According to Turner, the mummified bodies, discovered in the Mata'afa residence in Amaile, consisted of a mother, father and two children aged between 8 and 12 years old.

The Ava Root

Manu'ans and Samoans believe the Ava root came from Fiji, and the Vanuatuans say they introduced it to the Fijians.

Samoans and Manu'ans have several legends about the origin of the Ava plant, saying it was brought from heaven by Tagaloalagi. Folklore has it that, prior to discovering the Ava, whether from heaven or from Fiji Island via the Vanuatuan, Samoans had been experimenting with mixing various roots and tree barks to make an intoxicating drink. For example, oral history tells stories where tree bark from the Vi fruit was said to have been scraped and mixed with water or coconut juice for a drink. But it appears that Samoans and Manu'ans were not aware of the Ava plant drink and its ritual ceremonies until they were introduced to them by Fijians and other Melanesian people.

The Ava itself is a root-based alcohol-like drink, the Samoan equivalent of the "nectar of the gods" and sacred drinks in other cultures. Keepers of Samoan and Manu'an oral traditions believe it came into being through the legend of the son of the god Tagaloalagi, at the "formation" of Manu'a and Samoa.

How the Ava Came to Samoa

The Samoan legend of Futi and Sao tells of a couple who came from Fiji to have their daughter, Sinalalotava, wed a smart Samoan called Tagatapopoto. Instead, she ended up marrying his brother Lauifia, begetting Mausautele who became the progenitor of one of the royal houses of Gatoa'itele and Vaetamasoaali'i. The legend says this is the couple that brought the ava plant with them and gifted it to the village of Safotu, Savai'i.

Another version of the legend is this:

In the village of Vailele, in the district of Tuamasaga on the Island of Upolu, there lived a couple with two daughters, Sinapoula and Sinafaalua. Their father, Faoulusau, went hunting for fruit pigeons in the mountain forest behind the village, which bordered the village of Siumu.

After an extended period of time, when he still had not returned, the mother sent the two daughters to search for their father. In their quest, the daughters crossed through to the villages of Siumu and district of Safata, and continued westwards on the Island of Upolu.

When they felt the search was in vain, the daughters decided to return home, following the coastal route around the district of A'ana. Upon reaching the village of Mulifanua, they saw a catamaran heading out to sea. The girls stood on the beach and motioned and waved for it to stop and return for them to catch a ride to their village.

The boat returned and picked up the girls. The girls inquired of the sailors, who they were and where they were going. The sailors introduced the girls to the captain, who was the Tuifiti (the Fijian king), and explained that their journey was in search of a remedy for the king's illness. But the search had been in vain, and they were returning to their homeland, Fiji.

Shortly after the girls joined the ship, the Fijian King suffered an attack of his illness, and the sailors and servants were filled with fear that their king might lose his life to this sickness. The sisters remembered the old Samoan remedy of taking a ripe green coconut—not one of the dark-brown ones—and opening a tiny hole in the top, so seawater can be added inside, then shaking it thoroughly for about half an hour until it is well mixed, in a similar manner to modern-day cocktails.

The sisters strongly insisted that the king should drink this concoction to relieve his illness. The king reluctantly accepted the drink, and before long he began to feel strong, and his health returned to normal.

The Fijian king was extremely pleased. Filled with elation and desire for the Samoan sisters, he took both girls to be his wives. Sinapoula gave birth to a son, Suasamiavaava—which means juice-of-sea water and ava roots—and Sinafaalua bore two children, a boy named Soatateteleupegaofiti, and his sister, Muliovailele.

The Tuifiti found great pleasure in his children borne by the Samoan sisters. His joy was short-lived, however, in that, not long afterwards, his son Suasamiavaava took ill and died. On his deathbed the son asked his mother and aunt to promise him that, if he passed, a plant that grew up and out of his grave would be uprooted and taken to Samoa and planted there in memory of him and of their sojourn in Fiji.

The plant that sprang forth from the grave of Suasamiavaava took on a shape of a man's fingers and became an attraction to the people of Fiji. This plant (Piper methysticum, from the Latin for "pepper" and the Greek for "intoxicating") was named the ava.

Muliovailele and her brother Soatateteleupegaofiti wished to visit their mother's homeland, Samoa, so they took with them the ava plant. They landed at the beachfront of their mother and aunt's village, Vailele, Upolu. It is during the course of this journey that they visited various villages in the Samoan chain of islands, where they gifted the ava plant to be planted.

How the Ava Came to Manu'a

A different legend of the ava plant is told by Manu'ans, involving the god Tagaloalagi and his Ava ceremony in his residence in the tenth Heaven; this is clearly a different kind of story, like the Manu'an story of creation: Tagaloalagi's grandson, TagaloaUi, sneaked up and stole the Ava, despite its being tapu (forbidden) because of its sacred nature. Then TagaloaUi brought the Ava down onto Earth for the first Tuimanu'a.

This shows a creative way of imagining the "origin" of the Ava, for the Manu'an is ever aware there has to be an "origin" and beginning for everything, just as in the mythology of creation. So, to their credit, in the absence of a legend that tells where the Ava originated (other than that it's from another island such as Fiji) Manu'ans understood and accepted that everything originated in Heaven and was administered by the will of Tagaloalagi.

The well-known legend of the first Ava ceremony begins with TagaloaUi and a man named Pava. The "half-human half-spirit" TagaloaUi was having an Ava ceremony with Pava, a plantation owner. And Pava's son, a three- or four-year-old, was playing and running around, making a lot of noise and disrupting their ceremony. He was being... rather annoying and, after couple of orders to keep the boy quiet and well-behaved were shrugged off, TagaloaUi became angry and grabbed the boy; he literally "split the boy in half" and laid him down in front of himself and Pava. Then TagaloaUi said, "This is our 'meal' for the Ava ritual ceremony." This is the first time the "meal" was to accompany the Ava ceremony. But, of course,

TagaloaUi had observed the whole ceremony up in heaven, when he sneaked up to steal the Ava for Tuimanu'a down on Earth, on Manu'a.

Pava was shocked and petrified, not to mention full of sorrow and heartbroken, and he begged for boy's life to be returned, because TagaloaUi was a deity. TagaloaUi thought that this was a learning moment, so he restored the two halves of the boy, and the boy came back to life. Afterward, Pava went out to fetch taro, palusami (baked taro leaves and coconut milk juice), bananas, and different types of fish for their meal.

Because of Pava's lackadaisical way of conducting the Ava ceremony, TagaloaUi banished him to a village now called Falealili, Upolu.

This legend reminds me of the story of Heracles of Anticlides. It is said that, after returning from the completion of his Labors, Heracles was invited with others to a sacrifice celebrated by Eurystheus. When the sons of Eurystheus set the best portions of food before themselves, but placed a humbler portion before Heracles, he, deeming that he had been insulted, slew three of the sons--namely Perimedes, Eurybius, and Eurypylus.[clxxxi] So much for the patience and temperance of the gods!

Some people believe that this Ava ceremony was done in the village of Pavaia'i, Tutuila Island, hence the somewhat eponymous village name. The legend does not say they consumed the boy's body, of course, and the reference to cannibalism simply illustrates the need for a meal to accompany the Ava ceremony. Also, it demonstrates TagaloaUi's spiritual power to restore life.

There was still no mention of any foreign persons or people involved with the Ava ceremony in this story, reaffirming the Manu'an version of the origin (in Heaven) of the Ava.

In another legend, Tagaloalagi has two sons from one of his many wives, one called Avaavaali'i and the other So'oso'oali'i. The legend follows the same storyline as with the King of Fiji and the two Samoan sisters from Vailele. In this case Avaavaali'i dies and the ava plant grows on his grave, with five branches that resemble the fingers of a man's hand. The people of Tagaloalagi called this plant Ava, in memory of Avaavaali'i, the son of their god Tagaloalagi.

Libation Ceremonies around the World

Out of Africa

It turns out that the origin of religious ceremonies around the ritual of "Libation" in a group setting is as old as the "Out of Africa" migration story. The story began in Central Africa and, it appears, travelled with the human migration across the world. It was adapted and practiced by the Egyptians, Indians, Mesopotamians, Jews, Romans, and many more cultures. Obviously, every culture added a little of their own protocol into the ceremony.

To start with African cultures, the traditional religious ceremony of "pouring a libation," to give homage to the ancestors and in reverence to the gods or God, goes back to early civilizations. The libation is typically some traditional wine (palm wine for example), mixed with water and or milk; it is mixed by hand, by a designated chief who is appointed to perform this function; and not just anyone can touch it, because it is a sacred "Libation" of the gods or God, and of the Chiefs and guests of honor.

The religious ritual always begins with a prayer, to the gods or God, for blessing, for good health and good life, and for the purpose of the particular celebration. Such a ritual takes place, for example: at the installation of kings, queens, and chiefs; at marriages, childbirth and funerals; and at formal meetings of family and village. In the words of Chief Yagbe Awolowo Onilu, who is among the most distinguished group of tradition-bearers of the African diaspora, libation connects words with relationships, with people, with the dead, with the gifts of the divine. It is an ancient form of prayer.[clxxxii]

In various cultures in Africa, libation offerings and ceremonies honor the Earth, Heaven and the Cosmos; also air, water, ocean, fire, foods, animals, harvest, lands, and environment, etc. That is why it is a most sacred religious ceremony to the Africans. It remains so in Samoa, and for the same reason, the Samoan House of Parliament opens with prayer followed by the Ava ceremony.

Egyptian Libation

When the human migration arrived in Egypt, the Egyptians adopted the same religious ritual of offering libations to honor the various divinities, sacred ancestors, humans—alive and dead—and the environment. It is suggested that this offering of libation to the gods began in the upper Nile Valley and spread out to other regions of Africa and on to the world.[clxxxiii] It is in Egypt that the people began to mimic the flow of the Nile, as life and spirit flowing through human veins, giving sustenance and life. On a bronze libation vessel it was written: To be spoken by Nut: "O Osiris Nut, take the libation from my own arms! I am your effective mother, and I bring you a vessel containing much water to satisfy your heart with libation."

As we have learned, the Nile meant everything to the Egyptians. It dictated the economic calendar, based on when the Nile floods and or runs low; and it helped build a kingdom that was the envy of the known world at that time.

After the reign of the last priest-king of Egypt, Hephaestus, the Egyptians were free from having a king over them. But the people, once again, could never live without a king. So, they divided Egypt into twelve portions and installed a king over each, so that now the country had twelve kings. At the very first establishment of these multiple lordships, an oracle was given to them, that whoever poured a libation from a "bronze vessel" in the temple of Hephaestus should be King of all of Egypt.

Now the twelve kings were living in peace and, as time went on, they came to sacrifice in Hephaestus' temple. On the last day of the festivities a special ceremony, for the pouring of libations to end of the celebration, was to be prepared by a high priest. The high priest brought out the wrong number of golden vessels, only eleven instead of twelve. So the last king, Psammetichus, got no vessel, at which Psammetichus took off his bronze helmet, held it out and with that he poured the libation.

Although the other eleven kings were prepared to pass judgement on Psammetichus to put him to death, they recalled the oracle's proclamation about the bronze vessel, and they decided to spare his life. Instead they chased him away into the marshes, and commanded that he not concern himself with the rest of Egypt.

After several attempts to reclaim his kingship authority, Psammetichus finally succeeded with the help of the Ionians and Carians, who landed on the coast of Egypt looking for provisions but ended up staying for a longer period of time. For Psammetichus, this was the fulfillment of the oracle; he made friends with Ionians and Carians, promising them great rewards if they would ally with him. Then, having won them over, and with aid of other Egyptians allies, he deposed the eleven kings.[clxxxiv]

The pouring of libation is important to protocol and standing. In our own village of Afega in Upolu, our Chief Council Ava ceremony protocol requires any Orator Chief to be able to perform this very sacred function of "pouring," or directing and distributing, the ava drink. For the Islands of Samoa and Manu'a, the Paramount Royal Chiefs and families have designated and declared a special orator or high chief to preside in the Ava ceremony.

The Old Testament

When the human migration crossed the Nile Valley and continued into the Saudi Arabian desert and the Levant, reaching ancient Israel, Judaism also instituted a libation ceremony. As stated in the Old Testament of the Bible, in Genesis 35:14, "Jacob set up a pillar in the place where he had spoken with him, a pillar of stone; and he poured out a drink offering on it, and poured oil on it."

Hinduism and Libations

In Hinduism, the libation ritual is part of "Tarpan" which is performed during Pitru Paksha (the Fortnight of the ancestors), during the Bhadrapada month, around September and October, of the Hindu calendar.[clxxxv]

Chinese Libation

In Chinese customs, rice wine or tea is poured in front of an altar or tombstone, pouring horizontally from right to left with both hands, as an offering to the gods and in honor of deceased.

Libation in Greek Tradition

By the time the Greeks discovered the "Libation" ceremony, it had become an all-male ritual, usually restricted to the wealthy, and to philosophers and orators and sophists, who gathered to contemplate the pursuit of wisdom in an epicurean setting. The Greeks would call this a Symposium. Some say that literary works that describe or take place at the Symposium include two Socratic dialogues, Plato's *Symposium* and Xenophon's *Symposium*, as well as a number of Greek poems such as the elegies of Theognis of Megara.

The particulars of the ceremonial ritual observed by the Greeks were a lot more elaborate and formalized, with strict etiquette—and poetry contests. Philosophy and orations were offered as a form of intellectual and literary entertainment. Athenaeus, in his *Deipnosophistae*, describes Homer's idea of inviting the "best men and those who are held in great esteem," while Hesiod prescribes also inviting the neighbors. Athenaeus continues by telling how Epicurus—a Greek philosopher from Samos who lived in 341 B.C. to 270 B.C.—would invite prophets to the symposium, while Plato and Xenophon—the ancient Athenian historian and philosopher—would advocate having people of different age groups present, including young men who aspired to arts and literature.[clxxxvi]

Eubulus (355-342 B.C), in a fragment from his 375 B.C. play, *Semele or Dionysus*, shows the god of wine, Dionysus, describing proper and improper drinking habits, and listing the "Kraters" or cups provided: For sensible men he would offer three Kraters—the first for health, the second for love and pleasure, and the third for sleep—suggesting wise men should go home after the third Krater. The fourth Krater is for bad behavior; the fifth is for shouting ; the sixth is for rudeness and insults; the seventh is for fights; the eighth is for breaking up the furniture; and the ninth is for depression. Which leave the tenth, which would be reserved for madness and unconsciousness.[clxxxvii]

Libation in Roman times

The Roman equivalent of the Libation Ceremony was called Convivium.[clxxxviii] And the Etruscans embraced the Libation/ symposium ritual as an academic conference or meeting.

The Americas

In the Americas, in the Quechua Aymara cultures of the Andes, it is common to pour a small amount of one's beverage on the ground before drinking, as an offering to Pachamama, or Mother Earth. The Libation ritual is commonly called "challa" and is performed quite often, usually before meals and during celebrations.

In Japan

In Japan, the drink offered in libation is called Miki, "The Liquor of the Gods." When the ceremony is performed at a Shinto shrine, it is usually done with sake. At a household shrine, fresh water can be used, though it should be changed every morning. The drink is served in a white porcelain or metal cup without any decoration.[clxxxix]

Comparison with the Ava Ceremony

So, do we draw a parallel between the Ava ceremony and other Libation rituals because the ava root resembles the wine, "nectar," and "ambrosia" of the gods, or because of the custom of serving and protecting the royal gods? For, as we have learned, the history of libation ceremonies, similar to the ava drink and ritual, is as ancient as the human migration "Out of Africa."

Our conclusion about the origin of the Ava ceremony, and how Samoans and Manu'ans came to embrace it, presents another example of how Polynesian culture consists of an amalgamation of influences from the other cultures and ethnic groups that they encountered along their migration path. The Ava drink and ceremony would have originated in North Africa and traveled with the first "Out of Africa" migration, going through India and following the Indian coastal route around till the people and ceremony arrived in the Asiatic Archipelago. It is here that native people continued to maintain the tradition in a primitive way, until other cultural clans adopted the religious ritual and carried it with them, eventually settling in Vanuatu, New Caledonia, Micronesia, Solomon Island, and down to Fiji Island.

The parallel path of Ava libation rituals, traveling up the Levant into the high culture societies of the Mediterranean, shows how these societies developed their own elaborate rituals and ceremonies in a more sophisticated social tradition.

Clearly, cultural diffusion, through human migration, is evident even in comparative legends of the Ava libation.

Tattooing

Tattoo or Tatau

Just as libation ceremonies have been practiced across the globe, so has the art of tattooing. It has been practiced since at least Neolithic times—the late phase of the Stone Age around 8000 B.C.—and is characterized by the birth of agriculture and the making of polished stone implements. Tattooing is evidenced in mummified preserved skin, ancient art, and archaeological records.[cxc] But how did it come to Samoa, and will that help us trace the migration path of the Navigators?

The oldest discovery of tattooed human skin to date is dated between 3370 and 3100 B.C., found on the body of Otzi the Iceman.[cxci] While documenting the "Otzi the Iceman" tattoos in 2015, Aaron Deter-Wolf, an archaeologist of the Tennessee Division of Archaeology, referenced other tattooed mummies that have been recovered from at least 49 archaeological sites, including locations in Greenland, Alaska, Siberia, Mongolia, western China, Egypt, Sudan, the Philippines, and the Andes of South America. These include: tattoos of Amunet, Priestess of the Goddess Hathor from ancient Egypt (2134-1991 B.C.); multiple tattooed mummies from Siberia, including the Pazyryk culture of Russia; and examples from several cultures throughout pre-Columbian South America. So the ancient history of tattoos follows the path and the timeline of human migration—a journey that started out of North Africa, crossed the Nile to the Saudi Arabian desert and on to India, turning westward to the Levant and eastward toward China, and on down to Southeast Asia and the Asiatic Archipelago.

Joann Fletch, a research fellow in the department of archaeology at the University of York in Britain, noted that the earliest known body tattoos were, for a long time, Egyptian, and were present on several female mummies dated at around 2000 B.C. According to Professor Don Brothwell of the University of York, a specialist in ancient tattoos, much evidence has been observed, from figurines dated around 4000 to 3500 B.C., that women had tattoos on their bodies and limbs—occasional female figures are represented in tomb scenes around 1200 B.C., and in figurines from around 1300 B.C., all with tattoos on their thighs, and all from Ancient Egypt. Thus it seems tattooing may have been an exclusively female practice in ancient Egypt.

Of course, initially, in the male-dominated field of archaeology, excavators assumed the women were of "dubious status," or "marked" as prostitutes. But new evidence shows they were royal and elite, including even high-status priestesses such as those of Amunet (as revealed by funerary inscriptions).

The etymology of the word tattoo, from the 18th century, shows that it derives from the Polynesian word "Tatau," meaning "to write." It is a word that is common throughout Samoan, Tongan, Tahitian, Maori and other Polynesian islands.

The Samoan Legend of Tatau

The Samoan legend of the origin of *Tatau* or Tattooing is the story of twin girls Taema and Tilafaiga, descendants of Ulufanuasese'e and Sinalalofutu-i-Fagaiofu, of Falelatai, Upolu. These are the girls who were originally conjoined twins:

The twins' journeys took them to Solosolo village in Upolu, and on to Manu'a and Tutuila, where Taema married Chief Togiola and bore Le'iatotogiolatu'itu'iotoga, after which they continued travelling on to Fiji Island. After some period of time, the twins desired to return to Samoa. In their farewell parting with the Tuifiti—the Fijian king—they were given a gift, a little box containing the tools and apparatus for tattooing the body. This was originally for tattooing women and not men. As the twins journeyed to Samoa, they sang their song as follows: "Tattoo the women and not the men."

The twins arrived at the seaside village of Falealupo in Savai'i, and one of them looked down to the bottom of the ocean and saw there a trident shell—the Samoan word—*Faisua*—really means a very large oyster. She dived down after it and brought it up into the boat. In the process she forgot the song, and so she asked her twin sister how the song went. Then the sister said, "It goes like this: 'Tattoo the men and not the women.'"

It is not clear whether the meaning of this incident is that the sister really got confused and changed the verse from women to men, or whether there is some symbolism attached to the oyster, relative to the women, that motivated the change in the practice.

The twins arrived in Safotu, Savai'i, where Paramount Orator Chief Lavea resided. The twins called out to Chief Lavea: "Hey there! We have a skill we brought with us on our journey from Fiji." But Chief Lavea did not pay any mind to the women, and so their journey continued on to the village of Salelavalu, Savai'i, to the residence of High Chief Mafua. But he too wanted nothing to do with women's gift box.

The twins went on to the village Safata, Upolu, where Chief Su'a lived, and they were kindly received by the chief's daughters. When they arrived, Chief Su'a was out at work in the plantation. So the chief's daughters had the twins welcomed to the house, served with fresh water to drink, and invited to rest for a moment, while they ran off to get their father. When Chief Su'a arrived home, he immediately greeted the ladies with kind, honorific remarks, and the twins were very impressed with the generosity of the Su'a family. They then told Su'a about their gift box from Fiji and how the purpose of it is to tattoo the body. The twins, desiring to express their thanks for the Su'a family's kindness and generosity, gifted the skill box to Chief Su'a. The gift included: the architectural design of the tatau (tattoo) and construction implements as his heirlooms, and his Ava cup name which must be called out during the protocol as to when he should receive (be served first) his Ava drink in the ceremony of tattooing or of a house (maota) dedication. This came with the following decree:

"This is the container and in it are all the tattoo hammers. These hammers are our tools; we will gift it to you, Chief Su'a, and your family. When the Ava ceremony is served, during the ritual you shall have the first cup to drink before every chief's term. Your Ava cup is called *Logotaeao* (to welcome in the morning), and your sacred meeting grounds shall be named Tulau'ega, Lalotalie and Fagalele and Fa'amafi in Safata."

After this the village ladies presented the twins with gifts of barkcloth and curcuma yellow, and the twins were elated.

The Time of Tattoos

The time frame for when tattooing was imported to Samoa by the twins, Tilafaiga and Taema (also called Pi'ilua), is around 1200 A.D., based on their genealogy being in the tenth generation, as posited by Dr. Krämer. Thus myths, cultural traditions, and genealogies work together to give a timeline of history and to help us find the migration path.

However, the genealogy of the twins, being descended from Saveasi'uleo and Ulufanuasese'e, sons of Taufaalematagi and Alao, goes much farther back, all the way to the story of the original people that migrated from the Indonesian Archipelago—it is the continuation of the legend of PapaAtea and Papa'ele and Papatu (the mythology of creation, told in the mythology section of this book). This implies that the importation of tattooing to Samoa could have taken place in early- to mid-1st century A.D.

Legends in Toga hold that Samoa, at that time, was under the Togan yoke for 400 years, from 825 A.D., and that tattoos were already common attire in both indigenous Polynesian cultures. Thus, we have a timeline for migration of the art of tattooing to the Tahitians, Hawaiians and the Maoris, indicating that it occurred after the legendary arrival of tattooing in Samoa.

The Use of Tattoos

As with the ancient tattoos noted in other ancient cultures, tattoos usually covered the whole body. Samoans and Manu'ans have always held onto the belief that Tatau is the "clothing of civilized men." Several explorers—including Jacob Roggeveen in 1722, and members of the expedition of Lois-Antoine de Bougainville in 1768—noted that, from a distance, the native males appeared to be clothed in a wrap-around material, until they came closer; then they realized that the native men were not wearing material clothing, but rather the explorers were observing their tattooed bodies only.

We have noted how ancient Egyptian women appeared to use tattoos as a form of cosmetic decoration—and also, perhaps, for medicinal purposes like acupuncture treatments. But, as we have seen, tattooing was now for men also. And today, young men are eager to have a tatau put on them, so they can serve the chief council and be proud young warriors.

Women can still have a tattoo, but a woman's tattoo is called the *malu*, and it is done on the thighs above and just below the knees, when the young woman shows signs of entering adolescence and experiencing puberty.

The procedure is this: when a man decides to get a tatau, then a female member of his family, such as a sister or a female cousin, can be a dual tattoo partner; they then accompany each other during the practice of this painful ceremonial ritual. This is one of only two occasions whereby the boundary taboo, between a male and his sister, is lifted. That is, the sister would be the only one to assist the tattoo architect, to help with the brother's tattooing while he is naked. The other exemption from this taboo is when a brother passes away and the sisters are to prepare him with his burial attire.

Practical Skills

Navigational Skill

A sense of direction and the ability to describe directions are essential to ocean navigation. The Samoan's basic concept of direction is North, South, East and West. It is related to the direction where the sun rises and sets, and the direction toward the mountains versus the ocean. So, the Samoans would say:

a) *sisifo* (west)
b) *sasa'e* (east)
c) *gauta* (always point to the mountain)
d) *gatai* (always point to the ocean)
e) *gag'ifo* (westward)
f) *gaga'e* (eastward)
g) *saute* (south)
h) *matu* (north)

There are no Samoan words for northward or southward, nor for northeastern, northwestern, southwestern, or southeastern. These directions are identified by celestial bodies or wind direction. So, the eastern trade wind (blowing from east to west) is the dry wind blowing from northeast to southwest. If the trade wind is cool and wet, it's blowing from southeast to northwest. Thus the common lexicon for directions is derived from wind directions and the sun, moon, stars, etc.

So, when a Samoan would ask where you just came from, the answer might be "I came from *sisifo* (the west)," with answers such as, "I came from Apia town," representing a relatively new development in language and culture.

Further directions, needed for travel between islands, were derived by association with heavenly bodies—such as the sun, moon, and stars; also including the wind direction in different seasons of the year. For example:

a) the Southern Cross (*sumu*) with its two Centauri (*luatagata*), provided the cross stands in the Meridian, or the Great Bear (*le anava*), if they are all visible
b) Orion's (*amoga*) girdle
c) Venus (*fetuao*)
d) Jupiter (*tupua legase*)
e) Mars (*matamemea*)
f) the Milky Way (*aniva*, sometimes *aolele* or *aotea*)

The people did not know the difference between planets and stars, but they were well acquainted with their appearance and could use their respective behavior for navigational purposes. Thus these celestial bodies were reconciled with:

a) the ocean (*ua soū le vasa*, violent Ocean)
b) waves (*galutetele*, violent waves)
c) tides (*tai o'oo'o,* high violent tides)
d) the weather (*aso timuga*, monsoon)
e) wind directions (*tuaoloa*, the cool trade wind from the southeast)

The language was developed to match and promote the navigational skills of the Navigators. For the Navigators of the Pacific Ocean knew the clouds for launching; the stars for sailing; the paths of fish; the winds for their bearings; the ocean swells for the current; the sea birds, fishing schools, and landmass directions; the rooster crow for the dawn of day and signs of land; and their language reflected this.

Weaving Skill

Weaving cloth, pandanus or coconut leaves, and tree-bark fibers (barkcloth) is a skill that goes back to when humans first began to find covers for themselves, to protect themselves from the weather. In particular, the whole of the Austronesian people practiced barkcloth-weaving, as a necessity for clothing, and carried that skill with them.

Anthropologist Paul Tolstoy, from the Department of Anthropology, University of Montreal, Quebec, writing about the tools used to beat the barkcloth, found that archaeological reports date Mesoamerican stone beaters as early as the 1st millennium B.C. Reports from Formosa and the Philippines could be dated as early as the 2nd millennium B.C.[cxcii]

Yale anthropologist, Raymond Kennedy, suggests that the "technology and techniques between central Sulawesi and eastern Polynesia date to the time of close contact or common origin."[cxciii]

And according to Roger Green, who studied early Lapita art from Polynesia and Melanesia, Polynesian barkcloth designs resemble those found in Sulawesi, and have also been matched with designs found on Lapita pottery dated between 3200 and 2400 B.C.[cxciv]

A 1963 paper by Ling and Ling in Taiwan noted that the use of barkcloth in China dates back to as early as the 6th century B.C.[cxcv]

The consensus, then, is that barkcloth traveled from the mainland to the Malay and Indonesian Archipelagos. Barkcloth, tapacloth, or the Samoan's siapo was used for clothing. And the "fine mats" woven from pandanus (or coconut) leaves were used for special occasions and celebrations.[cxcvi]

The important thing to note is that everything about the skills needed to build and to operate tools and weapons, and to create domestic products (such as clothing) and aid in provisioning (growing crops, caring for domestic animals, and preparing food) were long primed, honed and preserved by the Navigators before they took the "leap of faith" in crossing the Wallace Line to East Pacific Ocean. All this detailed planning was necessary for this kind of long distance journey with an unknown ocean ahead.

Geography and Geology

The study of how the earth is formed, and how its formation affects human and animal populations

The Malay Archipelago

The Malay Archipelago was born around 13,500 years ago, when the earth's last glacial occurrence lowered the ocean water level some 400 feet, exposing some of the landmass connecting the peninsula with the Southeast Asian Sundaland landmass. Geologists E. Sathiamurthy and H.K. Voris of Chulalongkorn University describe how Palawan was part of Sundaland, while the rest of the Philippine Islands formed one large island, separated from the continent only by the Sibutu Passage and the Mindoro Strait.[cxcvii] At this time, of course, the Australian continent was connected to the New Guinea and Tasmania Sahul landmass. Between Sahul and Sundaland lay the peninsula of Southeast Asia, which was comprised of present-day Malaysia and western and northern Indonesia; leaving an archipelago of islands known as Wallacea. The exposed landmass turned out to contain newly formed islands across the peninsula, including Indonesia and its 8,400 islands.

Thus God's creation, the foundation to the whole of the Pacific basin, results in the geological formation of the Malay Archipelago of the Indonesian Peninsula. According to geologist Debbie Guthrie Haer, this is the result of the tectonic subduction of the Indo-Australian plate under the Eurasian plate. The tertiary ocean floor, made up of ancient marine deposits including an accumulation of coral reefs, was lifted above sea level by the subduction. Layers of tertiary limestone, lifted from the ocean floor, are still visible in areas such as the Bukit peninsula, in the huge limestone cliffs of Uluwatu, Bali, or in the northwest of Bali at Prapat Agung.

Haer describes how local deformation of the Eurasian plate created by the subduction encouraged fissuring of the crust, leading to various volcanic phenomena. Thus a string of volcanoes lines the northern part of the Indonesian Peninsula, aligned west to eat, where the western part is oldest and the eastern is newest. The highest volcano, at over 10,000 feet, is the active stratovolcano Mount Agung.[cxcviii]

The Haer study further indicates that volcanic activity has been intense through the ages, affecting most of the surface of Bali; outside this area, the Bukit Peninsula and Prapat Agung have been covered by volcanic magma. Some deposits remain which are more than a million years old, while most of the central part of the Island of Bali and many islands in the Indonesian Peninsula are covered by young volcanic deposits dating from less than a million years ago.

Volcanic activity, which generates thick deposits of ashes and improved soil fertility, has also been a strong factor in the agricultural prosperity of the islands in the Indonesian Peninsula—Bali, Southwest Java, the Timor group, etc. and Debbie Guthrie Haer points out that, because of the subduction, the island of Bali is also at the edge of the continental Sunda shelf, just west of the Wallace line; it was at some time connected to the neighboring island of Java, particularly during the lowering of the sea level in the Ice Ages.

The Wallace Line

What is the Wallace Line?

The combination of periodic collisions between the Pacific tectonic plate and the Eurasian Plate created the "Ring of Fire" chain of submarine volcanoes in the Pacific Ocean. And the Wallace Line runs from the Australian continent all the way up to the Philippine Sea, along a deep valley under the ocean floor, which resulted from the volcanic activity.

Anthropologists have long been aware of the Wallace Line as the Indonesian Archipelago's equivalent of the Sahara Desert or the Himalayan mountain range—both of which represent major obstacles to traveling migrants. While these other major obstacles are land based, however, the obstacle facing the colonizers of the East Pacific—the Wallace Line—lies within the biggest ocean in the world. It acts as a defining geophysical line that separates families of people, animal species, plants, and other indigenous living things, one side from the other.

Named after Alfred Russell Wallace, the father of biogeographical science and co-founder of the theory of natural selection (with Darwin in 1840 to 1860), the Wallace line is a result of rivers, desert, forestry, and mountain range, as well as of ocean depth and the grouping of islands on different oceans.

Alfred Wallace, a naturalist, postulated an invisible dividing line in the Indian Ocean that could explain the differences in the types of plants, animals and species thriving in one geophysical area as compared to another. While searching for evidence of evolution in Southeast Asia and South America, he located the phenomenon in the center of the ocean around the Indonesian Archipelago, imagining a line that followed the architectural structure of the volcanic line underneath the northeast Pacific Ocean, later known as the "Ring of Fire." The presence of this line would later be confirmed, and it was named the Wallace Line.

This invisible line lies underneath a group of more than 8,000 islands in the Indonesian Archipelago—out of 17,000 islands stretching in and around the equator. The Wallace Line separates these islands from the East Pacific Ocean.

The Science Behind the Wallace Line

There is a scientific explanation of how the phenomenon of the Wallace Line came about, though Alfred Wallace did not know this at the time, as limited research had been done, and knowledge in the fields of geology and oceanography did not yet cover the impact of the last glaciation on land and ocean floor. It takes an understanding of all the above sciences, plus biology, ethnology and anthropology, to clear up the Wallace Line's conundrum.

At an ancient time, around 335 million years ago, when the earth's surface consisted of very few continental units, there existed a continuous landmass or supercontinent known as Pangaea. But Pangaea began to break apart about 175 million years ago. This process caused the separation of the landmass, forming new continental units, and the separation of the oceans, causing the emergence of major rivers.

This process also reshaped the landscape of the continental units and the floors of the various oceans. So, when the landmass connecting Sahul (Australia) and Sunda (Borneo, Java, and Sumatra and surrounding islands)—often referred to as the Sundaland or Sundaic region—was covered by rising seas around 13,000 years ago, during the last melting of icecap (the last Glacial Maximum), the ocean floor configuration resulted in some islands being situated in shallow ocean water to the west, while others moved toward the deeper ocean water to the east—these would include New Guinea and other islands off the Bismarck Archipelago.

This process also helps explain how original native species of animals and plants separated with the continental breakup and established new ecosystems in their newly formed homelands.

Crossing the Wallace Line—the Theory

The accepted idea, now, is that the Austronesian or Polynesian seafaring people were island-hopping in the east to northeastern Indonesian Archipelago all throughout the Pleistocene (1.8 million-18,000 B.C.), Holocene (11,700-8,000 B.C.) and Neolithic (3,200-250 B.C.) periods.

In early 2019, Shimona Kealy, Sue O'Connor, and a team out of Indonesia and the Australian National University were given permission to explore Obi, in Indonesia's Maluku Utara province, for possible tool evidence suggesting that humans arrived on the tropical island of Obi at least 18,000 years ago. Prehistoric axes, sharp blades, and beads were found, apparently used for hunting and possibly marking canoes for voyaging between islands.

Perhaps even more profound than the tool evidence is the confirmation of a crucial staging post for the seafaring people who lived in this region—a place where they could contemplate their "leap of faith" before crossing the Wallace Line to the East Pacific while the last ice age was coming to an end. [cxcix]

Crossing the Wallace Line—the Men

New understanding of this biogeographical region allows us to appreciate the challenge undertaken by the Navigators in crossing the Wallace Line to colonize the rest of the East Pacific islands. It's not the same as island-hopping in the somewhat shallow ocean water in the Indonesian Archipelago. The degree of difficulty in navigating across the Wallace Line's deep ocean water, coupled with that of negotiating the largest body of salt water the Austronesians had ever encountered, necessitated careful planning and organization, and moreover a "warrior" task master. It's important to remember that these sea mariners were not experienced ocean navigators. Prior to this they traversed close to landmass shores when seeking other destination islands in the Malay and Indonesian Archipelagos. The arduous journey on the open Pacific Ocean would require many more years spent in honing the navigational skills to do it.

Crossing the Wallace Line—the Women

This eye-opening discovery—recognizing the challenges the environmental obstacles that the Wallace Line imposed on the colonizers of the East Pacific Ocean—added to the fact that the Navigators are a matrilineal and matrilocal society, sheds light on the long-standing conundrum of how to reconcile the DNA, linguistic, and cultural differences and similarities found among Polynesians. This conundrum is sourced in the fragmentation of Polynesian DNA and its haplogroup markers, as we shall see when we turn our focus to DNA, where one study concludes that the ancestors of Polynesians can be traced to mainland Southeast Asia, while another traces them to Melanesia. We will cover the cultural implications more closely my second book, but I have chosen to comment about it here to footnote the importance of the eye-opening discoveries of the Wallace Line.

Samoan family structure is matriarchal from its ancient beginning. The female family members always carry the family genealogy. The male inherits the title of Chief, but the female inherits the genealogy and directs the operation. Also females are the custodians of all family heirlooms and cultural customs and etiquette. A sister carries the Princess title and is honored to share the "head of family" leadership. She co-leads with the holder of the Chief title in the family, village, and clan. The Princess title-holder can even ask for pardon on behalf of a punished violator of *tapu*—violator of a taboo—a punishment over which only the only High Chief has authority.

The history of the Navigators is full of folklore evidencing the matriarchal structure. Even today, the center of the village of Saoluafata, the main village proper (where the sacred meeting ground, the *Malae* is) holds the residences of the two princesses of the Paramount Chiefs Tagaloa and Sagapolutele, while the chiefs live in an adjacent property. The boundary between these residences illustrates the honorifics given to the two matriarchs of these major families.

Samoan history noted that the first consolidated Paramount High Chief of all of Samoa (not including Manu'a) was a female, Tafa'ifa (or Queen) Salamasina—she is the first Tafa'ifa of Samoa, as orchestrated by the Warrior Queen Nafanua. The two matriarchal royal crowns (or titles) of Gatoa'itele and her daughter Vaetamasoaali'i, were decreed by Malietoa Uitualagi (1300-1380) to become two Paramount royal crowns (the two female Papas) through the lineage of Gauifaleai and Totogata, wives to his son Malietoa La'auli. Gatoa'itele is the daughter of Gauifaleai, and Vaetamasoaali'i is the daughter of Gatoa'itele. The two male Papas are TuiAana (or TuiA'ana) and TuiAtua. And then, of course, there was Nafanua herself, the Warrior Queen who helped consolidate the regal crowns through assisting in war, in the battle to acquire the royal crowns and titles.

The role of women in Samoan culture—as leaders and custodians of family lineage, custom, and formalities—is elaborated in detail in my next book—*Forging a Culture*. The characteristics of Samoan and Manu'an family structure are very much consistent with those of tribes in the interior of the Timor, Sulawesi, Maluku, Kai, Tanimbar, Aru and Barat Daya Islands, and other islands in the archipelago. This provides further evidence that the origin of the Navigators was in this area, among the islands of Southeast Asia.

Expansion into the Islands

An Amalgamated People

We have seen how an amalgamated people, from the Pontic-Caspian steppe and Deccan Plateau of India, navigated through the Greater Eurasian steppe and snaked through the continent of China to arrive in the Asiatic or Malay Archipelago.

We should recall, the Indian Archipelago, before it was called the Malay Archipelago, was already occupied by the North African/Indian Dravidian people from that first migration that arrived some 60,000 to 30,000 years earlier. These people were called the Negrito, from the Spanish for a short and small-framed African negro, formerly called

"Semang." They comprised the Negritos of Malaysia and the Philippines, and the Melanesians, who extended westward from their own core region around New Guinea into the eastern islands of Indonesia. The Australoid-Melanesians, as some anthropologists would call them, are the Orang Asil, meaning "original people" or "first people," the aboriginal and tribal inhabitants of the Malay Archipelago.

The Native Indonesians, or Pribumi, meaning "inlanders," are the foundational aboriginals of the Indonesian Archipelago. The short-statured Negrito population of the region is comprised of Peninsular Malaysians, inhabiting the mountainous region from Pahang north to the Thai border, and the Negrito of the Philippines, who inhabited both coastal and inland localities, in pockets of Luzon, northern Palawan, Panay, Negros, and Mindanao.[cc]

But cultures clashed. The acrimonious relationship between the newly arrived migrants and the Negrito populations of the Malay Peninsula became a source of warring conflicts. Anthropologists have concluded that this resulted in driving the indigenous Negrito populations deep into the forest and up into the mountainous areas, hence the term "inlanders." It's from the Orang Asil aboriginals that the origin Polynesians were born.

This multiethnic group, composed, as it was, from highly diverse ethnicities, is believed to have entered this landmass between 6,000 and 8,000 years ago. Linguistically, they divide into two groups—the Austroasiatic and the Asian. The interbreeding of the Dayak (the indigenous tribes of the Borneo islands) and the Kadazan (indigenous to the Sabah) and the Ibans (indigenous tribes of Sarawak, Borneo Island) created the foundational ethnicities of the people of the Malay or Indonesian Archipelagos.

The Impetus to Migrate

The isolated islands of Bali and Lombok provided refuge to warring tribes in the Malay Archipelago as they escaped from being defeated and being pushed out of their home territory.[cci] Thus, island-hopping became popular with the people in the peninsula, not only for refuge, but also as impetus for the spirit of discovery and colonization.

As these islands became more populated and settled, further travel among the people expanded into inter-island trade. The inter-island movement toward trade and fishing continued to hone their already well-practiced seafaring craft, a skill that eventually gave them the confidence to venture out even further into the South Pacific.

Understanding the environment in which these "amalgamated" island people (those we now refer to as the Polynesians) lived in the Malay Peninsula is important to gaining an insight into their psyche and their motivation for eventual migration to and subsequent colonization of the various islands in the South Pacific Ocean. The struggle for survival and territorial acquisition appears to have been a way of life in the Malay Peninsula, through many different tribes and at different time periods.

Understanding the layers of civilization and time periods of these different migration waves into the Malay Peninsula will allow us to isolate and focus on the particular people that will, eventually, be known as Polynesian, and to analyze their migration into the eastern Pacific Ocean.

The Ocean Seascape

The oceans surrounding the Malay Archipelago and the Indonesian Peninsula are as follows:

- the Indian Ocean to the southwest
- the Bay of Bengal to the northwest
- the Gulf of Thailand to the north above Malaysia
- the Java Sea between Java and Borneo
- the South China Sea, Celebes Sea, and Banda Sea north of Timor-Leste
- the Timor Sea north of Australia and south of Timor-Leste
- the Arafura Sea west of Papua New Guinea
- the Bismarck Sea northwest of Papua New Guinea
- and the Solomon Sea west of Solomon Islands

The importance of understanding the ocean seascape, in the archipelago and the Indonesian Peninsula, is to shed light on Polynesian familiarity with the science of ocean navigation—a familiarity that allowed them to establish trade routes and ultimately colonize Polynesia. This amalgamated group of people, with very similar cultures and ethnicities, occupying this group of islands in the peninsular archipelago, eventually made the ultimate decision to migrate to the Eastern Pacific, where they discovered the vastness of the Pacific Ocean.

Psychology

The study of the how the human mind affects human behavior

Taking the Modern Worldview

Navigators as Entrepreneurs

When I think about the Navigators of the Pacific Ocean, and their risk-taking venture over 1,500 years before Ferdinand Magellan "discovered" the Pacific Ocean in 1519, I'm reminded of the attributes of current Internet Technology entrepreneurs, who Professor Howard Stevenson, "the godfather" of entrepreneurship studies at Harvard Business School, Harvard University, documents in his study, noting the following: that they (the entrepreneurs) all seem to have a tolerance for ambiguity, keen perceptiveness, tactical ingenuity, and salesmanship. Perhaps an ability that is critical, but is not mentioned in Professor Stevenson's list, is also their keen ability to read market opportunity, as applied to, for example, the timing of a launch.

Professor Stevenson defines entrepreneurship very simply as "the pursuit of opportunity beyond resources controlled."[ccii] And to launch a journey across an ocean, without knowing its size or what conditions would prevail, in a direction to a place that may or may not exist, without knowing how long the journey will take, also taking into account limited food and fresh water resources, is surely a great entrepreneurial undertaking, clearly displaying a tolerance for ambiguity, and an ability to navigate through the maze of detailed planning to the final execution of an intrepid trip.

Does it make sense, then, to view the Navigators' psyche, using the current platform of an age of ubiquitous information and knowledge, in order to understand their risk-taking constitution? Surely it is reasonable to ask: How much planning did they undertake? What human resources and decisions about provisions did they make? What organizational structure did they build? What kind of risk assessment analysis did they undertake?

We know, today, that organizational behavior in corporations is a function of the culture within the company, as any student of the famous Professor Peter F. Drucker (1909-2005) understands.[cciii] We also know that behavioral modification is most effective when influenced by the community to which a person belongs, as seen in the Samoan and Manu'an cultural practices of thousands of years, observed by the illustrious author Margaret Mead in *The Coming of Age In Samoa*. And, we know, the quest for adventure—the search to find new land—will be motivated by physical conditions, economics, safety, and colonization aims, and will be driven totally by the leaders' "tolerance for ambiguity."

Also, we now have a much greater appreciation for the Polynesians' knowledge of ocean currents and wind directions at different times of year, and of cyclical ocean patterns caused by changes in trade winds. However, in spite of their recognized experience and knowledge set (which was probably limited to just a few navigators), the Pacific Ocean's vast size and its violent and unpredictable behavior would always render major challenges, even to an experienced adventurer.

This can only increase our reverence for these Navigators and their accomplishments. Why would we not study this migration, giving it the same prominence as the study of adventurers and colonizers during the period of Enlightenment? The answer to my rhetorical question is, of course, we would.

A Mystery Since 1776

The story of the Polynesian's great migration is a mystery that scientists have been trying to unravel for the last two hundred years, ever since Captain Cook discovered these islands in 1776. The Polynesian migration presents a narrative which, to be complete, must include why, where, how, and when it began. It has to answer the question of motivation. It has to recognize how challenging the preparation for the arduous journey must have been, particularly in an era so lacking in resources and "management know-how" to carry out such a task.

This incredible story began thousands of years before the Navigators entered the Pacific Ocean. It began, as we have seen, in a period around the Bronze Age, when human migration had moved eastward from Anatolia toward the Caucasus mountain range and the steppes of Mongolia and the Deccan Plateau (the Deccan is the largest plateau in India, covering most of the southern part of country). The spirit of unity, the need to persevere in protecting their genealogy and cultural identity, and the urge for survival throughout the dangerous journey itself, were of paramount importance.

Sometimes it is easier to tell a story when you have more data points and information. The vicissitudes of time, and the myriad results of research studies from ethnology, archaeology, linguistics, and anthropology (to name but a few) have produced more information—more colorful stones to add to this mosaic story of the Polynesians in general, and the Navigators in particular. Thus the passage of time and the events in history bear witness to this mysterious migration into the South Pacific.

Chiefdom and Family-Centric Culture

The arduous journey of Polynesian migration was driven by the spirit of entrepreneurship, to use a modern term. Perhaps in ancient times it might have been more the spirit of discovery and of settling a new abode. But the launch of a migration trip, to look for a new "place to call home," is a very deliberate decision. It requires careful planning and preparation. It requires organization and the delineation of responsibility and authority. It requires the accurate calculation of resources to support the journey. Logistical preparation must be thoroughly thought through (as opposed to merely read about), given the oral culture of the period—that is, everything must be orally repeated and frequently rehearsed.

To accomplish this comprehensive exercise in planning and preparation, the chiefdom organizational structure was developed and used, a system that already long existed in Polynesian culture. Such hierarchical structures had been well-established, and their use was thoroughly ingrained with the people over hundreds of years before the great migration eastward to the vast Pacific Ocean. Indeed, the family-centric sense of unity was integral to the culture and religion. An agricultural economic system had long been established and was practiced in the family-centric cultural model, a vital part of the amalgamation of customs and religious practices acquired from neighboring cultures and tribes. No further assignment of titles had been created at this period other than Paramount Chief. Other titles were a later refinement of the chiefdom protocol after settling the Pacific.

Fundamental to the Navigators' existing culture was a well-developed and much-practiced oral language, brought over with the people from the far Northwest. And this is the very essence of what W.H.R. Rivers was gravitating toward with his theory of kinship structures as a way to glue together the functions that drive an organization structure.[cciv] It is what the Navigators called Family-centric Culture. In this terminology, "genealogy" represents the bones (roots + genes) that are used to construct the architectural form and structure of the family organization, and thus the culture. We see that without this "genealogy system" there will be no construction materials to build the organization. Then the question remains, how does this type of elementary organization adopt changes, both on the immediate or short term and the long term.

Homeland: Price and Identity

In the words frequently cited by Samoan orators, *Ua lau i ula le vasa i Tamaali'i ma Tulatoa o le Atunu'u na saili malo au ni manu mo Samoa ma Manu'a*—"The mighty ocean is covered with precious fine mat carpets, with the pandanus leis of Warriors who have died in the course of conquering the mighty Pacific Ocean, during their adventurous journey to find new islands and explore fish migration paths for a better way of life."

Facing overwhelming odds against them—unforeseen difficulties and potential calamities, either from nature or the will of the gods—nothing could deter them from the quest to discover new islands for their colony and find a potential new home. The price paid for this "homeland" is... "priceless."

So, when Samoans and Manu'ans say, "A person, his or her self, is identified with family, village, district, country, and family land, all the way to the core of the earth," we can comprehend the profound clarity of this personal identification. Indeed, this might even give us an understanding of the geopolitical and internal conflicts in many countries, stemming from land and country identification—

For example, almost all of the Middle East nations, thanks to the Picot Agreement, were put together by "foreigners" without regards to ethnicity, national, geographical contours, culture, genealogy, history, and more; and we wonder why there is turmoil plaguing the region.

Taking a Global Perspective

A Biased History

The documented history of Samoa and Manu'a was originally undertaken by European missionaries around the beginning of the 19th century, during the second European Exploration and Colonization period. Their perspective was driven by a Christian message, with scientific (and social) observations having auxiliary importance. So now I can paint what they achieved with a large brushstroke: a "history," based on Christian dogma, that fast-forwards to the people's current abode, and continues to perpetuate the missionaries' insistent vantage point of Christian virtue, repentance and salvation... and "forget your ancient history because it's mythology." Thus, their interpretation of observations made on the oral history of Samoans and Manu'ans is inherently biased.

In our alternative approach, we can continue to chisel through the archaeological rocks, clear the overgrown vines of tropical rainforests, and seek on the bottom of the Pacific Ocean for the mosaic that lies underneath. This way, we may find handprints and footprints of the Navigators' ancestral "mystery" migration.

Despite the risk of overzealous credulity distorting their history, each time a scientific discovery is made relating to the Polynesian migration, the data points are mounting, and the true picture of the mosaic is getting more complete than ever before.

The Global Perspective

The view of local or regional issues, in isolation from neighbors, can now be supplemented with a global perspective, giving rise to recognition of the reality: that the world can be viewed as a series of "dots," representing the interconnectivity of one whole cohesive system. In an age of electronically driven information, this makes the world, metaphorically speaking, quite small. Meanwhile the journey that started with the beginning of man, follows through many different increments over time, and continues even today.

We have come to understand, thanks to the age of ubiquitous information, that human migration snakes through and across national and geographical boundaries, in "waves," at different times and in different environments, and, of course, under different circumstances.

Each wave of migration is marked, or identified, by remnants of its footprints and etched into memories of the distant past. Different processes cross national borders, continents, and geographical and oceanic locations, and are critical to our understanding of human migration. The diffusion of cultures and religious ideas, the spread of food products and livestock, the transmission of disease, the spread of economics and technology—all are integral to finding the mosaic image that reveals the ancient history of a people, country, and culture. For Manu'ans and Samoans, close examination of these processes will, I believe, yield even more colorful stones of the mosaic image of their ancient past.

The Personal Perspective

For me, this intriguing inquiry into actual discoveries, uncovering subsequent developments in culture and a complete way of life, has long been a lingering ache, an itching nerve.

The image of the mosaic, as fragmented as it seems, revealing the image of the Navigators' migration, appears even more complex and enigmatic than previously imagined. For truly, in the words of Thomas Mann, "Deep is the well of the past. Should we not call it bottomless? ... and the deeper we sound, the further... we probe and press, the more do we find that the earliest foundations of humanity, its history and culture, (genealogies and language) reveal themselves unfathomable."[ccv]

"The influence of cultural diffusion cannot be minimized," says Joseph Campbell. The imprints, whether "elementary, simple and basic" or at an "ethnic or cultural group" level, are fundamental to the human psyche. This idea was put forth by Adolf Bastian (1826-1905) back in 1868. It was elaborated upon by Carl Jung in his *Psychology of the Unconscious*, where he writes about the "personal unconscious and collective (cultural group) unconscious, also known as archetype," saying, "it exists in our dreams and images as (a prototype) in our creative unconscious mind, that eventually becomes the rapture in our imagination."[ccvi]

The discovery of the procedures and processes integral to the collective functioning of a community is borne from these imprints, both innate and environmental; it is "regressed," or stored and recalled over time. Thus Campbell concludes, as people continue to move and cross geographical boundaries, the processes, customs, and religious rituals become permanent in the culture. These imprints and mythologies continue to travel along with the people.[ccvii]

The real value of drawing parallels between specific cultural attributes, organizational structures, and mythologies is to emphasize the power of influence. The modern idea of adopting "best practices" is still in play, as people move and make contact with various ethnicities and cultures along their migration path. Thus, if a group can maximize the value of the individual and the community as whole, their influence will most likely be adopted.

This accumulated knowledge, acquired over time, provides an advantage. The learning process is reaffirmed, as well as the wisdom that will protect the individual and community throughout their long and difficult migration.

Semiotics

The study of how signs and symbols are used and interpreted

The Written Record

First Writing and the Bible

Just as there are few statues and monuments to reveal the history of Manu'ans and Samoans, so there is a lack of written records. The first "writing" arises with the original Samoan team of experts, who worked with the missionaries to translate the Bible into the Samoan language and had to use Greek (a Hellenic language), Latin, Aramaic, Hebrew and, of course, English versions of the Scriptures to derive the Samoan translation. They followed the historical sequence of Bible documentation. That is, they had to first understand the Aramaic and Classical Hebrew (an archaic form of the Hebrew language) version first, followed by Hebrew, then Greek, then Latin, and finally English.

Paramount Chief Fuimaono Na'oia covers the history of the Samoan Bible translation project as part of the history of the village of Avao, Savai'i, where a memorial church stands dedicated to the translation project. The project was led by Rev. George Pratt, Rev. Turner, and six Samoan Chiefs: Mala'itai Leuatea of Safune village, Leota Penitala of Avao, Talavou Malietoa of Sapapali'i, Va'aelua Pettaia of Lalomalava, Laupu'e Gagamalo of Samauga, Maiava of Sato'alepai village (all in Savai'i).[ccviii]

Using these profound original translations, as opposed to just the more modern English King James version, speaks to an iconic effort undertaken by these translators. It also illustrates the level of proficiency of these authors of the Samoan language, and it speaks to the richness of the language itself.

Bible Translation

When the first translation of the Holy Bible into the Samoan language began to roll off the archaic printing press in 1842-44, it represented a milestone in Samoan culture. The monumental efforts of the missionaries, Rev. Pratt and Rev. Turner, and six Samoan Chiefs, begun in 1838, marked a major paradigm shift in Samoan culture, a culture which had existed since the ancient ancestors colonized the island chain about 3,000 years before.

My main reason for mentioning this here is because, when we get into the Language section of this book, we will see there is already a "shadow reference point" lying in the distant future. Samoans and Manu'ans developed, maintained, and sustained their language orally over a very long period. But several of the language innovations, which we will discuss in detail later, would now facilitate the transition or transformation of oral culture into a written language, allowing a rapid completion of the Bible translation, which took only two and half years of actual time worked.

First Writing and Tattoos

In Dr. Krämer's *The Samoa Islands, Volume II*, under his discussion of "Tattoos and Bark Cloth designs," he makes some very important observations regarding Roman letters and markings made with spellings inverted.[ccix]

In particular he mentions names spelled out in Roman letters found on war clubs and barkcloth and tattooed on the bodies of men and women, specifically on their lower arms. Quite frequently, the names appear to be inverted. Thus one may read the word ELAV on someone's arm, i.e. VALE inverted with the "L" upside down, or, as Krämer found on a very beautiful barkcloth presented to him by Mata'afa Iosefa on his departure from Samoa, the long word *Fa'amamafana*, could be written completely in reverse. The words are not always inverted, but the practice is often repeated, leading Krämer to ask how this can be explained?

To answer, we need to refer back to the history of writing.

It is well-known, for instance, that the old Greek manner of writing developed from old Semitic forms, going from right to left as in old Semitic script, whereas Latin script goes from left to right. What if Samoan tattoos were done in the same right-left manner?

Naturally this does not have to apply to cursive script—the handwriting style of calligraphy—since, due to the missionaries, the Samoans learned to write exceptionally well in the Latin way, from left to right, using their right hands. (Semitic people, by contrast, decided to write their letters with their left hand.) But this could apply to capital letters or to block printing.

As Dr. Krämer points out, ancient people engraved their first inscriptions in stone, holding the chisel in their left hand and the hammer in their right hand. In the same way the Samoans, in tattooing, hold the instrument in their left hand and the mallet in their right hand. A written word would begin at the left of the line and proceed toward the right, simply because of the implements being used. But with different implements, writing from right to left, it would, for example, be more natural to extend the arm of an L toward the left, rather than toward the right, and to write the letter N with the slanted line in the opposite direction. It is interesting that the N and L of old Samoans is written, as in Old Semitic, in this "inverted" direction.

In writing from left to right, holding the pen like a schoolchild and working slowly, the downward lines (drawn toward the body) would be heavier than upward lines. This is a purely natural matter. But again, it is interesting that people who, a few years earlier, had no writing, would progress as did the ancient Greeks through such a logical sequence.

Krämer makes note of another unique phenomenon, which should be mentioned here, that Samoans prefer to look at pictures or photographs sideways or even fully upside down.

If this explanation for the inverted symbols is to be valid, it must have been at its most pronounced in written symbols of inverted writing of the Greek symbols, which is indeed the case.

A History of Semiotics

Signs and Marks

I have not found, nor heard of, any study of the Samoan Tatau in the area of "semiotic" science—a science which explores the study of signs and symbols, as a significant part of communication and, of course, linguistics.

So I ask, were the Navigators on the cusp of solidifying their own writing, or communication of messages, through their pictorial tattoo scripts?[ccx] Perhaps this was a pre-stage to the Rongorongo, the un-deciphered hieroglyphic tablets found at Easter Island.

The Greeks first coined the word sēmeiōtikos, meaning "observant of signs or mark."[ccxi] And historians have attributed early exploration of the relationship between signs and the world to Plato and Aristotle, first in the field of philosophy and later in psychology.

This field of "semiotics," the study of "signs and marks," began to flourish in the late 1600s when an English physician, writer and scholar, Henry Stubbe (1632–1676) first used the term in English to denote the branch of medical science relating to the interpretation of signs.[ccxii]

The illustrious philosopher John Locke used the term in his concluding edition of *An Essay Concerning Human Understanding* (1690), in which he explained semiotics as the "the doctrine of signs" to be observed and made understood, in diagnoses and in finding cures in medicine.[ccxiii]

The Rosetta Stone

Egyptian hieroglyphs were first deciphered in 1822, by a team of scientists led by the French Egyptologist, Jean Francois Champollion

(1790-1832). The Rosetta Stone, as it is known, contains the same information written in three languages, including Egyptian hieroglyphs and Greek text. Champollion discovered that the writing praised the good works of Pharaoh Ptolemy V, and that the stone itself was carved in 196 B.C., using a script made up of small pictures that were found originally in ancient Egypt for religious texts.[ccxiv]

The Triadic Approach

Charles Sanders Peirce (1839-1914), the world-renowned American philosopher, logician, and mathematician—called the "father of pragmatism"[ccxv]—picked up Locke's philosophical thread, and referred to semiotics as a "formal doctrine of signs," which abstracts how signs are used by an "intelligence capable of learning by experience," and provides a "philosophical logic pursued in terms of signs and sign processes." Charles Peirce's philosophical perspective on the study of semiotics revolves around the logic inherent in signs, relative to the respective messages conveyed by the object, as interpreted by the recipient—a "tri-relative" or triadic approach, involving sign, object and interpretant (immediate, dynamical, and normal), where all three are critical to the encoding, transporting, and decoding of messages.

Peirce's philosophical theory rests upon a logic whereby the object has an agreed-upon meaning, based on the immediate, dynamical, and normal interpretation of it, which is trusted by the recipients. To put it another way, this is a philosophy of simple tool designs and art patterns—for example, a house architecture made inherent in signs. The practical meaning and interpretation of the intended message is rather like the application of various traffic signs for prevention, detection, and correction of violations of traffic laws. That is, if you fail to obey the sign, and you are caught by law enforcement, you will be cited, and you will be punished by imposition of a fine or jail time—assuming you didn't get yourself killed by another vehicle. Philosophically and pragmatically, when applied to traffic signs, this is a system of controls to govern the liberty (well-being) of the population in the usage of public roads and freeways.

In the 1900s, according to Michael Caesar (1999), the Italian semiotician and novelist Umberto Eco (1932-2016) "proposed that every cultural phenomenon can be studied as communication" in the field of semiotic anthropology.[ccxvi]

Semiotics Today

Computer "Messages"

The Internet has ushered in the revitalization of sign usage, with "icons" used to convey message instructions to the reader. Thanks to Steve Jobs, innovations in color graphics together with pictures and numerous icons—and the use of the mouse on his Apple Macintosh computer—have forever changed the science of designing software and hardware. Use of signs has mushroomed across web application development, generating colorful and intuitive graphical user interfaces. All of this reaffirms the idea that humanity's understanding of signs preceded the development of the vocal cord—i.e. preceded the creation of sounds that represent the observed sign, as observed by Daniel Everett in *How Language Began* (2017).[ccxvii]

Tatau "Messages"

As mentioned above, the field of reading and interpreting signs, marks, and pictures as they relate to human communication has long been a subject of erudite scholastic debate. So following up on Dr. Krämer's philosophical thought process—that the Samoan tattoo or tatau has cultural messages that are communicated through its detailed design and patterns—seems more relevant and possible today, given the abundance of information available on the Internet. The detailed analysis and documentation undertaken by Dr. Krämer in his *The Samoa Islands, Volume II* gives evidence of his probing into the possibility of the tatau's standard designs and patterns being cultural "symbols" and "semiotic" messages, being passed down from ancient ancestors.

The usage of animal shapes (such as birds and centipedes) and objects (such as the architectural beams of houses), together with patterns whose designs memorialize the cultural history and journey, drives the "cultural semiotics" perspective, as opposed to the "linguistics viewpoint" of language. These are not letter "symbols," but rather "pictorials" depicting the objects themselves.

The Navigators' legends and mythology are corroborated and memorialized by the tatau fabric, which reminds them of events from their ancient history, as depicted in the tatau mythology. The tatau design is "fixed," meaning it has never changed since the mythology of its importation by the "twins, Taema and Tilafaiga" around the 12th century. By sacred decree it is "tapu" to make any change to the tatau's design and ceremonial protocol.

Spoken Language

The French writer, Charles de Brosses (1709-1777), author of *Histoire des Navigations*, coined the words "Polynesia" (in 1756) and "Australaise." His writing[ccxviii] provides a materialistic theory of the origin and evolution of language, where the meaning of words is considered as an image of the physiological articulation of sounds (the Sound Symbolism field).[ccxix]

In his Reith Lectures in 2000, Vilayanur S. Ramachandran describes research into the links between brain structure and function, where his theory "may explain how humans create metaphors and how sounds can be a metaphor for images."

Everything about the Orators' oration is focused on the poetic construction of speech. The words are borrowed from mythology and folklore's proverbial phrases. The emphasis is on eloquence and the usage of an ancient lexicon, from which ancient historical events perpetuate the language and thus the culture. The obsessive usage of metaphors arises because metaphors represent the parallelism of images of historical events.

This is not how primitive, ancient, and isolated people use language, but rather it represents the process of evolutionary development in all aspects of culture and language, the same across every culture and society around the world. The Navigators are no different. Hence, the orators' oration begs for more in depth examination.

Unchanging, by Decree

The decree to the Su'a Family clan, as custodian of the Tatau design, its implements, and its construction, has been etched into the fabric of the ancient history of Samoan and Manu'an cultures. These are heirloom assets of the culture, which have withstood the test of time, avoiding any temptation to change in almost 1,000 years. This shows the resiliency of the people, to so uphold their cultural identity.

The message to the Su'a Family clan is not to commoditize or sell sacred assets that are a property of the culture and Samoa. For there are only few families in all of Samoa and Manu'a that were decreed with the country's cultural heirlooms, as single custodians of such a gift. This is the case with the Su'a family and the Tatau (its architecture, design, and production).

Similarly, Pili and his wife Sinaletava'e gifted the seed-planting stick to Tua (the founder of Atua) to farm with and feed the county; the war club to Ana (the founder of A'ana) to fight with and protect the country; and the Orator staff and scepter to Saga (the founder of Tuamasaga) to orate the language for the culture. And so the Su'a family was given the Tatau to clothe the country.[ccxx]

Thus, the Orator staff and scepter have been decreed to our Tuamasaga district and, since Orator Chiefs Fata and Maulolo are the Elder Orator Chiefs of the district, we guard this sacred gift with utmost care.

We have always viewed the gift of oration as being vested in our village Orator tongue. Hence the reminder to the custodian of our Tatau, because of what it represents: culture, art, clothing, hieroglyphs, language, communication, technology, history, chronology, genealogy, architectural blueprints for vessels, houses, and tools etc. It's the whole Culture of our Country.

Linguistics

The study of languages and how they evolve

Why Language is Important

Language as Identity

The most important gift from the gods is language or rhetoric, says the Greek philosopher Plato, and it turns out also to be the "greatest weapon" ever gifted to man. It is used to secure food, protect and defend the family and homeland, conquer new land and people, proselytize with a gospel or cultural belief (Hellenic, Christianity and other religions), build empires, and identify or brand a race.

Language gives identity to a group of people or race. It encourages separatism and isolationism. It promotes dependence on the group as a unit, or on ethnicity and community. It encourages avoidance of interaction or mixing with other groups or ethnicities. It guards against invasion from alien people.

Because of language, reclusive isolationist behavior tends to grow in a developing society if it is not infused with new "blood" or ideas. In a closed society, language development is internally dependent, thus limiting the creative process and stifling growth. This is the opposite of the rule that too much of anything can paralyze growth.

This need for communities to have their own identities led to the development of over 6,500 languages spoken around the world, though many of these have only a small number of speakers. It is said, for example, that on the Island of Papua New Guinea it is not unusual to have several spoken languages (sometimes more than 5) within a radius of less than five miles. Compare that to the Mandarin Chinese language that is spoken by over a billion people.

The need to be different and separate is a human tribal phenomenon. As the world becomes more closely integrated—in trade, communication and travel—languages begin to gravitate toward merging with competing languages, until eventually we may have fewer than 10 languages spoken around the globe—which has huge implications for the future of self-identity of races (or of ethnic groups), and for the erosion of national "brands." But, while this phenomenon persists, there remain many small, isolated ethnic groups who are rekindling the fire, revitalizing their respective languages—for example, Hawaiians, many tribes of American Indians, indigenous tribes of Taiwan, and others around the world.

The more we want to be different, the more we find commonality with everyone else. And so with the Samoans; the more they think they are different from other Polynesians, the more they discover they are of the same stock.

Words as Character

Words... once spoken, they set expectations about the actions induced by the message(s) they proclaim. Words originate from thoughts. They represent images and symbols of objects and actions which together form message(s). These messages, once breathed out of human lungs—through the larynx (or vocal cords), through the trachea (or windpipe), and through bronchial tubes—are encoded by the senders (speakers) and decoded by the recipients. Words set up a series of action steps dictated by their message. So they set expectations for action or response. When action is taken, this produces results. And, depending on the results, words turn into a practice. Depending on the quality of the practice, it might become a habit. A habit becomes part of your character. Your character defines you and your destiny. And so the words you used and heard have determined your identity.

The Origin of Language

The Bible's account of the story of the Tower of Babel, in Genesis 11:1-9, says that the Lord recognized that the tower was being built so humans might make a name for themselves, and so that they wouldn't be scattered over the face of the earth, since at that time the people all spoke one language. And the Lord came down and saw that if they could do this, when speaking in one language, nothing would be impossible for the people to do. So the Lord said, "Come, let us go down and confuse their language there, so that they will not understand one another's speech."

Depending on your religious belief, this incredible account becomes the "primary motive" for the chorus of linguists and anthropologists seeking the origin of man and his language. A consensus within the above disciplines agrees that language was, and still is, the most effective and powerful weapon or tool man has created, to facilitate human beings' development and migration around the world.

The creation of an idea in the "pineal gland" of the human brain, and the transformation of the idea into guttural and sibilant sounds in the vocal cords, forming an "interjection" that can be understood by a mate or family member and deciphered as a message, is an incredible step in human development. The process of creating and encoding a message, in a language that can be decoded and comprehend by a receiver, is the birth of human speech.

Plato's "gift of the gods" is not wasted, for language was decreed to the oracle, and subsequently passed down to the orators, and studied in Rhetoric and Philosophy by the Greeks.

It is not known whether language originates in the respiratory control of air flow in and out of the lungs, passing through vibrations in the larynx or voice box, and on to the tongue, lips and the rest of the vocal organs, or, as Charles Darwin speculated, it begins in signs and gestures. In 1871, Darwin wrote: "I cannot doubt that language owes its origin to the imitation and modification, aided by signs and gestures, of various natural sounds, the voices of other animals, and man's own instinctive cries."[ccxxi]

Symbol and Grammar

Dr. Dan Everett, author of *Dark Matter of the Mind* and *How Language Began*, explained that language, in its fundamental definition, is composed of "symbols and grammar." Dr. Everett summarizes this as follows, writing that "signs" are divided into three categories:

- Index: in the same way as "smoke" is an index for fire-related messages.
- Icon: where the symbol is associated with a specific meaning, such as a piece of art or a deity.
- And symbol: for example, where a shovel indicates digging the earth.[ccxxii]

Everett goes on to define grammar, initially, as the arrangement of very simple sounds with words in a linear fashion. At a time before the verb and noun were differentiated, the simple sentence might be something like "go I."

A second level of grammar came into being through the development of inflections of linear grammar, so a sentence has more words, and their order implies their specific meaning.

Vibration and Sound

As the old Samoan belief says, the Spirit Wind gave birth to a vibration and a discernable sound.

We learn from a basic introduction to music theory—or, for example, from a course on Harvard and MIT's edX—that sounds originate from vibrations. The speed of the vibration creates the pitch. An unchanging pitch produces a continues humming (a traveling longitudinal wave). The wavelength and the speed of the sound wave determine the frequency of the sound, recognized as the "note" being played or heard. Frequency measures the sound in terms of the sound wave, and pitch describes low or high sounds as they are heard. Thus frequency and pitch describe the same thing from different points of view. Frequency (pitch) is determined by the speed (of sound) divided by the wavelength.

A continues humming sound, or a sound with constant pitch, evokes a companion spiritual message. These "soundbites" are the foundation of music, prosody, poetry, and rhetoric in human language development, in any ancient culture. Prosody describes those elements of speech that are not individual phonetic segments—not vowels and consonants. Prosody looks at syllables and linguistic functionality—for example, intonation, tone, stress, and rhythm.[ccxxiii]

Music and Sound

So... is music foundational to speech and therefore to the development of language? I believe it is. I believe this is the source of differences in musical orchestration in different cultures or native tongues, paralleling the differences in native languages. Thus sounds precede the development of monosyllabic language.

The Western world is only schooled in mathematically based music—that is, the so-called "modern" music, which is composed using mathematical note- or pitch-arrangements. This is the reason why the Western world often fails to have a greater appreciation of many different forms of indigenous music. But we have always accepted that sound pitch conveys messages. It could be a sound of fear, or some other sound that is recognized because you have a message to convey. Music, therefore, carries messages, making it more than entertainment therapy; it encapsulates wellness in living.

The Indian sage, Panini, was an ancient Sanskrit philologist and grammarian in the 4th century B.C. He said—referring to the continuous "hummm"—that it is the first spoken sound in the Rig Veda language, and so in the Religious Hymns.[ccxxiv]

Speech and Linguistics

The origin of speech and language has been a subject of controversy and constant debate since the Classical period when Aristotle wrote his treatise *On Rhetoric*, dating from the 4th century B.C.[ccxxv] This was a time when orators had not paid much attention to voice, considering it a subject only of concern to actors and poets.

Aristotle defined voice control (volume, rate, pitch, and prosody) as critical to conveying messages to be clearly understood by the recipients. However, he did not go into how to produce specific voice, or tone, in one's voice, which may perhaps indicate a mild disdain for the topic as a whole.[ccxxvi]

Much has changed in this area of speech- and linguistics-studies. Modern scholars have explored voice more extensively. And linguistics has been enjoying a rather productive era of remarkable grammatical tradition in India and Greece, under the heading of rhetoric and philosophy.

The beginning of the 19th century ushered in the modern era of the study of linguistics. The discovery of the notion that languages have a common ancestor, and therefore the need to trace the origin of these languages to their common ancestors, led to reconfirming the path of human migration across the globe. This naturally led to the usage of "comparative methodology" to define and ascertain ancestor relationships of languages.

And this, of course, provides more evidence for the Navigators' origin and migration path.

Language Categories:
Malay / Polynesian / Austronesian

Migration and Language

The exhaustive work of the Indian grammarian, the sage Panini, in analyzing and dissecting Sanskrit language and grammar, around the 4th Century B.C., became a catalyst for a whole new field of research into the origin of language and comparative linguistics, as it relates to tracing human migration. Frits Staal, department founder and Emeritus Professor of Philosophy and South/Southeast Asian Studies at the University of California, Berkeley, documents that Panini's theory of morphological analysis (the structure of words, including phonetics and phonology) was more advanced than any equivalent Western theory before the mid-20th century. And indeed, Panini's analysis of noun compounds still forms the basis of modern linguistic theories of compounding, all which have borrowed Sanskrit terms.[ccxxvii]

Franz Bopp (1791-1867) took up the cause in the early 1800s, focusing his work on comparative linguistics of Indo-European (Aryan) languages. His comprehensive coverage includes the classification of the Austronesian Oceanic language family, in which he further includes the Malay/ Polynesian language category in 1841.

Languages of the Pacific

Prior to Franz Bopp, in 1834, the British historian and linguist William Marsden was able to speak of languages, such as Malagasy, as "Hither" Polynesian, and of the languages of the central and eastern Pacific as "Further" Polynesian.

It should be noted that the earliest European documents on languages of the Austronesian family are two short vocabularies collected by Antonio Pigafetta, the Italian chronicler of the Magellan expedition of 1519-22. He notes that the Dutch ships, bound for the islands of Southeast Asia, stopped to restock in Madagascar—a contact that resulted in his almost immediate recognition of the relationship between Malagasy and Malay, soon after the first expedition reached Indonesia in 1596.[ccxxviii]

During the 17th century, the Dutch—in Indonesia and Taiwan—and the Spanish—in the Philippines and Guam—compiled the first substantial descriptions of the Austronesian languages. Then, by the beginning of the 18th century, the Dutch scholar Adriaan Reland was able to suggest an eastern extension of Malay-like languages into the western Pacific.

James Cook's observations, made during his three voyages from 1768 to 1780, show the similarity of Polynesian languages to one another, and likewise their similarity to Malay. This became the widely accepted belief: it is where William Marsden picked up the theme of language similarity between Polynesian and Malay, leading Wilhelm von Humboldt to coin the name Malay-Polynesian. But it was Franz Bopp who published the ideas in 1841.

This milestone, in classifying the Polynesian language together with the Malayan language, had a profound impact, misguiding all subsequent studies of the Polynesian language, and fixing a false belief in Malayan origin. The frequent error, made by early linguistic experts, was the assumption that the higher the number of words common to both languages in spelling (approximation) and meaning, the firmer would be the confirmation of the hypothesis that the Malayan language is the foundation for the Polynesian language. This belief existed for centuries, and it was commonly held by the lay population.

The fact is, as some seers have argued, that the existence of words with a common spelling and meaning does *not* confirm the origin and age of both languages. The origin must be traced to the lexicon and grammatical root stock for each language, and then compared to see if both versions share a common origin in the archaeological timelines of the people's existence, as argued by Fornander, Humboldt, and Gaussin.

It was Robert Codrington, a leading English scholar of the languages of Melanesia, who objected vehemently to the designation of Malayo-Polynesian, on the grounds that it excludes the darker-skinned peoples of Melanesia. He referred instead to the "Ocean" family of languages. And in 1906, the Austrian anthropologist and linguist Wilhelm Schmidt proposed that the Munda languages of eastern India and the Mon-Khmer languages of mainland Southeast Asia might form a language family, which he christened Austroasiatic (meaning "southern Asian") and later coined as "Austronesian." This designation was purely based on similarities in verbal affixes, with nothing about grammar and structure. This was the beginning of the Austronesian language as a major language family in the world, and of the Malay-Polynesian family as its subgroup.

So, the Austronesian language family is an amalgamation of the numerous languages spoken by different indigenous populations of countries and islands in the Asiatic Archipelago. It consists of 1,200 languages, spoken by 350 million people in Southeast Asia.

The major Austronesian languages, with the highest number of speakers, are Malay (Indonesian and Malaysian), Javanese, and Filipino (Tagalog).

Language History

Panini's illustrious foundational work, in delineating the structure of Sanskrit grammar and phonemes, has influenced the study of modern linguistics—the study of grammar, root, lexicon, phonemes, and governing rules-structure of Indo-European languages.

Historians believe that Panini did not use writing to conduct and document his analysis and rules construction, but rather relied on his students to memorize them. It wasn't until the beginning of the 19th century that modern linguists focused on Panini's work. Franz Bopp (1791-1867)—a German linguist and professor of Oriental literature and general philology at the University of Berlin—is credited with establishing the importance of Sanskrit in the comparative study of Indo-European languages. And later, Ferdinand de Saussure (1857-1913)—Professor of Sanskrit at the University of Geneva (1891) and widely known as the father of structural linguistics in modern European languages—and Charles Sanders Pierce became the major fathers of semiotics and semiology.[ccxxix]

Professor Ferdinand de Saussure came up with a proposed set of rules of language in 1894, which was further developed by Noam Chomsky in 1957. However, it is the work of Franz Bopp that we are interested in here, because of his pioneering work on the languages of Far East Asia and Southeast Asia, which include what is now called Austronesian.

Austronesian Languages

The Mis-Classification of Austronesian Languages

Bopp's comparative language analysis of Oceanic in general, and Malay/Polynesian in particular—comparing their language structure and development to that of the Proto-Indo-European languages—laid the foundation for the mis-classification of the Polynesian language as a "child" of Malay.

The approach and rules Professor Bopp used, to derive this conclusion, were based on comparison of similar words, grammar, and roots to old Sanskrit, comparing them to the new Sanskrit language and to the Indo-European languages.[ccxxx]

It is widely recognized that the sage Panini's lifework defines the beginning of Classical Sanskrit around 300 B.C., at the end of the period of Old Vedic Sanskrit. Linguistic historians have now agreed that Old Vedic is a language of hymns or "sound humming." This was practiced by the priests and close custodians of the religion. So, before sound could be converted into scripts, the message content must have been clearly understood by the priests.

It is now estimated that Old Vedic is foundational to Proto-Indo-Aryan (2,000 B.C.), which is borne out of the Proto-European language. Proto simply means what came before it; the languages themselves are unknown. We cannot substantiate exactly what language existed prior to the European language family, so we call it Proto-Indo-European. Likewise, Proto-Sanskrit, Proto-Chinese or Proto-Sino-Tibetan, Proto-Austronesian, Proto-Oceanic, Proto-Formosan, and Proto-Malayan are language names indicating that we do not know all the details of the language that came before.

So what language came before Austronesian? The answer is we do not know. Could it be derived from Proto-Chinese or Proto-European, or maybe Proto-Rig Vedas, or, perhaps, Proto-Tamil? While the major language family of Austronesian encompasses many diverse indigenous people, the yearning to find one's language heritage, and thus identity, is compelling. But the fact that there are many similarities in the indigenous languages of these diverse people, in this vast geographical area, does not necessarily mean they are kin. And so, the search for one's origin goes on.

We now know that Austronesian came out of China (the Asian continent) around 5,000 B.C., with other, more ancient civilization layers dating back even further into Taiwan, its peninsula, and surrounding islands such as Formosa. This means the Austronesians arrived in Taiwan and Southeast Asia before the period of the Rig Vedas, and surely before Classical Sanskrit around 300 B.C. This puts it in the time-period of the Proto-Rig Vedic and Proto-European languages; also, of course, there is the Proto-Dravidian-Tamil language.

Based on comparative linguistic methodology, the Austronesian language family has been established on the basis of cognate sets— meaning sets of words which are similar in sound and meaning, which can be shown to have descended from the same ancestral word in Proto-Austronesian, according to regular rules.

The internal structure of the Austronesian language family is complex. It consists of many similar and closely related languages, with large numbers of dialect continuums, or dialect chains, which spread across geographical areas in such a way that neighboring language varieties differ only slightly. The differences accumulate over distance, so widely separated variations on the language are not mutually intelligible.

According to Dyen's classification model,[ccxxxi] the greatest genealogical diversity is found among the Formosan languages of Taiwan, and the least diversity among the islands of the Pacific. This classification appears to support the dispersal of the language family from Taiwan or China.

Further Mis-Classification of Austronesian Languages

This is a good staging point for the framework of Judge Fornander's passion, but his is a faint voice, coming from 60 million square miles of Ocean far, far away. His passion led him to write a two-volume set of books on the Origin of the Hawaiians and Polynesians—*An Account of the Polynesian Race, its Origin and Migrations, and the Ancient History of the Hawaiian People to the Times of Kamehameha I.*

The importance of noting the difference between old and new Sanskrit is that Vedic Sanskrit turns out to be a much closer relative of the original Proto-Aryan language, borne from the "starburst" of Proto-Indo-European languages, such as Greek, Latin, Germanic, etc.[ccxxxii] This generational difference is crucial in tracing back the ancestral origin of the Polynesian language.

So, returning to Professor Bopp's foundational work, it was really Wilhelm von Humboldt, the Prussian philosopher, diplomat, and linguist, who first "established on an impregnable basis the fundamental relationship between the Malagasy, East Indian, and Polynesian groups of languages, to which we can now add Micronesian," as W.D. Alexander says in his preface to Fornander's *Account of the Polynesian Race: Comparative vocabulary* book.[ccxxxiii] In this book, the Honorable Judge Fornander tells us Humboldt observed that a large class of Sanskrit words existing in the Malay area—used by Javanese and the Bughis—was lacking in other languages of this stock. Humboldt concluded that these words must have been introduced to the Malay language after Malagasy and Polynesian separated from other branches of the Oceanic language family. These words were determined to be "pure and genuine" Sanskrit, arriving before the Malay language became corrupted with other languages (such as Polynesian originally, and much later by Arabic).

Judge Fornander cited the Rev. Archibald Henry Sayce (1846-1933), a pioneering British Assyriologist and Linguist from the University of Oxford, saying, "But it is to the period of Aryan speech, when... 'the cases were not as yet sharply defined,' and... when the relations of nouns were indifferently expressed by prefixes or suffixes, when people said 'love-I,' instead of I love, *ama-yo*, contracted *amo*, 'speak-I,' etc., as Polynesians express themselves to this day: *lofa-a'u*, 'love-I,' *fai-a'u*, 'say-I,' *fai-oe*, 'say you.'"

Fornander continued building the case to delineate the Polynesian language from the Malay. The death of ancient Sanskrit in 300 B.C.—according to the Sanskrit scholars Bopp, Humboldt, and Gaussin—occurred right around the time of the flowering of the Indian civilization of Java. But there is no evidence of a relationship between Javanese and pre-Classical Sanskrit Polynesian.

W. D. Alexander and Judge Fornander both point out that Javanese "mythology and decorations of its magnificent temples"—both proof of its great antiquity—show no trace of Polynesian. This signifies that the

Javanese arrived after the Polynesians had emigrated further northeast of the Indonesian Archipelago.

Aside from the late infusion of Sanskrit words into the Malay language, Humboldt did also identify a second class of Sanskrit words that extends to "remote dialects" such as Tagala, Malagasy and Polynesian. He attributed this wide diffusion of words to an older form of Sanskrit, or a "pre-Sanskrit-Vedic" or Proto-Sanskrit-Vedic language.

It is at this juncture, according to Judge Fornander, that Professor Bopp took the initiative in postulating that the Polynesian language "is but the degraded remains of a once highly organized language like Sanskrit." At the same time, he made a similar comparison with modern languages in Southern Europe that grew up out of the ruins of the Latin language, whose grammatical structure had crumbled to pieces; so, likewise, he said, this great family language "had arisen out of the wreck of the Sanskrit."

Fornander, observing Bopp's analysis, records that Bopp further stated that the dissolution of Sanskrit into the Oceanic family of languages was more thorough than its Latin counterpart, in that Latin's daughters, while preserving much of the old system of conjugation, had only completely abandoned the treatment of nouns. These Oceanic dialects, according to Bopp, "had entirely forsaken the path in which its Sanskrit mother moved; they have taken off the old garment and put on a new one, or appear, as in the Islands of the Pacific, in complete nudity." This observation well occupied Judge Fornander's sedulous legal mind, leading the Polynesian language expert to argue the contrary; that the Polynesian language had not "forsaken the old garment" after its separation from the mother language, whether it be the Proto-Aryan language or some other proto-ancestral language.

Re-Classifying the Polynesian Language

W.D. Alexander (in his preface) cites the observation of M. Gaussin, saying the renowned linguist "has clearly shown from internal evidence the extremely primitive character of the Polynesian language," in that its words "express sensations or images, while most abstract terms are wanting," adding that "he demonstrates the primitive character of its grammar, and proves that some of the formative particles have even yet hardly ceased to be independent words."[ccxxxiv] For example the Samoan directive particles—*mai, atu, ane, ifo, a'e, ese*—versus particles denoting tenses—*e, te, ua, sa, na, o.*

Alexander continues: "Everything about this language shows that it is in its childhood, so to speak, and that instead of having lost its inflections, it has never had any to lose. Having been at a very early period separated from the rest of the human race, destitute of metals or beasts of burden, and deprived of nearly all the materials and incentives which develop civilization, the Polynesians seem to have remained nearly stationary, and their language to be still in its infancy as regards to its degree of development."

We should note, the language would have separated, as we've seen earlier, when the people crossed the Wallace Line, which was originally dated around 2,000 B.C. but is now re-dated to 4,000-6,000 B.C.

Foundation of Vowel Variation

The sage Panini, studying and formalizing the grammar of ancient Sanskrit, wrote a sutra-style treatise containing "verse" or rules on linguistics, syntax, and semantics. His first two sutras were as follows:

1. vrddhir adaiC
2. adeN gunah

In these sutras, the capital letters are special "meta-linguistic" symbols, called IT markers. In the two sutras above, the C and N denote lists of phonemes, (ai, au) and (e, o) respectively. Technically, both sutras should be written with the technical term (vrddhir and gunah) at the end, but vrddhir means "prosperity" in its non-technical usage, so placing it at the beginning offers "good luck."

Thus the two sutras each consist of a list of phonemes, and a technical term. Their final (linguistic) interpretation states that:

1. The phonemes (a, ai, au) are called vrddhir (which mean "growth" in Sanskrit), making them correspond to lengthened Indo-European "ablaut grades," while
2. (a, e, o) are called guna (which means "string, thread or strand," or "excellence, merit, or virtue," or "quality, peculiarity, attribute, or property" in Sanskrit), making them correspond to full Indo-European "ablaut grades."

In these definitions, "ablaut grades" are regular vowel variations. At its simplest, one might think of lengthened grades as corresponding to long vowel sounds, and full grades to short vowel sounds.

These terminologies, as we shall see, are fundamental to the foundation of vowel variations across the Austronesian language family. Sanskrit may not be the origin of the language development, because of the timeline difference whereby Austronesian may very well be much older than Sanskrit, but Sanskrit might be foundational to understanding the evolutionary development of Proto-Indo-European and the Proto-Austronesian language family.[ccxxxv]

Survival of the Primeval

Judge Fornander took up the thesis, put forward by Professor Sayce, that the natural stages of development growth in a language are monosyllabic and disyllabic, followed by agglutinative, analytic (isolated) and then, finally, inflected systems of grammar. Agglutinative refers to the gluing together of words or affixes, and inflection refers to the modification of a word to express different grammatical categories, such as tense, person, gender, mood, or meaning.

Sayce concluded that a supposed ancestor of the Proto-Aryan languages must have gone through these stages in its grammatical development, "much like the Polynesian or Austronesian of today."

Alexander writes: "It was at that distant period 'in the night of the time' that the ancestors of the Oceanic race separated from the Aryan stock, somewhere in central Asia." And Fornander pointed out the parallel between this separation and that of Iceland, where "the old Norse tongue has been preserved with little change." In the same way, according to this point of view, "the Oceanic languages have remained in a state of arrested development as a survival of the primeval language of Aryans; as, in fact, a 'living specimen' of that ancient form of speech."[ccxxxvi]

I was particularly intrigued with Judge Fornander's passionate work, because of his considerable knowledge of the Polynesian language and of the overall field of linguistics, an area he frequently comments on with reference to his contemporaries (Bopp, Sayce, and others).

Tracing the Language Path

Quenching the thirst of curiosity will lead to the "well of the ancient past," says Thomas Mann, for there we will find water.

My quest to trace the origin of the Polynesian language stems from the fact that I have been led, ever since I can remember, to believe that the Polynesian language originated from the Malayan language. But when I began to research the foundation of this claim, I immediately found out that the majority of the literature points to a group of Polynesian islands (Samoa, Tonga, and others in this cradle area of Polynesia) as the origin of the Polynesian language.

There is a language family, in the classification of languages, called Austronesian. This is widely dispersed throughout maritime Southeast Asia, in places such as Madagascar and other islands of the Pacific Ocean, together with a few members in continental Asia. Austronesian languages are spoken by about 360 million people, making this the fifth-largest language family in the world, measured by number of speakers—standing behind only the Indo-European languages, the Sino-Tibetan languages, the Niger-Congo languages, and the Afro-Asiatic languages.

The Malayo/Polynesian classification includes the Polynesian, Melanesian, and Micronesian languages, with further subdivisions for:

- the Admiralty Islands (Yapese)
- the St Matthias Islands (Western Oceanic, Temotu)
- and Central-Eastern Pacific—the Southeast Solomons (Southern Oceanic, Micronesian and Fijian-Polynesian)[ccxxxvii]

One can see the challenge of tracing a single thread back to its origin, in the multi-colored fabric of this language family. But tracing this thread will further reveal the origin and path of the Navigators' migration

The Polynesian Language

Current Research into the Polynesian Language

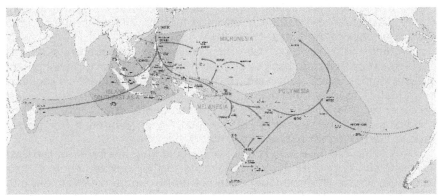

Figure 10 Chronological dispersal of Austronesian people across the Pacific (per Benton et al, 2012, adapted from Bellwood, 2011) [ccxxxviii]

Current research into the Polynesian language focusses, for the most part, on the historical development of the language after the Polynesians arrived in the South Pacific Ocean in 2000 B.C., and during the subsequent eastward expansion to other islands of the Pacific around 1000 B.C. These research initiatives are based on the assumption that the linguistic classification of the Polynesian language has already been made, placing it under the umbrella of Austronesian. This classification was initially postulated by Professor Bopp, the distinguished Indo-Europeanist, back in the first half of the 19th Century.

It was Professor Bopp who coined the "Malayo-Polynesian" classification—initially identified by that illustrious linguist, Wilhelm von Humboldt (1767-1835) as "malayisch"—to describe the relationship between Indo-European and Austronesian. This was further taken up by Otto Dempwolff, a German linguist and anthropologist (1871-1938), who extensively explored Austronesian using "comparative" methods. Another German linguist, anthropologist, and Roman Catholic priest, Wilhelm

Schmidt (1868-1954), coined the German word "austronesisch"—which comes from the Latin *austere*, meaning "south wind," plus the Greek *nesos*, meaning "island." The name Austronesian was formed from the same roots.[ccxxxix]

While many modern linguists have taken up the challenge to examine how the various language families and subfamilies are related to each other, and to study their development cycles using comparative methods, very little effort is devoted to discovering where each family originated. The Austronesian languages all appear to originate in the Asiatic Archipelago and in the indigenous language of Taiwan. Many references, regarding mainland Asia and the Levant as language influences on Austronesian, point to Sanskrit and Arabic. These two languages are more dominant in the Malay and other sub-families in the Asiatic Archipelago. But this is not the case with the Polynesian language.

There are remnants of Malay in the Samoan lexicon, but these do not give a definitive determination of whether Malay initially adopted Polynesian words, adding either Sanskrit and or Arabic corruptions to them, or whether Polynesian adopted Malay words. Hence that echo from a faint distance in the chronicle authored by Hon. Judge Abraham Stoke Fornander back in the late 19th Century.

Arguing vehemently that the Polynesian language still has characteristics that date back to antiquity—back to the early development of the Indo-Aryan language family—Judge Fornander's sedulous investigation reveals evidence of the Polynesian language being the last specimen of a language in its early developmental stage—the only one remaining since the separation of the Indo-Aryan (European) languages such as Germanic, Romantic, Latin, etc.

This being the case, the Polynesians would have migrated to the East Pacific Ocean and settled with little to no further development of their language. That is, their language did not go through a development into an "inflectional" or "synthetic" stage, but rather it stayed, from its earliest days, "agglutinative" or "analytic," as it is today.

Can a Language Determine the Ancestral Origin of a Race?

The question is: Can a language determine the ancestry and origin of a race?

Does an abundance of words with exact or similar spelling and meaning, between two different languages, constitute a kindred relationship between the two languages and the people speaking them? Or does it arise purely from coincidence, with words acquired through neighborly influence?

To echo Judge Fornander: It takes more than a language's origin to determine the ancestry of a race. Theories must be corroborated with geological evidence, with ethnological comparison, and finally—to quote the old saying "blood will tell"—with DNA. But my interest, in tracing the origin of the Polynesian language, is to corroborate the evidence as to where the people came from when they ultimately discovered and colonized these islands in the Pacific Ocean. Where did they begin their intrepid migration? Knowing this would illuminate their migration path and the timeline of their journey. It would help us to dig down further to the depths of the "well of the past" to understand their ancient ancestry. It would allow us to unravel the mystery of their survival in isolation.

Professor Bopp's famous monographs on the relationship of Malayo-Polynesian with the Indo-European languages, and later the Caucasian languages, were published in 1840 and 1846. But, according to the collective view of some of the leading philologists and linguists of the time—such as Professor W.D. Whitney, 1870; Professor A.H. Sayce, 1880; and Professor B. Delbruck, 1880—"the impetus of his genius led him to the wrong track."[ccxl] The most salient criticism of Bopp's proposition, rendered by these savants, is that the procedure of comparing "roots" of words, in both the Malay and Polynesian languages, to roots, in the Caucasian or old Indo-European languages, was not an accepted methodology of comparative linguistics at the time.

Fornander continues, pointing out that the presumption that Malayo-Polynesian represented a backward leap from the Indo-European languages was surely premature, without first determining what the parental and kindred relationships might be between Malayo-Polynesian and the Aryan languages such as old Sanskrit or Vedic.[ccxli] And several critics of Professor Bopp—for example Sayce, Fornander, and Whitney—suggest he was not sufficiently proficient in Sanskrit, Malay, and the Polynesian languages to effectively perform such analysis and derive his subsequent conclusion.

While Bopp's proposition stirred up debate on comparative linguistics and language family classifications, leading to the Austronesian language family, it was his core objective of fixing the origin of the Polynesian language to the Indo-European language which led him to conclude, erroneously, that Polynesian is a "child" of the Malay language; hence the coining of the phrase "Malayo-Polynesian" which became a catalyst to other savants in the field, seeking to pursue the origin of the Polynesian language.

Judge Abraham Stoke Fornander:
An account of the Polynesian Language

Judge Abraham Stoke Fornander (1812-1887), of the Island of Kauai, was a Swedish-born immigrant, arriving in 1844. He was schooled in a Swedish Gymnasium—a school where gifted students studied languages and the Greek classics. He swore allegiance to King Kamehameha III and became a citizen of Hawaii in 1847. During his 43 years of service to the Island Kingdom, he became an important Hawaiian journalist, a judge, and an ethnologist. He married a native Hawaiian princess of royal genealogy and became fluent in the Hawaiian language, becoming the

Island Kingdom's most erudite expert in Polynesian legends and history. His book *An Account of the Polynesian Race, Its Origins and Migrations and Comparative Vocabulary of Polynesian and Indo-European Languages*, published in 1884, was a direct attempt to advance from Professor Bopp's proposition with added vigor and factual evidence.

Judge Fornander's assiduous comparative analysis of word roots and his refocusing the issue on determining the ancestral relationship between the Malay and Polynesian languages, rather than comparing the language to Vedic-Sanskrit and Classical Sanskrit, is compelling. As Hon. Judge Fornander pointed out, Professor Bopp's error is not in his methodology, as his critics vehemently claimed, but rather in the fundamental assumption he made—because it was widely accepted at that time that "the Polynesians were the descendants, the degenerate and brutalized rejetons (scions or offshoots) of the Malay race or family." Actually, Fornander applauded Bopp's "genius" in that "he perceived that there was a connection between the Polynesian and the Indo-European (languages), but he failed to demonstrate it."[ccxlii]

Bopp, having found a large number of Sanskrit words—in a more or less well-preserved condition—in Malay and Javanese, and having found the same and other Sanskrit words—in, as he thought, a less well-preserved condition—in Polynesian, argued that Malay was a corrupted daughter of Sanskrit, and that Polynesian was a still worse corrupted "granddaughter." But Judge Fornander continues, while Professor Bopp clearly hears "the true ring of Aryan metal in both Malay and Polynesian," he nevertheless "failed to discriminate between younger and older, and failed to detect... that the Aryan element in the latter—the Polynesian— was genuine and inborn, and in the former—the Malay—was adventitious and imported."[ccxliii]

Plenty of evidence swayed earlier linguists to pursue the idea that the Malayo-Polynesian languages are next-of-kin descendants. The similarity of cultures, the shared geography of the Indonesian and Malay Archipelagos, and the commonality of languages, particularly when noting words that have same meaning and differ little in spelling, all led linguists to believe that the Polynesian language is an offspring of the Malay.

Rev. George Pratt:
The Samoan Dictionary and Grammar

We should note that documentation of the written Samoan language was commissioned by Rev. John Williams and accomplished by a small team of Samoan language experts in 1832; it was first published in the first edition of the Samoan Holy Bible in 1842. These pioneering Missionaries were very busy documenting anything and everything in Samoan and Manu'an culture, history, language, everyday life activities, and family structure and genealogy.

The first documentation of Samoan grammar was written in 1875 by Rev. George Pratt, in addition to the first edition of his *Samoan Dictionary* printed at the Samoan Mission Press in 1862. It was George Pratt who first made the observation that the *Hebrew Grammar* by Nordheimer, in many points, resembled the Samoan Grammar. This led Pratt to write his book showing the syntax of Samoan Grammar. Samoans and Manu'ans are forever indebted to these early missionaries for their efforts and their body of work.

Rev. Pratt summarizes his observations with a comparative review of the Malay and Samoan languages. He clearly recognizes how Arabic words and letters—dating back to the 9th century A.D. when the Arabs (and Muslims) migrated to Southeast Asia via the Silk Road—had inundated the Malay language. Referring to Marsden's *Dictionary of the Malayan Language,*[ccxliv] he points out that there are "multitudes of pure Sanskrit words."[ccxlv]

Pratt continues: "The Malayan abounds in reduplicated words as *lakilaki.* Reduplication is a characteristic feature of the Samoan verb. Nouns have no cases. Case is indicated by a preposition, e.g. *ka langit,* to the sky. *An* is suffixed to form the noun as *pilian,* choice, from *pili* [similar to the *ga* in Samoan]. Gender is denoted by adding male or female. The adjective follows the noun and is not otherwise distinguished. Numerals have many resemblances; *lima puluh,* five feathers, or fifty. In Samoan *lima fulu* [*limagafulu*], fifty."

Reverend Pratt noted that "all tenses in Javanese and in Malay are indicated by adverbs" and posits that "this is probably the origin of the verbal particles of the Samoan." Pratt goes on to explain the syntax, with the subject usually following the verb. For example: *E toa ono tagata* means there are six people, and it uses the word order: Verb then Adjective-Subject or Object. But in *'O manu e fa,* which means there are four birds, the sentence and word order is changed: verb auxiliary *'O* + the noun + the adjective. It should be noted that this represents a change since the translation of the Bible. The use of the verb auxiliary *'O* to introduced the noun (bird) followed by the adjective is new; in the old word order (Verb or Adjective-Subject-Object) we would have *E fa manu*— a numeral adjective follow by the noun object (birds)—and so, simply, Four birds—not *the* four birds, which would be a different sentence.

Also "Malay has a language of politeness; as does Samoan.

And "The Polynesians must have migrated before the Malay became corrupted" by the Arabic, Tamil and other later languages. "Their language, probably, is now nearer to the old Malay than the language at present in use by the Malays. Samoans have lost the *h* and softened the *k,* and changed *r* into *l;* but they almost alone have retained the *s,* and a language of politeness."[ccxlvi]

Words common to Samoan and Malay

I have lifted a few words from Pratt's *Grammar & Dictionary of The Samoan Language* (4th Edition 1911) that have the same meaning in both Samoan and Malay, with similar spelling. The following are example of some words that are common among the Samoan language and that of the Malay:

1. *Tala* (Samoan), Tarang (Malay): a tale, a narration
2. *Tagulu* (Samoan), Danagkur and Garu (Malay): to snore
3. *Tagi* (Samoan), Tagis (Malay): to cry, to weep
4. *Tagavai* (Samoan), Tuggai (Malay): an emblem in war
5. *'Alaga* (Samoan), Garrang (Malay): a shout
    a. Note the pronunciation Ah lā gā with a short cough on the ah as one would pronounce Allan
6. *Alelo* (Samoan), Delah (Malay): the tongue, a term of greatest abuse
7. *Asu* (Samoan), Asap and Taso (Malay): smoke
8. *Ate* (Samoan), Ati (Malay): the liver
9. *'Avapui* (Samoan), Java (Malay): ginger plant.
10. *Ia* (Samoan), Iya (Malay): he, she, you
11. *I'a* (Samoan), Ikan (Malay): the general name for fishes, except the bonito and shellfish (in Tutuila *I'a* is bonito)
12. *Ioe* (Samoan), Iya (Malay): yes
13. *O* and *Omai* (Samoan and Malay): Hey or Oh (singular or plural)
    a. as in Oh go, or Oh come: *O alu, O sau*
14. *Umiti* (Samoan), Umih (Malay): to bite, to suck, good food
    a. In Manu'a it is an offering
15. *Fuga* (Samoan), Bunga (Malay): flowers, blossom
16. *Fulu* (Samaon), Bulu (Malay): a hair, a feather
17. *La* (Samoan - capitalized), Laei (Malay): Sun – the celestial body
18. *la* (Samoan – not capitalized), Layer (Malay): a sail
19. *La'a* (Samoan), Langkah (Malay): to step, to pass over, to step over
20. *Lailoa* (Samoan), Lelah (Malay); to be tired, exhausted, pained
21. *Nei* (Samoan), Ini (Malay): this (as in *this* is; the plural is *lenei*)
22. *Nifo* (Samoan), Nifoa (Malay): a tooth, a tusk, a horn
23. *Sulu* (Samoan), Suluh (Malay): a torch—to shine a spotlight on something bad—a spy
24. *Sulu* (Samoan), Sulu (Malay): to plunge into (as a canoe in the waves), to take refuge in, or to fasten or tie a wraparound skirt—a *lavalava*.
    a. Also means "son" of a high Chief, or "suli" in the northwest side of Savai'i
    b. and a southwesterly wind
25. *Susu* (Samoan), Susu (Malay): the breast, the dug or teat of animals
26. *Tuli* (Samoan), Lutut (Malay): the name of a bird
    a. In Manu'a it is a name for the messenger bird of the god Tagaloalagi
27. *Tumu* (Samoan), Jumu (Malay): to be full, to be satiated

Samoan Sentence Structure

According to Tuitele and Kneubuhl's *Upu Samoa: Samoan Words,* there are seven Samoan sentence patterns that illustrate word order in Samoan sentence structure as follows:[ccxlvii]

1. Verb (*'O*) + noun. Example: *'O le la'au* (It is a tree); *'O Siaki* (He is Jack); *'O matou* (We are).
2. Verb (*'O*) + noun + verb (*'O*) + noun. *'O le tamaloa 'O Siaki* (A man is named Jack); *'O Siaki 'O se leoleo* (Jack is a policeman); *'O Ioane 'O le faifeau* (John is a minister)
3. Verb auxiliary + verb + noun. Example: *'Ua sau le tama* (The boy cometh); *Na moe ia* (he was sleeping); *Sa tamomo'e latou* (They were running). Note the verb auxiliaries are also particles—*'ua, na* and *sa.*
4. Verb auxiliary + pronoun + verb. Example: *'O lo'o matou 'a'ai* (We are eating); *'O le'a tatou tatalo* (Let us pray); *'Ua 'ou ma'i* (I am sick).
5. Verb auxiliary + pronoun + verb + noun. Example: *Na matou faia le fale* (We were the ones that built the house); *Na ia tusia le ata* (He drew the design of the house); *Sa lua faitauina le tusi* (The two of them read the book).
6. Verb auxiliary + verb + noun + *e* + noun (if two nouns come after the verb, the subject is marked by *e* while the first noun is a direct object). Example: *Na fasi le pua'a e matou* (The pig was butchered by us); *'Ua fau le laulau e Sione* (The table was constructed by John); *'O lo'o faitau le tusi e lo'u uso* (The book is being read by my brother). Also, the *e* + noun phrase in this pattern can come before the noun (direct object). It can also take a form of; verb auxiliary + verb + *e* + noun (subject) + noun (direct object).
7. Verb auxiliary (*E*) + pronoun + *te* + verb. Example: *E matou te o* (We are to go); or *Matou te o* (We go); *E matou o* (We are going). In this pattern, the *e* or the *te* can be dropped but never both at the same time.

These reveal valuable conclusions about Samoan sentence patterns:
A. Verbs (or verb auxiliary + verb) begin Samoan sentences.
B. Pronouns can come before the verb or after the verb.
C. Nouns can only come after the verb
D. If two nouns come after the verb, the subject is marked by *e*. The second noun would be the direct object.

The usage of verbal particles is unique to the Samoan language, in the sense that it is integral to the written and oral language. Likewise, the articles *le* and *se* are used in Samoan whenever an idea is definite in the mind, vis-a-vis the English indefinite article (reference: Rev. George Pratt 1892).

Samoan Word Order

So, there are seven sentence patterns (described by Tuitele and Kneubuhl) in the Samoan language; and all of them start with a verb or verb auxiliary. In fact, the older version of the Samoan language—which is spoken by the chiefs and sometimes referred to as the polite language—holds for the most part to a strict Verb-Object-Subject or Verb-Subject-Object word order.

Samoan cultural belief holds that the relationship of the sentence content to the Subject or Object should be described by the verb or verb auxiliary or by adjectives, since each describes an action, emotion, mood, tense, or occasion for the noun.

Samoan Polite Language

Word order is important to a Samoan orator, for in Samoan culture, the verb describes the occasion (the type of meeting for example) and the occasion dictates the contents of the speech and the structure of the message to be delivered. Because of the oral-based cultural customs and traditions, content must be constructed to include the relationships of the object or subject to the message—for example: *Tulona le mamalu o le Aiga Malietoa...*, meaning "Respectfully," or "the venerated Malietoa family...." That is, the verbal phrase, describing different occasions—such as a wedding, funeral, everyday meeting or dialog—would alert the speaker as to the appropriate lexicon and protocol in the content and method of delivery.

There are different sets of vocabulary words earmarked for each special occasion. The introduction is the salutation of the sacred residence and meeting ground, followed by the veneration salutations of the various families involved in the occasion. Thus, the occasion or the object of the day might be the wedding, but to the orator it is first the glory and honor of the families; their salutations are critical in the introduction of the speech. Each "family" and their respective chiefs have very specific salutations, or idiomatic words and expressions that describe the mood of the occasion.

This is where one can observe the difference between the common language and the formal, polite, or chieftain language. The old Chieftain's Samoan idiom holds that the "Samoan Culture was built on Words" (or rhetoric)— *'O Samoa na fau i upu*, where he verb *'O Samoa* is built, *fau*, with rhetoric or oration, *upu*. So, anything can be resolved through words or oratory. Smart and eloquent can be a panacea to discord in human conflict.

Another phrase says, "Samoans live and survive through their oratory, their dignities and honorific titles, and through respect to one another." An elaborate system of gift-giving and reciprocity (you give gifts, and the recipient in return gives you gifts) keeps the peace within village and clan.

Ultimately, in Samoan thinking, it is of utmost importance to understand the inextricable nature of their relationships to things, people, and the physical world. The subject or object of a sentence will become obvious from the verb describing it.

The isolated disposition of Manu'ans and Samoans, in these very small islands, naturally resulted in intermarriages throughout their history, and therefore in close kin relationships. Thus knowledge of kinship, together with knowledge of the type and nature of the occasion, makes it even less important to lead a sentence in the European way, with the subject or object: For example, at a wedding or funeral, everyone already knows the subject and object—they are obvious.

Verb Subject Object or Verb Object Word Order Obsession

"Verb Subject Object" or "Verb Object" (VSO / VOS) word order is not a rule in linguistic development. The only known theories postulate the development of languages through monosyllabic, to polysyllabic, agglutinative (the gluing together of words or affixes), and finally to inflection (the modification of a word to express different grammatical categories, such as tense, person, gender, mood, or meaning). But the Samoan language has followed a particular developmental path that was driven by the oral culture, history, mythology, folklore, customs and formalities, and family genealogies. So understanding the natural boundaries and relationships of all things to one another becomes the foundation to how Samoans receive and respond to message contents. It is all about content.

Samoan word order, therefore, is fundamentally different from word order in those societies or (Western) cultures that use subject-verb-object (SVO) word order, which would be called an "Object and Subject (or Noun) Obsession."

As we have seen, the orator views an "occasion" in terms of how effectively the protocol is delivered. The gathering of the families, together with respecting the relationships or genealogies of the families, is paramount. Every special, ceremonial occasion in the culture requires a recitation of the genealogical connections of the families involved. So a real test of an orator chief is how much he or she knows of the family genealogies. Some can recite up to 55 generations, say, in the case of the TuiAtua family, and 42 generations on the Malietoa title.

The Ava ceremony is the immediate "object" or prerequisite to the gathering of Chiefs. But to the orator clan, the protocol and procedures for the conduct of the ceremony are the most important thing. And the sanctity of the Ava protocol sets the stage for the sacred meeting.

Culture Protocols

In accordance with the culture's protocol, the Ava ceremonial process "opens" the gathering of Chiefs and formal meetings or symposia. The Ava drink and ceremonial protocols "define" the guests attending the conference. This is the reason why the Ava Salutation is the Prologue of any formal speech given at formal occasions. The only exception to this protocol is when it's superseded by "Praising or giving thanks to God" for the beautiful day.

Even if the actual Ava drink is not present or performed at an event, the body of the formal speech will still acknowledge its protocol process in order to commence the occasion, and this will be articulated just as though the speaker were actually performing the Ava ceremony. The same eloquence applies, and the same serving of cups to the guests, by their Salutations, as well as to dignitaries present. This signifies to the audience that the Orator has opened the conference, and the speech now moves through all its other sections until closure.

All this is of utmost importance to the "Orator clan," which is the academy (to borrow the English term) of Orator Chiefs in all of Samoa and Manu'a. It is of this group that I asked indulgence in the opening Salutation of this book.

Some argue there are 13 foundational families in Samoa and Manu'a; others say only eight. But we all agree, by decree, that they are the pillars of the organizational structure of Samoan and Manu'an Government. These foundational families have their princes and princesses that, in their own families' rights, have become the source of strength and authority within their mainline families. These princes and princesses may very well inherit the Paramount Chief title and reign for several generations before passing it on to the next part of the family genealogy.

Because of the emphasis on protocol-oriented custom, great attention is directed to the conduct of these rituals and norms, and the proper execution of the protocol's procedure. In contrast with Western culture, which views the "object" as logically separate from the verb applied to it, in the Samoan view, the object is integral to the message. Thus, great emphasis is placed on training and being proficient in these procedures and in the specific protocols of each custom, ritual, and formality. This is often the yardstick used to measure competence, hence the steep learning curve for a new Chief.

The Importance of Action Words

Action words and examples of a "phrasal verb particle idiom" are found in oratory. We should remember that each phrase below should be viewed through the prism of the active verb:

- *Fesili* (verb) *muli mai ia mua mai*, meaning "He who came last should ask him who came first."

- *E le o le* (verb particles) *lau a manu a'o le fa'amuli o atu*, meaning "Don't be distracted and follow the seabirds and forget about the school of tuna fish."
- *Seu* (verb) *le manu ae taga'i i le galu* is a well-known saying meaning "Don't get too anxious in catching the seabirds, but keep your eyes on the on-coming waves, for one might carry you out to sea." (A contest by Tu-i-Manu'a and Malietoa Uitualagi catching seabirds with small hand nets took place in Tutuila Island.)
- *E, le o le Sua i Aiga po'o le Tamali'i, a'o le tapenaga o le ta'iiga o le fa'aaloalo*— a well-known saying about the Sua. The Sua is the formal word for a "meal" of the Chiefs, and in *E, le o le Sua*, the verb auxiliary *E* and the negation *le* mean no or not followed by the meal. Thus it's not the Sua (the meal) that's most important to *Aiga* (family) or to *Tamaali'i* (high Chief), but rather the conduct, *tapenaga*, of the protocol procedures to serve, *ta'iiga*, that praise the honor, *fa'aaloalo* of the guests. It's all about praising and lifting the emotions (or ego) of the participants.

The point I am illustrating here is not the phrases themselves, of course, but the Samoan usage of verbs. They are "action words" that "describe" content, because this further describes the environment. The description—of the environment of an occasion—dictates the attitude; it dictates how the occasion is to be conducted. It influences the course of action and decisions. The Samoan sees the object or subject through the prism of the verb or action or content.

Comparing Samoan and Western Word Orders

The philosophical difference in how the Samoan uses language, stemming from the word order VO or VS as opposed to the Western obsession on the object or subject, carries all the way to its grammar—to the innovation of verb particles or phrasal verb particles. Thus, when a Westerner converses with a Samoan or Manu'an, it is important to keep in mind the difference in point of view. For example, while the Westerner or European is focusing on the occasion or object, the Samoan or Manu'an is viewing it from the verbs describing the actions and protocols of the object.

My observations of the SVO word order is that Western languages tend to view the object as a separate and distinct item. By contrast, Samoans view the object as an integral part of the overall environment. So a Samoan doesn't just see the wedding or funeral as single, isolated unit, but rather a Samoan sees the totality of the ceremonial process of the occasion. Therefore the relationships of things relative to the whole is paramount to the Samoan psyche.

The "boundaries" of things "relative to the whole" form the rules that must be adhered to for the culture to survive. It's not the individual, but rather the family that comes first. The individual is defined in relationship to the family. Hence the Samoan and Manu'an national salutations: *Tulouna le paia o Aiga ma o latou Tama, Tama ma latou Aiga*, meaning "Honorable families of Samoa/Manu'a, and their respective princes and princesses, and their respective families." The first families referred to are the major families of the Island nation. The second set of families refers to the prince's respective family.

As is often said, a language is the mirror of a culture. This is perhaps even more true in an oral-based culture, as compared to one based on written documents. It is vital for Samoans and Manu'ans to have clarity in how they see the world around them through their own prism first, before viewing it from other cultures' perspectives. It is important to master the perspective of your own culture's language, before trying to master multi-cultural perspectives. It is, however, equally important to eventually achieve multi-cultural understanding, for this allows us to be better citizens of the world around us. But this would be more effectively achieved if first we have an excellent grasp of our own culture and language.

Comparing Samoan and other language Word Orders

A structural characteristic found in many Austronesian languages that share commonality with the Polynesian Samoan language is word order.

For example, the great majority of Formosan and Philippine languages (both are members of Austronesian) are classified as verb-subject-object (VSO) or verb-object-subject (VOS) based word order. This is true for all Formosan languages, with the minor qualification that auxiliaries and markers of negation may precede the main verb.[ccxlviii]

This is exactly the same with the Samoan language—e.g. including auxiliaries), verb auxiliary + verb + noun, as in *'Ua sau le tama; Sa tamomo'e latou*—the boy, *tama,* came; they, *latou,* were on a run, *tamomo'e.* In fact, this is the standard word order for Taiwanese and Chinese languages, with which Formosan has had its longest contact.

Formosan uses the third-most common word order among the world's languages, after subject-verb-object (SVO)—as in English and Mandarin—and SOV—as in Hindi and Japanese. The language families where all or many of the sub-families are VSO include the following:

- Celtic languages (including Irish, Scottish Gaelic, Manx, Welsh, Cornish, and Breton)
- Biblical Hebrew
- Arabic
- Filipino,
- Tuareg-Berber
- Middle-Egyptian,
- Assyrian and few others.

Verb-Object-Subject (VOS) languages include:
- Malagasy

- Baure and
- Proto-Austronesian.

Most languages of western Indonesia are subject-verb-object (SVO) word order, including:

- Malay
- Javanese
- Balinese.

However, there is a smaller number of languages that begin a sentence with verb-subject-object (VSO) word order such as:

- Malagasy,
- the Batak language of northern Sumatra,
- and Old Javanese.

Importance of Linguistics to Timelines

The importance of understanding the fundamental characteristics of historical linguistics—classification, sound change, reconstruction, and cultural history—together with synchronic linguistics—sound systems, lexicon, morphology, syntax—is to assist in postulating the timeline of the Polynesian Samoan language before their migration into the East Pacific Ocean.

If, at this junction in their migration path, the Samoan language was already an evolved language dialect and a member of an amalgamated Austronesian language family, we can reasonably assume that the Navigators departed at an early time during the Proto-Austronesian epoch. We look back to the developmental metamorphoses of language order—that is, first monosyllabic, followed by disyllabic, and then agglutinative or inflectional language—and we observe the time when the most basic, first sentence spoken by man is "love I," a verb-object or verb-subject-object word order. The Proto-Austronesian language was at a developmental stage. And the Polynesian Samoan language may very well be the last specimen of such a language existing today. It may very well precede Formosan, Malayo-Polynesian (Western Malayo-Polynesian and Central/ Eastern Malayo-Polynesian), Oceanic, and Asiatic proto-languages in their developmental stages.

Although much work is being carried out by various linguists—such as Dr. Blust (1991) out of the University of Hawaii-Manoa; Reid (1978) at the University of Hawaii; Zorc (1986) at Canberra: Pacific Linguistics; Starosta (2002) at Canberra: Pacific Linguistics; and others—they are focused on the ancestry migration path of the Malayo-Polynesian language from Taiwan (around 5000–4300 B.C.) to the immediate islands in the Southeast China Sea—islands such as Formosa, the Batanese islands, and Luzon—followed by a subsequent dispersal further east to the Philippines, and south to Borneo, Sulawesi, the Malay Peninsula, Sumatra and Java. In particular, Dr. Blust has been reconstructing the Proto-Austronesian language through sub-family groups in the (Proto)-Malayo-Polynesian family, such as the Batanic languages—Yami, (Orchid Island, Taiwan),

Itbayat (the Philippines), Ivatan (the Philippines), and Babuyan (the Philippines).

The value of this body of linguistic work is great, offering numerous resources. For my own purposes, it gives us a "harbor light" as we trace back to the origin of the Polynesian Samoan language migration path and timeline.

Re-Tracing the Language's Migration Path Backward

I would like to return now to my initial methodology of stepping backward from where we are today—the known language (Polynesian-Samoan)—and following one footprint at a time, to see how far back we can trace the origin of the Polynesian language.

The First Footprint—Samoan, Manu'an and More

In the not so distant past, the people living in Upolu already recognized a slight difference in how they speak Samoan, as opposed to how it's spoken by the people in Savai'i, as well as how Samoan is spoken on the island of Tutuila and, of course, by Manu'ans. There are different words referring to the same objects and distinct accents that separate the islanders' usage of the Samoan language. In the case of Manu'ans, the difference in the spoken language is quite significant, particularly when listening to Orator speech. One must really pay attention to the pronunciation of words and understand the difference in terminologies and structures of the speech and in the phraseologies.

The Second Footprint—Fiji Islands

The next "footprint" would be the Fiji Islands—more specifically, Rotuma island. Rotuma is believed by Manu'ans and Samoans to be the island where they sojourned in Fiji. At this juncture, the actual Fijian language is absolutely different and, in fact, not even mutually intelligible to Samoans. But, in the wisdom of the world's linguists, the Fijian and Samoan languages are classified under the same language family, i.e. Austronesian. For that matter, languages in the complete Polynesian triangle—from the Maori of New Zealand in the south, to the Hawaiian Islands in the far north, and as far to the east as Easter Island—are all classified as members of the Austronesian language family.

Linguists have already determined that the Fijian language is part of Melanesian, loosely related to their Polynesian neighbors to the east, and is different from the Samoan language. In fact, the standard language of the indigenous Fijian people is Bauan (Eastern dialect) or Bauan Fijian— Bau, or Mbau, is an island of the Fijian chain that was politically dominant during the reign of Chief Mataiwelagi.

Archaeological evidence shows that Fiji was settled and populated initially around 5,000 years ago, by the Melanesians, and then by the Lapita trading people from Southeast Asia around 2,000 B.C., followed by Austronesian Polynesians.

The Third Footprint—Solomon Island Archipelago

The relationship of the Fijian language to the languages of the next group of islands on the migration path would be important, to see if it proves to be of the same kin. The next stop on the Navigators' migration path is the Solomon Island Archipelago. There are seventy languages spoken on the archipelago, and the adopted common language (the lingua franca) is Pijin or Pidgin. Solomons Pidgin describes the language spoken in the Solomon Islands, and the language is closely related to Tok Pisin spoken in Papua New Guinea and to Bislama spoken in Vanuatu. In fact, they might be considered as dialects of a single language. Pidgin is also related, though more distantly, to Torres Strait Creole.[ccxlix]

The Solomon Island Archipelago's ancient history goes back around 35,000 years, and the large number of language dialects across the many islands seems indicative of the numerous tribal clan settlements throughout the islands in the archipelago.[ccl]

The Next Footprint

We now arrive in the heart of the group of islands that is collectively categorized as the outlier of Melanesia. The big island of New Guinea is, of course, included in the same category as Melanesia. So, can we compare the Polynesian (Samoan and Togan) languages to Melanesian languages, to confirm kinship of the two groups?

We already know that, according to the world's anthropologists, linguists, ethnologists, and geneticists, these people are of two different races, sharing a common geographical continent of Southeast Asia. The following is only a partial list of major language categories (400) in Melanesia:

- Melanesian pidgins
- Hiri Motu
- Oceanic language
- Fijian language
- Gedaged language
- Bambatana language
- Bugotu language
- Mota language and
- Rotuman language

While there are close relationships between the Polynesian and Micronesian languages—studied by R.H. Codrington (1871-77), H.N. van der Tuuk (1864-67), Hendrik Kern (1880), Renward Brandstetter (1906-15), and Otto Dempwolff (1934-38)—the best summarization of this relationship came with Otto Dempwolff's breakthrough in subgrouping the Austronesian languages to include Proto-Melanesian or Proto-Oceanic as it is known today. His "Oceanic hypothesis" proposes a common decent from a single protolanguage for nearly all Austronesian languages east of a line at approximately 138 degrees East longitude, running through Indonesian New Guinea, but leaving out Palauan and Chamorro in western Micronesia. These languages would all have resulting from the initial breakup of Proto-Austronesian.[ccli]

More Footprints—Austronesian

At this juncture the audit trails of the Polynesian language cease to exist in this central-eastern region of the Solomon Island Archipelago, Vanuatu and New Caledonia. Very few people living in coastal island communities in the eastern part of Vanuatu and the Solomon Islands speak any form of the Polynesian language. Thus, there are no significant signs that would indicate the Navigators—the Polynesians—settled in any of the Melanesian Islands for any significant period of time.

The classification of all languages of Southeast Asia into a single family, called Austronesian was made for scientific convenience. But it complicates efforts to find the "needle in the haystack" which represents the path of the Navigators of the Pacific.

The best we can determine is that the Polynesian language is borne out of the dispersal of Proto-Oceanic, which itself was most likely borne out of the Proto-Formosan language, and finally Proto-Austronesian. Beyond that, the Proto-Taiwanese language contributed to sourcing the Austronesian language family, together with languages of the Asiatic Archipelago.

Going further—Proto-Sino-Tibetan

The next logical, external, ancient language that might have a kinship or ancestral relationship to the Austronesian language would be Proto-Sino-Tibetan. Beyond that would be Proto-Indo-European (PIE), or Proto-Sanskrit or Rig Veda (the language of oral religious prayer-hymns, which is contemporary to the Proto-Indo-European language).

If we look to mainland China's Chinese language as a possible ancestor of Proto-Taiwanese, then we must understand that the language family of origin that includes ancient Old Chinese is the Sino-Tibetan language family. The Sino-Tibetan languages—also known as Trans-Himalayan in a few sources—are a family of more than 400 languages spoken in East Asia, Southeast Asia and South Asia. Thus

Proto-Sino-Tibetan is the second largest language family, next to Proto-Indo-European (PIE). There are 1.3 billion speakers of different varieties of Chinese languages, 33 million Burmese, and 6 million speakers of Tibetic languages.

It was Brian Houghton Hodgson (1801-1894), a pioneer naturalist and ethnologist working in India and Nepal, who identified the parallels and similarities between the Chinese, Tibetan, and Burmese languages. And in 1856, James Richardson Logan, writing *The Ethnology of the Indian Archipelago: Embracing Enquiries into the Continental Relations of the Indo-Pacific Islanders*, coined the "Tibeto-Burman" family group classification.

Logan and other mid-19th century social scientists studying the "Indo-Chinese" languages of Southeast Asia discovered that they comprised four families: Tibeto-Burman, Tai (or Zhuang-Tai or Tai-Kadai), Mon-Khmer and Malayo-Polynesian.[cclii] After much debate on the inclusion of Thai, Mon, and Vietnamese, August Conrady and Ernst Kuhn, in 1896, defined the Indo-Chinese language to consist of two branches, Chinese-Siamese and Tibeto-Burman.[ccliii]

The importance of continuing our audit trail, tracing Polynesian back to the next major language family, Sino-Tibetan, is to understand and appreciate the migration path of those who eventually occupied Taiwan. If these migrants came with their respective language, would that be the origin of the Sino-Tibetan languages?

Where did Sino-Tibetan come from?

There are many proposals about the homeland of the Sino-Tibetan family. In 1991 James Matisoff—Professor of Linguistics at the University of California, Berkeley, and noted authority on Tibetan-Burman languages—placed the origin on the eastern part of the Tibetan plateau in around 4000 B.C., with various groups migrating out down the Yellow, Yangtze, Mekong, Salween, Irrawaddy and Brahmaputra rivers. In 2005, George van Driem—a Dutch linguist at the University of Borne—proposed that Sino-Tibetan originated in the Sichuan Basin before 7000 B.C., with early migration into northeast India, and a later migration, north of the predecessors of Chinese and Tibetan.

In 2009 Professor (then Doctor) Roger Blench—from the University of Cambridge, Cambridge, England—argued that, since agriculture cannot be reconstructed for Proto-Sino-Tibetan, the earliest speakers of Sino-Tibetan must have been highly diverse foragers rather than farmers; this implies an early date.[ccliv] In 2014 Dr. Blench and Dr. Mark Post of the University of Sydney, Australia—both linguists studying the ancestry of and migration to Sino-Tibetan—proposed that its homeland is in northeast India, the area of greatest diversity, around 7000 B.C.

The point I want to emphasize is that the geographical area, here, is the junction of the major rivers in the Greater Asia continent, which became foundational to sourcing many great cultural societies in central, eastern, and southeastern Asia. Three major rivers of India—the Indus, the Ganges, and the Brahmaputra—together with their many tributaries, merged into other rivers here. This helped facilitate and, to some degree, accelerate human migration eastward through the Asian continent.

Peiligang Culture (about 7000-5000 B.C.), Laoguantai Culture (about 6000-5000 B.C.), Beixin Culture (about 5300-4100 B.C.) and Cishan Culture (about 6500-5000 B.C.) are representative of the ancient (Neolithic) Yellow river civilizations. They came out from the great migration from these rivers.

There is currently a highly controversial debate concerning the reconstruction of the Proto-Indo-Tibetan language family. In time, this debate will yield great tidings from "the well of the ancient past." But it would be too far-fetched, until the scientists complete their research, to insist on a parallel, or to postulate that the Proto-Austronesian family is definitely kin to the Proto-Indo-Tibetan language family.

Proto-Sino-Tibetan and Samoan Parallels

It should be noted that a few scholars disagree over the extent to which the agreement morphology in the various languages can be reconstructed for a proto-language.[cclv] But I am encouraged to learn that the Austroasiatic (formerly known as Mon-Khmer) family is being studied (reconstructing Proto-Austroasiatic) and is being accepted as a language family of mainland Southeast Asia.

In 2005 Laurent Sagart proposed a Sino-Austronesian family with Sino-Tibetan and Austronesian (including Ka-Da as a sub-branch) as primary branches of the language family.[cclvi] Stanley Starosta extended Sagart's proposal to include a branch called "Yangzian," joining Hmong-Mien and Austronesian.[cclvii]

It appears there are remnants of Proto-Sino-Tibetan developments of dialects and languages that have parallels with the Samoan language.

- The monosyllabic and bisyllabic root characteristic of Sino-Tibetan, requiring prefix and suffix to classify word meaning—as noted by Dai Qingxia in 1977—is very similar to the usage of particles and verb particles in the Samoan language.[cclviii]
- The word order—studied by Matthew Dryer in 2003[cclix]—was originally Object-Verb (OV) before acquiring the Subject-Verb-Object (SVO) form from neighboring languages in the linguistic areas of mainland Southeast Asia. However, Dyer noted, unlike all other VO languages in the world, Chinese and Bai place relative clauses before the nouns they modify. This is the same with the Samoan language, with the use of relative clauses (or particles) to modify the nouns.

This research, in my opinion, will allow further tracing of the many indigenous language subgroups of the Proto-Austronesian family, through Austroasiatic and on to the Proto-Indo-Sino-Tibetan language family. I believe this will yield results consistent with the DNA genetic-test results of the various subgroups of Austronesian, including Polynesian, which traced the Lapita DNA to mainland Asia.[cclx]

The logic is that the farther back we trace through reconstructing the Proto language families, the more commonalities we should find in the phonology and morphological structure of the grammar and roots.

Linguistic Development of the Samoan Language

It is difficult to summarize such a complex body of linguistic works. The acid test is the identification—through innovative developments in phonology (language system and rules of sounds) and morphology (form, structure, and relationship of words) of the specimen languages—leading me to believe the Samoan language predates the migration on to the Eastern Pacific.

According to Blust (writing in 1991 and 1994),[cclxi] the relevant phonological innovations are as follows:

- The Proto-Austronesian "t" and "c" merged as "t" in Proto-Malayo-Polynesian. This is true with the Samoan language.
- The Proto-Austronesian "l" and "n" merged as "n" in Proto-Malayo-Polynesian. In some cases this is true with the Samoan language.
- The Proto-Austronesian "s" and "h" merged as "h" in Proto-Malayo-Polynesian. This does not show up in the Samoan language, but it is found in the Toga and Hawaii dialects.

The merging of "l" and "n" can be observed in the Proto-Austronesian word, *tula* (meaning freshwater eel) which becomes *tuna* in Proto-Malayo-Polynesian. Meanwhile the merging of "p" and "f" can also be seen in the Proto-Austronesian word *pitu* (meaning seven), which becomes *pito* in Proto-Malayo-Polynesian (or Itbayat) and *fitu* in Samoan.

The merging of "t" and "c" can be observed in the Proto-Austronesian word *calina* (meaning ear) which becomes *talina* in Proto-Malayo-Polynesian (Itbayat) and also *talina* in Samoan. Likewise the Proto-Austronesian *maca* (meaning eye) is *mata* in Proto-Malayo-Polynesian (Itbayat), and *mata* again in Samoan.

The Samoan language went through several phonological and morphological innovations in the Indonesian Archipelago, before the great migration into the Eastern Pacific. These changes include, for example, the development of a higher language (a language of politeness) as distinct from the common language, and the obsessive adoption of the verb-object word order. Again, VSO or VOS was the common word order characteristic in those Proto-Malayo-Polynesian languages close to the epicenter, when they first left mainland China and moved on to Taiwan, continuing to the South China Sea and the East Pacific. This seems to indicate that the Samoan Polynesians were part of the original group of migrants, before the Malayan migration (around 550 B.C.) into the area.

It is seen in Blust's effort to reconstruct the Proto-Austronesian language (in 1991) that reduplication (CV, or consonant + vowel) is characteristic of an earlier innovation, and thus existed in the Proto-Malayo-Polynesian language before the great eastern Pacific migration.

Developments and innovations that took place in Polynesian Samoan, in the East Pacific Ocean, include the use of particles, glottal stops, and macron (long or stressed vowels, written with a printed mark) for sound pronunciation, the dropping of the "h" sound, and removing the difference in the sounds of "k" and "t" in both formal polite language and common everyday speech.

And, of course, their focus on oral language is how the Samoans and Manu'ans were able to hone those weapon skills and other skills critical to their survival. Language was fundamental to their culture and their peaceful existence.

Language Conclusion

Timelines

I believe the timeline of the arrival of the original Homo erectus into the Asiatic Archipelago and Indonesian Archipelago will add more ancient colorful stones to the mosaic of Austronesian history. The idea that there were ancient humans roaming and navigating the ocean in the region, many thousands of years before modern humans (Homo sapiens and our cousin, the Neanderthal) were born, causes us to re-examine the timeline of human and cultural developments in the region.

In addition, this drives us to re-examine the development of languages in the region. Scientists have confirmed that Homo erectus had language around 800,000 years ago. However, assuming that sailing followed language, this could more likely be 1.5 million years ago, based on extensive travel and tool standardization. The resurgence of efforts to re-examine the origin of language now has a more scientific basis, given that Homo erectus had the capacity to navigate the ocean, make plans, and organize a well-trained group of sailors to oar the vessel.

Learning from mistakes made in previous efforts, and correcting errors of the past, is a critical aspect of the cognitive process. This hones our perceptiveness, encouraging better recognition of events, patterns, situations, and potential outcomes. The prerequisite to these cognitive developments is having a language to formulate and decode messages effectively within the team, group, family, or clan.

Professor Daniel Everett, Bentley University in Massachusetts, in *How Language Began*, describes the evolutionary process—from symbols and sign language, to "mere sounds" or interjections (spontaneous emotional outbursts), then to the cognitive recognition that a particular pitch has a pattern learned over time (regression) that is "believed" and "trusted" to repeat the same "pattern," and will by consensus be the message.[cclxii]

Müller, in 1861, said that "Language begins where interjections end."[cclxiii]

So the major impact here, in my opinion, is on our understanding of the developments of the Austronesian language family. If the Austronesian language family is rooted in a more ancient language development, sourced from the ancient Homo erectus in the region, then we must accept the reality that it is a foundational native language of the region, and that subsequent modern human migrations, with their respective tongues, were the additional language ingredients added to the region's native language. This seems to explain the very deep common structural characteristics of the different languages of the whole of Southeast Asia and Oceania.

In conclusion, to achieve an understanding of our origin and our journey, through the past 2 million years, one must accept both faith and the miracle of science.

The Gift and the Miracle

"In the beginning was the Word, and Word was with God, and the Word was God. He was in the beginning with God." John 1:1-2 (NRSV). So said the written record in the Hebrew Bible around 586 B.C.—though many scholars still debate the date; convincing evidence that these words could have been written around 800 B.C. was recorded in the 2016 study by doctoral students Shira Faigenbaum-Golovin, Arie Shaus, and Barak Sober, led by Israel Finkelstein, Professor of Archaeology at the Tel Aviv University.[cclxiv]

The whole story of God's Creation in the Book of Genesis began with verbal commands, where God said, "Let there be light," and there was light. Christian theologians and scholars, particularly in Christology, have exhaustively debated the translation of the Greek word "Logos" to mean "Word." But it is a word with more than one meaning. It's often translated into English as "Word," but it can also mean thought, speech, reason, principle, logic, and other such terms.[cclxv]

Some 2,000 years before the composition of the Hebrew Bible, the text of the Memphite Priesthood of the creator-deity (the mummy-god) Ptah was written in the language of the Old Kingdom of Egypt. Professor Joseph Campbell comments on the essence of this text, repeating the theory that the heart of God brings forth creation and the tongue of God repeats what the heart has thought.[cclxvi] If indeed all words come from the thought of the heart and the commandment of the tongue, the eyes see, the ears hear, and the nose breathes, then they report to the heart. The heart brings forth every idea, and the tongue repeats the thoughts of the heart, thus fashioning all the gods, even those of Egypt.[cclxvii]

How the human brain deals with speech and language, and with the creation and recognition of language, is complex, and we are far from clearly understanding how it all works in a co-operative manner. We know, to some degree, how the various regions of the brain function in a co-operative manner to create, transmit, process, translate, and hopefully understand messages—this is carried out in a very complex series of networked neurons, that transmit signals containing messages to every region and functional center of the brain. This gives us the intellect, or self-awareness, which distinguishes humans from most other species—in psychology, self-awareness is defined as metacognition, or the awareness of one's own ability to think.

According to the Mayfield Clinic, the left hemisphere of the brain is generally responsible for speech and language; it is called the "dominant" hemisphere. The right hemisphere plays a large part in interpreting visual information and performing spatial processing.[cclxviii] But the idea that the heart might be the master of the "Word," in concert with the left hemisphere and other all-encompassing functions of the brain, is hard to fathom. After all, the brain is what directs and regulates the lungs to take in oxygen and release carbon dioxide, as a way of creating energy needed by the body, so that the heart can continue beating to regulate the flow of blood through the body's anatomy. It's the miracle of Creation and a gift from God.

Is the brain itself the gift and the miracle, designed together with its intricate and complex functions? Or will we find we have been studying and using the gift—a different gift—for centuries, while we searched for God's answers. The brain is the source that creates the anatomy of language. And the Gift is Language. Language kept the Navigators and the rest of the Polynesians alive for thousands of years.

Genetics

The study of heredity and DNA

DNA and the Navigators

Difference Matters

Now I move on to how the modern science of genetics helps trace and confirm the Navigators' migration path.

I want to preface this important section of my quest by saying I have come to the conclusion that the science of genetics is the study of "differences" rather than of commonalities in the human species. The analysis of patterns found in genetic differences is the most significant issue. These differences are caused by genetic mutations which permanently alter the DNA sequence of a gene.

Regression analysis is important to this kind of study. It is a statistical method that allows large amounts of data to be effectively analyzed. This type of analysis looks for which differences in the data are important, and how differences interact with each other. Genetic sequencing is combined with regression analysis to look for the most important genetic "differences" and their patterns over populations.

Diversity is fundamental in humanity's definition of who we are and what we are. Thus our obsession with uniqueness, and with defining our unique characteristics, may very well stem from our makeup as a species of diversity. Preoccupying ourselves with the pursuit of uniqueness automatically results in a preoccupation with defining differences. And, as we shall see, scientists have labored to decipher the statistical code of these "differences," using breakthroughs in DNA and Y-chromosome analyses on the human genome. Today this diversity leads us to seek the DNA characteristics of Polynesian ethnicity.

The Diaspora of the Navigators

The target audience, which I hope to reach with this endeavor, is those Samoans who now speak only the English language, due to whatever circumstances or for whatever personal reasons. About 40% of approximately 200,000 Samoans born and living in New Zealand, and about 80% of about 189,000 Samoans and Manu'ans born and now living in the United States, all speak English, while few to none speak Samoan. This is the diaspora of the Navigators of the Pacific Ocean.

These Samoans are interested in learning about their ancestry and origin, if for no other reason that just to confirm their identity, particularly in light of today's obsession with identity. They use, for example, ancestry.com, one of the fastest growing websites on the Internet in the US—many similar websites are springing up across the globe.

A second, and very important issue I wish to address is the void in the availability of detailed literature on our ancient history, prior to the birth of Christ, and on the architectural development of our culture, which I will address in more detail in my second book.

What is DNA?

I believe it is important to bring together all the evidence, provided by all the various genetic studies of Polynesian DNA, in order to "connect the dots" and produce a cohesive narrative summary describing the Migration of the Polynesians, or the Navigators, into the East Pacific.

The hereditary material in the human organism is defined by four molecules, or chemical bases (A, G, C and T), which come together to describe our unique genetic code. The order of these bases in the DNA defines the genetic code. They are the building blocks, metaphorically, in a human book of about 3 billion letters—a book that makes up the human species.

Decoding DNA

The Wall Street Journal wanted to find which innovation has had the most profound impact on humans and society, globally, during the last millennium. They polled many experts on "innovation" for their article on "The Most Influential Innovation."

Overwhelmingly, respondents voted that the top breakthrough—the most influential achievement—is the successful completion of the Human Genome Project, begun around 1990, which was finally able to sequence the DNA of the human genome, after thirteen plus years of labor. Thanks to more powerful computers, which made it possible to analyze massive amounts of data, this task was accomplished within our lifetime.

Our knowledge of human DNA began with the discovery of *nuclein* (now called DNA) in 1869 by Friedrich Miescher MD, a professor of physiology at the University of Basel, Switzerland. In 1953, James Watson and Francis Crick discovered the structure of DNA—the double helix shape—for which they were rewarded with the Nobel Prize.

But what is DNA? The short answer is that DNA stands for *Deoxyribonucleic Acid*, and it is contained in every one of your body's cells.

It is a complex molecule that contains all of the information necessary to build and maintain an organism.

DNA itself is carried in chromosomes. All living things have DNA within their cells. And whenever organisms reproduce, a portion of their DNA is passed along to their offspring.

DNA is a double helix, made of two long twisted chains of molecules, called nucleotides, which tell each cell what proteins to make. Each nucleotide contains a sugar molecule attached to a phosphate group, and a nitrogen-containing base. The four types of nitrogen bases are Adenine (A), Thymine (T), Guanine (G) and Cytosine (C). The order of these bases is what determines the DNA instructions, or the genetic code.

What is DNA—the Long Answer

In my quest to really understand and appreciate the complexity of this science, I found some of the most basic literature, such as *Genetics For Dummies*, very helpful.[cclxix] I believe it would benefit any readers not proficient in basic biology to learn some of this. Much of the following I feel compelled to reproduce with minimal editorial remarks:

A piece of DNA is rather like a very long sentence that uses only four letters, called nucleotides (A, T, G, C). The DNA is made from two strands which fit together, rather like the two sides of a zipper. The "teeth" of the zipper are nucleotides, labeled A, T, G and C. The nucleotides come in pairs, called "base pairs," where A always links to T, and C always links to G. In this way, the two strands can be pulled apart, or unzipped, and each individual strand holds all the information needed to recreate the complete double strand. This is how DNA copies itself.

Imagine a short segment of DNA. If one strand of the sequence is CTGGAC, then the other strand must be GACCTG. Together they would look like:

```
C—G
T—A
G—C
G—C
A—T
C—G
```

When they are split apart, the cell's machinery finds new pairs (in italics below) for each of the nucleotides, giving:

```
C—G      C—G
T—A      T—A
G—C      G—C
G—C      G—C
A—T      A—T
C—G      G—C
```

We now have two exact copies of the DNA sequence we started with. Only one strand is needed to convey all the information, and our exact (very long) combination of these letters is the human genome sequence.

There are around 3 billion nucleotides in the human genome. As you can imagine, making copies of 3 billion nucleotides every time a cell multiplies is no easy task. The cell uses enzymes to make copies of its DNA. Even though these enzymes are very precise, mistakes do happen, and the wrong letter gets placed in the sequence. Such a mistake can be either harmless or fatal to the cell depending on where the mistake was made. To keep mistakes to a minimum, the cell uses another set of enzymes whose job is to check the new copy and repair any mistakes.

What is a Gene?

The anatomy of a human being is one cohesive, integrated, interdependent, sets of sub-networks all working in unison, much like an orchestra where all the many instruments are integral to the production of a beautiful piece of music. The key in any instrumental composition—whether small or large and however complicated and sophisticated—is the orchestration which binds all the instruments into a cohesive, functional unit. Similarly, given the integrated and interdependent characteristics of human anatomy, one cannot speak on one aspect without saying something about the other functions which are a part of the total network.

We've covered briefly, above, a general and simple description of the basic function of our DNA. But we cannot speak about DNA without also considering the questions: what is a gene? what is a cell? and what is an allele? All these things are needed to complete an accurate description of the genome sequencing process.

In a nutshell, the human body is a complex, multicellular organism. Our bodies are made up of over 30 trillion cells, at the latest count.[cclxx] In addition to the enormity of this number, there are about 200 different types of cells, with different types of purposes, all ensuring that the systems of human anatomy work as expected. And it's expected that an estimate of the number of bacteria in the human body might be even greater than the number of cells.

So, to start with the gene: Genes are small sections of DNA. Each gene contains the instruction for a specific protein, much like a "cookbook recipe" for making the proteins in the cell. And proteins are the building blocks for everything in the human body—bones, teeth, hair, earlobe, muscles, and blood are all made up of proteins.

What are Chromosomes?

Now for the relationship of genes to chromosomes: Thousands of genes make up each chromosome. Chromosomes can be thought of as being made up of strings of genes (DNA that codes for proteins) with non-coding sections of DNA between them. Therefore chromosomes, like the genes, are made from the chemical called DNA. They contain very long strands of DNA, coiled up like a ball of string.

Chromosomes are found in the nuclei of all body cells, with the exception of red blood cells as these have no nucleus and therefore do not contain chromosomes. Chromosomes are also found outside the nucleus, in very small compartments called mitochondria. These are the "energy warehouses" of the cell and are found scattered outside the nucleus. The strands of DNA in mitochondria are much smaller and have very little non-coding DNA.

Scientists today estimate that each gene in the body makes as many as 10 different proteins. That's more than 300,000 proteins. And, since the chromosomes (which contains strings of genes) come in pairs (one from each parent), there are also two copies of each of each gene. The chromosomes which don't come in pairs are the X and Y "sex" chromosome.[cclxxi]

What are Alleles?

So, now we know that strings of genes are contained in chromosomes, and that genes and chromosomes are made up of a chemical substance called DNA. The genes code for particular proteins. Genes, with alternate forms, code for the same proteins, and arise from mutations at particular locations on the chromosome. There can often be more than one alternate version of a gene—i.e. different versions of a known "mutation" at the same place (or location) on the chromosome. An allele is an alternative, or variant form of a particular gene.

An allele is a variant form of a given gene, or a variant collection of sequence variations among the several hundred base-pairs in the genome that codes for a protein.[cclxxii] These small (harmless) differences contribute to each person's unique physical features or traits.

If alleles arise from mutations (from changes in the makeup of a gene), then we might see that the study of these mutations—in particular taking into account the rate of occurrence of mutations that might occur in the lifecycle of DNA making up the gene—could give us a window into the characteristics and history of an organism or people. So we cannot complete the description of the allele without also looking at the cause and result of mutations.

What are Mutations?

Mutation is the word for a change that has occurred in a gene, giving rise to an allele. Mutations can range in size from ones affecting only a single DNA base-pair to ones that affect multiple genes in a large segment of a chromosome. But let's not forget that each gene contains the "cookbook recipe" for how proteins should be built to do their job efficiently. What if the recipe is wrong?

Unfortunately, it turns out that proteins do not always work efficiently in the functioning of this complicated system called human anatomy.

While some mutations contribute to a person's unique features, others can be harmful.

If a change occurs in a gene's instructions for making a protein, this mutation can cause the protein to malfunction, or even not to exist. Thus, if a mutation (change) alters a protein that plays a critical role in the body, it can stop the normal development of the body or cause medical problems with the functioning of the body. Medical conditions caused by mutations in one or more genes are called genetic disorders.[cclxxiii]

Genes and Populations

How Genes are Inherited

Genes are organized and packaged in units called "chromosomes," which we inherit in pairs from our parents. Humans have 23 pairs of chromosomes; they are tiny structures, found within your cells, which contain the DNA information and instructions that define who you are—what you look like, how your body works, and even what genetic diseases you might have.

Humans normally have 46 chromosomes—23 pairs of chromosomes which scientists have numbered 1 through 22 (called the autosomes), with the 23rd pair (the allosomes) determining the sex. Hence the 23rd pair is called the sex chromosome—men have an X and a Y sex chromosome and women have two X chromosomes.

How Inheritance Works in Families

Our inheritance is determined by our chromosomes. One autosomal chromosome from each pair (the first 22 pairs) comes from our mother and the other from our father. That is, we get half of our DNA from our mother and half from our father. Thus, each chromosome we possess is a combination from our parents' own pairs of chromosomes, which they got from their parents (our grandparents).

The way human biology works is that the pairs are not "expressed" in us evenly—we are not made up of 50% mother and 50% father, but rather we have pairs of chromosomes which come, one from the mother and one from the father. Each chromosome from the mother is a unique "combination" of her two matching chromosomes. Similarly, each chromosome from the father is a unique combination of his two matching chromosomes. So each person is unique.

The pairs of chromosomes mean the child has two copies of each gene available, but only one will be "expressed." But if a gene from one parent is "dominant," the chance of that parent's gene being expressed is higher—for example, brown eyes are dominant over blue eyes.

Simplifying this complex process, traits may disappear over many generations. Or you might be more "related" to one of your grandparents than the other. The apparent "randomness" of this distribution process may result in your having an exact copy of one of your parent's genes and expressing no portion of the other's genes.

How Inheritance Works in Populations

The miracle of life is that Y-chromosome DNA is inherited only from the father (since the mother has no Y chromosome) and is passed on to his son. Mitochondrial DNA (mtDNA), on the other hand, is inherited only from the mother—it is found on the X chromosome, but it turns out that, shortly after the process of fertilization, the sperms' mitochondrial DNA dies away, and the embryo is only left with only the maternal mitochondrial DNA (from the egg). This is a complex mechanism that includes dilution of sperm mtDNA within the fertilized egg.

According to the science, mtDNA is passed down nearly unchanged from generation to generation. So we share the same mtDNA as our mother, our maternal grandmother, our maternal great-grandmother and so on. In fact, science tells us that the exact same mtDNA code will track a direct genetic line, defining a population.

How Mutations affect Populations

Remember that an allele is an alternative version of a gene located on a particular part of the chromosome. We know that about three billion pairs of DNA nucleotides, or "letters," serve as an instruction manual, or cookbook, for how to assemble a human. These strings of DNA letters spell out the information required to build proteins, including enzymes, which do much of the "heavy lifting" work in human cells.

Geneticists say that only about 2% of the human genome encodes proteins and a somewhat larger fraction is involved in gene regulation. The rest of the genome, as yet, has no known role.

According to the science, the overall genomes of any two people are extremely similar, with a difference in only about one out of 1,000 nucleotide pairs. Thus the sites where one nucleotide pair substitutes for another are referred to as "single-nucleotide polymorphisms" or SNPs. The alternative versions of the DNA at SNPs are called alleles.

Because most of the genome does not encode proteins or regulate genes, most SNPs probably have no measurable effect on the individual. But if an SNP occurs in an important region of the genome, it may affect the structure or function of a protein, or where and how much of the protein is made. In this way, SNPs can conceivably modify almost any trait, be it height, eye color, ability to digest milk, or susceptibility to diseases such as diabetes, schizophrenia, malaria, and HIV.

When natural selection strongly favors a particular allele (variant or mutation), this allele becomes more common in the population with each generation. Likewise, a disfavored allele (such as one generating susceptibility to disease) becomes less common in the population with each generation.

An example of a favorable allele is the one discovered, about 10 years ago, in sequencing the genome of the Tibetan people. This gene mutation allows the production of red blood cells in Tibetans to be more tolerant to the low oxygen levels found 14,000 feet above sea level. The mutation is estimated to have occurred sometime when humans first left Africa, around 60,000 years ago (an estimated range of 50,000 to 100,000 years ago). It turns out such a phenomenon takes many years to evolve—from 100 to 200 generations. [cclxxiv]

A study, undertaken to trace early human migration "out of Africa" some 60,000 year ago, in collaboration with a team from Stanford University, identified three major, favored allele patterns that lay down the foundation of DNA and resulting haplogroup distribution across the world:

1. All non-African populations: the adaptive allele pattern appears and begins to spread, shortly after leaving Africa.
2. West Eurasians: a favored allele occurs at high frequency in all the populations of Europe, the Middle East, and Central and South Asia.
3. East Asians: the favored allele is most common in East Asians, as well as Native Americans, Melanesians, and Papuans.

The last two patterns appear to have occurred after West Eurasians and East Asians split off and went their separate ways. It is not known precisely when this occurred, but probably around 20,000 to 30,000 years ago, according to the study. [cclxxv]

What's clear is that advantageous, as opposed to disadvantageous, alleles are found as a result of natural selection's enigmatic effect on the human evolutionary process. Environmental factors can influence the process, then, when the environment is stable, the population "adopts" the mutation as a permanent part of the overall system. This is how mutations affect family, tribe, clan, culture, ethnicity, society and nation, as in the case of the Tibetan mutation.

The process of mutation takes a lot longer than initially thought, particularly in the case of disadvantageous alleles (those causing susceptibility to disease). Additionally, human migration paths and their geographical trajectories can result in a permanent split in human populations (in their different mutations), which affects how mutations are passed on. But all these affects are taken into account in the research.

Mitochondrial DNA can be used to track a genetic line all the way back until the point at which a natural mutation in mtDNA occurred—the point where a population "split" from whatever group it used to be a part of. This sort of mutation was believed to occur about every 20,000 years, though now the timescale is believed to be longer.

What is a Haplotype?

If, on average, a natural mutation of mtDNA occurs every 20,000 years, how can we trace our genetic code to the first humans (130,000 to 200,000 years ago)?

This is where we look to the sciences of archaeology, anthropology, ethnology, and genetics, searching for ancient human remains to determine their DNA codes and to establish generational DNA "haplotypes" and "haplogroups." Such groups should appear in a genetic population or group of people who share a common patrilinear or matrilineal ancestor. The most commonly studied are Y-chromosome (Y-DNA on the male or the father) haplogroups and mitochondrial DNA (mtDNA on the female or the mother) haplogroups.

Remember, an "allele" is a variant form of a given gene, arising through mutation, that is responsible for hereditary variation—that is, a variant of a gene, or copy of a gene, of the same trait (such as blue eyes or brown eyes).

A haplotype is a group of "alleles" in an organism that are inherited together from a single parent. Because they are inherited together, the "variations" of the genes, over multiple generations, allow computer models to trace the historical path of human heredity.[cclxxvi]

Tracing the DNA family tree

The Study of Changes

The study of gene variations, or the "changes" in genes over times and populations, is a major focus of statistical analysis in the field, with multiple regressions undertaken on sample data to identify the patterns. The resulting haplogroups are assigned letters of the alphabet, with refinements consisting of additional number and letter combinations: For example, the R1b tree, also known as Hg1 and Eu18, is a Y-chromosome haplogroup, most frequently occurring in paternal lineages in Western Europe and some parts of Russia and Central Africa.[cclxxvii]

Tracing human DNA is analogous to following the family tree, starting from the leaf—or current generation—to the branch of the tree—or family—to the stem, and on to the main trunk down to its roots. It is also like an upside-down pyramid, with the vertex at the bottom being the foundational ancestor of the whole pyramid. There are children, parents, grandparents, great-grandparents and so on in the hierarchical tree structure of a person, a family, tribe, village, and ethnicity.

The nomenclature is complex for tracing a person's or people's Y-DNA and mtDNA haplogroups and respective refinements (variations in the branches). The analysis of "refinements" or "branch variations" is, again, a focus of present study. The "layers" of the tree's branches are numerous, for this ancient tree of life is older than 2 million years. And the Samoan would say a person has more roots than a tree—*e tele a'a o le tagata lo a'a o le la'au. Tulou le mamalu o le la'au ma ona lau*—E (verb auxiliary), *tele* (many) *a'a* (root) of a *tagata* (person) than the *a'a* (roots) of a *la'au* (tree).

So, it is expected that the Polynesian Samoan DNA, Y-Chromosomes, and mtDNA will contain ancestral DNA that could trace back, initially, 3,000 to 5,000 years. Now the research is tracing it back 20,000 to 50,000 years, and perhaps 60,000 to 130,000 years. There might be an allele pattern for long-distance seafaring among the people of the Pacific Islands. Someday in the not so distant future, geneticists may uncover it. And we'll know the arduous environment in ancient times may have contributed to its occurrence.

Haplogroups of Polynesian Ancestry

According to the FTDNA (Family Tree DNA), ISOGG (International Society of Genetic Genealogy), and published papers,[cclxxviii] the Polynesian Y-Chromosome DNA of 75% of those reporting a direct Polynesian paternal line falls into these haplogroups:

1. Haplogroup C2 (M38): This is the haplogroup of 34% of those who report their paternal line as Polynesian. The C2 haplogroup is found in Polynesia, Melanesia, New Guinea, and Indonesia.
2. Haplogroup O (M122) is the marker of about 24% who report their paternal line as Polynesian. The O haplogroup is typical of populations of East Asia, Southeast Asia, and culturally Austronesian regions, with moderate distribution in Central Asia (ISOGG Tree-O3 M122).
3. Haplogroup K (M9) is the haplogroup of about 18% who report their paternal line as Polynesian. K is the haplogroup of an old lineage presently found only at low frequencies in Africa, Asia, and in the South Pacific. One descendent line of this lineage is restricted to aboriginal Australians, while another is found at low frequencies in Southern Europe, Northern Africa, and the Middle East.[cclxxix]

The mtDNA results for around 93% of males and females reporting their maternal line as Polynesian show they belong to haplogroup B. This lineage is found in eastern and southern Eurasia, Native American Indians, and Polynesia. Haplogroup B is estimated to be the mtDNA haplogroup of about 93% of the males and females living today who report their maternal line as Polynesian.

The group of mutations 16189C, 16217C, and 16261T collectively define the "Polynesian Motif" (PM), a special subgroup of haplogroup B which is found almost exclusively in Polynesia. This "PM" subset of B is estimated to be the haplogroup of more than 75% of the males and females living today who report their maternal line as Polynesian.

It should be noted that the above mutations are based on the Cambridge Reference Sequence (CRS) which was further based on mitochondrial DNA sequenced first in 1981.

Technological Convergence

It should not come as a surprise to note there are many layers in the fabric, and many branches to the tree of human ancestral DNA, all the way to the first man and woman. We owe a lot to scientists from many disciplines for their indefatigable efforts to find the origin of humanity and their journey. The sheer number of technological innovations that had to be developed and put to use—such as computing, satellites, geo-spatial mapping, telecommunications, the Internet, and others—all converging at the same time to make these studies possible, is incredible. Much of this momentum took place in the last 150 years, initiated by the late 1700s' industrial revolution. And the importance of the convergence of these various technologies cannot be minimized.

The Importance of Data

The field of statistical analysis is often subjected to debate concerning how the various elements and statistical entities are applied in the authors' model. But the scientists who have labored in sequencing Polynesian DNA in the past 50 years have been the experts in the field, and thus their collaborative efforts and conclusions are accepted with high credibility.

The basis of any scientific study requiring the analysis of historical and current data is a sufficient quantity of good and relevant data. For the application of statistical methods to haplogroup studies, it is necessary to have an adequate sample size of empirical data, and a logical stratification of the populations in which the data were collected.

For example, the relevant population data for Polynesians should be gathered from the relevant island populations such as Tonga, Samoa, Niue, To'elau, Funafuti, Elise, Rarotoga, Rotuma, and others. The more recent studies have included these indigenous peoples in the sample data as the bases for the above studies.

The Importance of Genetics

Colin Renfrew coined the term archaeogenetics, describing the study of ancient DNA using various molecular genetic methods and DNA resources.[cclxxx] And we must not minimize the importance and complexity of these highly specialized scientific fields, called genetics and DNA sequencing, to the search for Polynesian origin.

The implications of sequencing the human genome to the wellbeing of human life are far-reaching. Such study extends our understanding from the beginning of life to the vast extent of all creatures' life on earth. The idea that we might identify our ancient ancestral brethren through matching relationships of human DNA—Y-Chromosomes (via the father) or mitochondrial DNA (via the mother)—represents an innovative breakthrough in biological science.

It is now a scientifically established conclusion that the human race can be traced back to a "Scientific Adam" and "Scientific Eve" who once lived in a North African village, some 150,000 to 200,000 years ago.[cclxxxi] Thus, the beginning or birth of humans in North Africa, with Scientific Adam and Eve, and the subsequent journey undertaken by the whole human race, that took them from there to the rest of the world, is the most intriguing and mysterious story, be it folklore, or even mythology, that has occupied the imagination of the human race since its beginning.

Likewise with the Polynesian migration from Africa: Theoretically, at some time within the scientifically established human timeline, this migration crossed the Nile River through the Persian Gulf and followed the coastline of Saudi Arabia, continuing up through the Levant—the Fertile Crescent (currently Iraq)—and northeast to Anatolia. They turned east toward Asia until they split, when some turned south (toward the Indus Valley) and others southeast (toward the Tibetan Eurasian Steppe), until they rejoined again in the Asiatic Archipelago. This is the migration path generally postulated by the scientific world as one of the routes taken out of Africa by our early ancestors.

Genetics and the Taiwan Connection

Geneticists have labored to trace the ancient ancestors of the Polynesians through matching genome DNA. Initially, analysis of the Y-chromosome (paternal DNA) showed matching relationships with other Polynesians (Tongans, Cook Islanders, Hawaiians, Tahitians, and others), Melanesians (from Papua and Fiji, Vanuatu, and Solomon Island), and Micronesians (from Palau, Guam, Pohnpei, Marshall Islands, and others). Also, significant relationships were noted with the Taiwanese.

Researchers at the University of Texas Health Science Center, in April 2001, expanded the data analysis and noted that the aboriginal Taiwanese carried distinctly different genetic markers from Eastern Polynesians or Southwestern Pacific Micronesians. The Micronesians and Polynesians were more related to Southwest Asians (islands in the Indonesian Archipelago) than to the Taiwanese.

The University of Hawaii's Professor Rebecca Cann has been focusing on mitochondrial DNA (maternal DNA) in her search for Polynesian ancestry and origins. Her team looked at the relationships of three different groups of Polynesians, with the Hawaiians, Samoans, and Tongans in "group one." The Hawaiians, Samoans, and Cook Islanders were in group two. And group three consisted of Samoans and

Indonesians. The study found that 95% of all Hawaiians are in all of these groups, and 90% of Samoans and Tongans sampled were in all groups. The third group showed the relationship of Samoans to Indonesians.

Cann's genetic study shows that the Polynesian expansion began in mainland Southeast Asia and took place around 6,000 years ago. Professor Cann theorizes several migration waves moving from Asia into the Eastern Pacific Ocean, with Micronesia being settled later than Polynesia.[cclxxxii] This is contrary to what most anthropologists have claimed.

Dr. Geoffrey Chambers, of Victoria University of Wellington, New Zealand, analyzed DNA data which had originally been collected for a study on genetics and alcoholism. He noted that there is less genetic diversity in Polynesian groups than in others. For example, the chance of finding two people with the same DNA is 1 to 112 million for Asians, 1 to 47 million for Caucasians and 1 in 6.7 million for Polynesians.[cclxxxiii] The lower rate of genetic diversity among Polynesians means that they were pretty much in isolation from the rest of the continental world, in the largest ocean in the world, once they arrived in the Eastern Pacific and began to colonize it. But what was their migration path?

Dr. Chambers concluded that the migration that came from China down to Taiwan and the Philippines continued down to the islands of Southeast Asia in the Indonesian Archipelago, then on to West Polynesia and East Polynesia.[cclxxxiv]

However, researchers from Leeds University, in the United Kingdom, published different research findings in 2011.[cclxxxv] According to their research, the long-accepted body of knowledge of a Polynesian link to Taiwan could no longer stand up to scrutiny.

In fact, the Leeds analysis of a much larger sample concluded that the mitochondrial DNA (inherited maternally) of Polynesians can be traced back to migrants from the Asian mainland into the Malay Archipelago—migrants who had already settled the islands in Indonesia and those close to (northern and northeastern) New Guinea, in what is now known as the Bismarck Archipelago, some 6,000 to 8,000 years ago.

Previous studies on mitochondrial DNA had used only pieces of mtDNA. But the Leeds study research was on sequencing complete mtDNA genomes gathered from some 157 people of the Pacific Islands, the islands of Southeast Asia, and islands in the Bismarck Archipelago. They wanted to determine the relationships and variability of the genomes.

The Leeds data and analysis suggest an origin in mainland Southeast Asian coastal areas for the Pacific islanders, with a timeframe around the mid-Pleistocene era (1,640,000 to 10,000 years ago). They concluded that settlement in the Bismarck Archipelago took place around the Holocene period (about 10,000 years ago, post ice age).

Somehow, in this convoluted conundrum of scientific research, we arrive at the two coastal areas where the original "out of Africa" migrations arrived at in the Asiatic Archipelago.

The Leeds Study

A Search for Genetic Signatures

The Leeds study looked for genetic signatures that would allow scientists to classify DNA into different lineages, to enable dating when these lineages dispersed around the world.

The researchers looked at the variability of (mitochondrial) mtDNA in specific geographical areas, to see how much it might have changed since the population's arrival, and to what degree variations were caused by the impact of other populations' DNA. This involved looking into what they called the "molecular clock," dating the changes, by studying the degree of variability in order to observe the time period. Evidence from related analysis—of food particles, soil composites, rock composition, etc.— revealed details of what took place during each period representing a change in the sample, providing insight into the "time clock."

The real message, emanating from the study, is that there is a high degree of relationship between Polynesians, Micronesians, mainland Asians, and Southeast Asian Islanders, but a negligible DNA relationship with Melanesians. This seems to imply that the precursors of the Polynesians settled and interacted with the islanders of Indonesia for some considerable time, then continued moving eastward and northeastward until they reached the Bismarck Archipelago, where the Lapita Trading Network began to take shape, launching from there to the other islands of the South East Pacific.

So, the Polynesian migration into the South Pacific was launched from the Molucca Sea, Ceram Sea, and Halmahera Sea, and then into the Bismarck Archipelago. The accepted idea is that the Austronesian or Polynesian seafaring people were island-hopping east to northeast of the Indonesian Archipelago all throughout the Pleistocene (1.8 million-18,000 B.C.), Holocene (11,700-8,000 B.C.), and Neolithic (3200-250 B.C.) periods.

In early 2019, Shimona Kealy, Sue O'Connor and a team out of Indonesia and the Australian National University were given permission to explore Obi, in Indonesia's Maluku Utara province, looking for possible tool evidence to suggest when humans arrived on the tropical island of Obi. Prehistoric axes, sharp blades, and beads, which were apparently used for hunting and possibly marking canoes for voyaging between islands, were found, dating to at least 18,000 years ago. But perhaps even more profound is the confirmation of this as a crucial staging post for the seafaring people who lived in this region, where they contemplated their "leap of faith" across the Wallace Line to the East Pacific, while the last ice age was coming to an end.[cclxxxvi]

Such evidence seems to indicate that the Polynesians, once they launched their intrepid journey into the South Pacific, moved on rapidly, without long extended stays or interactions with the Melanesian islanders along the route, until they arrived on the Island of Fiji, where they stayed for 700 to 1,000 years.

DNA analysis of Lapita skeletons (specimens from Vanuatu and Toga) confirms and corroborates the Leeds study. And this break-through, from the University of Leeds, supports the timeline and the concept of many layers of migrants into the Malay Archipelago, beginning with the Melanesian Negritos (Spanish meaning "small blacks") who were descendants from the first migration into the Asiatic Archipelago from North Africa, via India and the southeast coastal route, 66,000 to 45,000 years ago. This migration was followed by a group of people who came from the Deccan region of India, of pre-Indo-European race, who were members of the Harappan (an ancient, sophisticated, peaceful culture in the north Indus Valley) and the Mohenjo Daro (west of the Indus River) culture and ethnicity. These two archaeological sites are now undergoing new efforts in excavation, and scientists are re-dating these ancient, cultural societies to 5,000 to 4,500 B.C., though they could be even more than 8,000 years old.

Archaeological Confirmation of the Leeds Study

Reports in 2018 described the unearthing of a 10,000-year-old civilization hidden beneath the soil atop hillocks in the Konkan region of Maharashtra. Experts concluded that the carvings, known as petroglyphs, were created by a hunter-gatherer community, because many of the images were drawings of animals. But many of the animals were not native to the area, and instead the depictions showed animals prevalent in Africa, suggesting the civilization could have migrated to India from Africa.[cclxxxvii] It is also interesting to note that the incredible images are very much reminiscent of the Nazca Lines in South America.

This is important in dating the migration route of the Polynesians and other Austronesians from North Africa through Asia and the Asiatic Archipelago and the Indonesian Archipelago. The time when the Austronesians crossed the Wallace line into East Pacific Oceania, around 2000 B.C., must be reconciled with the timeframe in which they immigrated into the Indonesian Archipelago, and the time of the Taiwanese Austronesian migration down to the islands of Southeast Asia.

The next wave of migration came from the Pontic Steppes, through the Eurasian Steppes, through China, and down through South East Asia via Laos, continuing on to the Malay Archipelago and the Bay of Bengal via Burma. This was followed by the Taiwanese migration down the Malay Archipelago and the Indonesian Archipelago and the North Pacific.

Finally, the last major ancient migration into the Asiatic Archipelago is comprised of Mongoloids from the Eurasia/Tibetan Steppes. This is the group that pushed the ethnic group, of which Polynesians are a part, to the East into the Indonesian Peninsula, where they settled the various islands and continued moving eastward and northeastward until they reached what is now known as the Bismarck Archipelago.

DNA Confirmation of the Leeds Study

In 2007, an article in *Human Genetics* described the analysis of DNA recovered from human remains in archaeological sites of prehistoric people along the coastal area of the Yangtze River, China.[cclxxxviii] This DNA also showed high frequencies of Haplogroup 01 in the Neolithic Liangzhu culture, linking them to the Austronesians and TaiKadai people. Haplogroup 01 was absent in other archaeological sites inland. The authors of the study suggested that this showed evidence of two different human migration routes peopling East Asia; one coastal and one inland, with little genetic intermixing in them.

The Leeds mtDNA study also confirmed the migration path from mainland Southeast Asia, down through the Malay Archipelago, through Sumatra, Java, Bali, West and East Nusa Tenggara, and on to Timor-Leste and the northern island group of Sulawesi and North and South Maluku Islands. This could have taken place around 6,000 to 9,000 years ago, right after the last icecap melting took place, around 13,000 to 15,000 years ago.

Additionally, the study confirms there were different migrations, layered together along different timelines with other migrations into the Indonesian Archipelago. This, of course, makes it more difficult to decipher the mystery of the Polynesian migration into the Eastern Pacific.

The study also implied that the Taiwanese migration south to the Indonesian Archipelago took place during the time when the Polynesians were on their way up to the northeast to what is now called the Bismarck Archipelago. This is where the spoken language of the Polynesians received its last influence, at the time of their launching on to the East Pacific Ocean. From here they continued moving southeast into the East Pacific Ocean.

The conundrum of deriving Polynesian genetic identity very much parallels the challenge of sorting through the fabric of layered threads in their migration path—through cultural influences, language diversity, and crossing many ethnicities and geographical areas.

The Leeds study made clear that there is a lack of mtDNA (maternal) markers for Melanesian in the maternal DNA of the Polynesians. This may be due to the Polynesians not stopping at any of the Melanesian Islands for an extended period of time, thus limiting intermarriage with the indigenous population of Papua New Guinea, Solomon Island, and Vanuatu.

However, several genetic studies noted the presence of Melanesian Y-DNA (paternal) in the Polynesian Y-DNA. This could be explained by the adventurous nature of traveling Polynesian males, who might customarily take on wives and then leave them and their children in their original homeland.

In fact, the oral history and folklore of Polynesians tell stories that the Melanesians were unfriendly and violent toward the Polynesians or any uninvited guests (and that they were practicing cannibalism). So

Polynesian traveling parties were even more motivated to push onward on their journey.

The oral traditions of Samoans and Manu'ans also corroborate a practice where the mother and children anchored a family, while the male (father) sought adventure. Such adventure was often decreed by the head of the family: for example, the "Decree by Lealali" to his children—Salevaogogo (*Sa,* big family, *le vao gogo,* of the might tern of the forest), Sausi, Tupa'imatuna, Tupa'ilelei and Tupa'isiva—and also the well-known decrees at the beach of Mata'ena'ena in Savai'i, where Saveasi'uleo and his brother, Ulufanuasese'e parted ways and became the founders of several major families in Samoa and Manu'a.

This is the story of Lealali's decree: Lealali married a woman from Iva in Savai'i, and also Malelegaaleto'elau the daughter of Tuisafua, and begat the brothers that caused the division of Savai'i. The first marriage produced two sons, Salevaogogo, and Sausi. The second marriage produced the brothers Tupa'imatuna, Tupa'ilelei and Tupa'isiva. Lealali decreed that Salevaogogo and Sausi should become the head of government in Leulumoega all the way to Savai'i and Falealili. Then he decreed that Tupa'imatuna, Tupa'ilelei, and Tupa'isiva should become High Paramount Chiefs in all of Savai'i.

Slow Boats and Out of Taiwan

It is time now to describe the two theories of Polynesian migration that have often held sway.

The "Slow Boat" vs. "Express Train" or "Out of Taiwan" theories about the Polynesians' (sometimes referred to as the Proto-Polynesian) migration across the East Pacific Ocean are two different propositions as to when and where the migration took place. I specifically avoided mentioning these earlier because I didn't want to get tangled up with the debate between them, and so lose sight of the direction of my own research and analysis. Still, to summarize the two propositions: The "Slow Boat" theory proposed that the Polynesians or Proto-Polynesians lived in and around the islands of the Indonesian Archipelago for over 20,000 years, and then made the "leap of faith" crossing to the East Pacific about 10,000 years before the present day. The "Out of Taiwan" proposal says that the Polynesian migration came from the mainland China migration, crossing over to Taiwan and on to the East Pacific around 3,600 to 4,400 years before the current period.

Interestingly, researchers commenting on biases in the research have pointed out that the geographic emphasis has long been influenced not by science, but by access, funding and tradition. And in fact, if we move back the timeframe for "out of Africa," taking the southern route—crossing the Nile and then entering the southern part of India and following the coastal route to the Asiatic Archipelago—it could mean that when the migration reached the Asiatic Archipelago, the travelers were able to continue to the Australian continent. But when the ocean water covered up the landmass connecting Australia and the Asian continent, I believe humans started to move up through mainland Asia going north. Thus, humans came up to populate China and perhaps South India before the populations from ancient Levant crossed over to the Pontic Steppe and Indus valley. This northwest migration could change how we view the directions and timelines of human migration.

My approach is to look for clarity on the amalgamation of indigenous peoples who immigrated into the Asiatic Archipelago, to trace their movements in the region, and then to isolate the Polynesian thread among them. We have to keep in mind that earlier migrants, the Negrito, were already in the archipelago, because they came on the first or perhaps the second migration wave, dated 40,000 to 65,000 years before the current period. So, if we just try to imagine what these people might have been doing for 30,000 to 50,000 years in the region, wouldn't the answer be that they were constantly moving around the region? For example, they could have continued journeying to the Australian continent (65,000 B.C.), Papua New Guinea (40,000 B.C.), and Solomon Island (20,000 B.C.), and have moved north toward China and Taiwan (45,000 B.C.) then on to the Philippines (around 37,000 B.C.). This would be 20,000 to 40,000 years before the amalgamation of different people from the Deccan, the Pontic Steppe, the Eurasian Steppe, and the land around the major rivers of Asia, descending into the Asiatic Archipelago.

The problem with these theories is they do not account for the anatomy of the Polynesians' way of life as they began their migration— their culture, language, tools, weapons, foods, religions, social interactions etc. They actually conquered the Negrito and settled the area for a significant period of time. It took them several thousands of years to cover the whole of the Asiatic Archipelago (from Madagascar to the islands of the Indonesian Archipelago, to Taiwan, Formosa Island, and the Philippines).

There was life before the great migration. There were warring factions undertaking colonization and fighting to hold onto a kingdom in the midst of a rather busy "migration lane" in the Malay and Indonesian Archipelagos. To assume "all things being constant," and then pick a launching place and time for Polynesian migration across the East Pacific, does not reflect reality. The reality is that these people were searching for a permanent place to call their own.

It became obvious to me why the Melanesians of Papua New Guinea and Solomon Island never explored the East Pacific Ocean. There was no motivation for them to do so. They had already found their Island Kingdom, and a large one at that. Do we not see the obvious: the only ocean that had not been explored was the East Pacific Ocean and it was time?

Genome sequencing of the Lapita specimen shows the initial migration wave took place between 2000 and 1200 B.C., using, as evidence, the Mainland Southeast Asia marker. Call it Proto-Polynesian, if you will, but it is the same group of indigenous peoples that were traversing the Malay and Indonesian Archipelagos for 10,000 years before the current period. The subsequent migration across the Wallace Line comes from children or descendants of the Polynesians who were island-hopping in the Indonesian Archipelago. This I cover in detail in my description of the Polynesians moving through the Java Peninsular Strait, when the Malayans violently pushed them eastward through the Java Peninsula. Genome sequencing points it out with the mtDNA marker of the Melanesian thread.

The matriarchal culture was such that women would intermarry with Melanesian men and produce descendants who pushed forward and migrated onto the East Pacific. Modern Polynesians are descended from this later wave of migration.

It should be noted that the Polynesians, or Navigators, also continued "island-hopping" in the Bismarck Archipelago and Solomon Island and Fiji Archipelagos for a period of 600 to 1,000 years before settling in Manu'a and Samoa.

Corroborating Evidence

The combination of linguistics, archaeology, and genetics from ancient DNA tells us a lot about the human population of the past. It helps piece together the mosaic schema of past cultures and migrations, from how they evolved to who they are today.

Pedro Soares, in searching for the Polynesian origin, pointed out that while the Leeds study does not support the "Out of Taiwan" hypothesis, it also doesn't rule out a linguistic relationship between the language of indigenous agricultural Taiwanese and the Austronesian family of languages.[cclxxxix]

His study (with Teresa Rito, and Martin B. Richard) further confirms findings from the Leeds University research study (which used 4,750 samples) in that it doesn't support the so called "slow boats" theory of Polynesian migration to the Eastern Pacific.

The study reiterates the fact that linguistics and geology together cannot ascertain the ancestral origins of a race. But they can corroborate the DNA and cultural similarities.

The language comparisons were discussed elsewhere in this manuscript, where I have taken the position that, although there are many words that are common among the Austronesian family languages, the grammar does not agree.

Also integral, in looking at any migratory population, is the issue of cultural similarities, but it still does not prove kinship. As I am trying to show, during the long path traveled, over a long period of time, crossing many cultures and ethnicities, every people and place will have had a profound impact on the Polynesian culture and human psyche.

Polynesian Migration Recorded in DNA

The Mystery Deepens

The mystery of Polynesian migration appears to be much older, and more of a conundrum, than was declared by the conventional wisdom of past years. The multilayered footprints on the mosaic of the Polynesian migration map evidence the real complexity of retracing a human migration that goes back 150,000 to 200,000 years. So, the "Out of Taiwan" and the "slow boat" theories, dating the migration to around 4,000 years ago, are now being redefined. My hypothesis, based on advances in science and analysis, is that normal routine sailing expeditions took place before the glacial period, around 25,000 years ago, and were propelled further by the icecap melting, around 10,000 years ago, causing a global climate change that profoundly impacted the Polynesian migration.

Climate Change and Migration

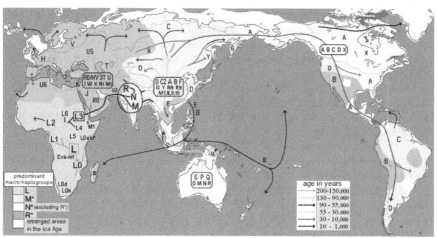

Figure 11: Human migrations and Mitochondrial Haplogroups[ccxc]

Dr. Oppenheimer, co-author of the study "Climate Change and Postglacial human dispersal in Southeast Asia,"[ccxci] proposed that migration of populations was driven by climate change during the Ice Age around 7,000 to 15,000 years ago. The effect of climate change was a rise of 4 to 6 meters (12 to 18 feet) in sea level, which submerged the ancient "Sundaland Peninsula" that previously extended the Asian continental landmass as far as Borneo, Java, and Sumatra. The final impact of this flooding and submergence was the creation, in the Java and South China Seas, of the thousands of little islands that today make up Indonesia and the Philippines. Population dispersal took place at the same time as the rise in sea level, resulting in migrations from the Philippines as far north to Taiwan in the last 10,000 years, and furthering the Polynesian eastward migrations to the newly formed Bismarck Archipelago.

Genetic analyses, by many scientists, have narrowed the focus, and research from the Leeds University finally corroborated this migration through the Malay or the Indonesian Archipelago. So now it is evident, from a multitude of genetic analyses of Polynesians, that there were different waves of migration from mainland East Asia down to the Malay Archipelago; and that, after a period of 3,000 to 4,000 years or more, the Polynesians embarked on a journey to the East Pacific Ocean. It is also clear that the original human migration down to Melanesia and Australia took place around 55,000 years ago, settling the Australian continent, followed by a migration that settled what is currently known as the Bismarck Archipelago around 33,000 years ago.

But the real issue, concerning DNA analysis, is the genetic relationship with groups outside of Polynesian—such as Indonesian, Malayan, Melanesian, Japanese, and others in the Asiatic Archipelago—for knowing those relationships will allow us to continue tracing the migration path of the Polynesians backward to their origin.

Samoans and Manu'ans are already aware of their kin and brethren—Tahitians, Hawaiians, Togans, Marquesans, and Maoris—and of relationships by intermarriage with Fijians. And Manu'ans have always had a belief that all the other islands were colonized by Samoan warrior explorers, such as Fitiaumua, Pili, Maui (all Manu'an) and others. But there is no reminiscence or remembrance to help retracing the genealogical ancestry back into to the Asiatic Archipelago and up into mainland Asia.

DNA Across the Wallace Line

Results of various DNA analyses show that the DNA of samples from modern Polynesians do not indicate a presence of Taiwanese or Asian DNA, implying that mainland Southeast Asian DNA never crossed the Wallace line into the East Pacific Ocean. However, a more recent study, by an international multi-disciplinary team, analyzed DNA extracted from the skeletons of four ancient women, from the islands of Vanuatu and Tonga, dated between 2,300 and 3,100 years ago.[ccxcii]

The four specimens of ancient women are directly associated with the Lapita culture, dated at 1,500 B.C. They come from a distinct population that appears to have been completely separate from the ancestors of people living today in Papua New Guinea. Instead, they share ancestry with indigenous peoples in Taiwan (the Atayal) and the Philippines (the Kankanaey).

Co-author Pontus Skoglund, a postdoc in David Reich's lab at Harvard Medical School in Boston, concludes that there is no evidence of Papuan ancestry in the Lapita group. This conclusion conflicts with the modern Polynesian DNA sample that shows Melanesian and Austronesian DNA and none from mainland Asian or Southeast Asia (Taiwan). So, are Polynesians (part of the Lapita culture) related to Melanesians (including Papua New Guinea) or not?

To reconcile the differences between the ancient women's DNA and modern Polynesian DNA, it is important to recognize the time difference between the Lapita culture and these ancient women (500-1,000 years) and the multiple waves of voyagers migrating across Oceania. Many scientists and authorities in Polynesian migration have now confirmed the Lapita trading network was centered in Vanuatu and is the original development site of the East Pacific trading system. Thus, this was very likely a landing port for early migrating voyagers. The later migrations—those of the Austronesians/Polynesians between 1,000 B.C. and 500 A.D.—resulted in offspring from intermarriages between Polynesian matriarchs with the Melanesian males. This is the DNA that crossed the Wallace line into the East Pacific Oceania.

Hence the diversity of modern Polynesian DNA, which includes the presence of DNA from the islands of Southeast Asia (Austronesian DNA) and Melanesian DNA, which led to confusion in pinpointing Polynesian ancestry in Southeast Asia. It is their (Austronesian) offspring who entered Oceania and settled in with the indigenous population there, while the matriarchs stayed and established the family structure, culture, and development of their Austronesian language. Over several thousands of years, the indigenous language and DNA would eventually be influenced by the Polynesian or Austronesian language and DNA, to the point of complete erosion.

A Warning

The studies reaffirm the need for other studies to connect the dots—as we have done in looking at the behavioral patterns of matriarchal society among the Polynesian Navigators at the period and in the vicinity of the Lapita trading network. Our explanation goes further, but we should remember the Orator's warning to "be careful when you open the family or the Chief's bamboo receptacle or container, for it holds all the fisherman's heirlooms such as, hooks, bait, feathers, medicinal items, speech, genealogy, history, and wisdom. For it's said that it can tell the story of not only the Samoan but all of mankind"—*Sa'a fa'aoti le utu a le faimea*—To open the bamboo receptacle of the Chief is to empty the bamboo container of the old wise fishermen's heirlooms. And so, be careful when opening old family lineages and tales, because they are sacred.

Close Proximity, but Different DNA

One would presume the DNA from the offspring of the intermarried population in the Indonesian Archipelago would be carried forward by colonizers of the East Pacific Ocean. So, what happened to the DNA of migrants from mainland Asia into the Indonesian Archipelago?

It turns out that the key to unravelling this conundrum is the cultural family structure of these islands' populations. Differences in the cultural family structure—matriarchal vs. patriarchal—and the corresponding cultural practices led to isolation and completely different genetics, language and dialect, and ecosystem, in spite of their close island or village proximity. The differences in the DNA of these islands' populations, in spite of their close proximity, makes it difficult to pinpoint the Polynesian migration path and origin in Southeast Asia.

According to J. Stephen Lansing—an anthropologist—and Herawati Sudoyo—a medical-geneticist and Director of the National Science Foundation Eijkman Institute for Molecular Biology Complexity Institute at Nanyang Technological University—the diverse DNA of the populations of the islands of Southeast Asia consists of mainland Southeast Asian, Melanesian, and Austronesian. The most interesting finding is the absence of mainland Southeast Asian DNA (tested for using the Y-Chromosome, mtDNA, X-Chromosome and autosomes) among Polynesians. This seems to indicate that the Asian DNA did not dominate the Navigators of the East Pacific Ocean.[ccxciii]

The key to deciphering this conundrum is the matriarchal nature of the societal structure of these clans or tribes that moved into these Indonesian Islands—the launching pads of the last link in the great human migration—around 4,000 years ago, prior to the last great migration. This matriarchal structure (tribal and cultural) did not originate in the Indonesian Archipelago, but rather these people brought it with them from mainland Southeast Asia. In fact, the matriarchal structure goes even further back to the Himalayan mountain range, the Tibetan steppes Plateau, back to the Deccan, the Levant, and, finally, across the Nile and back to North Africa.

The convergence of many tribes and clans, immigrating into the Indonesian Archipelago and settling on the various islands, created an atmosphere of seclusion and isolation, based on the family matriarchs. They each brought with them their language or dialect, which explains the numerous languages or dialects that coexist in this small geographical area. For example, in Papua New Guinea it is not uncommon to find two village tribes, living two or three miles apart, where each speaks two or more languages completely different from each another.

In anthropologist Stephen Lansing's research, we see that, within the key stepping stone islands to the launching pad of migration to the East Pacific Ocean, there are cultures such as Sumba (with a patriarchal structure), Flores (with a matriarchal structure), and Timor (where interior villages show a predominantly matriarchal structure). Thus the mitochondrial DNA, which descends from the female relationship, is more consistent in these matriarchal villages, rather than DNA in the male Y-Chromosome.

This matriarchal family structure is fundamental in untangling the story of Polynesian migration and cultural development. In family structures with a female head, women anchor the family, and men are the providers of food, security, and conquering warriors. Men seek new lands, and populate the clan through marriages, extending the family and genealogy. This transient role of the male contributes to spreading DNA from the Y-Chromosome across the islands of the Pacific Ocean, while the females end up marrying the indigenous males from other populations. In the cases of these matriarchal villages, some females ended up marrying Papua New Guinean males. The offspring of these marriages produced a mixed DNA population, with the X-Chromosome coming from mainland Southeast Asia, Austronesia and Melanesia.

It's this generation of offspring that would eventually take the leap of faith into the East Pacific Ocean to colonize the islands.

Congested Traffic in Malay and Indonesian Archipelagos

Surprisingly, genetics, combined with other sciences, can even point us to the reason for this leap of faith migration. Geneticists step in to illustrate the biodiversity of the population demographic of the Indonesian Archipelago. The population mix in the Strait of Malacca and the Java peninsula was very much "unknown" to social scientists for a long time, since early discovery of the region, because very little was known about these people, let alone their migration path to the archipelago. But as more threads of this colorful tapestry unfold, revealing the demographic of the Strait of Malacca, we are now learning just how busy the traffic was there and how diversified the population.

For my purposes, the more we understand the diversity of the population in the past, the more we can understand the path and motivation of the Navigators' island-hopping migration throughout the archipelago. But postulating the origins of different people and cultures will not provide definitive clarity on the overall demographic of this crossroads to the Pacific Australasian corridor. We need a scientific way to tell us the kinship story. And again, thanks to the convergence of multiple technologies, through collaboration and corroboration of various scientific disciplines, efforts can now be made to illustrate the real story behind our conundrum.

As we've seen, several genetic studies have covered the different populations of mainland and Southeast Asia, looking specifically at Austronesians, Melanesians, Micronesians, and Polynesians. More recently, they have begun to, quite succinctly and simply, lay out the salient genome markers for the key foundational population groups. A summary of these findings, published by *Nature Publishing Group*,[ccxciv] confirms the timeframes of migration waves into the archipelagos, using the genome markers for the group in each major wave. This gives clarity to the demographic of the region and provides a window into possible ways of life at the time of migration.

The preface to this study notes that, even today, the indigenous population still has a tendency to view themselves (or their demographic) as being split between "pribumi," or natives, and "pendatang," or foreigners—i.e. indigenous vs. migrant residents of the archipelago. While it's not clear which part of the demographic most subscribes to this attitude, relating migrant data to the approximate arrival times in the archipelagos lets one deduce that the early wave of tribal indigenous people, whose presence goes back several thousand years, might be most likely to feel this way.

It would be naive to think these people did not intermarry, but it's equally naive to think some tribes or clans would not have insisted on maintaining racial purity through prohibition of intermarriage with other tribes or people, an attitude the Navigators and many other Polynesians practice.

So, to summarize the study:

- Sequencing of mtDNA found haplogroups M, F, Y2 and B in the western part of the Indonesian Archipelago. People in these groups are mostly speakers of Austronesian languages, spoken in Southeast Asia, Madagascar, and the Pacific Islands.
- In the eastern part of the Indonesian Archipelago they found haplogroups Q and P. These are non-Austronesian speakers.
- More interestingly, on the islands of Mentawai and Nias (off the west coast of West Sumatra), the haplogroup E can be grouped together with the native people of Formosa Island (off the coast of Taiwan)— i.e. these are Austronesian speakers who traveled south around 5,000 years ago (a date that is now redated to between 8,000 and 4,000 years ago).

The haplogroups M, F, Y2 and B represent Austronesians occupying the west to Madagascar. And haplogroups Q and P show people moving toward Papua New Guinea and the Nusa Tenggara corridor.

Additionally, the haplogroups (or macrogroups) M and N represent the first stage of the "out of Africa" dispersal, around 50,000-60,000 years ago. The second stage of migration also comes from mainland Asia and carries mtDNA markers B4a, B4b, B4c, B4c1b3, B5a, B5b, B5b1, D, and E, dating to around 10,000-40,000 years ago. Within this group, there is a group whose marker traces back to the region around the Yangtze River and Hunan.

The third migration stage, or wave, takes place in the Neolithic period around 3200B.C.-1 A.D. with representatives of haplogroups M7b3, E1a1a, M7c3c and Y2. This is the period when cultural flowering and the spread of language diffused throughout the archipelagos. The leading cultural development found in this period is strong evidence of matrilocal and matrilineal organizational structures of family and clan. Also at this time, considerable maritime movement between islands increased diversity throughout the region.

Increasing migration traffic into the two archipelagos (Malay and Indonesian) and, more specifically, into the Strait of Malacca and the Java Peninsula, between 40,000 B.C. and the first century A.D., had a swamping effect on the gene pool in this epicenter (or watershed) of migrant population. At the same time, rising sea levels during the melting of the icecaps around 13,000 years ago buried the landmass between Southeast Asia and the Australian continent, further squeezing the migrant population in this geological region. Then the rapid growth in population density in the archipelagos fueled gene pool diversity and competition for homesteading. So by the Neolithic period (3100-100 B.C.) the "island-hopping" Austronesian/Polynesian behavior reached its full flowering.

This environment is the backdrop for the Navigators' journey, migrating across the East Pacific. And now, just as I make my last minute editing corrections and additions to this book, an article pops up on my mobile phone saying: "Ancient DNA is revealing the genetic landscape of people who first settled East Asia." So I feel compelled to mention and cite this article before I go to publishing.

The crux of the article published by *The Conversation*[ccxcv] is the confirmation, through DNA sequencing studies, of the history of the peopling of Southeast Asia and specifically of the Malay and Indonesian archipelagos. And it's critical to have this sort of clarity about what was going on in this corridor, in order for us gain clarity about the psyche of the Navigators, relative to their arduous migration.

The science advances, even as I write, and more threads of the fabric are revealed.

DNA Conclusions

Why it Matters

In my introduction of this DNA Section, I mentioned my belief that the whole analysis of genome sequencing is really the study of changes or mutations in the genes at specific locations on the chromosomes. What we can say is that the various DNA sequencing studies have indicated several key findings about the genetic makeup of Polynesians and have shed light on the route they took in their migration path through the Indonesian Archipelago.

DNA analysis confirms the island-hopping approach of the Polynesians, up and down the Eastern Indonesian Archipelago. The association with Melanesian shows not only a geographically close proximity, but also the presence of markers of Polynesian "motif."

The sequencing of the genome is still at a fragmented stage; it still needs more data and more complete examples of both ancient and current specimens. This would allow scientists to home in on mutations that might tell us more about traits, gene types and their variants causing physical disorders and diseases, and maybe even genes that combat viruses.

The idea of traveling across the Pacific Ocean, over distances requiring weeks or months without adequate water and food for sustenance, speaks volumes to the genetic makeup of the Navigators. There has to be something special in their genes to have let them endure this kind of consistent physical-body workout for generations. Perhaps comparing the Polynesian genome to that of other long-distance migrants of the past might reveal valuable knowledge—looking, for example, at Vikings, Bedouins, and others who have a history of traversing long distances in other parts of the world.

My memory of Samoa in the olden days—from observing my grandparents and others in the same generation—is of physical characteristics that were thin and lean; medium to tall in height (from my actual observations, I'd say they were really quite tall); with dark brown or black, straight or wavy hair; dark brown eyes; a long torso; long skinny legs; long skinny hands with long fingers; broad shoulders; and a short neck with a medium-sized head. These characteristics are often described in family folklore and legends of Samoans and Manu'ans. So a question that comes to mind is: could these be the characteristics of an architecturally well-structured body, built to endure long distances of intrepid ocean travel?

Our quest is to look to all the sciences for answers on where the Navigators originated, who they are, and who they're related to. And we look to genetics to understand their human anatomy and genome makeup, so we can appreciate who they really are. This is another critical aspect of the enigma of their migration mystery.

A Burgeoning Field of Research

This burgeoning field of genetics is only minimally explored in our brief journey in search of the Navigators and of the ancestry of the Polynesians. We didn't set out to conduct a comprehensive review of genome sequencing for the whole Polynesian population, but rather to acquire an understanding of their evolutionary biology—of how different the Polynesian markers are from those of ethnicities found along their migration path. We have not come close to covering the many areas and disciplines in the field of genetics—for example, the application of genetics to medicine, forensic biology, biotechnology, and virology (research into the source of viruses, cause, effect, and implication on vaccine development) in general; nor applications of genetics to the ecology, epidemiology, and microbiology of Polynesians and Navigators in particular. However, genetic sequencing is of critical value in quenching our thirst for more definitive information about the Navigators' origins.

With limited specimens of genetic material from ancient Polynesians, and specifically from ancient Samoans and Manu'ans, there is not enough to allow the sequencing of a complete population profile. Nevertheless, the progress made to date in this area is nothing short of miraculous. The biotechnology being used for gene sequencing today is giving us constantly more data, describing more clearly our genetic "motif," and filling in the missing pieces of our beautiful mosaic.

What We have Learned

We can summarize the storylines on the Navigators' genome as follows:

Mitochondrial DNA (mtDNA) resides in the cell cytoplasm and contains DNA that is inherited only from the mother. Various efforts to look into the genetics of Polynesians and the Navigators through maternal DNA (specifically mtDNA) have helped us understand their kindred relationships with various populations of Austronesians in Southeast Asia. The timeline revealed by these respective DNA sequencing efforts may very well allude to a storyline that explains the actual movements of Polynesians in the region.

For example, while the Leeds University study (with Professor Martin Richards and Dr. Pedro Soares in 2011) does not confirm the "Out of Taiwan" origin of Polynesians, its analysis does reveal "Out of Mainland Southeast Asia" DNA. The Leeds Study also did not confirm or deny the so called "slow boat" migration supposition, vis-a-vis the "direct fast boat" argument. But it did, nevertheless, add to the storyline which pieces together the mosaic.

There are clearly many layers to Polynesians migration in Southeast Asia and the Malay and Indonesian Archipelagos, covering 8,000 years of sojourn in the region. The window—the porthole, as it were—afforded us by genome sequencing biotechnology and by geneticists has only confirmed one piece of a long-fragmented strand of that helix called DNA. The reality is that earlier human migrations moved from south to north on the mainland, followed by a much later movement, of a more advanced human population, going south from Taiwan to the Malay and Indonesian Archipelagos.

Cultural Past Confirmed in the Genome

We have learned several new cultural attributes that were not evident in Samoans and Manu'ans today. The matriarchal culture was the original structure of society. But when the Navigators arrived, they began building and expanding their family and cultural practices, and the men began to curtail their daily ocean journeys; at this point the Navigators' emphasis moved toward the male chieftain authority, derived from the family, and to family responsibility and authority as it is today. Genome sequencing enlightened us as to how this results from the island-hopping movement of Polynesians in the Indonesian Archipelago.

Manu'ans and Samoans have never suffered from an "identity crisis," colloquially speaking. They have always been clear as to who, what, and where their ancient beginning and ancestors are. What was missing was scientific confirmation of their legendary story. The missing link—that of human migration across the East Pacific Ocean, even touching the Americas, accomplished by the Polynesians—has long been a subject of debate. But I believe we have finally put this to rest. The Polynesians' oral traditions, added now to scientific evidence of their origins and migration details, sets their story and history in place in the annals of World History.

The tidings that the Navigators brought with them as gifts from the gods—such things as culture, language, innovation and creativity, genetic traits, mannerisms of reticence, open-arm generosity, oratory eloquence, unwavering beliefs, and commitment to responsibility toward their culture and family structure—all combined together, have defined and will define Samoans and Manu'ans from their beginning up to today, tomorrow, and forever.

Meanwhile, what is also clear, via genome sequencing, is that the Navigators are citizens of a much bigger ancestral group called Austronesian, one which collectively encompasses over half a billion people in Southeast Asia. Although this population has increased significantly in the last 300 years, it has added exciting new mutations recognized in the genetic markers of a beautiful people.

Closing Salutation

Eureka

Eureka! Oh you Navigators, Eureka! Oh you Navigators of the Pacific. You have found it! You have found it!

God's blessing and gifts to you lie at:

Latitude: -13 degrees 48 minutes and 26 seconds South

Longitude: -171 degrees 46 minutes 30 seconds West, for Samoa;

and at:

Latitude: -14 degrees 18 minutes 23 South

Longitude: -170 degrees 41 minutes 42 seconds West, for Manu'a and American Samoa.

This is your permanent address, an address that is defined from the highest point in the landmass to the core of the Earth, an address that is a place you call home—a gift to all your generations past, current, and future till the end of time.

For even Archimedes, perhaps the world's greatest scientist, who famously said, "Give me a lever and a place to stand, and I'll move the world"—he was the greatest scientist in the classical age; Archimedes of Syracuse, on the Island of Sicily, who lived in the third century B.C.—but even he did not know that the Navigators had already been given the Koa tree, the Pacific Ocean, the Wind, and the Heavenly bodies, as they conquered the Pacific Ocean.

Archimedes' "Eureka!" moment came when he discovered the principle of buoyancy, or how ships float in the water.[ccxcvi] But this, oh Navigators, is yours.

Oh, Navigators, your Kingdom is in the South Pacific, an Island Nation that stands ready to be counted among the Nations of the World.

Oh you Navigators of the Pacific, there may not have been a welcoming committee, but the feeling of Eureka and euphoria must have been overwhelming. Yet the humility, from quietly internalizing the euphoria of seeing their god's gift and blessing, is a behavior pattern that remains characteristic of the Navigators forever.

Conclusion

Fate's Last Movement

It's purely a coincidence that this year (2020) the world's classical music lovers are celebrating the 250th anniversary of Ludwig van Beethoven's birthday. As we return to our earlier "Symphony of Fate" metaphor (from Beethoven), we see that we have just negotiated the third movement, with the Genetics section of this book, and now comes the impending finale, where the risk-takers are rewarded with the euphoria of triumph over adversity. It evokes a pandemonium of Eureka!— of discovery.

With this grand finale, the composer Beethoven achieved his masterpiece. His creative approach, weaving and orchestrating the motifs and themes of the 5th Symphony throughout each movement, reveals what experts will forever enshrine as brilliance. The way he wove that motif in a pianissimo thread—at times like a faint distant sound, like the wind whispering—reminds us that fate hovers and knocks on our subconsciousness always, whatever undertaking we choose to pursue. And the outcome can be predictable, because it is based on how dedicated, smart, and resilient you are as you pursue it to the end.

The illustrious Greek sage, Solon, advised King Croesus of Lydia, using a metaphor that, in a wrestling match the winner cannot be declared while still in the ring. He implied that the match is not over until no competitors remain in the ring. (This discourse is told in one of my favorite Greek myths, recorded by Herodotus.)

At the time, King Croesus was soliciting accolades and confirmation of his wealth and status from his most esteemed guest, seeking recognition and affirmation to increase his extreme happiness. But to no avail. The Athenian lawmaker and philosopher put it simply: You should count no man happy until he dies.

The moral of the story is, as we know in the game of life, that it's not over until you are done with life, or life is done with you. And we all know the end of the story and the fate of King Croesus—he was by defeated by the Persian King Cyrus and was captured, and was about to be burned on a great pyre on the city square of Sardis, his city. As the flames started engulfing the king, Croesus tried to imagine what people would say of him after his death. Bursting into tears at the unpleasant thoughts, he suddenly remembered Solon's wise advice, and, almost too late, he cried out: "O, Solon, O Solon, O Solon, you true seer!"

Intrigued to ascertain the meaning of these words, Cyrus ordered that the fire be put out and Croesus be taken off the pyre and brought to him. Cyrus immediately inquired as to the meaning of Croesus' cry.

"I was just naming the name of a wise man," replied Croesus, "one who revealed to me a truth worth more than all of our riches and glory." Then Croesus told the story of his guest, the traveling sage Solon. It is said that Cyrus the Great was so moved by this tale that he pardoned Croesus and made him one of his favorite court judges.[ccxcvii]

So we have negotiated the themes of the arduous path, the environment, the language development, the culture mat, the religious Spirit, and finally the miracles of science and technology in genetics. And I can hear the raw power and overwhelming strength of the Polynesian motif arise in a crescendo of exaltation at their arrival.

The Witness

The Ocean Swell

As I stand here today, some 3,100 years since the Navigators traversed across the Wallace Line of the Indonesian Archipelago into the East Pacific Ocean, I am humbled to be a descendant of these warrior Navigators of the South Pacific Ocean. I look back, looking westward on the Pacific Ocean, and see no monuments, no footprints, no voyage path, no guideposts, no remnants of dilapidated vessels, no sign in the sky of their navigational path, no signs in the flight path of birds, nothing whatsoever other than the calm, massive, mighty Pacific Ocean. And this ocean's behavior is such that the waves build up a swell, but never break. This suggests a metaphor with oratory: the swells of the waves sound angry and look frightening, but a wave never breaks until it hits a large object or the shore.

In another metaphor, God's wrath can be devastating but His mercy is everlasting. Similarly, the Pacific Ocean is a silent killer when the weather is not cooperating. It consumes everything in its path. It is deep and wide, and its currents can be a major force with a mind of their own. The ocean has never been conquered by man. We have learned to use and navigate it, but we have never tamed it.

I'm reminded of the Biblical verse in Proverbs 30:1—"The words of Agur son of Jakeh. An oracle. Thus says the man: I am weary, O God, I am weary, O God. How can I prevail?" Verse 2 adds, "Surely I am too stupid to be human; I do not have human understanding" (NRSV). Verse 3: "I have not learned wisdom, nor have I knowledge of the holy ones." And verses 18 and 19 show us these four things that, I believe, even the great wisdom of King Solomon—the wisest man mentioned in the Bible—could not solve. To paraphrase the Scriptures, these are:

- the way of an eagle in the sky,
- the way of a snake on the rock,
- the way of a ship at sea, and
- the way of a man with a maiden.

So who am I to be so arrogant as to think I could actually do these things that, by their very nature, are impossible to do? Are we so arrogant, and so sure of our science and human intellect, that we claim the precision of our scientific measurements will tell us the whole truth?

The orator's idiom says: "Who was there to witness?" which is not being a "smart aleck," but comes from the recognition of how far away the distant past is—the distant past of the orator's history, culture, and language.

Nevertheless, we have searched the ocean for guideposts and for remnants of their ancient vessels; we have searched the sky for signs in the flight paths of birds; but we have found no definitive evidence. So we are left to the mercy of science and its inner workings to give us some answers about the anatomy of the Navigators' migration. And science gives us its small, porthole-like windows to interpret the fragmented indicators of what might have transpired in the Navigators' journey, but not the whole true story.

My belief is that the truth lies right in front of us. The people of Manu'a and Samoa are the descendants of the Navigators. To understand their origin, we have to look through the prism of their living descendants. Additionally, we have to touch on the Austronesians and their neighboring countries and societies, to get a view of how they influenced the Navigators on their journey through the region. Looking through this prism allows us to see and touch the flesh and bones, the culture and the way of life, which will illuminate our ancestors' colorful past and migration.

The Pain of Goodbye

We often herald the accomplished and are quick to give accolades and monumental rewards, but very few remember the pain and suffering that was endured by the Navigators while making their arduous journey.

I reflect now on my own experience of saying goodbye to my grandparents and all my family relatives in Samoa. We departed Apia, in the middle of the night, on a small inter-island boat, on our way to American Samoa, to complete our travel immigration papers to the United States, back in late 1962. I can still remember how painful it was, and the sadness of leaving my grandparents. I was devastated with the idea of leaving everything I had and loved, leaving everything I had known in my life to that point. The sadness of saying goodbye to the people who you love dearly is excruciating.

Then I'm reminded of other goodbyes that I witnessed, when other members of my family left for Tutuila, Fiji, New Zealand, Australia and, on rare occasions, for the United States. You see, the distance and remoteness of the islands make these farewells and goodbyes feel like eternity. At times I felt that the people—those departing and those staying—were sobbing so profusely, as though they were in a funeral procession.

As I think about it today, I realize that they were saying farewell, in a sense, forever. They knew these countries were so far away, on the other side of world, that they had very little knowledge about them—nothing other than cryptic news stories, legendary descriptions of those advanced societies that they received intermittently through the radio waves, and the words of traveling guests or relatives. So, yes, such goodbyes are almost equivalent to saying farewell to someone you love, who you may never again see in your lifetime.

That excruciating pain in your heart, on saying goodbye, is an integral part of the Navigators' migration journey. It must have been devastating for the Navigators and other contemporary immigrants. But I know, as one who was once an immigrant and business entrepreneur, that ambition for the journey and fixation on the dream of achieving the goal, or of arriving in a new exciting place, is a way of soothing and deflecting this excruciating pain.

Hope feeds the imagination, or as the German Marxist philosopher Ernst Bloch (1885-1977) said, hope is cast in our imagination, where our desires, dreams, and longings are given form.[ccxcviii] Peter Thompson, writing in the *Guardian,* explains how Bloch laid out the many ways in which hope and the very human desire for liberation and fulfillment are found together in everyday life.[ccxcix]

While optimistic about arriving at a new life in the United States at the age of 14 despite knowing nothing about the United States, fear and apprehension were my prevailing feelings at that time. But the idea is to push down or suppress the pain, so it won't be too dominant in your awakening consciousness.

To deliberately break away from a personal bonding with those you love is probably the most excruciating pain one can endure, whether the break is by choice or by death. I have noticed that we often hear people, in times of great suffering, utter their first cry for help, comfort, understanding, empathy, and compassion, rendered with questioning, blaming, and then crying to God.

The Pain of Job

I recall how God's faithful servant, Job, questioned God: "Why have you made me your target?" in Job 7:20. The Samoan Bible's translation of this verse is one of the most profound translations I have ever read: *Ua ou agasala; se a se mea ua ou faia ia te 'Oe, 'O le ua silasila i tagata?, se a ea le mea ua E fai ai a'u ma manulauti ia te 'Oe, ua fai ai a'u ma avega ia te a'u?*[ccc]

In this translation we see another example of word creation in the Samoan language. At the time of the Bible translation, which I will cover in more detail in my next book, *Forging a Culture*, there was no Samoan word for the English word "mark" or "target." But Samoans did have a phrase used to describe a contest of shooting, or of capturing a prize. For example, *Ua togi le pa tau i le ave* means "He threw the large whale bone fishhook to pluck down the breadfruit punch from the breadfruit tree for the maiden's father's request. And thus he wagers that whoever can throw and pluck without climbing to do it will win the maiden's hand in marriage." (This is found in the Legend of the contest for the hand of TuiAtua Leutelelei'ite's daughter).

There is also a chieftain contest whereby, when a small, fragile, beautiful-colored bird, a little bigger than a hummingbird, lands on a leaf of a ti plant, whoever can shoot it down with an arrow is the winner. It's the size of the target or mark on the tiny ti leaf that makes it a challenge in the contest. Hence, the "bird on a ti leaf" word, *manulauti*. And hence, in the translation of Job, "Why have you made me a *manulauti*, a mark against thee (or a mark on your contest), so that I am a burden to myself?" (Job 7:20). So, Job is referring here to God making him, Job, the mark or target of a contest wager between God and Lucifer.

Living Descendants

Looking through the eyes of these living descendants of the Navigators, and of all Polynesians as well as Austronesians, we can really appreciate the full impact of human migration through mainland Asia and across the Pacific Ocean. What we can confirm is that Samoans and Manu'ans are descendants of the Navigators. They originated from the Malay and Indonesian Archipelagos or Southeast Asia. Before settling Southeast Asia, they were an amalgamation of several people groups who came from as far away as Africa, across the Nile into the Fertile Crescent, then the Pontic Steppe, Deccan, around the south coasts of the Indian continent and into the Asian continent before settling in the Asiatic Archipelago.

Why did they Move?

As we have seen, in the beginning, from a simple cell and molecule, the resulting biological organisms are always in motion and have always seemed restless. The long process of evolution, leading to the development of the human brain, separates us from lower level species, and it also makes us always seems discontented, always fighting for survival. We are creatures of habitats. We, like the cells, are restless and constantly in motion. And, as we have observed throughout the history of mankind, this innate desire or ambition drives us to seek change.

Is it because we're always discontented with the status quo? Is it this propensity to evolve, almost seeming to be always in a state of dissatisfaction, that pushes us into a constant state of motion?

And then, is the "leap of faith" journey across this treacherous ocean guided by a higher God?

God and Creation

I recall the famous sermon of that eloquent African American, Reverend James Weldon Johnson.[ccci] His whole sermon consisted of his rendition of the story of creation from the Book of Genesis. To paraphrase what is now a profound and famous literary poem, he begins: When God stood out in space, He looked around and said, I'm lonely. I'll make me a world. And so God began His creation, day by day, as it is in the Biblical verses.

The reverend's version would end each day's work by saying, then God looked at... and He was pleased; but He was lonely still, and so He created His next creation, up until the end of the fifth day, when He looked and saw the beauty of His creation. But He was lonely still.

Then God said, I'll make me a man to enjoy all of this Creation. Then God gathered the earth's dirt and formed it into His image, and then He blew the breath of life, and man became a living soul. And then He put man to sleep and He pulled a rib bone out man, and He formed it on the earth and created a woman. And at end of the sixth day, God looked around and He said I am pleased and happy. And on the seventh day He rested.

The personal expressions of the African American reverend make the point, among others, that God may have had a real purpose and plan to His creation.

Do we now see that mankind's destiny is to evolve, then populate, migrate into, and inhabit the earth? Since the creation of the earth and mankind, the earth and the firmament of the heavens have been "open for business"—meant to be explored, exploited, and be made habitable.

I believe God intended for Adam and Eve to explore and appreciate His creation. Man, as an intelligent species, with his restlessness, his "always in motion" nature, was destined to roam the earth and explore, exploit, conquer, and settle it. So the Polynesian migration across the East Pacific Ocean didn't and shouldn't come as a surprise. The Pacific Ocean was destined be discovered and conquered, just like the other four corners of the world. Hence the story of our human migration.

It could have been the Chinese, Negritos, Indians, North and South American indigenous peoples... any of these people could have been the first to navigate the great Pacific Ocean; it was simply a matter of time. But they didn't; it was the Polynesians' destiny.

The Pacific Ocean was an obstacle and a challenge in the face of the Polynesians. It stirred them. It had to be conquered. It was no different from the Sahara Desert, the Pontic Steppe, the Eurasian Steppe, and all the other geophysical challenges that mankind had to conquer to make the world their habitat. So, while there are no monuments to celebrate their achievements, the world can still witness and maybe remember the Navigators and the rest of the Polynesians in the annals of world history, in the story of man's global migration.

The Journey Comes into Focus

As we walk through the path we've taken, on our journey to gain more understanding of Samoan and Manu'an origins and their migration to their present homeland, we may not trace the exact path of their vessels on the ocean. But the mosaic image, the image that lies under the abyss of the mighty South Pacific Ocean, is rapidly coming into focus, thanks to new initiatives in science and technology allowing us to excavate the ocean floor to unearth the stones of this mosaic.

The pieces of a fragmented mosaic design are coming together now, through more investigations in all the relevant sciences. Just as it is in history, the elapsed period between mythology and the time when science finally confirms the mythology is significant. The mythology of the Polynesian migration is thousands of years old—since that time when they first recited at dawn, when the first cock crowed, says the orator. And science, now, has taken over 300 years to confirm it.

We need not now regurgitate the scientific evidence of that migration, and we shall not recapitulate the myth and story of the migration, because these are, collectively, their Navigators' history. But what I will say is:

> Oh Navigators of the past, our ancestors, how we now know and understand your voice and messages to us. For clearly you are not mute, but your voice we hear from the wind. You speak to us, through plenty of evidence in our culture, language, religion, history and now genetics. And, perhaps more importantly, you speak through your descendants, for they bear witness to your mysterious migration and discovery of our home and our own Kingdom in the South Pacific Ocean.

Thus, we must seek the truth through the prism of the people. We can see and imagine the Navigators' trials and tribulations in their pursuit of their ambition. And we can find ourselves.

A Final Note

Finally, I am often reminded of the proverbial advice, rendered by the god of creation of the Navigators, Tagaloalagi, who said, in my own translation:

"When encountering sudden change in the wind's unpredictable behavior, and when the weather conditions become violent, the Captain (referring to the Chief) should command the sailors of the vessel to let go the rigging of the sails of the unpredictable wind and, instead, double weave the chain of the rope of the rigging—of the Old Wisdom and Experience of the Chiefs from the gods—to guide your vessel through the rough sea." *Lafoa'i le afa o le fua lagavale, ae so'omaea le afa o le fua o le tofa loloto.*

That's the "Old Wisdom and Experience" achieved only through hard honest work and through being a good servant of the family and people of the community. The same old wisdom is the tidings drawn up from the well of the past, to paraphrase Thomas Mann.

Then I recall the famous parting words of farewell, between the TuiManu'a and Tafa'ifa Malietoa Vaiinupo (around 1836-1827 A.D.), made as Malietoa sets sail to return to Samoa, after his brief visit to the Kingdom of Manu'a to share with Tuimanu'a the wonderful news of his, Malietoa's, receiving and accepting Christianity. The two leaders agreed to accept and to spread the word of God to all of Samoa and Manu'a. Hence the farewell ceremony and the words decreed by these Paramount Chiefs. As Malietoa makes his way to his vessel, Tuimanu'a reaches out to him and says:

"Honorable Malietoa, come, my friend, let us decree to remove our honorable titles and all the worldly glory and salutations that are vested in them, and let us lay them on the port side of your vessel; and let our citizens drive deep the oars of God's vessel carrying the message of peace" (my own translation). *Lau Susuga Malietoa, au mai o ta paia ma o ta mamalu e tatao i le ama o le sa lea ae laga i matau le fa'atofaali'iiga o le Atua ma lo na finagalo.*

Afterword

Afioga Vui Asiata Toeutu Faaleava, MPA, JD, PhD.
Director, McNair Scholars Program, Oregon
Assistant Professor, University Studies
Portland State University, Portland, Oregon.

Malo saunoa Fata, lau Susuga Fata ma Maulolo, le Tu'itu'i o le Gatoa'itele

I have known Orator Fata Ariu Levi for years. I admire his intellectual tenacity and knowledge of Samoan culture. He takes seriously his obligations as a guardian and teacher of Samoan culture and history, and he is a skillful and hardworking researcher who has been reading and teaching Samoan culture and history for years. His book, *Navigators: Quest for a Kingdom in Polynesia,* is a generous gift for the people of Samoa and Manu'a. Students will find, in Fata Ariu Levi's work, a well of perspectives and ideas about the development of the Polynesian cultural complex, over thousands of years.

Early European explorers were surprised to find the Pacific islands already inhabited with thriving established communities. They surmised that these people must have drifted to the islands by luck, but Fata Ariu connects the dots from many research undertakings in diverse fields, confirming instead that the migration into the Pacific Ocean was an intentional, organized, well-planned, and deliberate effort. He respectfully navigates his writing through deeply guarded stories, histories, and sacred heirlooms, sharing water from his lineage, and using his own family genealogy and mythology, wisely and carefully, to illustrate his case. Fata Ariu acknowledges there are many versions of stories, and there are contested claims. As a wise orator, he knows that the theater of Samoan perspectives is a dynamic and challenging space. But, with the help of DNA analysis and other technological advances, we may yet learn more about the Navigators who discovered Samoa and Manu'a.

Navigators: Quests for a Kingdom in Polynesia reminds us of the complexity of the Navigators' unparalleled achievement in sailing into and finding a homeland in the Pacific Ocean. As a descendant of both Samoa and Manu'a, Fata Ariu delivers this manuscript as a gift, to future generations, to help them navigate and untangle the knotted threads of their journeys, hopes, and yearnings, and recognize their own islands and kingdoms.

Afioga Vui Asiata Dr. Toeutu Fa'aleava
10/13/2020

TABLES

As I labored putting together a table of cultural similarities and parallel themes of mythology across the Polynesians migration path, an epiphany came to me, remembering the ancient Sumerian clay tablet translation and writing of Dr. Samuel Noah Kramer.[cccii] In my quest to show culture diffusion as foundational to the Polynesian or Navigators' cultural development, I found Dr. Kramer's list of the attributes he noted in the Sumer Tablets to be a comprehensive description of God's Grand Design, and thus a useful reference point for making my tables.

While Job, the Father of Faith, seems to jealously question God's Word in Job 7:17, 15:14 (NRSV), saying: "What are human beings, that you make so much of them, that you set your mind on them...?" and "What are mortals, that they can be clean? Or those born of woman, that they can be righteous?" Job's answer is found in Psalms 8:4 (NRSV) in the words, "What are human beings that you are mindful of them, mortals that you care for them?" (also in Psalm 144:3). The grand design is that Jesus will be born in human flesh and will be the sacrificial Lamb to cleanse our sin, in order to afford us a gateway to the Kingdom of God.

Let us take a look at the Sumerian account of God's grand design or, as Campbell says, "order of the universe," as evidenced on the tablets and itemized by Dr. Kramer. Professor Joseph Campbell, prefacing Dr. Kramer's list, points out the importance of each class of things and each behavior of man, in representing a God-given natural pattern. In Egypt, as we have learned, this was known as "maat;" in India as "dharma;" in the Far East as "tao;" and in Sumer as the "me."

Dr. Kramer tells his modern readers to try to forget their own ideas, even their own "common sense," instead letting the imagination reflect on each category as a permanent structure in God's world, representing perfectly God's design."[ccciii]

Kramer's list (also referenced in the "What is Mythology?" section of this book) is as follows:

1. Supreme lordship
2. godship
3. the exalted and enduring crown
4. throne of kingship
5. the exalted scepter
6. the royal insignia
7. the exalted shrine
8. shepherdship
9. kingship
10. lasting ladyship
11. the priestly office known as divine lady
12. the priestly office known as ishii
13. the priestly office known as limah
14. the priestly office known as kurgarru
15. truth,
16. descent into the nether world
17. ascent from the nether world
18. the office of the eunuch known as kurgarru

19. the office of the eunuch known as girbadara
20. the office of the eunuch known as sagursag
21. the battle standard
22. the flood
23. weapons,
24. sexual intercourse
25. prostitution
26. legal procedure
27. libel
28. art
29. the cult chamber
30. the role of the hierodule of heaven
31. the musical instrument called guilim
32. music
33. eldership
34. heroship
35. power
36. enmity
37. straightforwardness
38. the destruction of cities
39. lamentation
40. rejoicing of the heart
41. falsehood
42. the rebel land
43. goodness
44. justice
45. the art of woodworking
46. the art of metal working
47. scribeship
48. the craft of the smith
49. the craft of the leatherworker
50. the craft of the builder
51. the craft of the basket weaver
52. wisdom
53. attention
54. holy purification
55. fear
56. terror
57. strife
58. peace
59. weariness
60. victory
61. counsel
62. the troubled heart
63. judgment
64. decision
65. the musical instrument called lilis
66. the musical instrument called ub
67. the musical instrument called mesi
68. the musical instrument called ala

Table A: Mythological Themes[ccciv]

SUPREME GODS AND GODDESSES	
Levant, fertile crescent	Gaea, *goddess of Earth* Uranus, *god of Sky (husband and son of Gaea)*
China	Pangu, *first living being in the Universe, separates Chaos from earth* Nüwa, *goddess after the universe stabilized, created humanity*
Japan	Kamuy – first Deity in the Land of Kuniuni *Major and minor kami are the spirits, gods, and deities in Shinto* Korea: Hwanung *descended from heaven to a sandalwood tree of Baekdu Mountain.*
India	Brahma, *worshiped under many different names. When God is formless, He is referred to as Brahma*
Southeast Asia	Malay/Indonesia: Tua Pek Kong (Chinese) Kaei *the world was water and Kaei lived in the firmament* Vietnam: Ngoc Hoang Jade emperor. *Ruler of Vietnamese pantheon and heavenly home of the gods* Cambodia: The Churning Ocean of Milk (also called Samudra manthan in Hindi or Ko Samut Teuk Dos in Khmer) *gives rise to the birth of creatures, gods and goddesses and kings and kingdoms.*
Samoa Manu'a	Tagaloalagi
Bible	One God
OTHER GODS AND GODESSES	

Levant, fertile crescent	Kronos, Saturn or Cronus, *god of Time* Rhea or Ops, *daughter of Uranus and Gaea, sister of Cronus* Poseidon, *god of the sea* Zeus or Jupiter *king of the gods, last child of Cronus and Rhea* Hera *sister and wife of Zeus* Demeter *daughter of Cronos and Rhea, mother of Persephone by Zeus* Dionysus *semi-divine son of Zeus by a mortal, but twice-born, making him a god* Hephaestus *son of Zeus and Hera, god of fire and metalworking, married to* Aphrodite Ares *god of war, son of Zeus and Hera* Athena *god of strategy, daughter of Zeus—no mother. The children of Zeus:* Aphrodite, Apollo, Artemis, Hermes, Athena
China	Fuxi, *created humans with his sister* Nüwa, *invented hunting, fishing etc.* Jade Emperor, *ruler of the 30 heavens* Xiwangmu, *married to Jade emperor, tends to peaches of immortality, guardian of Daoist women* Chang'e, *goddess of the moon, stole immortality from husband,* Hou Yi Guanyin, *goddess of mercy* Kou Mang, Chu Jung, Ju Shou, Hsüan Ming, Hou Tu
Japan	Major Kami including Amaterasu-Ōmikami *Goddess of the Sun* Ame-no Uzume *Goddess of dawn & revelry, instrumental to the "missing sun motif" in Shinto.* Hachiman *God of War & protector of Japan and its people* Fujin *God of the Wind* Inari Okami *Goddess of rice and fertility* Seven Lucky Gods: Benzaiten *goddess of words, knowledge, speech, eloquence music, like the Hindu goddess Saraswati* Bishamon, *protector of the north, the righteous* Jurojin , *protector of the south, longevity* Hotei *Laughing Buddha, guardian of children* Fukurokuju *Wisdom and longevity* Ebisu *patron of fishermen and luck, born without bones* Dalkokuten *wealth in a successful harvest* Kichijoten *goddess of happiness, beauty and fertility* Korea: Habaek *sun god*

India	* Shiva * Brahma * Krishna * Vishnu * Surya * Rudra * Shakti * Kamadeva * Prajapati * Ushas * Devi (goddess)
Southeast Asia	Malay/Indonesia Bulan *goddess of the moon* Djalai *goddess of sky* Vietnam: Âu Co *(A beautiful fairy lady) from the mountains.* Lac Long Quân *(Dragon king) from the sea.* Khong Lo *(primordial giant separating sky and earth)* Giat Hai *first goddess, companion to Khong Lo* Thailand: God of Thai Buddhism * Vishnu God (Violin Heaven) * Garuda (Buddha Ruo) * Brahma God (Brahma) * Yak (Yasha) * Mock (Momotaro's monkey) * Shin (Guardian Dog) Cambodia: Sowathara (Goddess of Earth) Apsaras *(Celestial creatures – daughters of sky god, or Soraren – came to earth to entertain the Gods and Kings)*
Samoa Manu'a	Gai'o *(devil in creation story)*
Bible	Baal, Ashtera – *gods of surrounding areas*

HEAVENS

Levant, fertile crescent	Mount Olympus
China	30 heavens
Japan	The Land of Kuniuni
India	7 lokas: bhuloka, Bhuvar, Svarga, Maharloka, Janaloka, Taparloka, Satyaloka. Svarga *is a transitory place for souls who have done good deeds but not yet attained elevation*
Southeast Asia	Kahyangan, *the Abode of the Gods where the bird of paradise protects the sacred jewel* Ngoc Hoang *(Jade Emperor) rules the heavenly home of Vietnamese pantheon* Cambodia: Manimekhola *goddess of lighting and guarding of the Sea.* Myanmar: Thagyamin, *king of the spirits in 2nd heaven*
Samoa Manu'a	10 heavens
Bible	1 heaven

UNDERWORLD

Levant, fertile crescent	Hades, *brother of Zeus, god of the underworld* Elysium
China	Jade emperor *also rules the underworld*
Japan	Datsue-ba *old woman in the Underworld who removes the clothes or skin of the dead.*
India	Patala (*may be more beautiful than* Svarga) Naraka, abode of Yama god of death
Southeast Asia	Alam Ghaib (*The unseen realm*) Cambodia: *The war between* Devas *(Gods) and* Asuras *(Demons), seeking the Elixir of Immortality led to the defeat of the Asuras, who were banished and trapped in hell* Myanmar: Athurakal *lowest form of Deities which have pleasure half the day and suffer the other half.* Yama Yazar *A saint, often claimed as death lord who rules over hell.*
Samoa Manu'a	Pulotu – *all spirits*
Bible	Sheol (Old Testament) Hell – Satan and his demons (New Testament)

DEMIGODS

Levant, fertile crescent	Heracles/ Hercules Achilles
China	many
Japan	Minor Kami, including Amatsu-Mikaboshi *the kami of stars who existed before the Kotoamatsukami, distinguished from the heavenly Kami, the first gods which came into existence at the time of the creation of the universe*
India	many
Southeast Asia	Âu Co *from the mountains and* Lac Long Quân *from the sea beget 100 children, 50 on mountain and 50 on coast.* Khong Lo *and* Giat Hai *give birth to wind, thunder, stars, ocean, mountain peaks and islands.* *Demi-god* Thach Sanh, *son of* Jade Emperor, *fought monsters and rescued son of chief sea god Long Vuong*
Samoa Manu'a	Lufasiaitu Children of Tagaloalagi in 1st – 9th heavens
Bible	Angels

GHOSTS/ SPIRITS

Levant, fertile crescent	
China	

Japan	Abumi-guchi *A furry creature* Abura-akago *A ghost* Abura-sumashi *A Spirit with large head* Akabeko *Red Cow* Byako *Japanese version of the Chinese White Tiger* Bake-kujira *ghost whale* Jorogume *ghost woman shifts into spider form*
India	
Southeast Asia	Malay/Indonesia: Hantu galah: *a ghost with legs and arms as long and slender as bamboo poles.* Hantu kopek: *a female ghost with large bosoms who lures men who cheat on their wives.* Hantu kum-kum: *the ghost of an old woman who sucks the blood of virgin girls to regain her youth.* Hantu lilin: *a wandering spirit that carries a torch or a lit candle at night.* Hantu punjut: *a ghost that takes children who wander into the forest late at night.* Hantu tinggi: *"tall ghost ", a type of giant that will flee at the sight of a naked body.* Jembalang: *a demon or evil spirit that usually brings disease* Myanmar: Nat sein *a kind of spirits of humans, specifically those died violent deaths.* Ott-saunk *beings cursed to roam the earth due to their strong attachment to objects or places.* Thaik nan shin *spirits who, because of their greed for treasure when they were human, have been assigned to guard the treasures of the Buddha.* Peik-ta *beings punished with perpetual hunger or thirst.* Sone *hags or witches* Thayé *ghosts*
Samoa Manu'a	
Bible	*No communication with the dead*
HEROES	
Levant, fertile crescent	Alexander the Great

China	• Fu Hsi (*famous for the invention of symbols, on which the* Book of Changes *is based; he used nets for hunting and fishing*) • Shen Nung (*he "ruled the world" for seventeen generations*) • Yen Ti • Huang Ti (*he invented the fire drill, burned the forest to clear the brush, burned the marshes, and drove out wild animals*) • Shao Hao (*he reigned for seven years and introduced the ritual of regicide*) • Chuan Hsu (*he had eight sons. His son Kun, the "Great Fish" was unsuccessful in dealing with the Deluge. But Kun's son Yu, the Great Yu, was given the Great Plan from Heaven to solve the problem of the Deluge. Yu dug the soil and led the water to the sea.*) • K'u (*he had two wives who each conceived a son miraculously*). • Yao (*the Divine Yao, he was reverential, intelligent, accomplished, thoughtful, sincerely courteous, and obliging*) • Shun (*he reigned for 28 years and is an ancestor of a great house*) Yu (*son of Kun, son of Chuan Hsu;* Heaven gave him the Great Plan to solve the Deluge)
Japan	
India	
Malay/ Indonesia	
Samoa Manu'a	Many heroes and antiheroes listed in genealogies
Bible	The Patriarchs (Old Testament)

FEMALE HEROES

Levant, fertile crescent	The priestly office of "divine lady"
China	
Japan	Inari Okami *Goddess of rice and fertility* Ame-no Uzume *Goddess of dawn & revelry, instrumental to the "missing sun motif" in Shinto.* Datsue-ba *old woman in the Underworld who removes the clothes or, skin if unclothed, of the dead*
India	Devi *Goddess*

Southeast Asia	Mat Ga Trong *the Sun Rooster or Sun goddess in Vietnam* Tran Chim *the Moon Swan or Moon goddess* Thailand's greatest heroines: Phra Mae Thorani *mythological "Mother Earth"* Queen Chamathewi *a Mon Queen and ruler of the indigenous Lawa people of northern Thailand. She was found and raised by the hermit Suthep in a cave on top of the mountain.* Queen Suriyothai *defended her country from Burma invasion north of Ayuthaya.* Thao Suranari *known as* Ya Mo *(Grandmother Mo). The Thao Suranari, "Brave Lady" title bestowed her by King Phra Nangklao for helping defeat the Lao invasion by King Anouvong.*
Samoa Manu'a	Queen Nafanua
Bible	The matriarchs, Deborah the judge, Rahab, Esther, Mary

CREATION

Levant, fertile crescent	Chaos, *father of* Erebus *(darkness) and* Nyx *(night).* Night *brings forth* Aether *and* Hemera *(day)* Ki *(earth) is married to* An *(sky).* Enlil *(storms) separates* Ki *and* An *making a habitable earth,* Enki *(water and creation)* Isis *resurrects* Osiris *(kingship and succession)* Mary gives birth to Jesus (ushers in new creation)
China	World created on Chinese new year *with animals, people and deities created during 15 days.* *Many myths: includes creation from chaos, from dismembering, from world parents and from primordial being.* Lord of the Birds' Nest: *people lived on bird nests built in trees. Then the Lord, the Fire Driller starts the transition to eating cooked foods, followed by the Deluge of Kung Kung, followed by the Period of Highest Virtue.*
Japan	Creation from shapeless silent chaos. *Sounds comes first, then lightest particles rise to heaven; heaviest make the earth. Then Izanagi and Izanami created the Japanese archipelago and gave birth to other gods:* Hinko Island of Awaj, Iyo Oki, Sushima Sado Yamata. Korea: Hwanung *descended from heaven to a sandalwood tree on Baekdu Mountain, founded* City of God, *transformed bear and tiger into beautiful woman.* Hwanung *gave her a son,* Dangun *or Altar Prince.* Dangun came to P'yongyang and founded Gojoseon. Yuhwa, *daughter of son god* Habaek, *married Haemosu and gave birth to* Jumon, founder of Goguryeo
India	Different dynamic narratives including Hiranyagarbha (radiant womb), and dismemberment of Purusha, sacrificed by gods.

Southeast Asia	Malay/Indonesia: Kaei *the world was water and* Kaei *lived in the firmament* Vietnam: Âu Co *from the mountains and* Lac Long Quân *from the sea beget 100 children, 50 on mountain and 50 on coast.* Khong Lo *and* Giat Hai *give birth to wind, thunder, stars, ocean, mountain peaks and islands.* Cambodia: *In the beginning,* Devas (Gods) *and* Asuras (Demons) *were fighting for world domination. In search for the Elixir of Immortality at the depths of the cosmic sea, they solicited the help of* Naga Vasuki (king of snakes) *as a churning rope and* Mount Meru *as a churning stick to churn the* Ocean of Milk. *The Naga were a reptilian race believed to have been ruled by King Kaliya and are Central in both Hindu and Khmer creation myths. They inhabited s large empire somewhere in the Pacific Ocean until relocating to India where King Kaliya's daughter married an Indian Brahmana named Kaundinya from whom the Cambodian people originated.*
Samoa Manu'a	Tagaloalagi *summoned wind and waves, organized pebbles into islands, pulled more islands from the abyss of the ocean, weighed and measured and saw it was good, gave hands, feet, head, heart to creatures and brought down soul.*
Bible	"In the beginning was the word…" "God saw that it was good"

VIRGIN BIRTH

Levant, fertile crescent	Mary gives birth to Jesus *(ushers in new creation)* *Also* Uranus *born of* Gaea *etc.*
China	The yellow emperor, *conceived by lightning bolt* The abandoned one, *conceived from a god's footprint* An old man, conceived full-grown *from a falling star* *And others*
Japan	The peach boy *found in a giant peach.* Kagua-hime *born inside a glowing bamboo stalk* Korea: Hwanung created Woman *from bear and tiger and gave her a son called* Dangun or Altar Prince. *Dangun came to P'yongyang and founded Gojoseon.* Jeseok bon-puri *is impregnated by a supernatural Buddhist priest (a form of the sky god) and gives birth to triplets who themselves become gods.*
India	Creation myth of radiant womb
Southeast Asia	
Samoa Manu'a	
Bible	Mary gives birth to Jesus

DELUGE

Levant, fertile crescent	In the story of Creation, told in Hebrew, Egyptian, Mesopotamian (Gilgamesh), and Greek

China	Deluge of Kung Kung – *the majority of land was covered by water.* Gun-Yu *flood continued for two generations.*
Japan	Izanagi and Izanami are siblings, repopulate the world after flood wipes everyone out
India	Pralaya, when Vishnu warns the first man and advises him to build a boat.
Southeast Asia	Mal/Indonesia: A stick in the ground was actually a serpent, Seri Gumum. Water gushed from a hole in the ground where the stick was and created Chini Lake
Samoa Manu'a	After the deluge, pigeon and chicken were only remaining birds. Pigeon and loose rocks produced swamp, with fertile land produced first human, with light produced Lu
Bible	Noah's flood

EPIC STORIES

Levant, fertile crescent	Greek and Roman myths and legends
China	The Lord of the Birds' Nest The Lords, the Fire Driller The Deluge of Kung Kung
Japan	
India	Vedic Sanskrit texts were composed around 1700 B.C. to 1000 B.C. Rig Veda: - Mantra language - Samhita Prose - Brahmana Prose, Oldest Upanishads. - Sutra Language Vedic Period: Codification of a Vedic Canon. Vedic Civilization Period: Rig Vedas Comprises of; * Religious hymns, * Allusions * Myths * Stories.

Southeast Asia	Malay/Indonesia: Epics (hikayat) Stories and Legends of Heroism. Hikayat Abdullah Hikayat Amir Hamzah *encouraged Malay warriors against the Portuguese in 1511* Hikayat Andaken Penurat *prose poem of a prince and his beloved* Hikayat Anggun Che' Tunggal Hikayat Bayan Budiman Hikayat Inderaputera Hikayat Iskandar Zulkarnain, *exploits of king briefly mentioned in the Quran* Hikayat Isma Yatim Hikayat Malim Dema Hikayat Merong Mahawangsa Hikayat Muhammad Hanafiah, *battle of Karbala* Hikayat Panca Tanderan Hikayat Lima Hikayat Patani Vietnam: Thach Sanh - *Son of* Ngoc Hoang. *A demigod who fought the monsters and rescued the son of chief sea god* Long Vuong. Myanmar: Story of Thagyamin (king of spirits), a brahma named Ahthi, and a severed head; *weaves together with Hindu mythology and Myanmar's animism.*
Bible	

FIRE STOLEN FROM GODS

Levant, fertile crescent	Prometheus
China	The Lords, the Fire Driller – *tells the transition from raw to cooked foods.*
Japan	Basan *Fire-breathing chicken monster*
India	
Southeast Asia	
Samoa Manu'a	Ti'eti'eitalaga
Bible	

CELESTIAL WEAPONS

Levant, fertile crescent	Thunderbolt thrown by Zeus Trident held by Poseidon
China	
Japan	
India	* Astra form of an arrow that is to be hurled at an enemy. * Shastra represents personal weapons like swords, spades, bows, axes, spears and maces.
Southeast Asia	Malay/Indonesia: Parasurama (Hindu) championed gods with a bow and was rewarded with an ax.
Samoa Manu'a	

Bible	Fire and Brimstone in hell

CHARACTERS WITH LIKENESS TO PLANTS

Levant, fertile crescent	
China	First man *born from bamboo stalk*
Japan	The peach boy *found in a giant peach*. Kagua-hime *born inside a glowing bamboo stalk* Korea: Princess Bari *abandoned by her father, later resurrects her parents with a flower of life*
India	
Southeast Asia	Malay/Indonesia: Hantu Pemburu: *the Spectral Huntsman whose head is always looking upwards with a shoot growing from his neck.* Also Breadfruits (*Ulu*), *the coco palm tree, and coconut tree* Kinorohingan *and his wife* Suminundu *sacrificed their daughter* Huminodin *when the people were starving. Rice seeds grew from her body.* Myanmar: Yetkhat *benevolent guardians of buried treasures and those hidden in tree roots.*
Samoa Manu'a	Ava plant, coconut
Bible	

CHARACTERS WITH LIKENESS TO ANIMALS

Levant, fertile crescent	Semberani: pegasus
China	Sun Wukong *powerful magician in monkey form* Baihu *Chinese White Tiger*
Japan	Itsumade *bird with human face* Tengu *human and bird characteristics* Basan *fire breathing chicken* and more Akabeko *red cow* Byako *like the Chinese white tiger*
India	Crocotta *dog-wolf* Karkadann *aggressive unicorn* Korea: Hwanung *transformed bear and tiger into human woman*

Southeast Asia	Malay/Indonesia: Lycanthropic beings such as: Harimau hadrian or harimau akuan: *were-tiger, were-leopard or were-panther* Ular-tending jadian: *were-cobra* Lemon jadian: *were-bull* Malay/Indonesia: Mythical birds Geroda: *a bird made of water* Jentayu: *a bird made water* Cenderawashih: Bird of Paradise, *king of the birds. Guardian of the sacred jewel in Kahyangan, the Abode of the Gods.* Malay/Indonesia: Beasts Naga: *a dragon said to inhabit caves and watery areas* Raja udang: King of Prawns, *a very large prawn or lobster-like creature.* Hantu Belangkas: *a gigantic king-crab that attacks people at sea.* Bajang: *the Spirit of a stillborn child in the form of a civet cat (musang).* Bota: *a type of evil spirit, usually a giant.* Lang suir: the mother of a pontianak. *Able to take the form of an owl with long talons; attacks pregnant women out of jealousy.* Vietnam: Sun Rooster, Moon Swan and Bear God Cambodia: The Naga *were a reptilian race believed to have been ruled by King Kaliya. They are central in both Hindu and Khmer creation myths. They inhabited a large empire somewhere in the Pacific Ocean until relocating to India where King Kaliya's daughter married an Indian Brahmana named Kaundinya from whom the Cambodian people originated.*
Samoa Manu'a	Saveasi'uleo with a tail like an eel
Bible	Snake in the Garden of Eden

CHARACTERS WITH HUMAN LIKENESS

Levant, fertile crescent	Middle Eastern: * Jin: Djinn * Syaitan: Satan * Pari-pari or peri: Faries * Malaikat: Angel (Religion-related) * Bidadari/ Bidadara: Woman/ Man Angel
China	
Japan	Abura-Sumashi *spirit with large head*
India	

Southeast Asia	Malay/Indonesia: Orang Bunian: *"hidden people " or "whistling people" a race of exceptional beauty and grace.* Orang ketot: *humans with short stature, similar to dwarves.* Orang kenit: *small humans, often possessing magic power.* Gergasi: *giants or ogres* Gedembai or Kelebai: *an ogre who has the power to turn things to stone* Duyong: mermaids, *having a lower body of a fish and a woman upper body* Bidadari: *beautiful heavenly nymphs* Myanmar: Belu *man-eating humanoids capable of shapeshifting* Zawgyi *(alchemist)-a human alchemist with supernatural powers and often seen with a stick and red hat.*
Samoa Manu'a	Hobbits
Bible	Angels

SACRED ANIMALS

Levant, fertile crescent	Lions, bull, snake, lizard, pig, chicken
China	Same, and horse
Japan	Same, and horse, and elephant
India	Lions, bull, snake, lizard, pig, chicken, horse
Southeast Asia	
Samoa Manu'a	Pig, lizard, eel, chicken
Bible	Only perfect animals permitted for sacrifice

RELIGIOUS PEOPLE

Levant, fertile crescent	Priestly office ishi, limah, kurgarru Eunuch office kurgarru, girbadara, sagursag
China	Shaman
Japan	Shaman
India	Emerging of the Caste System: The system divides Hindu Religion into rigid hierarchical groups based on their karma (work) and dharma (word for religion) * Brahmanas (priests and teachers) * Kshatriyas (Warriors and rulers) * Vaisyas(farmers, traders and merchants) * Sudras (laborers) * Dalits (relegated to the forbidden work).
Southeast Asia	Shaman
Samoa Manu'a	Fa'ataulaitu
Bible	Priests and prophets

RELIGIOUS RITUALS

Levant, fertile crescent	Sacrifice, animal sacrifice, blood sacrifice, temple celebrations, temple virgins

China	Confucianism, Taoism and Buddhism
Japan	Hinduism, Buddhism, spirit gods, and worship of demigods
India	Hinduism and Jainism, followed by Buddhism,
Southeast Asia	Hinduism, Buddhism, spirit gods, and worship of demigods Temple of Angkor Wat Devata goddess temple
Samoa Manu'a	Tattooing, Ava ceremony, Chieftain bestowment, Sua (the baked pig for Paramount Chief), worshipping spirits and demigods.
Bible	Temple worship

COSMIC BODIES RELATED TO GODS

Levant, fertile crescent	Seven through ninth heavens in Hebrew and Mesopotamian mythology. Sun, moon, stars, wind, and sky were all perceived as supreme gods. The seven observable celestial bodies: Sun, Moon, Mercury, Venus, Mars, Jupiter and Saturn gave us the seven day week.
China	
Japan	Amatsu-Mikaboshi *The kami of stars who existed before the Kotoamatsukami, distinguished from the heavenly Kami, the first gods which came into existence at the time of the creation of the universe* Korea: Habaek *sun god*
India	
Southeast Asia	Malay/Indonesia: *Sky goddess* Djalai, *moon goddess* Bulan Vietnam: Mat Ga Trong *the Sun Rooster or Sun goddess* Tran Chim *the Moon Swan or Moon goddess* Con Gau *The Bear creates Solar and Lunar eclipses*
Samoa Manu'a	One through ten heavens of Tagaloalagi and sun gods. Winds and ocean are sacred
Bible	One God created the heavens and the earth

IDOL WORSHIP

Levant, fertile crescent	Worship of statues of lions, bull, reptile, humans and deities
China	
Japan	Korean Shamanism *(living traditions and literary myths).*
India	
Southeast Asia	Ong Lo *kitchen and hearth, or household god*
Samoa Manu'a	None
Bible	Forbidden, but often found

Table B: Culture and Daily Life

TOOLS	
Levant, fertile crescent	Rocks, stones, bronze, silver, iron, steel. Axes, levers, chisel, hammer
China	Scrapers, hammers Invented seed drill and wheelbarrow
Japan	Many stone tools, flaked blades, pebble tools
India	Stone tools, later blades (quartz)
Southeast Asia	Stone tools, sharpened tools
Samoa Manu'a	
Bible	Chariots and horses in later times

TRANSPORTATION	
Levant, fertile crescent	Water transport: Wooden boat by the Egyptians and Phoenicians. Land transport: Donkey Crossing River: Floating bridges
China	Land transport: Camel and horses Down-River transport: wooden rafts, then rafts from inflated (treated) pig and sheep skins. Up-River transport: initially by land. Sail invented later. Crossing Rivers. Floating bridges
Japan	Water transport: Dug-out Canoe. Land transport: Camel, horses, elephants
India	Camel, elephant, (followed by horse), dugout canoe, and wooden ship vessels. Crossed rivers with floating bridges
Southeast Asia	Camel, horses, dugout canoe
Samoa Manu'a	Dugout canoe
Bible	Donkey

ARTS AND CRAFTS	
Levant, fertile crescent	woodworking, metal working, scribe, smiths, leatherworker, builder, basket weaving musical instruments called, lilis, ub, mesi and ala.
China	Calligraphy, embroidery, statues, shrines, silk...
Japan	Metalwork, pottery, sculpture, painting, Chinese influence...
India	Rock art, paintings, sculpture
Southeast Asia	Cave paintings, statues, wood carving...
Samoa Manu'a	Tattooing, Mat-weaving—fine mats, tree bark mats (siapo), native house building, canoes building, native music and dancing

Bible	Weaving goat-hair for Temple covering Wood and gold imported for Temple

CUSTOMS AND FORMALITIES

Levant, fertile crescent	Cult chamber, elders, holy purification, ritual prostitution, celebration of victory
China	
Japan	
India	
Southeast Asia	The architectural design and structural alignments and measurements of Angkor Wat were based on narratives of mythology and spiritual guidance from the heavenly celestial gods and Cosmic Sea Mythology.
Samoa Manu'a	Respect and reverence toward chiefs, elders, people of authority, ministers, and women. Emphasis is placed on customs and formalities.
Bible	Temple worship (tent in wilderness, Temple building later)

GOVERNMENT STRUCTURES

Levant, fertile crescent	Legal formalities and procedures
China	Emperor (First Kingdom on Earth decreed by Heavenly God)
Japan	Emperor
India	Monarch and king (feudal system)
Southeast Asia	Almost all governed by kings and monarchs
Samoa Manu'a	Ancient Paramount Chiefs now Parliamentary Republic
Bible	Religious government with secular influence Great respect for religion

FAMILY ATTITUDES

Levant, fertile crescent	Value of straightforwardness, punishment for falsehood and rebellion
China	Matriarchal – The Mosuo (Lagu Lake) Tibet
Japan	Ainu culture is matriarchal Korean shamanism was originally exclusively female
India	Several matriarchal societies (Meghalaya, Khas in north, Nayar in south, the Garo...) Nepal- Newar Indigenous - matriarchal
Southeast Asia	The Minanggkabau, West Sumatra, matriarchal Thailand also matriarchal The Cham, descendants of ancient rulers of Southeast Asian kingdoms, are matriarchal. They spread from Vietnam, Lao, Cambodia and Thailand.
Samoa Manu'a	Family centric, initially matriarchal
Bible	Man has authority, woman is subservient

PHYSICAL APPEARANCE

Levant, fertile crescent	Similar to Polynesian (remember Mohenjo Daro figurine): The Levant people consists of North African, Indian, Moroccan, Arabian, Israelite, Egyptian, Canaanite.
China	
Japan	
India	
Southeast Asia	
Samoa Manu'a	Medium to tall in stature, slender build in the past, complexion ranging from dark to light olive-brown, black hair, thick texture, wavy to straight, long head and face, with narrow, relatively pronounced nose; eyes ranging from black to brown, characteristically large and open .
Bible	

LANGUAGE

Levant, fertile crescent	Proto-Indo-European
China	Proto-Chinese, part of Proto-Sino-Tibetan (second oldest language after PIE, covers East Asia, Southern Asia, central Asia, North Asia, Southeast Asia)
Japan	
India	Sanskrit, Veg Veda, Dravidian
Southeast Asia	Proto-Sino-Tibetan
Samoa Manu'a	Austronesian Language family . Agglutinative—each inflection conveys only a single grammatical category such as person, mood, tense, voice, aspect, gender, number, and case. 5 vowels and 14 consonants. High number of particles.
Bible	Hebrew

ECONOMY

Levant, fertile crescent	Agriculture, international trade in large city states
China	Agriculture driven by technological innovation—the wheel, gunpowder, compass, sadly stirrups, application of metallurgy to weaponry
Japan	Agriculture with ocean fishery
India	Local and regional, mainly agricultural driven by religious groups and practices, fueled by monarch and King embracing religion (Hinduism or Buddhism)
Southeast Asia	Agriculture with sea trading

| Samoa Manu'a | Agrarian, based on agriculture, and aquaculture. Domestically self-sustaining with well-defined division of labor within the family structure. Member of ancient trading system, the Lapita Network. |
| Bible | Tribal then kingdom |

DIET

Levant, fertile crescent	Wheat and barley. Meat, poultry, fish, vegetables, fruits. Rich sophisticated diet from fertile land and abundant food crops and livestock
China	Agriculture based – wheat, barley, rice, roots, meat, poultry, fish. Heavily dependent on rice. Pork became a mainstay.
Japan	
India	Vegetarian, poultry, fish, fruits, milk (first to be able to process lactose)
Southeast Asia	Chinese diet spread across East and Southeast Asia with emphasis on fish. Agriculture spread to island without wheat, barley, corn or rice, hence emphasis on roots like taro, yams, bananas, breadfruit in Polynesia
Samoa Manu'a	Native edible roots: Taro, Yam, Ta'amu, Ufi (Samoan Yam), bananas, bread fruits (Ulu), and variety of tropical vegetable and fruits. Fish, poultry, and pork (beef only came to islands with the Europeans)
Bible	Religious regulations about pork and other foods that would not keep well.

NAVIGATIONAL SKILLS

Levant, fertile crescent	
China	Sailed the rivers
Japan	Sailed the sea
India	Sailed the rivers
Southeast Asia	Ocean sailing becomes dominant because they occupy the coastline.
Samoa Manu'a	honed to perfection in ancient times, utilizing ocean currents, climate, wind direction, celestial bodies, bird migration, etc. Navigation used for fishing, exhibitions, and voyaging, and exploration.
Bible	Fought then traded with seafarers

Notes

IMAGES

[i] Admiralty Chart No 5216 South Pacific Ocean, Published 1942, John Edgell / Public domain

[ii] Christopher J. Bae, Katerina Douka, Michael D. Petraglia. Out of Africa migratory model. https://science.sciencemag.org/content/358/6368/eaai9067 / CC BY-SA (https://creativecommons.org/licenses/by-sa/4.0) Dec 8 2017 (https://creativecommons.org/licenses/by-sa/3.0)

[iii] https://commons.wikimedia.org/wiki/File:Pacific_Ring_of_Fire.svg Gringer (talk) 23:52, Feb 10 2009 (UTC) / Public domain

[iv] BlankMap-World-162E.svg: Lokal_Profilderivative work: Milenioscuro (talk) derivative work: Obsidian Soul] / CC0

[v] Denisovan Spread and Evolution, created from hand drawn pp map and inserted data by User:John D. Croft / CC BY-SA (https://creativecommons.org/licenses/by-sa/3.0)

[vi] "Copyright © 2015 the author(s), publisher and licensee Libertas Academica Ltd. This is an open-access article distributed under the terms of the Creative Commons CC-BY 3.0 License."

[vii] Ephert / CC BY-SA (https://creativecommons.org/licenses/by-sa/3.0) recreation of a map that can be found at the Kyushu Museum website that shows the human migration path and dates Out of Africa as proposed by Saitou Naruya (Japanese:斎藤成) professor at the (Japanese) National Institute for Genetics. http://www.museum.kyushu-u.ac.jp/WAJIN/113.html

[viii] Carte synthétiques des migrations en Océanie. Hiro-Heremoana / CC BY-SA (https://creativecommons.org/licenses/by-sa/3.0)

[ix] "Chronological dispersal of Austronesian people across the Pacific (per Benton et al, 2012, adapted from Bellwood, 2011).svg" Obsidian Soul / CC BY (https://creativecommons.org/licenses/by/4.0)

[x] Human_migrations_and_mitochondrial_haplogroups User:Maulucioni / CC BY-SA (https://creativecommons.org/licenses/by-sa/3.0)

PREFACE

[xi] Malinowski, Bronisław. *Argonauts of the Western Pacific*. London, G. Routledge & Sons; New York, E.P. Dutton & Co. 1922

[xii] de Bougainville, Louis-Antione. *A Voyage round the World performed by order of His Most Christian Majesty in the years 1766, 1767, 1768 and 1769*; trans. Foster, Johan Reinhold, 1772. pp.278-284

[xiii] Heibert, Fredrik. *National Geographic World History: Great Civilizations*. Cengage Learning. 2015

[xiv] Krämer, Dr. Augustin. *The Samoa Islands: An Outline of a Monograph with Particular Consideration of German Samoa: Vol 1*; trans. Theodore Verhaaren. Auckland. Polynesian Press Samoa House. 1994

[xv] Krämer, Dr. Augustin. *The Samoa Islands: An Outline of a Monograph with Particular Consideration of German Samoa: Vol 1*; trans. Theodore Verhaaren. Auckland. Polynesian Press Samoa House. 1994. p.529

INTRODUCTION

[xvi] Bullfinch, Thomas. *Illustrated Mythology*. Konecky & Konecky, 72 Ayers Point Rd., Old Saybrook, CT 06475. 1885

[xvii] Boschman, L.M; van Hinsbergen D.J.J. "On the enigmatic birth of the Pacific Plate within the Panthalassa Ocean." *Science Advances* 27 Jul 2016 : E1600022

[xviii] Pellegrino, Charles. *The Ghosts of Vesuvius: A New Look at the Last Days of Pompeii, How Towers Fall, and Other Strange Connections*. William Morrow 2004

[xix] Schulze-Markuch, Dirk; Irwin, Louis N. *Life in the Universe: Expectations and Constraints* Chapter 5: The Building Blocks of Life. Advances in Astrobiology and Biogeophysics ISSN: 1610-8957 Springer Verlag Berlin Herdelberg, 19 February 2005. Online ISBN 978-3-540-32453-9

[xx] Rao, Joe. (an instructor and guest lecturer at New York's Hayden Planetarium. A frequent writer about astronomy for *Natural History* magazine, *Farmer's Almanac,* and other publications). "Exploring the Famous Southern Cross Constellation" www.space.com May 19 2015

[xxi] Asimov, Isaac. *The Intelligent Man's Guide to Science volume 1: The Physical Science*. New York, Basic Books. 1960. p.16; also White, Michael. *Giants of Science. Galileo Galilei: Inventor, Astronomer and Rebel*. New York. Blackbirch Press. 1999. pp.3,18,19,35,38

[xxii] Shakespeare, William. *The Tempest*. 1611

[xxiii] Austen, Ralph A; Jansen, Jan. "History, Oral Transmission and Structure in Ibn Khaldun's Chronology of Mali Rulers." *History in Africa*, vol.23. 1996. pp.17–28. JSTOR, www.jstor.org/stable/3171932. Accessed 17 Aug. 2020.

[xxiv] Harris, William V. *Ancient Literacy*. Harvard University Press, 1880

[xxv] Kuriyama, Taro; Kissel, Adam ed. "Phaedrus Summary." *GradeSaver*, Mar 8 2008 Web. Jun 25 2020. https://www.gradesaver.com/phaedrus/study-guide/summary

[xxvi] Stille, Alexander. "Prospecting for Truth in the Ore of Memory." *New York Times*. Mar 10 2001

[xxvii] Harris, William. *Ancient Literacy*; reprinted Harvard University Press 1989. pp.324-25

[xxviii] Khaldun, Ibn. *Muqaddimah*. 1377; trans. Dawood N.J. Princeton University Press. 2015; quoted by Wikipedia contributors. "Muqaddimah." *Wikipedia, The Free Encyclopedia*. Wikipedia, The Free Encyclopedia, 7 Aug. 2020. Web. 11 Aug. 2020.

[xxix] Romm, James. *Herodotus*. Yale University Press; First edition, Dec 11 1998

[xxx] Swanson, Roy Arthur. "The True, the False, and the Truly False: Lucian's Philosophical Science Fiction." *Science Fiction Studies*, vol.3, no. 3. 1976. pp.228–239. JSTOR, www.jstor.org/stable/4239038. Accessed 11 Aug. 2020

[xxxi] Rawlinson, George. *The History of Herodotus*. New York. D. Appleton & Company, 443 & 445 Broadway. 1864

[xxxii] Krämer, Augustin. *The Samoa Islands: An Outline of a Monograph with Particular Consideration of German Samoa: vol 2: Material Culture;* trans. Verhaaren, Theodore. Auckland. Polynesian Press Samoa House 1994

[xxxiii] Campbell, Joseph. *The Mask of God: Primitive Mythology*. First Published. New York, NY. Viking Penguin Inc.1959. Revised edition 1969. Copyright renewed Joseph Campbell. 1987. p.388

[xxxiv] Admiralty Chart No 5216 South Pacific Ocean, Published 1942, John Edgell / Public domain

[xxxv] Cook, Martin. "Immigration and Ethics." *Markkula Center for Applied Ethics*, v. 7, n. 2. Spring 1996

[xxxvi] Christopher J. Bae, Katerina Douka, Michael D. Petraglia. Out of Africa migratory model.

https://science.sciencemag.org/content/358/6368/eaai9067 / CC BY-SA (https://creativecommons.org/licenses/by-sa/4.0) Dec 8 2017

[xxxvii] Mapping Human Genetic Diversity in Asia, BY THE HUGO PAN-ASIAN SNP CONSORTIUM, SCIENCE11 DEC 2009 : 1541-1545 Genetic analyses of Asian peoples suggest that the continent was populated through a single migration event.

[xxxviii] Soares, Pedro; Rito, Teresa; Trejaut, Jean; Mormina, Maru; Hill, Catherine; Tinkler-Hundal, Emma; Braid, Michelle; Clarke, Douglas J; Loo, Jun-Hun; Noel Thomson, Tim Denham, Mark Donohue, Vincent Macaulay, Marie Lin, Oppenheimer, Stephen; Richards, Martin B. "Ancient Voyaging and Polynesian Origins." *American Journal of Human Genetics*. Feb 11 2011

[xxxix] Flaum, E. *Discovery: Exploration through the Centuries.* Gallery Books, an imprint of W.H. Smith publishers Inc, NY, NY. 1992; also *Concise History*. National Geographic 2005; Herodotus *Book II* With an English Translation by A. D. Godley, Hon. Fellow of Magdalen College, Oxford. In Four Volumes I Book I and II. London. William Heinemann LTD Cambridge, Massachusetts. Harvard University Press. 1920. rev. 1926, 1931, 1946, 1960

[xl] Dio. *Roman History III (XXXVI-XL);* translation by Earnest Cary; *Concise History*. National Geographic 2005

[xli] Flaum, E. *Discovery: Exploration through the Centuries.* Gallery Books, an imprint of W.H. Smith publishers Inc, NY, NY. 1992

[xlii] *Concise History of the World: an Illustrated Timeline*; ed. Kagan, Neil; forw. Bentley, Jerry H. Washington, D.C., USA. National Geographic Society. 2006. Revised edition 2013

[xliii] Flaum, E. *Discovery: Exploration through the Centuries.* Gallery Books, an imprint of W.H. Smith publishers Inc, NY, NY. 1992

[xliv] Bardach, John E. et al. (Senior Fellow Emeritus Environment and Policy Institute East-West Center, Honolulu. Director, Hawaii Institute of Marine Biology, University of Hawaii at Manoa,1971-77. Author of *Harvest of the Sea*.) Editor of *Encyclopedia Britannica*. Jul 26 1999, Aug 25 2000, Jun 19 2008.

[xlv] https://commons.wikimedia.org/wiki/File:Pacific_Ring_of_Fire.svg Gringer (talk) 23:52, Feb 10 2009 (UTC) / Public domain

[xlvi] 1998-present PALEOMAP Project website, www.scotese.com

[xlvii] Neall, Vincent E; Trewick. Steven A. "The age and origin of the Pacific islands: a geological overview." Philos Trans R Soc Lond B Biol Sci. 2008 Oct 27; 363(1508): 3293–3308. Published online 2008 Sep 3. doi: 10.1098/rstb.2008.0119 PMCID: PMC2607379

[xlviii] Gregory, J.W. "The Geological History of the Pacific Ocean." *Nature*. 125 (3159): 750–751. 1930

[xlix] "Coral reefs around the world." Guardian.com. Sep 2 2009

[l] Wilkinson, Clive. "Status of Coral Reefs of the World." Global Coral Reef Monitoring Network and Australian Institute of Marine Science, Townsville. 1. 2004. Executive summary 2008

[li] Burke, Lauretta; Reytar, Kathleen; Spalding, Mark; Perry, Allison. "Reefs at Risk Revisited." World Resources Institute, Feb 2011

[lii] "Coral Reef condition status report for American Samoa." NOAA Coral Reef Conservation Program. 2018 with J. Thomas, C. Donovan, A. Fries, and H. Kelsey from the University of Maryland Center for Environmental Science

[liii] Ziegler, Maren; Quéré, Gaëlle; Ghiglione, Jean-François; Iwankow, Guillaume; Barbe, Valérie; Boissin, Emilie; Wincker, Patrick; Planes, Serge; Voolstra, Christian. "Status of coral reefs of Upolu (Independent State of Samoa) in the South West Pacific and recommendations to promote resilience and recovery of coastal ecosystems." *Marine Pollution Bulletin*. 129. 392-398. 10.1016/j.marpolbul.2018.02.044. 2018

[liv] BlankMap-World-162E.svg: Lokal_Profilderivative work: Milenioscuro (talk)derivative work: Obsidian Soul] / CC0

[lv] Gross, Grant M. *Oceanography: A view of the Earth.* Prentice-Hall. 1972; also Pinet, Paul R. *Invitation to Oceanography.* Jones & Bartlett Learning; 7th edition. Oct 17 2014

[lvi] Coomaraswamy, Dr. Ananda K. *Yaksas, Part II.* Washington D. C., Smithsonian Institution, Publication 3059, 1931, pg.14; also Campbell, Joseph. *The Mask of God: Oriental Mythology.* First Published. New York, NY. Viking Penguin Inc. 1962. Published in Penguin Books. 1976. Copyright renewed Joseph Campbell, 1962. p.147

[lvii] Childe, Professor V. Gordon *New Light on the Most Ancient East.* New York: D. Appleton-Century Company. 1934; also Campbell, Joseph. *The Mask of God: Oriental Mythology.* First Published. New York, NY. Viking Penguin Inc. 1962. Published in Penguin Books. 1976. Copyright renewed Joseph Campbell, 1962. p.148

[lviii] Mann, Thomas. *Joseph and His Brothers;* English translation by H. T. Lowe-Porter. New York. Alfred A. Knopf. 1948

[lix] Mann, Thomas. "Freud and the Future." *Life and Letters Today*, Vol. 15, No. 5. Autumn 1936. p. 89; ref by Campbell, Joseph in *The Mask of God: Primitive Mythology.* Prologue: "Toward A Natural History of The Gods And Heroes" note 14 and 15. First Published. New York, NY. Viking Penguin Inc.1959

[lx] Mann, Thomas. "Freud and the Future." *Life and Letters Today*, Vol. 15, No. 5. Autumn 1936. p. 89. Revised edition 1969. Copyright renewed Joseph Campbell. 1987

[lxi] Vial, Claude. *Inscriptions de Delo* (Index. tome 11: les Delian, Paris: De Boccard). 2008

[lxii] Fornander, Abraham Stoke. *Comparative Vocabulary of the Polynesians and Indo-European.* London. Trübner & Co., Ludgate Hill. 1885

[lxiii] Alexander, W.D. *the Brief History of the Hawaiian People.* Honolulu, Hawaii, 1891

[lxiv] Fornander, Abraham Stoke. *Comparative Vocabulary of the Polynesian and Indo European Languages.* Honolulu, Hawaii. Sep 8 1884

[lxv] Mann, Thomas. *Joseph and His Brothers;* English translation by H. T. Lowe-Porter. New York. Alfred A. Knopf. 1948

TRACING THE MIGRATION PATH

[lxvi] Campbell, Joseph. *The Mask of God: Oriental Mythology.* First Published. New York, NY. Viking Penguin Inc. 1962. Published in Penguin Books. 1976. Copyright renewed Joseph Campbell, 1962. p.152

[lxvii] Campbell, Joseph. *The Mask of God: Oriental Mythology.* First Published. New York, NY. Viking Penguin Inc. 1962. Published in Penguin Books. 1976. Copyright renewed Joseph Campbell, 1962. pp.153-4, citing Frobenius, Leo. *Indische Reise.* Berlin: Verlag von Reimar Hobbing. 1931. pp-221-22

[lxviii] Mann, Thomas. "Freud and the Future." *Life and Letters Today*, Vol. 15, No. 5. Autumn 1936. p. 89

[lxix] "Literary Terms." Literary Terms. Jun 1 2015. Web. Nov 3 2016. <https://literaryterms.net/>

ANTHROPOLOGY

[lxx] Parcak, Sarah H. *Satellite Remote Sensing for Archaeology.* Routledge. 1st edition. May 12 2009

[lxxi] Denisovan Spread and Evolution, created from hand drawn pp map and inserted data by User:John D. Croft / CC BY-SA (https://creativecommons.org/licenses/by-sa/3.0)

[lxxii] Bar-Yosef, Ofer. "The lower paleolithic of the Near East." *J World Prehist* 8, 211–265 (1994). https://doi.org/10.1007/BF02221050

[lxxiii] Serpell, James. *The domestic dog: its evolution, behavior, and interactions with people.* Cambridge University Press. 1995. pp.10-12

[lxxiv] Goren-Inbar, N; Alperson, N; Kislev, ME et al. "Evidence of hominin control of fire at Gesher Benot Ya'aqov, Israel." *Science*. 2004;304(5671):725-727. doi:10.1126/science.1095443

[lxxv] "Why Am I Denisovan?" National Geographic Society Project. 2017

[lxxvi] Zimmer, Carl. "Are Hobbits Real?" *New York Times* Jun 20 2016; also Brown, P; Sutikna, T; Morwood, MJ et al. "A new small-bodied hominin from the Late Pleistocene of Flores, Indonesia." *Nature*. 2004;431(7012):1055-1061. doi:10.1038/nature02999; also Sutikna T; Tocheri MW; Morwood MJ et al. "Revised stratigraphy and chronology for Homo floresiensis at Liang Bua in Indonesia." *Nature*. 2016;532(7599):366-369. doi:10.1038/nature17179

[lxxvii] Mijaresa, Armand Salvador; Détroit, Florent; Piper, Philip; Grün, Rainer; Bellwood, Peter; Aubert, Maxime; Champion, Guillaume; Cuevas, Nida; De Leon, Alexandra; Dizone, Eusebio. "New evidence for a 67,000-year-old human presence at Callao Cave, Luzon, Philippines." *Journal of Human Evolution Vol 59, issue 1.* Jul 2010. pp.123-132

[lxxviii] Bar-Yosef, Yosef. "The Natufian culture in the Levant, threshold to the Origins of agriculture." *Evolutionary Anthropology: Issues, News, and Review 6.* (6.5): 159-177. 1998

[lxxix] Liu, Hua; Prugnolle, Franck; Manica, Andrea; Balloux, François. "A Geographically Explicit Genetic Model of Worldwide Human-Settlement History." *The American Journal of Human Genetics.* Aug 2006

[lxxx] Wikipedia contributors. "Toba catastrophe theory." Wikipedia, The Free Encyclopedia. Wikipedia, The Free Encyclopedia, 11 Aug. 2020. Web. 17 Aug. 2020.

[lxxxi] Cowan, Angela M; Education Specialist and Curriculum Designer; Producers Andres, Katy; Brown, Julie (National Geographic Society); Michael, Alison (National Geographic Society); Brewer, Winn (National Geographic Education). *Ocean Currents and Climate*, 03.21.2013 www.nationalgeograph.org. Last updated Mar 21 2013

[lxxxii] *Concise History of the World: an Illustrated Timeline*; ed. Kagan, Neil; forw. Bentley, Jerry H. Washington, D.C., USA. National Geographic Society. 2006. Revised edition 2013; also History Magazine at www.nationalgeographic.com

[lxxxiii] Fornander, Abraham. *An Account of the Polynesian Race*. London. Trübner & company. 1880

[lxxxiv] Hays, Daniel. *From Every People and Nation: A Biblical Theology of Race*. IVP Academic. Jul 12 2003

[lxxxv] Gibbons, Ann. "Trail of tools reveals modern humans path out of Africa." *National Geographic online*. https://www.nationalgeographic.com/news/2015/2/150224-africa-stone-tools-modern-humans-arabia-emiran-nubian-origins/

[lxxxvi] "Copyright © 2015 the author(s), publisher and licensee Libertas Academica Ltd. This is an open-access article distributed under the terms of the Creative Commons CC-BY 3.0 License."

[lxxxvii] O'Connell, J.F; Allen, J; Williams, M.A; Williams, A.N; Tourney, C.S; Spooner, N.A., et al. "When did Homo sapiens first reach Southeast Asia and Sahul?" *Proceedings of the National Academy of Sciences of the United States of America*. 115(34): 8482-8490. August 2018; also Bellwood, Peter S. *Prehistory of the Ind-Malaysian Archipelago*, 3rd Edition. Canberra. ANU E

Press. 2007; also, for a comprehensive summary, Hatin et al. "A genome wide pattern of structure and admixture in peninsular Malaysia Malays." *The HUGO Journal* 2014, 8:5 http://www.thehugojournal.com/content/8/1/5

lxxxviii Oppenheimer, S.J; M. Richards. "Polynesian Origin: Slow boat to Melanesia." *Nature* 410 (6825). 2001. pp.166-7; also Hedrick, John D; Goodrich-Hedrick. "The Problem of Polynesian Origin" *Expedition Magazine* 14. 1972; also Dixon, Roland B. "A new theory of Polynesian Origins." *Proceedings of the American Philosophical Society*, 59. 1923 *** All three authors discussed this separately—Fornander in his *Account of the Polynesian Race Volume I* and Joseph Campbell both make reference to Piggott.

lxxxix Heine-Geldern, Robert. *Urheimat und früheste Wanderungen der Austronesier*. Anthropos, 1932 (loc. cit., pp.598-602); quoted by Campbell, Joseph. *The Mask of God: Primitive Mythology*. First Published. New York, NY. Viking Penguin Inc.1959. Revised edition 1969. Copyright renewed Joseph Campbell. 1987. p.44

xc Heine-Geldern, Robert. *Urheimat und früheste Wanderungen der Austronesier*. Anthropos. 1932 (loc. cit., pp.358-602.); quoted by Campbell, Joseph. *The Mask of God: Primitive Mythology*. First Published. New York, NY. Viking Penguin Inc.1959. Revised edition 1969. Copyright renewed Joseph Campbell. 1987. p.442

ETHNOLOGY

xci Campbell, Joseph. *The Mask of God: Primitive Mythology*. First Published. New York, NY. Viking Penguin Inc.1959. Revised edition 1969. Copyright renewed Joseph Campbell. 1987 (quoting Oswald Menghin and Professor Heine-Geldern); also Wells, S. *The Journey of Man: A Genetic Odyssey*. New York. Random House Trade Paperbacks. 2003 [2002]; also Appenzeller, T. "Human migrations: Eastern Odyssey. Human had spread across Asia by 50,000 years ago. Everything else about our original exodus from Africa is up for debate." *Nature*. 485(7396). 2012

xcii Campbell, Joseph. *The Mask of God: Oriental Mythology*. First Published. New York, NY. Viking Penguin Inc. 1962. Published in Penguin Books. 1976. Copyright renewed Joseph Campbell, 1962. p.158 (quoting Professor Piggot)

xciii Bar-Yosef, Ofer. "The Natufian Culture in the Levant, Threshold to the Origins of Agriculture." *Evolutionary Anthropology*. 6.5 (1998): 159-177. Print

xciv Campbell, Joseph. *The Mask of God: Oriental Mythology*. First Published. New York, NY. Viking Penguin Inc. 1962. Published in Penguin Books. 1976. Copyright renewed Joseph Campbell, 1962. p.158 (quoting Professor Piggot)

xcv Campbell, Joseph. *The Mask of God: Oriental Mythology*. First Published. New York, NY. Viking Penguin Inc. 1962. Published in Penguin Books. 1976. Copyright renewed Joseph Campbell, 1962. Pp. 158-159

xcvi Ephert / CC BY-SA (https://creativecommons.org/licenses/by-sa/3.0) recreation of a map that can be found at the Kyushu Museum website that shows the human migration path and dates Out of Africa as proposed by Saitou Naruya (Japanese:斎藤成) professor at the (Japanese) National Institute for Genetics. http://www.museum.kyushu-u.ac.jp/WAJIN/113.html

xcvii *Marathi language Rashtra Mimansa* (Nationalism); trans. N. Jayapalan. 2001; also Hansen, Thomas Blom. *History of India*. Atlantic and Dist. 1999. p.21; also "Imagining the Hindu Nation" *The Saffron Wave: Democracy and Hindu Nationalism in Modern India*. Princeton University Press. p.80

xcviii Witzel, Michael. "Autochthonous Aryans? The Evidence from Old Indian and Iranian Texts" (PDF) *Electronic Journal of Vedic Studies*. 7(3). 2001. p.69

xcix "The Vedanta Philosophy": An Address Before the Graduate Philosophical Society of Harvard University, Mar 25 1896 by Swami Vivekananda. New

York, The Vedanta Society. 1901; also Srila Vyasadeva. *The Vedas*. Vedanta is the 13th Chapter of Bhagavad Gita. Vedanta-Sutra

[c] Burrow, Thomas. "On the significance of the term arma-, armaka- in Early Sanskrit Literature." *Journal of Indian History* XLI, Pt. I : 159-166. 1963

[ci] Frawley, David. "The Myth of the Aryan Invasion of India." *The India Times;* also Frawley, David. "Hidden Horizons: Unearthing 10,000 Years of Indian Culture." Amdavad, India: Swaminarayan Aksharpith. p.×i-xiv. 2007

[cii] Trautmann, Thomas R. *Languages and Nations: The Dravidian Proof in Colonial Madras*. University of California Press. Nov 4 2006

[ciii] Arlotto, Anthony. *Introduction to Historical Linguistics*. UPA. Jan 9 1981; also Slocum, Jonathan. "Early Indo-European Online (EIEOL): Ancient language lessons in web page form," *Journal of Indo-European Studies 33, 3 & 4,* Fall/Winter. pp.315-323. 2005; also: liberalarts.utexas.edu The University of Texas at Austin: Linguistics Research Center: Topic: Jonathan Slocum Publications Journal Articles.

[civ] Mallory, J.P; Adams D.Q. *The Oxford Introduction to Proto-Indo-European and the Proto-Indo-European World (Oxford Linguistics)*. Oxford University Press. 1 edition. Nov 9 2006

[cv] Wikipedia contributors. "Pontic–Caspian steppe." Wikipedia, The Free Encyclopedia. Wikipedia, The Free Encyclopedia, 23 Jul. 2020. Web. 18 Aug. 2020.

ARCHEOLOGY

[cvi] Schmidt, Klaus. *Gobekli Tepe: The World's First Temple?* quoted by Curry, Andrew. *The Smithsonian Magazine*. Nov 2008

[cvii] National Geographic Channel. "Cradle of the Gods" (aired 01.11.2013), featuring Dr. Jeffrey I. Rose from the Archaeology and Antiquity department of Birmingham University, U.K.

[cviii] *Concise History of the World: an Illustrated Timeline*; ed. Kagan, Neil; forw. Bentley, Jerry H. Washington, D.C., USA. National Geographic Society. 2006. Revised edition 2013

[cix] High Chief Aiono Dr. Fanaafi Le Tagaloa. "O le Fa'asinomaga." Preface, Upolu, Samoa. Published Lolomia e le Lamepa Press. Senadofi Place, Alafua, Samoa. Nov 1997

[cx] *Pratt's Grammar & Dictionary of the Samoan Language*. Apia. Samoa. 1977 Edition.

[cxi] Wells, Spencer. *The Journey of Man: A Genetic Odyssey*. Random House. 2002. The Out of Africa common genetic marker, Y chromosome known as M168 (Haplogroup CT (Y-DNA). p.182f; also M130 (Haplogroup C (Y-DNA) new marker for Indonesia Archipelago indigenous. p.75

[cxii] *Concise History of the World: an Illustrated Timeline*; ed. Kagan, Neil; forw. Bentley, Jerry H. Washington, D.C., USA. National Geographic Society. 2006. Revised edition 2013

[cxiii] Campbell, Joseph. *The Mask of God: Primitive Mythology*. First Published. New York, NY. Viking Penguin Inc.1959. Revised edition 1969. Copyright renewed Joseph Campbell. 1987. pp.206-211

[cxiv] Kirch, P.V; Hunt, T.L. eds. "The To'aga Site : Three Millennia of Polynesian Occupation in the Manu'a Islands, American Samoa; Number 51." Contribution of the University of California Archaeological Research Facility Berkeley, California. 1993; also Clark, Jeffrey T; Michlovic, Michael G. "An Early Settlement in the Polynesian Homeland: Excavations at 'Aoa Valley, Tutuila Island, American Samoa." *Journal of Field Archeology* 23:2, 151-167, DOI: 10.1179/009346996791973927

cxv Green, Roger C; Davidson, Janet M. eds. *Prehistory of Alega, Tutuila Island, American Samoa.* 1993. pp.34-68; also Davidson, Janet M. "Settlement Patterns in Samoa Before 1840." *The Journal of the Polynesian Society* 78 (4): 399-420. 1969; also Davidson, Janet M; Green, Roger C; Buist, A.G; Peters, K. M. "Additional Radiocarbon Dates for Western Polynesia." *Journal of the Polynesian Society* 76(2) : 223-230. 1967

cxvi Davidson, Janet M. "Settlement Pattern in Samoa before 1840." *Journal of Polynesian Society*, Vol.78. 1969

cxvii Green, Roger C; Davidson, Janet M. "Radiocarbon Dates for Western Samoa." *The Journal of the Polynesian Society* 74(1): 63-69. 1965/7

cxviii Clark, Jeffrey T; Michlovic, Michael G. "An Early Polynesian Homeland: Excavations at 'Aoa Valley, Tutuila Island, American Samoa." *Journal of Field Archaeology* Vol.23: 151-167. 1996

cxix Dickinson, William M; Green, Roger C. "Geoarchaeological Context of Holocene Subsidence at the Ferry Berth Lapita Site, Mulifanua, Upolu, Samoa." *Geoarchaeology. An International Journal*, Vol.13, No.3, 239-263 (1998) CCC 0883-6353/98/030239-25. 1998

cxx West, Barbara A. *Encyclopedia of the People of Asia and Oceania.* Facts on File Dec 1 2008

cxxi Carte synthétiques des migrations en Océanie. Hiro-Heremoana / CC BY-SA (https://creativecommons.org/licenses/by-sa/3.0)

cxxii Summerhayes, Glenn. "Edward W Gifford and Richard Shutler Jr's Archaeological Expedition to New Caledonia in 1952 (review)." *The Contemporary Pacific.* 16. 461-462. 10.1353/cp.2004.0060. 2004

cxxiii West, Barbara A. *Encyclopedia of the People of Asia and Oceania.* Facts on File Dec 1 2008

cxxiv Pawley, Andrew. "The Origins of Early Lapita Culture: The Testimony of Historical Linguistics." Department of Linguistics Research School of Pacific and Asian Studies. The Australian National University Canberra, ACT, 0200, Australia. andrew.pawley@anu.edu.au

MYTHOLOGY

cxxv Kramer, Samuel Noah. *From the Tablets of Sumer*, pp.92-93; cited by Campbell, Joseph. *The Mask of God: Oriental Mythology.* First Published. New York, NY. Viking Penguin Inc. 1962. Published in Penguin Books. 1976. Copyright renewed Joseph Campbell. 1962. pg. 112-114; also Kramer, Dr. Samuel Noah. *The Sumerians: Their History, Culture and Character.* The University of Chicago Press. 1963

cxxvi Mann, Thomas. "Freud and the Future." *Life and Letters Today*, Vol. 15, No. 5. Autumn 1936. p. 89

cxxvii Evans, Bergen. *Dictionary of Mythology.* Centennial Press. 1970

cxxviii Wikipedia contributors. "Thomas Aquinas." Wikipedia, The Free Encyclopedia. Wikipedia, The Free Encyclopedia, 21 Aug. 2020. Web. 21 Aug. 2020.

cxxix Chenu, Marie-Dominique. Ecole partique des hautes etudes, Paris, 1945-51. "St. Thomas Aquinas: Italian Christian Theologian and Philosopher" published by Britannica.

cxxx Mann, Thomas. "Freud and the Future." *Life and Letters Today*, Vol. 15, No. 5. Autumn 1936. p. 89; ref by Campbell, Joseph in *The Mask of God: Primitive Mythology.* Prologue: "Toward A Natural History of The Gods and Heroes" note 14 and 15. First Published. New York, NY. Viking Penguin Inc.1959. Revised edition 1969. Copyright renewed Joseph Campbell. 1987

cxxxi High Chief Aiono Dr. Fanaafi LeTagaloa. *O le Fa'asinomaga.* Asu Village, Tutuila Island, American Samoa. Published Lolomia e le Lamepa Press. Senadofi Place, Alafua, Samoa. Nov 1997. p.84

[cxxxii] Krämer, Dr. Augustin. *The Samoa Islands: An Outline of a Monograph with Particular Consideration of German Samoa: Vol 1*; trans. Theodore Verhaaren. Auckland. Polynesian Press Samoa House. 1994.

[cxxxiii] *Aua Village, Tutuila Island, American Samoa. Tusi Fa'alupega O Samoa Atoa.* Published and Authored by Methodist Church Board of Trustees, 1985 edition. p.258

[cxxxiv] Frazer, James George. *The Golden Bough.* UK, Macmillan Publishers. 1890

[cxxxv] Campbell, Joseph. *The Mask of God: Primitive Mythology.* First Published. New York, NY. Viking Penguin Inc.1959. Revised edition 1969. Copyright renewed Joseph Campbell. 1987

[cxxxvi] Krämer, Dr. Augustin. *The Samoa Islands: An Outline of a Monograph with Particular Consideration of German Samoa: Vol 1*; trans. Theodore Verhaaren. Auckland. Polynesian Press Samoa House. 1994

[cxxxvii] Campbell, Joseph. *The Mask of God: Primitive Mythology.* First Published. New York, NY. Viking Penguin Inc.1959. Revised edition 1969. Copyright renewed Joseph Campbell. 1987

[cxxxviii] Campbell, Joseph. *The Mask of God: Primitive Mythology.* First Published. New York, NY. Viking Penguin Inc.1959. Revised edition 1969. Copyright renewed Joseph Campbell. 1987. pg.16. Also Sigmund Freud, *Totem und Tabu*, first published in two parts in Imago (Bd.1-2, 1912-1913); republished as a book by H. Heller und Compagnie, Leipzig, 1913; Gesammelte Schriften, Vol.X (Vienna, Psychoanalytischer Verlag); English translations by Dr. A. A. Brill, *Totem and Tabu*. New York. New Republic. 1931; also pub. by W. W. Norton and Company. 1952.

[cxxxix] Campbell, Joseph. *The Mask of God: Primitive Mythology.* First Published. New York, NY. Viking Penguin Inc.1959. Revised edition 1969. Copyright renewed Joseph Campbell. 1987

[cxl] Meleisea, Malama. *Lagaga: Short Story of Western Samoa.* Published: Institute of Pacific Studies and the Western Samoa Extension Center of the University of South Pacific.1987. pp.2-10

[cxli] Coomaraswamy, Dr. Ananda K. *Yaksas, Part II.* Washington D. C., Smithsonian Institution, Publication 3059, 1931 p.14; referenced by Campbell, Joseph. *The Mask of God: Oriental Mythology.* First Published. New York, NY. Viking Penguin Inc. 1962. Published in Penguin Books. 1976. Copyright renewed Joseph Campbell, 1962. p.147

[cxlii] Campbell, Joseph. *The Mask of God: Primitive Mythology.* First Published. New York, NY. Viking Penguin Inc.1959. Revised edition 1969. Copyright renewed Joseph Campbell. 1987

[cxliii] Chi, Li. *The Beginning of Chinese Civilization* Seattle: University of Washington Press. 1957. pp.3-4

[cxliv] Campbell, Joseph. *The Mask of God: Oriental Mythology.* First Published. New York, NY. Viking Penguin Inc. 1962. Published in Penguin Books. 1976. Copyright renewed Joseph Campbell, 1962

[cxlv] Campbell, Joseph. *The Mask of God: Oriental Mythology.* First Published. New York, NY. Viking Penguin Inc. 1962. Published in Penguin Books. 1976. Copyright renewed Joseph Campbell, 1962. pp.422-428

[cxlvi] Wikipedia contributors. "Eight Immortals." Wikipedia, The Free Encyclopedia. Wikipedia, The Free Encyclopedia, 31 Aug. 2020. Web. 3 Sep 2020.

[cxlvii] Campbell, Joseph. *The Mask of God: Primitive Mythology.* First Published. New York, NY. Viking Penguin Inc.1959. Revised edition 1969. Copyright renewed Joseph Campbell. 1987

[cxlviii] Krämer, Dr. Augustin. *The Samoa Islands: An Outline of a Monograph with Particular Consideration of German Samoa: Vol 1*; trans. Theodore Verhaaren. Auckland. Polynesian Press Samoa House. 1994. p.539.

cxlix Alexander, Neville E. *Studien Zum Stilwandel Im Dramatischen Werk Gerhart Hauptmanns,* Springer-Verlag GmbH. 1964

cl Campbell, Joseph. *The Mask of God: Oriental Mythology.* First Published. New York, NY. Viking Penguin Inc. 1962. Published in Penguin Books. 1976. Copyright renewed Joseph Campbell, 1962; citing Piggott, S. et al; also Heine-Geldern, R. "The Origin of Ancient Civilizations and Toynbee's Theories." Diogenes 4 (1956): 81-99. https://doi.org/10.1177/039219215600401307, Diogenes, No. 13; Frobenius, Leo. *Erlebte Erdteile,* Bd. I. Frankfurt, 1925 029; also Radcliffe-Brown, A. R. *The Andaman Islanders.* Cambridge University Press. 1922;also Frazer, J. G. *the Golden Bough.* UK, Macmillan and Co. 1890

cli Campbell, Joseph. *The Mask of God: Oriental Mythology.* First Published. New York, NY. Viking Penguin Inc. 1962. Published in Penguin Books. 1976. Copyright renewed Joseph Campbell, 1962; citing James Henry Breasted

clii Campbell, Joseph. *The Mask of God Book 3: Occidental Mythology.* Viking Compass Edition published 1970. Copyright @ Joseph Campbell. 1964. p.519

cliii Malinowski, Dr. Bronislaw. "Argonauts of the Western Pacific." *Studies in economics and political science,* no. 65. London, G. Routledge & Sons; New York, E.P. Dutton & Co. 1922

cliv *Concise History of the World: an Illustrated Timeline;* ed. Kagan, Neil; forw. Bentley, Jerry H. Washington, D.C., USA. National Geographic Society. 2006. Revised edition 2013

clv Hesiod. *Theogony/Works and Days;* trans. Evelyn-White, Hugh G. 1914

clvi Campbell, Joseph. *The Mask of God Book 3: Occidental Mythology.* Viking Compass Edition published 1970. Copyright @ Joseph Campbell. 1964

clvii Uktarsh. http://utkarshspeak.blogspot.com/2010/11/rooster-in-various-mythologies.html

clviii Krämer, Dr. Augustin. *The Samoa Islands: An Outline of a Monograph with Particular Consideration of German Samoa: Vol 1;* trans. Theodore Verhaaren. Auckland. Polynesian Press Samoa House. 1994. pp.118-9.

clix Campbell, Joseph. *The Mask of God: Primitive Mythology.* First Published. New York, NY. Viking Penguin Inc.1959. Revised edition 1969. Copyright renewed Joseph Campbell. 1987. p.61

clx Krämer, Dr. Augustin. *The Samoa Islands: An Outline of a Monograph with Particular Consideration of German Samoa: Vol 1;* trans. Theodore Verhaaren. Auckland. Polynesian Press Samoa House. 1994. pp.141-143

clxi Campbell, Joseph. *The Mask of God: Primitive Mythology.* First Published. New York, NY. Viking Penguin Inc.1959. Revised edition 1969. Copyright renewed Joseph Campbell. 1987. p.472

GENEALOGY

clxii Fornander, Abraham. *An Account of the Polynesian Race, volume 1.* London. Trübner & company. 1880

clxiii Fornander, Abraham. *Fornander Collection of Hawaiian Antiques and Folk-Lore: The Hawaiian Account of the Formation of Their Islands and Origin of Their Race, with the Traditions of Their Migrations, as Gathered from Original Sources;* trans. illus, with notes by Thrum, Thomas G. *Vol V Part 1.* Honolulu, Hawaii. Bishop Museum Press. 1918

clxiv Pratt, George. Genealogy of the Kings and Princes of Samoa. Report of the second meeting of the Australasian Association for Advancement of Science, Vol.II. 1890

clxv Fornander, Abraham. *An Account of the Polynesian Race volume 1.* London. Trübner & company. 1880. p.162

clxvi Lameko, Hon. Pule. Minister for Youth, Sports, and Cultural Affairs, Samoa. *Samoa Ne'i Galo*. 1994; also Lafai Sauoaiga F.S. Apenamoemanatunatu. *O le Mavaega I Le Tai*. Apia, Malua Printing Press. 1988; also references to Dr. Stuebel, Oscar. *Myth and Legends of Samoa-Tala o le Vavau, Samoan*. English translation by Brother Herman. Wellington, 1967; Muller, F.W.K. "Samoanische Texte." *Herausgegeben Veröffentlichungen aus dem königlichen Museum für Völkerkunde*. IV. Bd. 2-4 Heft. pp.62, 15; Bülow, W. "v. No. 19. Beiträge zu Ethnographie der Samoa-Inseln." I. A. E. XIII. 1900. p.66; Turner, G. "No. 2. A hundred years ago and long before." London 1884. p.222; Fraser, John. No. 1. "'O le tala ia Taemā and Nafanua - II Item." (Samoan Text). *Journal of the Polynesian Society (JPS)* of New Zealand. Wellington. V. 1896, p.171; Fraser, John. "No. 6. The Malayo-Polynesian theory." *JPS*. IV. 1895, V. 1896, VII. 1898; Stair, J. B. "No. 4. Flotsam and Jetsam from the Great Ocean or summary of early Samoan Voyages and settlement." *JPS*. IV. 1895; Stair, J. B. "No. 2. 'O le fale o le Fe'e (house of the eel) or Ruins of an old Samoan temple." *JPS*. II. 1893; Stair, J. B. "No. 4. Samoa: whence people." *JPS*. IV. 189; Krämer, Dr. Augustin. *The Samoa Islands: An Outline of a Monograph with Particular Consideration of German Samoa: Vol 1*; trans. Theodore Verhaaren. Auckland. Polynesian Press Samoa House. 1994

clxvii Pratt, George. *A Grammar and Dictionary of the Samoan Language*. Apia, Malua Press. 1977. p.325

clxviii Krämer, Dr. Augustin. *The Samoa Islands: An Outline of a Monograph with Particular Consideration of German Samoa: Vol 1*; trans. Theodore Verhaaren. Auckland. Polynesian Press Samoa House. 1994. pp.27-28. Also, Dr. Krämer adhered to v. Bulow #11. (See *the History of the Ancestor of the Samoan*. I.A.E. 1898 vol.XI. for more complete and reliable legend of Pili.)

clxix Krämer, Dr. Augustin. *The Samoa Islands: An Outline of a Monograph with Particular Consideration of German Samoa: Vol 1*; trans. Theodore Verhaaren. Auckland. Polynesian Press Samoa House. 1994. pp.9, 26-28.

clxx Krämer, Dr. Augustin. *The Samoa Islands: An Outline of a Monograph with Particular Consideration of German Samoa: Vol 1*; trans. Theodore Verhaaren. Auckland. Polynesian Press Samoa House. 1994; also Tonumaipe'a, Ape. *Mavaega i le Tai*. 1988

clxxi Fa'atonu, Liumanu: *Samoa Ne'i Galo*, "Samoa, Lest We Forget;" English translation by Su'a Julia Wallwork. 1994

clxxii Alexander, William De Witt. *A Brief History of the Hawaiian People*. American Book Company. 1891

ETHOLOGY

clxxiii Hart, Dr. Keith: "The 1898 Cambridge Anthropology Expedition to the Torres Strait's 100 years Celebration Conference" hosted by Dr. Hart Aug 10-12 1998. Published Online in *Science and Culture* in 1998

clxxiv Radcliffe-Brown, A.R. *The Andaman Islanders* 2nd printing; London: Cambridge University Press, 1933

clxxv Tibi, Bassam. *Arab Nationalism*. 1997, pg.139. The Muqaddimah is foundational work for the schools of historiography, cultural history, and the philosophy of history. Mohamad Abdalla Summer 2007. "Ibn Khaldun on the Fate of Islamic Science after the 11th Century," *Islam & Science* 5 (1), pp.61-70.

clxxvi Jung, Carl. *Psychology of the Unconscious*, English translation by Hinkle, Beatrice M. London. Kegan Paul Trench Trübner. 1916; cited by Campbell, Joseph. *The Mask of God: Oriental Mythology*. First Published. New York, NY. Viking Penguin Inc. 1962. Published in Penguin Books. 1976. Copyright renewed Joseph Campbell, 1962. Reference Notes: Part One: Chapter 1, note # 23: C. G. Jung, *Das Unbewusste im normalen und kranken Seelenleben*, first edition 1916, second, 1918, third: Rascher Verlag, Zurich, 1926; reprinted in Two Essays on Analytical Psychology. (London: Bailliere, Tindall and Cox, 1928; New York, The Bollingen Series XX, The Collected Works of C. G. Jung, Vol. 7, 1953)

[clxxvii] Jung, C. G. *Psychologische Typen*, Zurich: Rasher Verlag, 1921, p.598; cited by Campbell, Joseph. *The Mask of God: Primitive Mythology*. First Published. New York, NY. Viking Penguin Inc.1959. Revised edition 1969. Copyright renewed Joseph Campbell. 1987. Chapter 1: The Enigma of the Inherited Image, Reference Notes #1

[clxxviii] Rivers, W. H. R. "The Psychological Factor" *Essays on the Depopulation of Melanesian*. London. Cambridge University Press, 1922 pp.84-113

[clxxix] Williamson, Robert Wood. *The Ways of the South Sea Savage: A Record of Travel & Observation Amongst the Savages of the Solomon Islands & Primitive Coast & Mountain People of New Guinea*. Philadelphia. J. B. Lippincott Company; London: Seeley, Service & Co. Ltd. 1914. pp.111-127.

[clxxx] Taylor, Jean Gelman: *Indonesia: Peoples and Histories*. Yale University Press. 2003. pp.7, 30-2.

[clxxxi] *Athenaeus: The Deipnosophists* with an English Translation by Charles Burton Gulick, Ph.D. Elliot Professor of Greek Literature, Harvard University. In Seven Volumes: II. London: William Heinemann LTD. Cambridge, Massachusetts. Harvard University Press. 1928, rep.1957. p.219.

[clxxxii] https://yagbeonilu.com/libation-legend-myth-divinity/

[clxxxiii] James, George G.M. *Stolen Legacy*. Philosophical Library. 1954; also James, George G. M. Ph.D. "Stolen Legacy: Greek Philosophy is Stolen Egyptian Philosophy. *The Journal of Pan African Studies* eBook. 2009

[clxxxiv] Herodotus *Book II* With an English Translation by A. D. Godley, Hon. Fellow of Magdalen College, Oxford. In Four Volumes I Book I and II. London. William Heinemann LTD Cambridge, Massachusetts. Harvard University Press. 1920, rev. 1926, 1931, 1946, 1960 pp 455-6

[clxxxv] Hindustan Times, Oct 2010; also Spiro, Melford E. *Buddhism and Society: a great tradition and its Burmese vicissitudes*. University of California Press. 1982.; also "Monier Williams Online Dictionary" www.sanskrit-lexicon.uni-koeln.de.

[clxxxvi] *The Deipnosophists, Volume II, Book V*, English Translation by Charles Burton Gulick, Harvard University Press; Loeb Library Edition, 1st Printed 1928

[clxxxvii] Hunter, Richard L. *Eubulus: The Fragments*. Cambridge University Press. 1983

[clxxxviii] Garnsey, Peter. *Food and Society in Classical Antiquity*. Cambridge University Press. 1999

[clxxxix] Wikipedia contributors. "Libation." Wikipedia, The Free Encyclopedia. Wikipedia, The Free Encyclopedia, 31 Aug. 2020. Web. 31 Aug. 2020.

[cxc] Deter-Wolf, Aaron. (2013). *The Material Culture and Middle Stone Age Origins of Ancient Tattooing* 2013

[cxci] Deter-Wolf, Aaron; Robitaille, Benoît; Krutak, Lars; Galliot, Sébastien. (2016). "The World's Oldest Tattoos." *Journal of Archaeological Science*: Reports. 5. 19-24. 10.1016/j.jasrep.2015.11.007. 2016

[cxcii] Tolstoy, Paul. "Culture Parallels between Southeast Asia and Mesoamerica in Manufacture of Bark Cloth" *Transactions of New York Academy of Science*, Series II, 25(6):646-662. 1963

[cxciii] Kennedy, Raymond. "Barkcloth Cloth in Indonesia." *Journal of Polynesian Society* 43(4):229-243, 1934

[cxciv] Green, Roger. "Early Lapita Art from Polynesia and Island Melanesia: Continuities in Ceramic, Barkcloth, and Tattoo Decorations." *Exploring the Visual Art of Oceania: Australia, Melanesia, Micronesia and Polynesia*. ed. Mead, Sidney. Honolulu, University of Hawaii Press. 1979. pp.13-31

[cxcv] Ling, Shun-sheng; Ling, Mary Man-li. "Barkcloth, Impressed Pottery and the Inventions of Paper and Printing," Institute for Ethnology Academia, Sinica, Monograph no.3. Nankang, Taipei, Taiwan 1963

[cxcvi] Aragon, Lorraine V. "Barkcloth Production in Central Sulawesi." *Expedition Magazine* Vol 32 No.1 1990. The University Museum Magazine of Archaeology and Anthropology University of Pennsylvania

GEOGRAPHY AND GEOLOGY

[cxcvii] Sathiamurthy, E; Voris, H.K. "Maps of Holocene sea level transgression and submerged lakes on the Sunday Shelf." *Natural History Journal of Chulalongkorn University* Supplement 2: 1-43 2006

[cxcviii] Haer, Debbie Guthrie; Morillot, Juliette; Toh, Irene. *Bali, a traveler's companion*. Archipelago Press. Jan 1 2000

[cxcix] Shipton, Ceri; O'Connor, Sue; Kealy, Shimona; Mahirta, Syarqiyah, Indah N; Alamsyah, Nico; Ririmasse, Marlon; "Early Ground Axe Technology in Wallace: The First Excavations on Obi Island." PLoS ONE 15(8): e0236719. doi: 10.1371/journal.pone.0236719 Published Aug 19 2020

[cc] Bellwood, Peter. *Prehistory of the Indo-Malaysian Archipelago*. Canberra. ANU Press. 2007

[cci] Hatin et al. "A genome wide pattern of structure and admixture in peninsular Malaysia Malays." *The HUGO Journal* 2014, 8:5 http://www.thehugojournal.com/content/8/1/5

PSYCHOLOGY

[ccii] Eisemann, Thomas R. "Entrepreneurship: A Working Definition" *Harvard Business Review*. January 10 2013

[cciii] Wikipedia contributors. "Peter Drucker." Wikipedia, The Free Encyclopedia. Wikipedia, The Free Encyclopedia, 21 Oct. 2020. Web. Oct 24 2020

[cciv] Hart, Dr. Keith: "The 1898 Cambridge Anthropology Expedition to the Torres Strait's 100 years Celebration Conference" hosted by Dr. Hart Aug 10-12 1998. Published Online in *Science and Culture* in 1998

[ccv] Mann, Thomas. *Joseph and His Brothers;* English translation by H. T. Lowe-Porter. New York. Alfred A. Knopf. 1948

[ccvi] Jung, Carl. *Psychology of the Unconscious*, English translation by Hinkle, Beatrice M. London. Kegan Paul Trench Trübner. 1916

[ccvii] Campbell, Joseph. *The Mask of God: Oriental Mythology*. First Published. New York, NY. Viking Penguin Inc. 1962. Published in Penguin Books. 1976. Copyright renewed Joseph Campbell, 1962.

SEMIOTICS

[ccviii] Fuimaono Na'oia Fereti Tupua. *O Le Suaga A Le Va'atele (The Findings of the Big Canoe)*. Copyright @ 1996 by Fuimaono Fereti Tupua and The Samoa Observer Co. Ltd. p. 71

[ccix] Krämer, Augustin. *The Samoa Islands: An Outline of a Monograph with Particular Consideration of German Samoa: vol 2: Material Culture;* trans. Verhaaren, Theodore. Auckland. Polynesian Press Samoa House 1994

[ccx] "Pictorial Semiotics," the *Oxford Index*, Oxford University Press, n.d. Web

ccxi Liddell, Henry George and Scott, Robert. "Perseus" in *A Greek-English Lexicon* Clarendon Press. Later Printing Edition Jan 1 1961

ccxii *Oxford English Dictionary*. 1989

ccxiii Locke, John an *Essay Concerning Human Understanding* England. 1690; also *Stanford Encyclopedia of Philosophy*: John Locke (plato.standford.edu locke john) First published Sun Sep 2 2001; substantive revision Tue May 1 2018; also *The Clarendon Edition of the Works of John Locke*. Oxford. Clarendon Press. [N] An Essay Concerning Human Understanding, Peter H. Nidditch (ed.), 1975. dot:10.1093/actrade/9780198243861. book.1/actrade-9780198243861-book-1

ccxiv "Ancient Egyptian Hieroglyphics—The Rosetta Stone." https://www.artyfactory.com/egyptian_art/egyptian_hieroglyphs/rosetta_stone.htm

ccxv Webster's *Biographical Dictionary* 1943

ccxvi Caesar, Michael. *Umberto Eco: Philosophy, Semiotics, and the Work of Fiction.* Polity. 1st Edition. Aug 3 1999

ccxvii Everett, Daniel L; *How Language Began: The Story of Humanity's Greatest Invention.* Liveright. 1st Edition. Nov 7 2017

ccxviii de Brosses, Charles; Saillant, Chez; Vincent, Philippe; Desaint, Nicholas. *Traité de la formation mecanique des langues et des principes physique de l'etymologie.* Paris. Chez Saillant, Vincent, Desaint. 1765

ccxix De Brosses, Charles; Morris, Rosalind C; Leonard, Daniel H. *The Returns of Fetishism: Charles De Brosses And the Afterlives of An Idea.* University of Chicago Press. Jul 2017

ccxx Krämer, Dr. Augustin. *The Samoa Islands: An Outline of a Monograph with Particular Consideration of German Samoa: Vol 1*; trans. Theodore Verhaaren. Auckland. Polynesian Press Samoa House. 1994. pp.10-11

LINGUISTICS

ccxxi Wikipedia contributors. "Origin of speech." Wikipedia, The Free Encyclopedia. Wikipedia, The Free Encyclopedia, 1 Sep 2020. Web. 3 Sep 2020. Citing Darwin, C. *The Descent of Man, and Selection in Relation to Sex*, 2 vols. London: Murray, 1871. p.56.

ccxxii Everett, Daniel L. *Dark Matter of the Mind: The Culturally Articulated Unconscious.* University of Chicago press. 1st Edition. Nov 15 2016; also Everett, Daniel L; *How Language Began: The Story of Humanity's Greatest Invention.* Liveright. 1st Edition. Nov 7 2017

ccxxiii Wikipedia contributors. "Prosody (linguistics)." Wikipedia, The Free Encyclopedia. Wikipedia, The Free Encyclopedia, 24 Aug. 2020. Web. 3 Sep 2020

ccxxiv Staal, Frits (1996). *Ritual and Mantras: Rules Without Meaning.* Motilal Banaridass Publ. 1996

ccxxv Aristotle. *On Rhetoric: A theory of Civic Discourse*; trans. Kennedy, George A. Oxford. Oxford University Press. Jan 16 1991

ccxxvi *The Rhetoric and the Poetics of Aristotle*; trans. Roberts, W. Rhys; ed. McQuade, Donald. New York. The Modern Library. 1984

ccxxvii Staal, Frits. *Universals: studies in Indian logic and linguistics.* University of Chicago Press. Mar 1988

ccxxviii Pigafetta, Antonio. *Magellan's Voyage: A Narrative Account of the First Circumnavigation.* (Dover Books on Travel, Adventure) Dover Publications. Oct 25 2012

ccxxix De Saussure, Ferdinand; Harris, Roy. *Course in General Linguistics (Open Court Classics).* Open Court. Reprint Edition. Dec 30 1998 [ccxxx] Fornander, Abraham; Stokes John F. G. *An Account of the Polynesian Race: Its Origins and Migrations, and the Ancient History of the Hawaiian People to the Times of Kamehameha I.* Hawaii. Trübner & Company. 1878

[ccxxxi] Dyen, Isidore. *A Lexicostatistical Classification of the Austronesian Languages,* Issue 19. Waverly Press. 1965

[ccxxxii] Fornander, Abraham; Stokes John F. G. *An Account of the Polynesian Race: Its Origins and Migrations, and the Ancient History of the Hawaiian People to the Times of Kamehameha I.* Hawaii. Trübner & Company. 1878

[ccxxxiii] Fornander, Abraham. *An Account of the Polynesian Race: Comparative vocabulary of the Polynesian and Indo-European languages. With a preface by Prof. W. D. Alexander.* Trübner & Company. 1885

[ccxxxiv] Fornander, Abraham. *An Account of the Polynesian Race: Comparative vocabulary of the Polynesian and Indo-European languages. With a preface by Prof. W. D. Alexander.* Trübner & Company. 1885. p. viii

[ccxxxv] Fortson, Benjamin W. *Indo-European Language and Culture.* Blackwell Publishing. 2004; also Meier-Brügger, Michael; Fritz, Mathias; Mayrhofer, Manfred. *Indo-European Linguistics.* Walter de Gruyter 2003

[ccxxxvi] Fornander, Abraham. *An Account of the Polynesian Race: Comparative vocabulary of the Polynesian and Indo-European languages. With a preface by Prof. W. D. Alexander.* Trübner & Company, 1885. p. viii, ix

[ccxxxvii] Lynch, John; Ross, Malcolm; Crowley, Terry. *The Oceanic Languages.* Curzon, 2002

[ccxxxviii] "Chronological dispersal of Austronesian people across the Pacific (per Benton et al, 2012, adapted from Bellwood, 2011).svg" Obsidian Soul / CC BY (https://creativecommons.org/licenses/by/4.0)

[ccxxxix] https://www.britannica.com/contributor/Robert-Andrew-Blust/4317

[ccxl] Wikipedia contributors. "Franz Bopp." Wikipedia, The Free Encyclopedia. Wikipedia, The Free Encyclopedia, 27 Jul. 2020. Web. 8 Sep 2020

[ccxli] Fornander, Abraham. *An Account of the Polynesian Race: Comparative vocabulary of the Polynesian and Indo-European languages. With a preface by Prof. W. D. Alexander.* Trübner & Company. 1885

[ccxlii] Fornander, Abraham. *An Account of the Polynesian Race: Comparative vocabulary of the Polynesian and Indo-European languages. With a preface by Prof. W. D. Alexander.* Trübner & Company. 1885. p. 23

[ccxliii] Fornander, Abraham. *An Account of the Polynesian Race: Comparative vocabulary of the Polynesian and Indo-European languages. With a preface by Prof. W. D. Alexander.* Trübner & Company. 1885. p. 23

[ccxliv] Marsden, William. *A Dictionary of the Malayan Language in two parts.* London 1812

[ccxlv] Pratt, George. *A Grammar and Dictionary of the Samoan Language.* The London Missionary Society. 1893. Note 1

[ccxlvi] Pratt, George. *A Grammar and Dictionary of the Samoan Language.* The London Missionary Society 1893. Note 1

[ccxlvii] Tuitele and Kneubuhl. *Upu Samoa: Samoan Words.* the Department of Education, American Samoa. 1978

[ccxlviii] Blust, Robert. "The Austronesian languages." Canberra, Australia. Asia-Pacific Linguistics Research School of Pacific and Asian Studies, The Australian National University 2013

[ccxlix] Wikipedia contributors. "Pijin language." Wikipedia, The Free Encyclopedia. Wikipedia, The Free Encyclopedia, 10 Aug. 2020. Web. 8 Sep 2020

[ccl] Levinson, Stephen C; Dunn, Michael; Terrill, Angela; Reesink, Ger; Foley, Robert A. "Structural Phylogenetics and the Reconstruction of Ancient Language History." *Science.* Sep 23 2005

[ccli] https://www.britannica.com/biography/Otto-Dempwolff

cclii Logan, James Richardson. *Ethnology of the Indo-Pacific Islands*. HardPress. ISBN 1318683599, 9781318683598. a reproduction of the original artefact. These books are created from careful scans of the original, 2019

ccliii Douglas, Bronwen; Ballard, Chris. *Foreign Bodies: Oceania and the Science of Race 1750-1940*. ANU Press, 2008. [This book includes writing by Helen Gardner, Vicki Luker, Christine Weir, Stephen Anderson, Paul Turnbull and others.]

ccliv Wikipedia contributors. "Sino-Tibetan languages." Wikipedia, The Free Encyclopedia. Wikipedia, The Free Encyclopedia, 9 Sep 2020. Web. 9 Sep 2020

cclv Handel, Zev. "What is Sino-Tibetan? Snapshot of a Field and a Language Family in Flux." Wiley Online Library-Language and Linguistics Compass/Volume 2, Issue 3 onlinelibrary.wiley.com 03 April 2008; also ed. LaPolla, Randy J. *Sino-Tibetan Linguistics: Critical Concepts in Linguistics*. London & New York. Rutledge. October 2018; also *Language Structure and Environment: Social, cultural and natural factors*. eds. De Busser, Rik; LaPolla, Randy J. Amsterdam. John Benjamin's 2015 and *The Sino-Tibetan Languages*, 2nd Edition. eds. Thurgood, Graham; LaPolla, Randy J. London & New York. Rutledge, 2017

cclvi eds. Sagart, Laurent; Blench, Roger; Sanchez, Mazas. *The Peopling of East Asia: Putting together archaeology, linguistics and genetics*. London & New York. Rutledge Curzon. 2005

cclvii Starosta, Stanley. "A grammatical typology of Formosan languages." *Bulletin of the Institute of History and Philology*. Academia Sinica. 1988; also Starosta, Stanley "A grammatical subgrouping of Formosan languages. Austronesian Studies Relating to Taiwan;" ed. Li, Paul et al. Taipei. Institute of History and Philology, Academia Sinica. 1995

cclviii Dai, Qingxia; Liu, Yan. "Analysis of the tones in Guangka subdialect of De'ang." *The Mon-Khmer Studies Journal*, vol. 27. 1997. pp. 91-108.

cclix Dryer, Matthew S. "Plural Words." *Linguistics* 27: 865-895. 1989

cclx Skoglund, Pontus; Reich, D; Lipson, M; Pinhasi, R; Bedford, S; Valentin, F; Spriggs, M. "Revisiting ancient DNA insights into the human history of the Pacific Islands." *Journal of the Archaeology in Oceania* Vol. 54, Issue 1. 1 April 2019

cclxi Blust, Robert. "The Austronesian languages." Canberra, Australia. Asia-Pacific Linguistics Research School of Pacific and Asian Studies, The Australian National University 2013

cclxii Everett, Daniel L; *How Language Began: The Story of Humanity's Greatest Invention*. Liveright. 1st Edition. Nov 7 2017

cclxiii Müller, Max. *Lectures on the science of language. Vol.1*. London: Longmans, Green. 1861

cclxiv Ngo, Robert. "When was the Hebrew Bible written?" https://www.biblicalarchaeology.org/daily/news/when-was-the-hebrew-bible-written/ May 4 2020; citing Proceedings of the National Academy of Science

cclxv Wikipedia contributors. "Logos (Christianity)." Wikipedia, The Free Encyclopedia. Wikipedia, The Free Encyclopedia, 21 Jul. 2020. Web. 9 Sep 2020

cclxvi Campbell, Joseph. *The Mask of God: Oriental Mythology*. First Published. New York, NY. Viking Penguin Inc. 1962. Published in Penguin Books. 1976. Copyright renewed Joseph Campbell. 1962. pg.84

cclxvii Campbell, Joseph. *The Mask of God: Oriental Mythology*. First Published. New York, NY. Viking Penguin Inc. 1962. Published in Penguin Books. 1976. Copyright renewed Joseph Campbell. 1962; citing Breasted, Professor James H. *Development of Religion and Thought in Ancient Egypt*. London. 1912; also citing Frankfort, Henri. *Kingship and the God*. Chicago. 1948; also citing

Wilson, John. "The Memphite Theology of Creation." *The Ancient Near East.* ed. James B. Prichard. Princeton 1958

[cclxviii] "Anatomy of the Brain" www.mayfieldclinic.com

[cclxix] Robinson, Tara Rodden; Spock, Lisa; *Genetics For Dummies*. For Dummies; 3rd edition 2 Jan 2020

[cclxx] Article Source: Revised Estimates for the Number of Human and Bacteria Cells in the Body. Sender R, Fuchs S, Milo R (2016) Revised Estimates for the Number of Human and Bacteria Cells in the Body. PLOS Biology 14(8): e1002533. https://doi.org/10.1371/journal.pbio.1002533

[cclxxi] www.kidshealth.org.

[cclxxii] Wikipedia contributors. "Allele." Wikipedia, The Free Encyclopedia. Wikipedia, The Free Encyclopedia, 11 Jul. 2020. Web. 10 Sep 2020

[cclxxiii] U.S. National Library of Medicine, *What is a Gene mutation and how do mutations occur?* https://ghr.nlm.nih.gov/primer/mutationsanddisorders/genemutation

[cclxxiv] O'Luanaigh, Cian. "Mutation in key gene allows Tibetans to thrive at high altitude" *The Guardian. Genetics.* July 2010

[cclxxv] Prof. Pritchard, Jonathan K. "How we are evolving" *Scientific American Special Edition 22*, 1s, doi:10.1038/scientificamericanhuman1112-98. Dec 2012

[cclxxvi] Wikipedia contributors. "Haplogroup." Wikipedia, The Free Encyclopedia. Wikipedia, The Free Encyclopedia, 22 Jun. 2020. Web. 10 Sep 2020

[cclxxvii] Karafet, T.M; Mendez, F.L; Meilerman, M.B; Underhill, P.A; Zegura, S.L; Hammer, M.F. "New binary polymorphisms reshape and increase resolution of the human Y Chromosomal haplogroup tree." *Genome Research.* 18(5):830-8.doi:10.1101/gr.7172008. May 2008; also Fu, Q; Posth, C; Hajdinjak, M; Petr, M; Mallick, S; Fernandes, D, et al. "The genetic history of Ice Age Europe." *Nature.*534(7606): 200-5. Bibcode:2016Natur.534.200F. June 2016; also ISOGG-Y-DNA Haplogroup R and subclades https://isogg.org/tree/index.html - select R for haplogroup R

[cclxxviii] Kayser, Manfred; Brauer, Silke; Cordaux, Richard; Casto, Amanda; Lao, Oscar; Zhivotovsky, Lev; Moyse-Faurie, Claire; Rutledge, Robb; Schiefenhoevel, Wulf; Gil, David; Lin, Alice; Underhill, Peter; Oefner, Peter; Trent, Ronald; Stoneking, Mark. "Melanesian and Asian Origins of Polynesians: mtDNA and Y Chromosome Gradients Across the Pacific." *Molecular biology and evolution.* 23. 2234-44. 10.1093/molbev/msl093. 2006; also Oppenheimer, Stephen; Richards, Martin. "Fast trains, slow boats, and the ancestry of the Polynesian islanders." *Science progress.* 84. 157-81. 10.3184/003685001783238989. 2001

[cclxxix] Karafet, T.M; Mendez, F.L; Meilerman, M.B; Underhill, P.A; Zegura, S.L; Hammer, M.F. "New binary polymorphisms reshape and increase resolution of the human Y chromosomal haplogroup tree." *Genome Res.* 18(5):830-8.doi:10.1101/gr.7172008. PMC 233680. May 2008; also Rowold, Daniel J; et al. "On the Bantu expansion." Gene. 593(1): 48-57. doi:10.1016/j.gene.2016.07.044. 2016; also now appears common among some South East Asia island populations and Melanesia: Cox, Murray P; Lahr, Marta Mirazon. "Y-Chromosome diversity is inversely associated with language affiliation in paired Austronesian-and Papuan-speaking communities from Solomon Islands." *American Journal of Human Biology,* vol. 18, is. 1 (January/February), OP. 35-50. 2006

[cclxxx] Wikipedia contributors. "Archaeogenetics." Wikipedia, The Free Encyclopedia. Wikipedia, The Free Encyclopedia, 31 Aug. 2020. Web. 10 Sep 2020

[cclxxxi] Cann, R; Stoneking, M; Wilson, A. "Mitochondrial DNA and human evolution." *Nature* 325, 31–36 (1987). https://doi.org/10.1038/325031a0

[cclxxxii] Lum, J; Cann, Rebecca. "mtDNA lineage analyses: Origins and migrations of Micronesians and Polynesians." *American journal of physical anthropology.* 113. 151-68. 10.1002/1096-8644(200010)113:2<151::AID-AJPA2>3.0.CO;2-N. 2000

[cclxxxiii] Norrgard, K. "Forensic DNA fingerprinting and CODIS." *Nature Education.* 1(1):35, 2008; also Kaye, David H. "DNA Evidence: Probability, Population Genetics, and The Courts." *Harvard Journal of Law & Technology.* Volume 7, Fall Issue, 1993

[cclxxxiv] Edinur, Hisham; Chambers, Geoff; Dunn, Paul. "New insights into ancestry and health of Polynesians and New Zealand Maori." 2016

[cclxxxv] Soares, Pedro et al. "Ancient voyaging and Polynesian origins." *American journal of human genetics* vol.88,2 (2011): 239-47. doi:10.1016/j.ajhg.2011.01.009

[cclxxxvi] Shipton, Ceril; O'Connor, Sue; Kealy, Shimona; Mahirta; Syarqiyah, Indah N; Alamsyah, Nico; Ririmasse, Marlon. "Early Ground Axe Technology in Wallace: The First Excavations on Obi Island." PLoS ONE 15(8): e0236719. doi: 10.1371/journal.pone.0236719. Aug 19, 2020

[cclxxxvii] Konnur, Marathi Mayuresh. "Prehistoric art hints at lost Indian civilization." BBC news. https://www.bbc.com/news/world-asia-india-45559300 Sep 30 2018

[cclxxxviii] Li, Hui; Huang, Ying; Mustavich, Laura; Zhang, Fan; Tan, Jing-Ze; Wang, Ling-E; Qian, Ji; Gao, Meng-He; Jin, Li. "Y chromosomes of Prehistoric People along the Yangtze River." *Human genetics.* 122. 383-8. 10.1007/s00439-007-0407-2. 2007

[cclxxxix] Soares, Pedro et al. "Ancient voyaging and Polynesian origins." *American journal of human genetics* vol.88,2 (2011): 239-47. doi:10.1016/j.ajhg.2011.01.009

[ccxc] Human_migrations_and_mitochondrial_haplogroups User:Maulucioni / CC BY-SA (https://creativecommons.org/licenses/by-sa/3.0)

[ccxci] Soares, Pedro; Trejaut, Jean Alain; Loo, Jun-Hun; Hill, Catherine; Mormina, Maru; Lee, Chien-Liang; Chen, Yao-Ming; Hudjashov, Georgi; Forster, Peter; Macaulay, Vincent; Bulbeck, David; Oppenheimer, Stephen; Lin, Marie; Richards, Martin B. "Climate Change and Postglacial Human Dispersals in Southeast Asia." *Molecular Biology and Evolution*, volume 25, Issue 6, Jun 2008, pp. 1209–1218. https://doi.org/10.1093/molbev/msn068

[ccxcii] Skoglund, P; Posth, C; Sirak, K. et al. "Genomic insights into the peopling of the Southwest Pacific." *Nature* 538, 510–513 https://doi.org/10.1038/nature19844 2016

[ccxciii] Tumonggor, M; Karafet, T; Hallmark, B. et al. "The Indonesian Archipelago: an ancient genetic highway linking Asia and the Pacific." *Journal of Human Genetics* 58, 165–173 https://doi.org/10.1038/jhg.2012.154 2013

[ccxciv] Tumonggor, Meryanne K; Karafet, Tatiana M; Sudoya, Herawati; Hammer, Michael F; Cox, Murray P. "The Indonesian Archipelago an Ancient Genetic Highway Linking Asia and the Pacific." *The Journal of Human Genetics*, Volume 58. Nature Publishing Group. March 2013, pp.165-173

[ccxcv] Yang, Melinda A. "Ancient DNA is revealing the genetic landscape of people who first settled East Asia" *The Conversation.* CC BY-SA https://theconversation.com/ancient-dna-is-revealing-the-genetic-landscape-of-people-who-first-settled-east-asia-139458 Sep 15 2020

CLOSING SALUTATION

[ccxcvi] Ross, Rachel. "Eureka! The Archimedes Principle." https://www.livescience.com/58839-archimedes-principle.html Apr 26, 2017

CONCLUSION

ccxcvii Herodotus *Book II* With an English Translation by A. D. Godley, Hon. Fellow of Magdalen College, Oxford. In Four Volumes I Book I and II. London. William Heinemann LTD Cambridge, Massachusetts. Harvard University Press. 1920. rev. 1926, 1931, 1946, 1960 pp. 106-112.

ccxcviii Bloch, Ernst. *Das Prinzip Hoffnung*, Frankfurt am Main, Suhrkamp,1959; also Bloch, Ernst. *The Principle of Hope (3 Volumes)* trans. Plaice, Neville; Plaice, Stephen; Knight, Paul. MIT Press, Cambridge, Massachusetts, 1986. Vol. I.

ccxcix Thompson, Peter. "The Frankfurt School, Part 6: Ernst Bloch and The Principle of Hope (Volume I in 1954, II in 1955, and III in 1959)" https://www.theguardian.com/commentisfree/belief/2013/apr/29/frankfurt-school-ernst-bloch-principle-of-hope 23 Apr 2013

ccc Version 1985 reprinted from the edition of 1884, published by The Bible Society in the South Pacific, Suva, Fiji.

ccci Johnson, Wendell James. *God's Trombones*: "Creation." *Freeman Periodical.* 1920; *Seven Negro Sermons in Verse.* Viking Press. 1927; Viking Compass ed 1969; Penguin Books 1976.

TABLES

cccii Kramer, Samuel Noah. *From the Tablets of Sumer*, pp.92-93; cited by Campbell, Joseph. *The Mask of God: Oriental Mythology.* First Published. New York, NY. Viking Penguin Inc. 1962. Published in Penguin Books. 1976. Copyright renewed Joseph Campbell. 1962. pg. 112-114

ccciii Campbell, Joseph. *The Mask of God: Oriental Mythology.* First Published. New York, NY. Viking Penguin Inc. 1962. Published in Penguin Books. 1976. Copyright renewed Joseph Campbell. 1962. pg.113-114; also Kramer, Dr. Samuel Noah. *The Sumerians: Their History, Culture and Character.* The University of Chicago Press. 1963

ccciv Piggott, Juliet. *Japanese mythology* (New ed.) New York, N. Y. ISMN 0-911745-09-2. OCLC 9971207; also Jun'ichi, Isomaej-Thal, Sarah E. "Reappropriating the Japanese myths: Motori Norinaga and Nihon shoki." *Japanese Journal of Religious Studies.* 27(1/2):15-39. 2000; also Taylor, Edward B. "Remarks on Japanese Mythology." *The Journal of Anthropological Institute of Great Britain and Ireland*: 6:55-58. doi:10.2307/2841246.1877; also Hoffman, Michael. "Land of the sun Goddess." *Japan Times Online.* ISSN 044-5763. Jul 12 2009; also Kitagawa, Joseph M. "Prehistoric Background of Japanese Religion." *History of Religions.* 2(2):292-328. doi:10.1086/462466. 1963; also ed. Terrence James Vistorino. *Mythical Creatures in Burmese Folklore: Jataka tales, History of Burma, Yama Zatdaw, Ramayana, Asura (Buddhism), Rakshasa, Garuda.* Log Press. 108 pg. ISBN 978-613-6-67801-6. 2011; also Campbell, Joseph. chapters on "Japanese Mythology" and "Indian Mythology." *The Mask of God: Oriental Mythology.* First Published. New York, NY. Viking Penguin Inc. 1962. Published in Penguin Books. 1976. Copyright renewed Joseph Campbell. 1962Joseph Campbell: Oriental Mythology.

Made in the USA
Las Vegas, NV
01 December 2021

35794983R00167